Debating Political Reform in China

Rule of Law vs. Democratization

Suisheng Zhao, editor

An East Gate Book

D0223642

M.E.Sharpe
Armonk, New York
London, England

To my family and many friends
whose love and support have sustained my search for a better world

An East Gate Book

Copyright © 2006 by M.E. Sharpe, Inc.

All rights reserved. No part of this book may be reproduced in any form
without written permission from the publisher, M.E. Sharpe, Inc.,
80 Business Park Drive, Armonk, New York 10504.

Library of Congress Cataloging-in-Publication Data

Debating political reform in China : rule of law vs. democratization /
edited by Suisheng Zhao.
    p. cm.
"An East Gate book."
ISBN 0-7656-1731-5 (cloth : alk. paper)—ISBN 0-7656-1732-3 (pbk. : alk. paper)
1. China—Politics and government—1976–2002. 2. China—Politics and government—
2002– 3. Rule of law—China. 4. Democratization—China. I. Zhao, Suisheng, 1954–

JQ1510.D43 2006
320.951—dc22   2005030862

Printed in the United States of America

The paper used in this publication meets the minimum requirements of
American National Standard for Information Sciences
Permanence of Paper for Printed Library Materials,
ANSI Z 39.48-1984.

Library
University of Texas
at San Antonio

MV (c)   10   9   8   7   6   5   4   3   2   1
MV (p)   10   9   8   7   6   5   4   3   2   1

Debating Political Reform in China

WITHDRAWN
UTSA Libraries

WITHDRAWN
UTSA Libraries

Contents

Introduction

Suisheng Zhao

This book is a modest attempt to understand the connection between the rule of law and democracy, two key issues that face political reformers in China today as well as political leaders of many other countries in the process of political change.

Since China began revamping its economy in the late 1970s, the pressure for political reform has been building as it has become more and more difficult for the Communist regime to sustain a growing disconnect between a market-oriented economy and a dynamic society, on the one hand, and an anachronistic and authoritarian state on the other. As a result, political reform has not only been hotly debated and broadly discussed among Chinese intellectuals but has also become an official policy objective, listed on the agenda of the Chinese Communist Party (CCP) and governmental meetings and official publications. One of the key issues in the debate is whether single-party rule can adequately facilitate China's transition or if a multiparty electoral democracy is required. Many Western observers and Chinese liberal intellectuals want to see China's political reform lead to a multiparty democracy. Nevertheless, when Chinese government officials and some Chinese scholars talk about political reform, they propose improving the rule of the CCP, making the single-party system more efficient and providing it with a solid legal base so that the CCP will continue to be instrumental for maintaining political stability, which is seen as a necessary condition for rapid economic modernization. Such an understanding of political reform is very widespread in China, including among the Jiang Zemin and Hu Jintao generations of the Chinese leadership. Improving single-party rule by subjecting the system to the rule of law has been regarded as an urgent task of political reform, while movements to transform the system into a Western-style multiparty democracy have to be on hold for the time being.

Pan Wei, a Berkeley-trained Chinese scholar at Peking University, illustrated a scenario of political reform without democratization using his idea of a consultative rule of law regime in a paper published first in a 1999 issue of *Zhanlüe yu Guanli* (Strategy and Management), a Chinese journal with a large readership among China's elite. Pan has therefore become known as one of the leading "neoconservative" scholars among some Western observers and has gained both domestic and international attention because of his systematic and sophisticated presentation of political reform to improve rather than replace single-party rule in China. An international symposium was organized by University of Denver's Center for China–U.S. Cooperation to discuss Pan's paper in the summer of 2000. After the symposium, Pan's revised English version of the paper was published, together with the critiques of his paper by several participants at the symposium, in the *Journal of Contemporary China* in 2003. In response, more scholars joined the debate. This book is a collection of selected responses to Pan's controversial argument (contained in Chapter 1) and some empirical studies of the relationship between rule of law and democracy in China.

In his attempt to demythologize the Western concept of democracy and promote his consultative rule of law regime, Pan Wei identifies four types of linkage between democracy and rule of law in the contemporary world: countries with democracy but no rule of law; countries with rule of law but no democracy; countries with both rule of law and democracy; and countries with neither. Pan believes that the first type is the worst, since a democracy without rule of law is likely to result in chaos, corruption, and unsustainable development. The second type has been proven to be a viable political option, especially for countries without democratic traditions. Hong Kong and Singapore are examples of the second type, and they are well governed societies with efficient and clean government. Pan therefore argues that political reform in China has not and should not consist simply of democratizing the polity. Instead, China has worked to establish a "consultative rule of law regime," which is a rule of law regime supplemented by democracy rather than a democracy supplemented by rule of law. This is a "mixed" regime derived from the Chinese tradition of civil service via examination and the Western tradition of legalism and liberalism via the separation of power to form checks and balances. It represents the Chinese ideal of a political civilization, which is radically different from the liberal democracy of the Western world. Therefore, Pan suggests the consultative rule of law regime as an option for China's political reform, a feasible path for China to fundamentally improve the rule of the CCP within the single-party system. He believes that a legalist direction of political reform is a logical development in light of China's particular social setting and the related political culture.

Pan's provocative and sophisticated argument is refreshing not only to many scholars of Chinese politics but also to many students of law and democratization, whether or not they agree with him. While it is not difficult to find flaws in Pan's thesis, it is hard for even the most critical scholars to simply ridicule Pan's argument for the consultative rule of law regime because Pan's view represents some of the most influential thinking among Chinese elites on the issues of the rule of law and democracy today. It is not coincidental that China's reformers from Deng Xiaoping and Jiang Zemin to Hu Jintao have emphasized rule of law while avoiding democratization. Through a spirited debate, this book tries to offer the readers Pan's alternatives for political reform, which by the end are well critiqued and illustrated by the other contributors.

Chapter 2, by Suisheng Zhao agrees with Pan's assertion that incumbent Chinese reformers have looked upon the rule of law and political liberalization without democratization as an alternative solution to many of China's problems related to the authoritarian one-party system. This welcome first step in China's political reform has produced substantial, even dramatic, political changes and has been the catalyst for greater individual freedom and economic development. Although China's history reminds us that the course of change is never certain, recent political liberalization, together with the change in one-party rule, may slowly lay a foundation for democratization, which should be the ultimate goal of political reform. The long-term political stability, administrative efficiency, and economic development in China ultimately depend on the emergence of a genuinely representative government chosen by the people through a democratic process. From this perspective, while Pan's rule of law regime may be an alternative to democracy for the immediate future, it is important to see the transitional nature of the rule of law regime and the inevitability of democratic development in the long run.

In chapter 3, Randy Peerenboom, a prominent scholar of Chinese legal development, welcomes the bold attempt by Pan to chart a feasible path of political reform for China. Similar to Zhao, while sympathetic to Pan's basic approach and beliefs that the rule of law without democracy is the most likely path to political reform in the short term, Peerenboom suggests that, in the long run, democracy will be necessary to solve some of the divisive social issues that have arisen in China as a result of economic reforms and social changes. He also asserts that Pan's understanding of rule of law is overly simplistic and that his faith in the miraculous power of rule of law to put an end to corruption, resolve pluralistic conflicts, and produce a just and harmonious society is wildly exaggerated. Peerenboom expands the scope of Pan's proposal to explore various possible administrative law reforms and legal reforms more generally required to realize a rule of law in China but he cautions that ultimately their success turns on issues of power that exceed the limits of the law. Therefore, it would be impossible to have genuine legal reform without democratization.

Larry Diamond, one of the most prominent scholars of democracy in the West, puts even more emphasis on democratic reform than does Peerenboom. He indicates in Chapter 4 that China urgently needs political reform to deal with the rapidly mounting problems of corruption, abuse of power, financial scandals, rising crime and inequality, and declining legitimacy of the Chinese Communist Party. A rule of law, with an independent judiciary and other autonomous institutions of horizontal accountability, is vital if China is to rein in these problems and deliver better, fairer, more transparent, and effective governance. From this perspective, Pan's "consultative rule of law system" is a potentially important step along the path of political reform. However, says Diamond, Pan's rule of law system is in essence a liberal autocracy that goes only part of the way toward addressing the deficiencies of governance in China. It is therefore best viewed as a transitional framework. To work, horizontal accountability must be supplemented and reinforced by vertical accountability through competitive elections, which give local officials an incentive to serve the public good, and enable the removal of bad officials by the people. Agreeing with Peerenboom, Diamond shows why an independent civil service, along with the rule of law and a counter-corruption apparatus, which have worked to curb corruption in Hong Kong and Singapore and which Pan sees as a way to deal with China's corruption, will not be effective. Using the example of Taiwan, Diamond argues that democratic institutions are necessary in order to have the rule of law. Ultimately, China can only achieve adequate and enduring political accountability and stability by moving toward democracy.

Whereas Zhao, Peerenboom, and Diamond see some merit in Pan's argument, Edward Friedman is more critical. He argues, in Chapter 5, that while Pan wonderfully illuminates some conundrums of Chinese politics, he prescribes the wrong medicine to treat the problems. Instead of offering an actual alternative, Pan provides a cultural spin on the now discredited concept of "Asian developmental despotism." His solution, synthesizing the ancient wisdom of Chinese Confucianism and legalism, is not a way to attain the liberties and lawfulness that Pan seeks to achieve, but is likely instead to produce a despotic rule by law—the coercive imposition of authoritarian rules on a populace whose unaccountable rulers would still remain above the law. Based on a comparative study of the experiences of Russia, India, Japan, South Korea, Taiwan, Singapore, and Hong Kong, Friedman suggests that gradual democratization is the best way to maintain stability, prevent war, check corruption, and promote further economic reform because democracy is the most stable political system in the world and tends to be a harbinger of stability.

Chapter 6 by Gunter Schubert, a leading China scholar in Germany, reconstructs Pan Wei's basic argument for the consultative rule of law regime and discusses both its conceptual consistency and political practicability. According to Schubert, Pan provides us with a democratic theory translated into a concept of one-party rule that combines elements of the Western liberal tradition with the Chinese tradition of meritocracy. Pan's vision of erecting an institutional framework based on limited participation and the absolute authority of the law is noteworthy as it transcends to some extent the official understanding of "socialist democracy" by the implementation of a sound legal system. Schubert suggests that Pan's argument for reforming Chinese authoritarianism by implementing legal reforms, a modern civil service structure, and more mechanisms of political consultation might work because there is considerable space for the CCP regime to gain new legitimacy for quite some time if only some elements of Pan Wei's concept are rigorously implemented. From this perspective, Schubert believes that Pan's consultative rule of law regime might indeed be the most realistic variant of democracy in China that one can hope for in the near future. He also argues, however, that "consultative rule of law" cannot sustain one-party rule in the long run.

In a critical response to Pan's thesis, Baohui Zhang's Chapter 7 discusses the Chinese historical view of rule of law or rule by law in comparison with the Western view. Learning from the history of the rule of law in the West, Zhang posits that the rise of the rule of law requires conditions such as political and institutional checks and balances, a robust civil society, and a free press that can effectively restrain the power of the state and its leaders. Unique medieval conditions in Europe allowed the emergence of constitutionalism, which served as the foundation for rule of law in the modern era. However, China today does not have similar conditions. Its system of single-party rule is inconsistent with the basic tenets of rule of law. Zhang therefore argues that it is impossible for China to develop a rule of law regime without democratization. And although democracy does not guarantee the rule of law, it does stand a better chance than other forms of government. China can only develop the rule of law through democratization.

The best way to assess the feasibility of Pan Wei's argument is to empirically examine the compatibility of the rule of law and one-party rule in China. The chapters by Qianfan Zhang, Yongshun Cai/Songcai Yang, Yunqiu Zhang, Guobin Yang, and Tamara Shie present some empirical studies in this regard. According to their studies, for many centuries, China was ruled by man, not by law. Post-Mao reform has brought about some significant changes on the legal front. Although these authors differ in their assessments of the progress of the reform, they agree that law is still mostly an instrument for the state and the ruling Communist Party. Rule by law rather than rule of law has been the most prevailing practice in China. Citizens' legal rights are not yet strongly protected, and an independent judicial system is hardly established because of the CCP's monopoly on political power. The difficulty for the development of the rule of law in China raises a fundamental question to Pan Wei regarding whether or not the consultative rule of law regime can be built up and function effectively within China's one-party system.

In Chapter 8, Qianfan Zhang examines the limits of China's judicial reform and illuminates the constraints of Pan Wei's rule of law regime in China. His empirical study finds that, although China has made great progress on the road toward rule of law, it still has a long way to go before becoming a state truly governed by rule of law. His argument is supported by what he calls the "judicial syndrome" in China's judicial reform. The Chinese courts have been beset by a lack of impartiality and autonomy owing to the heavy political influence exerted by the ruling party, the shortage of well-trained judicial personnel, and, more generally, the absence of social respect for the traditionally insignificant judicial branch in a primarily administrative state. Thus the existing judicial system is woefully inadequate for sustaining Pan's rule of law regime, as it fails to meet the Weberian conditions for a politically neutral legal system that uniformly enforces the law. The uniform administration of justice is further jeopardized in China by the enormous diversity of local conditions and interests typical to a developing state, and by the intimate relations between the courts and local political branches. Zhang thus concludes that the most direct and fundamental limit to Chinese judicial reform is its political system: namely, the party directly interferes in judicial decisions. One-party rule is a barrier to the rule of law in China.

Chapter 9 by Yongshun Cai and Songcai Yang starts in agreement with Pan Wei that the rule of law is one of the most important components of future regime building in China because political and socioeconomic changes in China have assigned an unprecedented role to law. That is why the Chinese government has made serious efforts toward this end. However, in an exploration of how state power in China affects the development of the legal system, Cai and Yang find that the progress toward rule of law remains slow. Other than the problem of many inadequately trained and incompetent lawyers, the environment in which lawyers operate is still replete with social and political constraints. The most important constraint comes from the fact that the legal system in China is still seen as an instrument of the party-state to achieve social and political order. To this end, legal institutions remain in the "cage" of the party-state. For the same reason, lawyers' practice has also to be accepted by the party-state, which implies limited autonomy of lawyers when defending litigants against state actors. Based on a survey of about 290 lawyers, the authors reveal that, as a result of this constraint, Chinese lawyers are selective in taking on lawsuits due largely to the political risks. They are more willing to represent clients in litigation pertaining to economic and civil affairs as opposed to administrative litigation and criminal cases. For one thing, lawyers receive high payment for lawsuits of an economic nature. More importantly, there are political risks in taking on administrative litigation and criminal cases. Cai and Yang therefore confirm Qianfan Zhang's conclusion that because the power of state agencies, particularly the party committees, has affected the development of the legal system by influencing legal representation, achieving even a thin rule of law in China remains challenging.

In Chapter 10, Yunqiu Zhang takes a more positive view than the previous two chapters on the feasibility of Pan's rule of law regime. According to Zhang, Pan's proposal shows an acute understanding of some fundamental problems with the current Chinese legal system and offers corresponding remedies for them. He agrees with Pan that nonelected technocratic elites—"neutral" civil servants, "autonomous" judges, "independent" anti-corruption agents, "independent" auditors—should be central players in the rule of law structure. But he also finds a problem with the conspicuous absence of public participation—the participation of ordinary citizens—in Pan's regime. His chapter addresses the necessity and possibility of involving ordinary citizens in building the rule of law by examining the interactions between law and a specific social group—workers. In a case study of the impact of labor legislation on Chinese workers, Zhang tackles the issue of why workers do not adopt street protests as a major strategy in defending their interests or why there is a lack of radical or coordinated challenge to the regime from workers. He finds that labor laws, which have proliferated in the reform years as a result of vigorous state legislative efforts, have provided workers with a new channel to settle their disputes with management and to express their concerns or protect their interests. He indicates that this legal channel, state-sanctioned or -supported, is less risky than protests, which are not endorsed by the state and could likely incur state reprisals, and is therefore preferable to most workers and could serve as an alternative to protests. Based primarily upon his own field studies, especially interviews with workers and investigations of some labor lawsuits, Zhang argues that labor legislation had a positive effect on workers, providing them with a useful weapon for self-protection. Workers gradually developed an awareness of the rule of law and a willingness to use legal means in handling their disputes with management and, in so doing, they often succeeded. Admitting that the legal weapon proved too heavy for ordinary workers to wield, as they had to encounter enormous and often insurmountable barriers in lodging and winning lawsuits, Zhang believes that the elements of the rule of law emerged in the area of labor.

Although Yunqiu Zhang is more positive about the development of the rule of law in China, his study, like the other two empirical studies, identifies the unchecked state/Communist Party power as the major barrier for building an effective rule of law regime. To overcome the barrier, a more assertive civil society must emerge to challenge the one-party monopoly of power, as it will become more and more difficult for the CCP to sustain the authoritarian single-party rule in an increasingly pluralized and liberalized Chinese society. Indeed, an increasingly assertive civil society is arising, facilitated, among other things, by the information technology revolution, particularly the development of the Internet. Many China observers have expected a collision between the Internet and the Chinese authorities because the Internet has the potential to erode the leadership's monopoly on information and complicate the relations between the authoritarian regime and the emerging civil society.

Based on a case study of the impact of the Internet on civil society development in China, Guobin Yang suggests in Chapter 11 that the Internet has indeed affected three key areas of Chinese civil society: the public sphere, social organizations, and popular protest. The Internet has fostered public debate and problem articulation and demonstrated its potential to play a supervisory role in Chinese politics. In addition, the Internet has facilitated the activities of existing organizations while creating a new associational form, the virtual community. Finally, the Internet has introduced new elements into the dynamics of protest. Public debate, social organization, and protest that take place on the Internet in China are linked in numerous ways with the global community, including the Chinese diaspora around the world. Despite government efforts to block selected sites, Internet users in China may access Web sites overseas, or "link up" with overseas individuals and groups for information exchange, solidarity building, or protest. By using the Internet to speak up, link up, and act up, Chinese citizens have struggled for basic citizenship rights—the right to voice their opinions on government policies, to be informed of issues that affect their lives, to freely organize themselves and defend their interests, and to publicly challenge various kinds of authorities and social injustices. Yang concludes that protection of these basic rights, therefore, should be on the priority list for political reform. If Pan Wei's rule of law alone cannot guarantee these rights, democratization will be a must.

The Internet, however, does not simply represent a threat to CCP rule or a conduit for democracy. Tamara Renee Shie argues in Chapter 12 that the Chinese Communist Party has not only employed various measures in the attempt to control the Internet, from introducing numerous regulations to encouraging self-censorship, with some success, but it has also taken advantage of the Internet to make CCP rule more effective. For example, the Web provides an opportunity for greater communication and cooperation between provincial and municipal governments and the central government. Increased government accountability is a potential by-product of the information technology revolution. Moreover, the Internet has provided a forum to foster nationalism. In this case, the Internet will not bring democracy to China by itself. It is neither inherently revolutionary nor liberating; the impetus for political change must come from political action within the population, although cyberspace could be a vehicle to speed this change once it begins. Therefore, the embracing of the Internet and information technology in China can be seen as a win-win situation for both the civil society and the ruling party. Shie's conclusion agrees with Pan Wei that political reform toward the rule of law without democracy is a logical direction that an information technology–driven Chinese government should pursue.

It has been five years since Pan Wei presented his rule of law regime argument at the Vail Conference in 2000. During this period, China experienced a transition of leadership from the third generation led by Jiang Zemin to the fourth generation under Hu Jintao. In Chapter 13, which brings China's political reform up to date, Suisheng Zhao examines the direction of political reform under the current Chinese leadership. He points out that although scholars have disagreed among themselves about the feasibility of Pan Wei's proposal, political reform in post-Mao China has moved toward building the rule of law regime that Pan proposed. The transition of the PRC leadership in the early twenty-first century has not shown any sign that the CCP will adopt the principles of liberal democracy and open up political competition any time soon. The following three important aspects of political reform suggest a steady move toward building a rule of law regime (more precisely, a rule by law system):

1. institutionalization of the leadership system with an emphasis on normative rules and procedures,
2. the effort to make government more accountable to an increasingly pluralistic society,
3. the improvement of citizens' legal/constitutional rights.

Zhao concludes that while Pan's rule of law regime provides an option for China's political reform, this option may not lead the Communist leadership to embrace the democratic principles that would dismantle its monopoly on political power. Because political reform in China has so far tried to use law to rule the country and to improve the Communist Party's capacity to govern the economy and society, the question of whether building a rule of law regime without democratization will sustain the single-party rule in China remains unanswered.

About a half-decade after presenting his original argument for the consultative rule of law regime, Pan Wei wrote an afterword in response to his critics for this book. Of course, this is not a concluding chapter. It is only Pan's personal reflection upon this important debate. While admitting some regrets about his original presentation, he reaffirms his basic argument. The consultative rule of law regime, particularly the six pillars, in his opinion, has withstood the test of history. In his reflection, Pan goes further to "demythologize" the Western concept of democracy by characterizing it as an ideology belonging to the ideal world. His criticism focuses on the so-called "myth of free elections." Pan holds that the emphasis on free elections represents a "narrow," "parochial," and "simplistic" definition of democracy. According to him, it is the arrogant attempt to export "electoral democracy" that has led to a significant "conflict of civilizations." Pan believes that both "democracy" and "authoritarian regime" have become the two most useless concepts in academic research of our time. The rule of law, he believes, should become the direction of political reforms in China. Pan clarifies that the rule of law is an issue-driven and problem-solving process, not one concerning values. Once again, he warns China's reformers that it is dangerous to build an electoral system before installing the rule of law.

The idea for this book started from the Vail Conference on Pan Wei's paper in 2000. After the conference, Tom Farer, dean of the Graduate School of International Studies at the University of Denver, planned to solicit contributions and put together an edited book, but failed to find time to do so. I took over the book project and would like to thank Tom for his initiatives. I would also like to thank all the contributors for their cooperation and responsiveness to my requests to rewrite/update their chapters for the book. Assistance from Malissa M. Spero, DU China Center's project manager, is gratefully acknowledged. Finally, it has been a great pleasure to work with Patricia Loo at M.E. Sharpe during the publication stage.

Debating Political Reform in China

1

Toward a Consultative Rule of Law Regime in China

Pan Wei

Why has China not embraced democracy? Should we consider alternatives when the change in China is unlikely to lead to a democracy?

The pressure for political reform is again being strongly felt inside China. Unlike 1989, the current pressure is not derived from an eagerness to speed up marketization, but from strong resentment against the widespread corruption. The abuse of public office for private gain exploded in the mid-1990s, quickly conquered all levels and branches of the government, and clearly became the top concern among the general public.

The rampant corruption stems from the contradiction between China's newly installed market system and the party-state's unchecked power. The party possesses the final say over the judicial, legislative, and executive branches of government, and over the media, markets, universities, and particularly the promotion of officials. Moreover, economic decentralization has led to the feudalization of administrative power, and the power monopoly of the party has become the personal power monopoly of each chief administrator. Nearly all enterprises, social institutions, and officials at all levels try to buy their way up through bribery of some kind. Their competitiveness depends less on how well they compete in markets than on how much and how skillfully they bribe the appropriate higher authorities. The lack of a just order within the newly built market framework calls for a decisive political move. It is widely believed within the Communist Party that if the regime falls, corruption will be the most immediate cause.

Besides the critical issue of timing, however, there are profound disagreements about what direction the political reforms should take. For many in the West, the solution lies in the introduction of a democracy mirroring their own political machines. While most Chinese intellectuals support that proposal, most rank-and-file officials view it with deep suspicion. As the average Chinese people know little about polity options, what they mainly care about is an effective cure to corruption, so as to guarantee fair competition in markets. The top decision makers have given confusing signals that represent their indecision and fear—the fear of losing the power monopoly of the Communist Party and hence a Russia-like chaos and collapse. For a time, they seemed willing to try a democratic direction—gradually, from the village level. The 15th Party Congress in 1997 decided to "develop socialist democratic poli-

3

tics," even asserting that "without democracy there is neither socialism nor modernization."[1] However, their attention in recent years seems to have shifted to "rule by law." The official propaganda has been making a large outcry about that term. Three terms—Communist leadership, democracy, and rule by law—are used simultaneously in the official media. Chinese leaders are not ready to go anywhere, but they know that they need to go somewhere.

In this chapter, I will first clarify the concepts of democracy and rule of law (and "rule by law" later), and specify their different functions in order to demythologize the democratic option. Then I will compare the socioeconomic settings in China and the West, and argue that the differences will likely shape different polity options. Finally, I will propose for China some decisive political changes in the direction of "consultative rule of law," which is a rule of law regime supplemented by democracy instead of a democracy supplemented by rule of law.

Democracy and Rule of Law

Why should democracy be such a desired form of government that its spread is even promoted at the cost of fighting international wars? How can we even think of an alternative to democracy? In third world countries, a "pure" democracy would likely decay to social disorder and tyranny. Let me start with a theoretical discussion of democracy and rule of law.

What Is a Democracy?

Democratizing all the world's polities has become, for some in the West, a Crusade-like undertaking, like some kind of religious cause. In 1848 Tocqueville wrote in his twelfth edition of *Democracy in America* that: "This work was written . . . with a mind constantly preoccupied by a single thought: the thought of approaching the irresistible and universal spread of democracy throughout the world."[2] In the book's Introduction, he even asserted that resisting democracy "appears as a fight against God Himself, and nations have no alternative but to acquiesce in the social state imposed by Providence."[3] After World War II, Talcott Parsons, who might be qualified as the founding father of American political sociology, suggested that democracy an "evolutionary universal."[4] After the Cold War, the fanaticism for spreading democracy has reached a new height in terms of "democratic peace," implicitly attributing all international wars to nondemocratic countries no matter who was the aggressor.[5]

Although democracies have wonderful merits and achievements, democracy itself needs be demythologized. It is merely an instrument of governance and its efficacy is conditional—on rule of law and certain social settings derived from historical accidents.

How should we define democracy and rule of law? Rule of law as a concept is much more parsimonious than democracy—it means the supreme authority of the established legal requirements. The authority of law increases as the branches of the government are separated to allow "checks and balances" among themselves, and when the law enforcement agencies are made accountable to the law instead of representatives of interest groups. Even as early as Aristotle's time, scholars understood that rule of law is preferred to personal rule.

Defining democracy, however, appears rather difficult. Although we have a precise definition of autocracy as unlimited power imposed by a ruler, prevailing definitions of democracy are vague and cumbersome, *hardly usable to tell democracies from nondemocracies.* They often describe normative ends rather than practical means, and they add vague degree requirements, such as "minimum," or "effective." Robert Dahl defined democracy as: (1) effective participation; (2) equality in voting; (3) gaining enlightened understanding; (4) exercising final control over the agenda; (5) inclusion of adults.[6] It seems that the concerned theorists are reluctant to write a neat and clear definition. Scholars may disagree on definitions, but they all well understand the need for, and importance of, a precise and usable definition. Why do we allow ambiguous definitions in this important area of study? The most likely reason is that there are very backward countries that might qualify as democracies, for they feature periodic elections of top leaders, and the voting there may be no less equal than that in the U.S. federal system, under which the worth of the suffrage greatly varies.

Democracy is said to be "people's rule." If people could rule themselves, why is there the need for "government"? If there were no government, the Hobbesian state of nature would prevail, and people would be subject to the law of the jungle.[7] Safety in social order is the first and most important reason for the need of a government that is authorized with all the means of violence. The polity closest to "people's rule" was the Athenian direct democracy wherein all of the *demos* had a good and equal chance to participate in all major decisions. However, even the Athenian "direct democracy" was often said to be oligarchic in reality. Aristotle's "rule of many" against "rule of one" and "rule of a few" was not the rule of even all of the *demos,* although the number of participants in the business of government was far more than just "a few." The point is that a democracy must also be some kind of "-cracy." The modern representative government is not designed to be "people's rule," but people's right to periodically elect a few representatives who "govern" the people. Thus, the current "sovereignty of people" is not much more than a parliamentary sovereignty or, in the case of the United States, the sovereignty of the president plus Congress that Dahl has called electoral "polyarchy"—rule of a few out of pluralistic contentions.[8]

The mythologized definition of democracy often implies the function of a panacea —all evils in a society are often implicitly traced to the lack of (representative) democracy, or the lack of enough democracy. Dahl lists ten great reasons for desiring democracy that comprise all the good things one can imagine in this world, such as liberty, equality, prosperity, and peace.[9] Should we forget the American Civil War, slavery, and the Great Depression of the 1930s? Should we ignore the prosperity and social progress in Japan, Singapore, Hong Kong, China, and other nondemocratic countries? With vague and flexible definitions of democracy, ambivalent elements and qualifications are added, illusory ends justify means, and democracy by definition becomes an unchallengeable "universal value." We know that the democratic value is not universal. As to a polity option, democracy was a void even in Europe for two thousand years. It is often argued that the current democracy is imperfect, and that democracy is a "process" toward perfection. Communist propaganda tells that a communist society is the most perfect and ideal. If anything bad happens, by definition it must have been produced because the society is actually noncommunist or not communist enough. The perfect communist society belongs to another world, and so does a "perfect democracy" or a "process toward perfection."

Democracy is often said to treat its own people well. How can a democracy feature bad governance and poor socioeconomic performance? Sometimes India is labeled the "largest democracy in the world," and it is perhaps one of the most stable democracies in the third world. Yet the label is rarely mentioned due to India's many features of underdevelopment, including violent ethnic conflicts. President Clinton labeled Yugoslavia as a "fascist" country led by a "present-day Hitler" who carried out another "Holocaust." Yet that country under its "Hitler" not only held regular elections of leaders, but also allowed open operation of opposition parties and media even during the war with NATO. Despite free and regular elections, how can a country with constant ethnic wars be a democracy, and how can a "drug trafficker country" like Colombia be a democracy? It is often ignored that the United States had the bloodiest civil war of the whole world in the nineteenth century, and Britain during the Opium War was a much larger "drug trafficking country" than today's Colombia. Of course, some would argue that democracies in non-Western countries are not "liberal" democracies, and that only those in the West enjoy the key label "liberal." I will show in a moment that the "liberal" part is associated with rule of law rather than with elections, and rule of law overcomes the weakness of democracy.

Democracy is also believed to treat its neighboring people well. Athens of ancient Greece was far more democratic than today's democracies. However, it was clearly much more war-prone than Sparta. When Athenians asked Melos, a small city-state, to give up its neutrality in the Peloponnesian War, the Athenian envoy told the Melians, "You know as well as we do that right is in question only between equals in power, while the strong do what they can and the weak suffer what they must." The Melians surrendered their 700-year independence to the discretion of the Athenians. Yet, the Athenians "put to death all the grown men whom they took, and sold the women and children for slaves, and subsequently sent out five hundred colonists and inhabited the place themselves."[10] The Athenian invasion of democratic Syracuse was democratically decided. The battle was famous because it was the Waterloo of the Athenian empire. The post–World War II history of international relations finds little difference in the pattern of what makes a country more war-prone than others. Does any concerned scholar want to seriously argue which country is the most war-prone in today's world? The key problem in the statement "liberal democracies don't fight each other" lies in such an implication that all international wars should blame those that are not "liberal democracies," no matter who invades whom.

There can be a clear and neat definition of democracy. Modern representative democracy is a polity featuring *periodic elections of top leaders by electorates.* This is, of course, the only definition of democracy.

Many would disagree with my definition above, and would suggest the inclusion of a lot more "good" things in it, especially those in the category of rule of law. However, I am not the first or only one to define democracy as such, Joseph Schumpeter did the same.[11] When all the good things are thrown into the single basket of "democracy," democracy appears more like an ideology than a practical polity or an instrument of governance. Even if we define democracy as only "liberal democracy," and others are phony or childish, we still want to know what is an "infant" or "hybrid" democracy, and why others are "genuine" or "mature" or "developed," or "liberal."

There are three major reasons to define democracy as periodic elections of top leaders. First, the essential difference between autocracy and democracy lies in how the leaders are produced. Thus, the periodic election of top leaders is the core characteristic of all democracies, and all definitions include it, although they disagree on other features. Ardent advocates mainly spread democracy by demanding free elections of the top leaders. They take this as an essential of "human rights," and as the critical indicator of democratization. Second, other key factors, such as checks and balances and freedoms of speech, press, assembly, and association should be excluded, for they can be obtained without elections of top leaders. I also exclude factors that are mainly a matter of degree, such as "effective" and "free" political participation, so that the concept is made clear and usable. After all, how effective is "effective," and how free is "free"? Is the general election in India as free as that in the United States? In 1997 a provincial parliamentary seat in Pakistan was competed for by 107 candidates; was it "free" enough? Third, I exclude ends, which are often attached to definitions. All forms of polity claim noble ends, and the declared noble ends serve to mythologize a polity and ignore its means. Means are what polities are all about, and democracy's means are periodic elections of political leaders, which, as is shown below in a comparison with "liberal" democracy, serve fewer ends than often claimed.

Is Rule of Law an Inherent Part of Democracy?

Democracy in the West is supplemented by rule of law, and many believe that rule of law is an inherent part of democracy. Yet, "rule of the people" and "rule of law" obviously indicate two different things, and *one can exist without the other.* Their essential differences are as follows.

Democracy and rule of law differ in political philosophy. Democracy trusts "good governance" to the *extensiveness* of political participation motivated by people's concern for their welfare, hence the demand for the supremacy of people's power. In modern times, people's power is represented through people's elected representatives. Although people's contemporary welfare is democracy's major concern, those welfare concerns are divided and often conflictive, which leads to partisan politics. Rule of law, in contrast, trusts good governance to limiting government power within the boundaries of the law, so that people enjoy the liberty that is not clearly prohibited. Instead of partisan interests, rule of law emphasizes equality before the law and "universal justice" in the supremacy of the Basic Law.

Democracy and rule of law differ in basic approaches. Democracy is to authorize a few elected with the power to rule. The government can govern because it has obtained the consent of a relative majority of the people. Rule of law is to regulate a government instead of creating a government. How can laws "rule?" Laws can rule when government power is separated to form checks and balances. Checks and balances reduce the leaders' accountability to the electorate and increase their accountability to the Law. Checks and balances can be further intensified by some institutional-functional overlaps, so as to avoid either rule of people or rule of bureaucrats or judges. Rule of law tells government officials what they may do, and they may not do what laws do not clearly authorize. Thus, the people enjoy the right to do whatever the laws do not prohibit. Therefore, elections authorize a few persons to govern, while checks and balances force the government to be law abiding.

Democracy and rule of law differ in political agenda. Democracy emphasizes law *making;* laws are only fair when they are made with the agreement of a relative majority. Rule of law emphasizes law *enforcement* as long as it is "constitutional," namely, made in accordance with the Basic Law. As in the case of the United States, a law is enforced as long as it is a law in effect, even when it refuses, for whatever reason, one equal vote per qualified voter, and when it says, for whatever reason, the candidate who wins fewer popular votes could win in the presidential election.

Democracy and rule of law differ in institutional sources of power. The power base of democracy consists of elected law-making offices, mainly parliament and the elected chief executive. The institutional power base of rule of law consists of nonelected law enforcement offices, mainly the civil service and the judiciary.

Democracy and rule of law radically differ in game rules. Democracy features regular elections plus relative majority votes, while rule of law features regular examinations plus constant evaluations. The former is about a majority, and the latter is about a meritocracy. While partisan interests dominate the former game, the impartial loyalty to the Law dominates the latter. Professional civil servants and judges are not living in a vacuum—they cannot be totally impartial—but they are much more impartial than openly partisan representatives due to how they come to power and what they are held accountable to.

In sum, the Law can "rule" due to the implementation of three basic principles:

1. The supremacy of the Basic Law: all laws and executive orders must be made according to the Constitution; the concerned disputes should be subject to the judgment of a third party—impartial professionals of law.
2. The independence of judicial and law enforcement agencies: the separation of power to form checks and balances is the core method to balance politicians and enable rule of law.
3. The meritocracy of judicial and law enforcement: the system of meritocracy guarantees the impartiality of judicial and law enforcement agencies, so that the government is less partisan and more law abiding.

Democracy is rooted in the belief in the eventual election of "good" leaders. It is often believed that the chance of government turnover every four or five years protects the welfare of the "people." Rule of law is rooted in the nonbelief in "persons"; it trusts no one who holds power, hence emphasizing the mechanism that works every day to punish government officials in case they abuse the enormous power in their hands or simply fail to govern according to law. Democracy produces the government, but is unable to force government to be law abiding every day. Rule of law does not aim at governing the people; it aims at governing the government. It can govern the government because there are independent judicial and law enforcement agencies built inside the government. Only power can effectively control power, and only government power can effectively control government power.

Why are some democracies successful and others not? The "standard" answer is that the successful ones are "liberal" democracies and the others are nonliberal ones. With the above distinctions, we will find that "liberal democracy" is different from "pure democracy" in that the former enjoys rule of law in addition to the rule of people's representatives. Without rule of law, those who have won majority votes hold concentrated power, and they might turn a democracy into a tyranny of the majority that abuses the individuals' civil liberties. With the above distinctions, we also understand that "electoral democracy" is easy to build. Distributing ballot boxes is far easier than building checks and balances. That explains the many unstable and "low-quality" democracies in the world.

How Does a Democracy Become "Liberal"?

Even if we define "true" democracy only as "liberal," while others are hybrid or childish, we still want to know what characterizes an "infant" or "hybrid" democracy, and why others are "genuine," or "mature," or "developed," or "liberal."

"Liberal" democracies in the West feature not only periodic elections of top leaders, but also rule of law. The authority of law is built on the effectiveness of law enforcement, enforcing equality before law, checks and balances in the separation of government power, legal provisions for freedoms of speech, press, association, and assembly, as well as other laws made in accordance with the Constitution. The effectiveness of law enforcement depends on the systems of the civil service and judiciary that are of high quality and independent of the electoral machine. "Liberal" democracies exhibit many fewer signs of corruption or social instability than those "pure" democracies in the third world.

Are periodic elections associated with those "liberal" features? No. The above-mentioned "liberal" features of Western democracy are in fact obtained by solid institutional arrangements of rule of law instead of elections. Liberty is not obtained through liberty per se. To obtain liberty, we have to be slaves to the Law.[12] Liberty derives from strict and impartial law enforcement. Tyranny (by one, a few, or many) begins where the effect of the Law ends and when law enforcement is abused.[13] Here, "the Law" means the basic constitutional provisions of justice, and "law" or "laws" containing detailed regulations of daily life, which are supposed to be interpretations of the Law in the current routine. Of course, even the Basic Law is man made; yet it is not made according to the contemporary group interests, but instead to reflect the universal justice of the "Natural Law" born of the long-term and costly experiences of humankind. Of course, the contemporary "interpretations" of the Basic Law do often reflect current ideologies and group interests, but that is exactly why we need "impartial professionals" to interpret and enforce laws.

Although "free" elections are supported by the four freedoms of speech, press, assembly, and association, those freedoms are not the products of elections. Compared to the principle of majority vote, the clear provisions and effective enforcement of law are a much more secure source of, and protection for, those four freedoms. Without an independent and impartial civil service, and a judiciary that is loyal to the concerned laws, those who hold the majority votes tend to enjoy a concentration of power and deprive the minorities' rights to the freedom of speech, press, assembly, and association. Even in the United States, the tendency of the majority has at times threatened the four freedoms. Right after the "9/11" terrorist attack on the World Trade Center and the Pentagon in 2001, that tendency was clearly seen again. A democracy needs freedom of speech, press, assembly, and association, but it does not provide the means for obtaining them. Moreover, the four freedoms do not require democracy—they can be protected even without periodic elections of leaders. We can see that in the case of Hong Kong, both yesterday and today. Even with periodic elections, the four freedoms are still widely abused by governments in the third world. More often than not, this abuse occurs because of the ruling parties' need to win periodic elections. The rights to the four freedoms are written in constitutions almost everywhere, but they remain only on paper in most developing countries. The key lies in the checks and balances, in how independent the power of the nonelected law enforcement agencies is, in how they are made accountable to the concerned laws instead of the elected leaders, elected offices, or influential/powerful "civil societies."

Similarly, elections do not create checks and balances among government branches; laws do. In fact, checks and balances appeared in Europe way before democracy came into being, in the form of the separation of the Church and the secular power of kings and queens that the "oriental despotism" did not have. Moreover, neither the making of the judiciary-civil service nor the practice of "judicial review" is compatible with the democratic principle. Without being checked and balanced by an independent judiciary and law enforcement, even elected representatives could become merely money and/or power suckers. Among many new democracies today, elected leaders often hold the kind of power that is nearly "absolute" during their tenure, suppressing or pressuring the judiciary and civil service. It is not uncommon to believe that the winning of a greater electoral majority means the people's endorsement of the leader's greater power. Does an election make the elected leader more legitimate than a non-elected judge or civil servant? The belief in the legitimacy only of elected leaders often leads to the concentration of power in the hands of those leaders. Elections per se do not correct this; they are a major source of it. In short, checks and balances belong to the domain of rule of law, not electoral democracy.

Elections are said to permit "equal," "adequate," or "effective" political participation of all adults. But how can those who elect and those who are elected be equal in political participation? One has the power of a few minutes to cast a vote every two, four, five, or six years, but another decides policies for two, four, five, or six years. Public opinion can influence policy making, but the influence of public opinion is not necessarily a part of electoral democracy. More important, the question of whether we really want more and more equal political participation looms large. If major decisions were made by the "people," who would take the responsibility for wrong decisions, and who could punish the "majority" of the people? Don't we want a "responsible" government? It was a fundamental Athenian belief that the greater the number of people who participated in the affairs of government, the more likely the decisions made would be just. They confused the power of the people with justice to the people. In fact, whether the tyranny is of one, a few, or many makes little difference. Almond and Verba describe a kind of political indifference unique to the Anglo-Saxon political culture. They assert that political indifference is a main feature of a mature democracy.[14] If they are correct, "equal" political participation must be a fiction; and those ambiguous adjectives of degree, such as "effective," or "adequate," merely serve to further confuse people. When we carefully study the electoral arrangements of "liberal" democracies, we learn that their mass political participation is much more strictly—but legally—confined than that of "new democracies" in the third world, such as in Taiwan. For example, the American electoral arrangement has effectively prevented the influence of a third, weaker party.

Perhaps we do not assume equal political participation through elections; instead, we assume equal social status through the principle of "one man, one vote." Social equality has been greatly valued ever since the French Revolution. Yet, the issue mainly emerged in the context of European feudalism, which was not at all a universal phenomenon in the world, at least not in China. And I doubt that the principle of "one man, one vote" could claim more social equality than the grand constitutional principle that "All men and women are equal before the Law." Social equality has much less to do with the number of votes than with the provisions and enforcement of law, with the degree of social mobility, and with the distribution of wealth. Elections force the elected to be accountable to the demands of certain strong social groups, and they reflect changes in the balance of power of a certain social setting, but they have not contributed to social equality as much as many would like to believe, such as in the case of India. Equality in social status is easier to achieve under an effective rule of law arrangement that guarantees the strict enforcement of the principle "No one is above or below the law." That is, social equality is achieved and assured when the interpretation and administration of laws are independent from the influence of powerful interest groups. "Liberal" democracy provides means for that, while pure electoral democracy does not. In other words, rule of law provides means for that, while elections do not.

In new democracies corruption is often a central political issue, while it is rarely so among "liberal" democracies. Should we believe that the higher the degree of democracy, the fewer chances there are for corruption? This belief is the major reason why many Chinese intellectuals favor democracy.

Corruption means the *abuse of public office for private material gain*. Corruption has two related roots: an embedded human character of pursuing private gain, and the fact that there are people who hold public office. As such, nowhere can corruption be totally eliminated. However, corruption can be controlled to such a degree that it is not a major concern of the general public when opposing the government.

If corruption is defined as using public office for private gain, there are only three possible ways for corruption, namely, the power of public office, the desire for private gain, and the linkage between public office and private gain. Hence the three methods for curbing corruption: (1) retain the autonomy of each functionally specialized government branch so as to form checks and balances among public offices and reduce the concentration of power; (2) require higher moral standards for officials, making them refrain from seeking private gain; (3) reduce the linkage between public office and private gain with stricter regulations and smaller government. None of the three has much to do with elections, and in the current world of the market economy, checks and balances provide the most effective means to prevent the concentration of power that often leads to the abuse of public office for private gain.

Many believe that only authoritarian regimes feature a concentration of government power. Yet a democratic regime could also feature that—in the hands of the elected leaders. That happens when elections are believed to be the only source of "legitimate" power, and the autonomy of judicial powers and law enforcement cannot be sustained. Moreover, elections per se contain a built-in tripartite mechanism that creates the potential for corruption. (1) The more electorates the politicians want to reach, the more money they need. (2) There are always rich people who want to provide money in exchange for some government support. (3) Therefore, once elected, the public offices are to serve voters on the one hand, and money providers on the other.

With checks and balances, "liberal" democracies have effectively brought corruption under control. In contrast, despite more open and more frequent elections, corruption has increased in "pure" (electoral) democracies. The governments of both Singapore and British Hong Kong intervened relatively less in the economy than other governments (i.e., less linkage between public office and private gain), but both intervened intensively in social life due to the characters of their respective societies. This social intervention invited widespread corruption through the 1960s. Singapore built an independent system of anti-corruption in the late 1960s, and Hong Kong imitated it in the early 1970s. Both effectively reduced corruption within a few years.[15] Today both governments rank among the most honest in the world, despite the fact that they have only marginalized democratic institutions. An authoritarian regime comes to its end once the autonomy of judicial powers and a civil service is in place. That is why the nondemocratic regimes in Hong Kong and Singapore are radically different from authoritarian regimes. Sometimes Hong Kong and Singapore are said to practice "rule by law" instead of "rule of law." However, no leader would rule *by law* if he or she enjoys unlimited power. The key is institutional checks and balances among government offices.

Since corruption was also a serious problem in the West before, many believe that it only takes time for new democracies to become "mature." The point, however, is not about *when* the corruption will be brought under control, but *what* can control corruption.

In sum, the solidity of rule of law has little to do with the degree of democracy (the more extensive the mass participation and the more frequent the elections, the higher the degree of democracy). Only when "rule of the people (or people's representatives)" is combined with "rule of law" can a democracy become a liberal democracy. Liberty is obtained through the supreme authority of the Basic Law, not through imposing the will of the "majority" on the minority.

On the "Mixed" Regime

The advantage of democracy over autocracy lies not in that democratically elected leaders necessarily serve people's welfare better than tyrants, but in that democracy periodically provides chances to expel "bad" leaders. In other words, democracy is preferred because it cannot be "worse" than autocracy, although it might not be "better." However, despite democracy's obvious advantage, we are still witnessing the presence of autocracy even today—2,500 years after the Athenian democracy. In fact, the term "democracy" was ignored even in Europe for more than two thousand years. Up until the early nineteenth century, everyone knew what democracy was, but few supported it. Today, however, few know what democracy is, but everyone supports it. It is not that people of the past were less "enlightened" than the Athenians or us. People support "modern" democracy because of its excellent performance, and its excellent performance comes only when direct democracy is turned into representative government—rule of a few via popular elections—and when representative government is combined with rule of law. In short, modern representative government is "good" only when it is a mixed regime featuring rule of law and rule of a few via elections by many. We need a mixed regime because even a government of an elected few has crucial shortcomings, which can be overcome by rule of law.

We may all agree with Aristotle that a "mixed regime" is wanted. A "pure" democracy is little more than the tyranny of the majority, and a "pure" representative government is little more than the tyranny of a few elected by the (relative) majority. However, few people today are interested in why a regime should be mixed, what makes it mixed, and how it is mixed. A mixed regime could be a parliamentary democracy supplemented by rule of law, or a rule of law supplemented by parliamentary democracy. The two kinds are radically different.

The strong legalist tradition in the West allows for a sound mixture of parliamentary democracy and rule of law, but most developing countries have been unable to achieve this. Distributing ballot boxes is by far easier than building independent and

Table 1.1

Regime Type and Comparative Performance

	All Western countries	Most developing countries	The rest of the developing countries	Hong Kong, Singapore (Japan before 1993)
Democracy	+	+	−	−
Rule of Law	+	−	−	+
Performance	+	−	−	+

quality judiciary and civil service systems. Many would believe that with democracy it is only a matter of time before obtaining rule of law. However, democracy without rule of law is vulnerable to corruption and political decay; it could well become a gambling game of shifting dictators. A democracy is likely to sustain and foster "good governance" if built on the basis of rule of law.

By the presence or lack of democracy and rule of law, we may divide the world's existing regimes into four groups, and roughly evaluate their performance by three criteria—the presence of democracy, rule of law, and performance: (1) Those that enjoy both democracy and rule of law are Western democracies, and their performance is excellent. (2) Most "new democracies" in the third world lack rule of law, and their performance ranks among the poorest. (3) The rest of the third world countries have little democracy and rule of law, and their performance is generally better than the second group. (4) Two essentially Chinese societies—Hong Kong and Singapore—enjoy rule of law but have only marginalized institutions of democracy, and their performance is no less excellent than that of Western democracies (see Table 1.1). The regime in Japan since the Meiji Reform of the 1860s and until the early 1990s might also fall into this last category. Nineteenth-century Prussia might represent its early form in European history. There is room to debate the significance of the two small city-states, but I will do that later.

Knowledge of political sociology—even before Max Weber—tells us that rule of law is the most effective indicator of the transition from a "traditional" society to a "modern" society.[16] A society becomes "modern" when the dominant patron–client relationships are replaced by the dominance of legal relations, or "contracts," so to speak.

Like autocracy, democracy is also a type of personal rule. Personal rule means rule by political leader(s). In an autocracy, one or a few nonelected leaders impose their rule on the people. In a democracy, a few elected representatives rule the people. "Government of the people, by the people, for the people" has been a special pride for modern representative democracies; but the "of" and "for" may be no less applicable to regimes of other types. The question remains only with "by the people." Even if we challenge whether people can govern, we have to at least admit that democracy is government by the people's representatives. Even so, democracy is still a kind of personal rule. That is the essential similarity between democracy and autocracy. Rule of one, a few, or many all belong to "personal rule."

By contrast, a rule of law regime emphasizes the supremacy of law through separation of personal power to form checks and balances. It is based on nonelected offices that explain laws, enforce laws, and are accountable to laws. Thus, rule of *law* differs from *personal* rule. In Japan, ever since the Meiji Reform, one could hardly find clear "political leaders" to take responsibility on top of the bureaucracy. So the Japanese government is said to be a "truncated pyramid." Similarly, ever since the early 1980s, Hong Kong has not had a clear political leader. And since the early 1990s, Singapore has not been under anyone's dictatorship. Of course, a "pure" rule of law regime has fatal shortcomings. It is either a stagnant regime, allowing little change, or it could become a government of judges/civil servants.

Why should we be alert to the rule of political leaders when they are popularly elected and hence accountable to their electorates? We have two major worries in building a pure representative democracy without the authority of law being established first: we worry not only that the concentration of power surrounding elected leaders might allow them to abuse their public offices, but also that a representative democracy is likely to breed the potential for social disorder.

As to our first worry, unlike the principle of meritocracy, the principle of the majority in an electoral democracy justifies an institutionalized game of power politics. The powerful groups have the legitimacy to win the right to govern, and the less powerful groups are supposed to gracefully accept their failure. What is the problem with power politics? Since some groups are unavoidably better organized, hence more powerful, their demands tend to obtain more representation, often disproportional to the number of people that they represent. The "minority" could well become hopeless under the principle of the majority, and would have to seek solutions by either nondemocratic means, or special arrangements of a nondemocratic nature.

The conflict of the minority with the democratic principle of the majority offers us room to think about the rights of the minority. While nondemocratic polities are supposed to have a built-in legitimacy problem, the power politics of a democracy is said to be naturally legitimate. What if the legitimacy of the majority principle is challenged in certain cultural establishments? Are we to believe that a government is "legitimate" whenever its leaders are elected? The legitimacy of elected leaders is based more on a belief than on sound logic. How does winning a certain proportion of popular votes on one single day relate to justice in governance over several years? The question is not answered, but rejected with "what else is a better alternative?" There are, of course, easy alternatives. When democracy fails, autocracy is a feasible and widespread alternative. A rule of law regime, like those in Japan, Hong Kong, and Singapore, is also a practical alternative. Why do we consider nonelected judges "legitimate" and trust them to make judicial decisions? The general public in the West deems the game of open power competition among social groups as just and fair—the powerful should gain their due. In most cases, and it is unavoidable in the game of numbers, the game winner represents only a "relative majority," namely, a de facto minority in terms of the total size of the electorate. The game is only "fair" when the general public is in consensus with the game's rules. This consensus, however, is culturally unique. Shall we obey the decision of certain people simply because they are backed by a relatively "larger" number of people? Why should it be a "universal" value? People in the world of science, education, and enterprise have never followed the principle of the majority. In Chinese civilization, belief in the majority is not only alien, but also problematic. In the Chinese language, the word "politics" (*zheng zhi*) is written like "the governance of justice," or the "governance of righteousness," not the government of a certain number or kind of people.

The culturally unique consensus on power politics is crucial to the success of democracies. There are cultures in which people do not identify with the powerful and with the balance of power, and that lack of consensus is by no means culturally inferior. The lack of consensus may derive from certain social settings. Some social settings may not feature clear boundaries among social groups. Sometimes even a boundary between "state" and "society" might not exist. Under such a different social setting, it could be very dangerous to play the power politics of social cleavage, stirring up social conflicts by enlarging social cleavages. In China, "class struggle" turned out to be a Hobbesian war of all against all. None of the involved parties respected or accepted any "legal procedure," and the losers did not "gracefully" accept their failure, but fought to the bloody end. Without a chance for even corporatism, only populism, violence, and dictatorship were left. In China, a different socioeconomic setting enabled examinations as an easy alternative to elections. While elections depend on social cleavages, examinations blur them. Therefore, in the Chinese social context, nonelected officials tend to enjoy more respect than elected ones, as long as they govern according to the principle of justice.

Our second concern regarding pure democracies is this: Unlike Western societies, in which group or class politics may quickly reach a balance of power in the society, the power politics of periodic elections in many third world countries leads to easy politicization of social issues and enlarges social cleavages, making a divided society more divided and a vulnerable social order more vulnerable. Moreover, without a tradition of legalism, this "class struggle" leads to little more than an accumulation of social chaos. Rather than the consideration of universal justice, the periodic open contention for government looms large in the daily work of the legislature, executive, and even judiciary, politicizing nonpolitical issues and linking political issues directly to winning the next round of election. If we agree with "modernization theory" that "nation building" is the first important step toward development in many third world countries, democracy has not been an effective way of approaching a unified national identity. More often than not, it is detrimental to it, as in the case of India. Politicians exploit the most sensitive or even explosive issues in the society, such as religion, ethnicity, and historical hatred. When politicians try to exploit social cleavages to win the right to govern, and when democracy fails to neutralize sensitive issues, the results have been dire: we see how the tribal rifts in Rwanda were handled, how the fire in the former Yugoslavia was extinguished, how the historical hatred in central Asia was revived, and how the conflicts in Indonesia became violent. The interesting point is not how long those conflicts had already existed before democratization, but how they were not explosive without democratization. Many believe that electoral democracy is good at neutralizing sensitive issues since politicians want the largest number of votes and hence are forced to adopt the central line. This is a fallacy because it has to assume that the majority votes are around the center—that there exists a *dominant* middle class. What happens if there is no such "middle class" in most developing countries? A strong consensus makes a democracy work, but democracy per se creates neither a middle class nor consensus. Despite a strong "middle class," it is the equality before the law instead of electoral politics that has been creating and maintaining a consensus between Singapore's 70 percent ethnic Chinese and 30 percent ethnic minorities. Politicians do not have to take a central-line position. More likely, they try their best to exploit all potential social cracks to win a certain proportion of votes—in the name of "liberty." As such, democracy without rule of law demonstrates a tendency of self-destruction, leading to an easy decay from democracy to autocracy.

The crucial shortcomings of democracy force us to consider a mixture of democracy with rule of law. The justification for rule of law has been strong throughout Western civilization. The logic is simple and powerful. Liberty means people's freedom to do whatever they want to do. It is self-rule, so to speak. However, self-rule invites the rule of "the law of the jungle," so there comes the need for a "government." People need a government first and foremost for order. Therefore, the government is authorized with the power to monopolize all means of violence. Yet whenever a government is in place, its existence per se becomes *the* major threat to a *fair* order. In the name of order or "long-term social interests," those who hold government offices often deprive individuals of key liberties. The people have no reason to trust anyone who is authorized with the tremendous power of government, whether or not he or she is elected. Thus, there must be a mechanism of checks and balances to make sure that the government is law abiding, namely, that it acts according to the basic social norms, and strictly follows the principle that people can do *all* that the laws do not prohibit and the government can do *only* what the laws allow it to do. With such a mechanism, officials will be punished whenever they do things other than what they are allowed to do by law. Government maintains social order, and rule of law maintains a just order.

In a society of class or group politics, however, laws often strongly reflect the interests of strong or influential social classes or groups. Thus, representative democracy is an effective way to correct laws unfair to certain groups of people. In a largely undifferentiated society without a stable consciousness of social cleavages, representative democracy can also help in improving laws and making laws reflect social progress.

In our era of the triumph of representative democracy, the danger is that elected leaders will abuse the tremendous power in their hands, and that this power abuse will lead to an unjust order that creates potential for social disorder. For example, despite the fact that the American people elect their leaders in fair elections, American leaders are obviously abusing the power of the United States, creating an unfair world order that fosters rebellions and a new world disorder. That derives from the fact that no other country can check and balance the tremendous power of the United States. If there is no way to correct this international political imbalance short of the emergence of a multipolar international power structure, we can clearly infer that the power abuse in a domestic context could likewise be prevented by a mixed regime. Elected leaders could be checked and balanced by the nonelected agencies produced under the principle of meritocracy, such as the judiciary and civil service. The nonelected offices are, therefore, as "legitimate" as the elected ones. When the elected leaders and the nonelected judiciary and law enforcement rule together, we call it a "mixed regime" of democracy and rule of law. A *pure* democracy comes into being whenever the discourse on elections as the only source of legitimacy prevails, and whenever elected leader(s) can inundate the judiciary and civil service. A pure democracy is not far from autocracy. On the eve of the eightieth anniversary of the founding of the Communist Party of China, there was a very terse press passage that gave an official interpretation of the current Chinese polity. I quote it here to show how close the rule by people's representatives is to an authoritarian form of government, or that the extreme end of democracy is the starting point of autocracy.

> Separation of power is not a democratic principle; rather, it represents the elites' rule against the rule of the people. China does not practice separation of power because we seek the most thorough and extensive people's democracy. All powers belong to the people, and all state power must be exercised in a unified manner by the People's Congress, and must never be shared by any other organs. All other organs, such as the judiciary and inspection, are generated by the People's Congress and are accountable to it, being placed under its supervision. There is a division of duties, but no separation of power.[17]

When all the power belongs to the people's representatives, China could legally maintain one-party rule as long as the party enjoys a dominant majority in the parliament. Many fascists came to power through fair elections, and the most important signal of their rise was the disabling of some key constitutional rights of individual liberty in the name of "majority people's desire." The real enemy of autocracy, therefore, is not democracy, but rule of law.

A democracy without rule of law can easily decay into the trap of corruption and social disorder, which turns autocracy into an attractive and practical alternative. So come the seemingly endless cycles of democracy and autocracy in the third world, as well as the practical difficulties there in distinguishing a democracy from an autocracy.

There is no such belief in the West that elections are the only source of legitimacy, although that belief is widely advocated in the non-Western countries to defeat autocracy. Liberal democracies in the West are not merely the "-cracy" of people's representatives, but also that of judges and law enforcement agents. In both Western Europe and the United States, the term *rule of law* enjoys almost the same authority as *democracy*. They are the two pillars of "liberal" democracy. Liberal democracy as such enjoys the best performance in today's world, demonstrating a beautiful balance between order and liberty, and representing the highest achievement so far in the political civilization of humankind.

However, people in the West tend to refer to their mixed regime democracy or liberal democracy, and they thus take the rule of law for granted, often forgetting that their performance is not derived from democracy only, and they believe that they differ from the backward countries due to the latter's lack of democracy. How many Americans understand the significance of the fact that their president-elect cannot assume his office without taking the oath to observe the Constitution, which must be witnessed by the nonelected Supreme Court justices? The U.S. president has to "swear in," no matter how many people have elected him. Since the Cold War, people in the West tend to forget their own strong legalist tradition on which the "liberal" democracy was founded. They are too carried away by the idea of spreading democracy, and thus ignore the critically important issue of a mixed regime and the sequence of priority. Moreover, now and then democracy is used as an unprincipled foreign policy instrument, and double standards are seen everywhere. The recent joke, of course, is the official U.S. reaction toward the military coup in Venezuela against the democratically elected president in April 2002.

Democracy can be created with little rule of law, and rule of law can be created with little democracy. They are not naturally integrated, but can be combined. Because of their contradictory natures, each balances the other. Rule of law reduces the authority of the people's representatives, forcing them to be law abiding. Democracy reduces the rigidity of the established legal system, making it less stagnant and more adaptable to a changing society. While elections are easy to hold, rule of law is difficult to build, for rule of law is very far from the personal rule of one, a few, or many. Without a legalist tradition, the authority of law has to be planted; and building independent and quality judicial powers and a civil service is much more difficult than distributing ballot boxes across the country.

As Western democracies were built on an already solid belief in the authority of law, the third world new democracies are built with little legalist tradition. Having obtained the tremendous power of "representation," the politicians in the third world are reluctant to yield their power to laws and the authority of law enforcement. Rather, they tend to manipulate the judiciary and civil service, and manufacture laws for their own convenience. Democracies in Asia, such as those in India, Philippines, and Taiwan, have weakened their traditions of legalism that originated in the time of colonialism or authoritarianism. In most developing countries, modernity depends not on replacing the rule of one with the rule of a few or many, but on the authority of law. What really differentiates the developed and developing countries is not whether they are democratic, but whether they are "liberal"—namely, whether they have rule of law. This also means that sequence is critical. Due to the differences in sequence, the transitions from socialism in China and the Soviet Union have obtained radically different results. In the post–Cold War world, acknowledging the importance of sequence requires that the intellectual world demythologize democracy by understanding what it actually does. Therefore, whatever is the favorite choice in the West, China cannot regret its different choice from the Russians, and the people of Hong Kong do not feel any inferiority about their polity vis-à-vis the democratic regime in Taiwan.

Different conditions require different proportions in the "mixture" of rule of law and representative democracy. The feasibility of a particular balance depends on the social setting and cultural tradition of a particular nation. After all, one cannot leave the earth by pulling one's own hair. As the grounds beneath people's feet differ, so people are not all the same. If we truly tolerate and respect cultural diversities, including the diversities of political culture, we cannot only justify and tolerate the need for a uniquely conservative American system, but also tolerate unique systems in other cultural backgrounds.

Due to the lack of a legalist tradition in China, building the authority of law is the priority in the current Chinese context. Building the authority of law is the most effective way to overcome tyranny and protect liberty in its rudimentary markets. The problem in China is not *who* should rule, but *what* should rule. So my argument is that China needs a mixed regime. The regime I suggest is a mixed one, but mixed in a unique way: it is neither a pure democracy nor a democracy supplemented by rule of law, but rule of law supplemented by democracy.

Polity Options in Different Social Settings

With the above understanding of the differences and different functions of democracy and rule of law, I am now ready to explain why China has not embraced democracy.

Let us begin with the contrast between rule by law in feudal Europe and rule by morality in traditional China. In feudal Europe, personal rule was more or less justified with the Law of Divinity. In traditional China, personal rule was justified more or less by moral principles. How did the difference between the two civilizations arise?

Over one thousand years ago, the Frankish kingdom started European "feudal" society with large plantations as its economic basis, a rigid system of estates as its social basis, and highly fragmented administrative entities as its political basis. Manors, or seigniors, and small kingdoms competed with each other and collaborated with a unified church system. This feudal society had four major characteristics: (1) a lack of economic freedom in the selling of land and labor; (2) a lack of political equality that denied the lower classes participation in government; (3) a strong tradition of power politics derived from competition among the decentralized political entities and fragmented societies; (4) a strong tradition of legalism that recognized the authority of law, which was rooted in the belief in the authority of the Divine. The justification for government was a matter of "contract" with God, and later in modern times, with the "society" or "people."

How Was China Different from Europe?

In 356 B.C.E., the Shang Yang Reforms began Chinese "traditional" society. Its economic basis consisted of small and self-sufficient family farms. Its social basis was made up of equal farmer families without a clear or stable differentiation of social status. Due to the lack of primogeniture and the agricultural interests in giving birth to as many sons as possible, "No rich family could be sustained for more than three generations [*fu bu guo san dai*]," as a Chinese proverb says. The political basis of Chinese traditional society was a unified kingdom under an emperor. The emperor led a centralized, hierarchical, and very secular government of civil service that governed in collaboration with local gentries, who led their communities via the bounds of lineages in natural villages. This traditional society also had four major features: (1) an embedded tradition of economic liberty; (2) a unique tradition of political equality; (3) a tradition of governance that depended mainly on persuasion instead of power politics; (4) a tradition of authority/legitimacy that was based on moral principles instead of laws or God.

What do those sharp contrasts imply for politics? Some further descriptions of the Chinese features will be self-explanatory.

1. China enjoyed a very strong tradition of economic liberty.[18] The freedom to sell land and labor was legally provided for by the Shang Yang Reforms (356 B.C.E.) in the country of Qin—one of the seven states in the period of the Warring States (475 B.C.E.–221 B.C.E.). Shang Yang's method soon socialized the other six countries. In 221 B.C.E.,135 years later, Qin unified the whole of China and built China's first unitary dynastic regime—the Qin Dynasty. In the following 2,200 years, except during the first three decades of Communist rule, freedom to sell land and labor was generally upheld as a natural principle. It is not surprising that in the past seven years economies in both Hong Kong and Singapore have been rated as the "freest" in the world, freer than the American economy. In Taiwan, the government tried hard to block economic exchanges with Mainland China, but the effort has been understandably ineffective, although it should have been easy for the island. It is quite natural that China's command economy was extremely hard to maintain and easy to set free. Today, witnessing China's huge imports by smuggling and the dramatic difference between nominal tax rates and the actually collected taxes, we can easily find very high incentives inside China to reduce government intervention, open up to the outside world, and support free trade. Historically, Chinese traditional government tried to block linkages with the outside world, but it was exactly during that time that Chinese immigrants opened up Taiwan and filled Southeast Asia. A similar tradition of economic freedom made the United States independent from Great Britain and led it to become the stronghold for free trade between world markets. In the foreseeable future, the Chinese tradition of economic freedom may well allow China to replace the United States as the free trade leader in the world.

For certain social strata in Europe, there would be no economic freedom without democracy, yet in China economic freedom took deep roots without any understanding of democracy. This difference was mainly derived from a unique Chinese social setting—the undifferentiated small-farmer society. And that nonfeudal social setting was closely related to the early maturity of agricultural knowledge. However, democracy is not just for economic liberty. How can people access government without democracy?

2. China enjoys a unique mechanism of political equality. To adapt to an undifferentiated small-farmer society, China invented a system of civil service. Through civil exams, the government, excepting the emperor, was institutionally open to competition among rich and poor, young and old, and even native and foreign. There was no wealth limit, age discrimination, or even nationality requirement for attending civil exams. The system was built in the Sui Dynasty (581–618 C.E.) and was institutionalized in the Tang Dynasty (618–907). It lasted for 1,300 years until its abolition in 1905. The examination system was the dominant approach for political participation and was popularly deemed fair. Prime ministers were often born into poor farmer families, and even the poorest farmer could expect to become a government official if he worked hard to master the contents of the examination. Lineages often financially supported their most promising (smartest) boys—not necessarily from the rich families—for school learning, so as to guarantee the success of the lineage. A Chinese proverb describes the miraculous social mobility through civil exams: "A common farmer in the morning can become an official beside the emperor in the evening [*zhao wei tian she lang, mu deng tian zi tang*]." No matter how true the social mobility was, ideology blurred social cleavages via the examination system. Just like the United States, no matter how big the gap is between the rich and poor, the *consciousness of status* is comparatively low due to the belief in social mobility. China's social cleavages were further blurred by the lack of primogeniture. Successive generations did not necessarily become wealthier. The open regime thus enjoyed such a legitimacy that no peasant rebellion or foreign conqueror before the twentieth century ever tried to abolish the system. Rebellions were always targeted at "bad" emperors and corrupt officials, not at the system of political participation via examination. Revolutionaries of the twentieth century challenged the content of the examination, but not the fairness of the approach. Even during the Communist rule of the past fifty years, passing the national college entrance exam has still been the most important qualification for government office.

Most people in China today agree that the national college entrance exam is the fairest thing, or perhaps the only fair thing, that still remains of the old system. No nation in the world takes examination and the skills of examination as seriously as the Chinese do. In the summer of 1997, the countryside of southern China was suffering the worst flood of the entire twentieth century, and many people fled to rooftops or trees. This happened during the national college entrance examination season. Military boats came to the flooded area in the early morning of the first examination day, with soldiers shouting, "taking examinees!" If one had an examinee certificate, he or she was saved, for the examinees "had to attend the national exam," and nothing was more important than that. No one objected, and the military was highly praised. On the national examination day, Beijing municipal government sends government vehicles to pick up examinees trapped in traffic jams. Vehicles bearing the "examinee" sign have the privilege to ignore traffic rules, including red lights and "one way" signs.

Because of the long-standing belief in "equality before examination," the Chinese have a natural doubt about class politics or "group politics," in which a stronger social group obtains greater political influence. It is common sense in rural China that villagers often do not respect the authority of the elected village leaders, for the majority principle is "unfair": a person from a larger lineage will always obtain the position to make key decisions. Chinese villagers would rather respect the mediation by the "learned" (knowledgeable) ones, such as senior or fair (neutral) people who are, or used to be, officials. The village election in China is highly publicized in the world media, yet few know that it has been a top-down effort for nearly ten years, and villagers often do not come to the election if they are not paid to attend. The same thing happens in Chinese students' and scholars' associations in American universities. Although each association represents hundreds or even thousands of students and scholars from China, each year's election in each university often draws fewer than ten participants, including candidates. A similar indifference to elections is also found among Chinese Americans, despite the fact that they should have high incentives to cast votes under the structural pressure of power politics. It is neither a surprise that the general public in both Hong Kong and Singapore supports the concept that civil servants should institutionally enjoy higher authority than that of elected politicians. Have bureaucracy or partisan politics dominated Japan? There was little doubt about it from the Meiji Reform until 1993, when Japan started "democratization."

In Europe, due to the feudal tradition, certain social strata were legally excluded from political participation, and democracy effectively solved that problem. In China equal opportunity of political participation took deep roots without democracy, and the lack of feudalism again explains that. It was elite politics, but the process of elite selection was open and equal. We might say that modern representative democracy also contains the elite selection, hence a somewhat elite politics—through elections though. However, without elections, how can people's desires be represented?

3. In a country of scattered and undifferentiated villages, as in China, governance heavily depended on persuasion instead of power politics. This persuasion was mainly carried out through indoctrination of moral principles via the examination system, and people could, in an orderly fashion, climb up the ladder of social prestige. Both Confucius (551–479 B.C.E.) and Plato (427–347 B.C.E.) thought that moral principles could rule, but both failed as their world fragmented into "warring states." Confucius's ideas, nevertheless, had a chance of success in a huge and unified kingdom of small farmers. In 130 B.C.E., 350 years after Confucius's death, Liu Che (Han Wu Di), the fifth emperor of the Han Dynasty (206 B.C.E.– 220 C.E.), adopted Confucianism as the official ideology, which was henceforth followed by nearly all the Chinese emperors throughout the dynastic history. In a fragmented feudal Europe, there was never a chance to implement Plato's idea, although it has continued to fascinate Westerners till today and is taught in all Western universities. Confucius told the rulers "to govern with moral principles [wei zheng yi de]." He explained: "To lead the people with administrative order and punish people with laws, people shall obey only for the fear of punishment, but they would not have a sense of right or wrong. To lead with moral

principles and sincere rituals, social order shall be easily maintained with people's strong sense of righteousness [*Dao zhi yi zheng, qi zhi yi xing, min mian er wu chi. Dao zhi yi de, qi zhi yi li, you chi qie ge*]."[19]

The traditional Chinese government's reliance on persuasion instead of power produced two results. The first was "small government." The traditional government in China was so small and lean that it did not have a separate institution for collecting taxes or for judicial affairs, and often it did not even maintain a standing army. At the county level, most of the time there was only one state-paid official, and this official was in charge of public order, judicial affairs, conscription, and taxation. The size of a county in traditional China was at least two times larger by area than it is today. China, with roughly the same area as that of the United States, has nearly 1,800 counties today. One emperor in the Ming Dynasty (1368–1644) was famous in that he did not attend to administrative affairs for thirty years, completely depending on his small government of civil service. Most common farmers never saw a state official in their lifetimes. The polity was authoritarian in form, but liberal in reality. A Chinese proverb so describes the people's freedom under that regime: "Heaven is high, and the emperor is far away [*tian gao huangdi yuan*]." Chinese farmers thus enjoyed the liberty of "limited government." The actual mechanism of rule can be summarized as follows: A villager passed the civil exam and became an official. When he retired, he returned to his village to become a local "gentry" with one foot in the state and another foot in his local community, helping local officials to maintain social order.[20]

The second result of the reliance on persuasion instead of power was that the "state–society boundary" was alien to Chinese people. The reliance on gentry blurred the state–society boundary to the point of being almost nonexistent due to the ideology of China being one big family. The "state" that the farmers dealt with consisted of gentries with the double identity of state official and communal leader, and the two identities were so integrated in the concept of a big "family" that even the gentries themselves would have a hard time distinguishing them unless a political crisis occurred and they had to choose between supporting or opposing the emperor. In the Chinese language, both state and country are still translated with one term, namely, *guojia,* which literally means "a country of families." The state had the right to do anything to its people, like a father leading a family, and it had the right not to do anything, like a father spoiling his kids. This "family" concept implies that state and society are one and shall not be pitted against each other. Until today, the grassroots authority in both urban and rural China is still not a formal level of government, but widely considered a level of government that deals with everyday state–society relations. As there is no clear boundary between state and society, the power politics of status or groups has lost its conceptual basis.

In Europe, class or group desires could not be protected or promoted without representative democracy. In China, without democracy, the blurred state–society boundary still somehow led to effective accountability. The lack of feudalism and the solidity of a small-farmer society meant that people's desires (interests), whether more or less diversified than European ones, were definitely less confrontational. They did not need to compete for the power of representation to protect or promote their interests. Thus, there was no word for election in the Chinese language until modern times. There existed the possibility of liberty under a small government, and the small government could govern by persuasion and maintain itself as long as the principle of justice—basic social norms of the time—was upheld. However, what were the social norms of the time? Without democracy, how could government officials observe and enforce the social norms instead of abusing the centralized and potentially tremendous power in their hands?

4. Moral principles, instead of laws or God, were the source of authority/legitimacy. In a society of scattered and self-sufficient farmer families, upholding moral principles was enough to maintain social order under a unified kingdom, and the state relied on local gentry's help to rule, rarely intervening in communal affairs. Unlike in a commercial society of intensive interdependence, laws made little sense in a stagnant society of self-sufficient farm families. A member of the gentry won allegiance from his community not because of his family wealth, but because he received an intensive indoctrination in Confucianism, passed the first, second, or even the third level of civil exams, and was a retired official, hence the "teacher" of many current officials and an incarnation of Confucian moral principles. The content of civil examinations was mainly four things: (1) the Chinese history of governance; (2) the social moral principle (respecting hierarchical social order of emperor, officials, and father/husband—*jun chen fu zi*); (3) the rulers' moral principle ("The people's welfare is of the most importance, the country is the next, and the emperor is the least important"—*min wei ben, she ji ci zhi, jun wei qing*); and (4) the personal moral principle (benevolence, righteousness, courtesy, intelligence, and credibility–*ren yi li zhi xin*). A gentry was loyal to the state because he was indoctrinated to respect the hierarchical order that allowed him to become successful. He was also loyal to his communal interests because he was educated with the moral principle of governance.

The Confucian teachings thus featured a kind of reciprocity of rule. The emperor and local government could be "legitimately" overthrown when the ruler "loses his sense of morality" (*shi de*). And so came another proverb. "People take turns to become emperor, and it is my family's turn next year [*huang di lun liu zuo, ming nian dao wo jia*]." Kang Xi (1654–1722), an early emperor of the Qing Dynasty, ordered that the farmland tax should be fixed forever to the level of his time (*yong bu jia fu*). Until the end of the dynasty in 1911, not a single Qing emperor dared to increase the farmland tax by even a cent, not even after China was forced to pay 450 million taels of silver—one tael by every old and young, male and female Chinese—as the war indemnity to the eight foreign countries that invaded China in 1900 to put off the Boxers. To collect the money, the Qing government sold the titles and ranks of government offices, and borrowed from domestic and foreign banks. It was to respect ancestors, and also for the welfare of farmer families. The motto for all Chinese emperors ever since the Tang Dynasty of 618–907 C.E. was, "The boat [royal family] was both supported and sunk by water [people]" *zai zhou fu zhou*). Due to the legitimacy and effectiveness of rule by moral principle, Chinese people bore a very weak sense of law. Unlike laws, however, the constraint of moral principles on personal behavior was always very "soft," and patron–client networks permeated the society and government in the form of kinship, lineage, community, locality, and guild. Restricting the use of public office for private gain relied mainly on moral teachings and self-restraint. The widespread natural worship of ancestry, local superstitions, cults, customs, and habits loosely held the society together. A traditional society as such, like a plate holding a large amount of sand, was very vulnerable to modern kinds of tremors, especially when being challenged by modern organizations born out of industrial markets, such as the military, accounting system, and the organization of modern industries.

In Europe, power could be abused to support the interests of certain social groups or classes, and rule of law could prevent that. In China, the lack of clear or stable social cleavages allowed the idea of universal will (*tian li*—a kind of "natural" moral principles) to dominate the state–society ties. However, it is true that the soft moral control of the officials and emperors became more and more problematic as they stayed in power longer. And abusing public office for personal gain had long been a central issue in China's history of governance. Although some sophisticated regulations were invented under China's civil service system, such as periodic office rotations and performance evaluations, as well as the strict rules to prohibit officials assuming office in their home counties, corruption periodically exploded due to the personal concentration of power. That problem became chronic when the society became commercial and competitive, hence the collapse of moral restraints.

China before the twentieth century was more of a category of culture than a "nation state." It had no lack of economic and political freedoms, but lacked the capability to mobilize and organize the scattered and equal farmer families, which were self-sufficient. Before the encounter with the Western powers, there was little need for such a capacity to organize or mobilize the stagnant traditional society. The need came into being when China met with Great Britain. In 1840, with the purpose of protecting the British liberty to sell opium to the Chinese, a few thousand British soldiers came from two oceans away and defeated a country of 400 million people. From then on, humiliations and defeats became part of Chinese life. Therefore, the twentieth-century Chinese revolutions aimed at neither economic liberty nor political liberty, but at mobilizing and organizing farmer families for "modernization." The agenda in China was shaped by the social crisis out of that sudden encounter with the West. The difference in agenda shaped the differences in polity. And democracy was thus not within the Chinese choice.

Different Polity Choices

The choice made in Western civilization has been democracy, but democracy after "modernization." Clear cleavages among large social groups constitute the social basis of this democratic polity, such as three or four social estates in feudal Europe, tripartite "corporatism" in today's Northern Europe (union, business, and executive), and huge interest groups and "civil societies" in North America. The cultural basis of this polity is a belief in the fairness of power competition among social groups, and a firm belief in the authority of law. The modern social revolutions in Western Europe were largely class based, and American politics has always been group based. History is path shaping, and the social crisis in both feudal and modern Europe shaped the choice of a Western-style polity. It is thus natural and unavoidable that democracy was on the top of the Western political agenda.

China has made a different choice, and is likely to make a different choice in the future. The Qing government was overthrown not because it was "authoritarian," but because it failed to mobilize farmers to effectively resist imperialism and build modern industries. Qing emperors tried to imitate Japan's Meiji polity; "northern governments" after the Qing imitated the European parliamentary system. Both failed in no time. The KMT (Kuomintang) under Dr. Sun Yat-sen announced a three-stage revolution: military dictatorship (*jun zheng*), authoritarian rule (*xun zheng*), and constitutional rule (*xian zheng*). Sun's party did not achieve very much until his successor, Chiang Kai-shek, imported German advisers and adopted de facto fascist rule. Yet the KMT's failure in mobilizing farmers led to its inability to put off the communist rebellion, and its defeat by Japan helped the rise of communism. Eventually, KMT rule in China ended in a fiasco and the imitation of Russian communism prevailed. The communist regime won popular support not because it was anti-authoritarian or democratic, but because of its capacity to mobilize and organize farmers in the civil war, the Korean War, and industrialization. The legitimacy came from the fact that the communist regime made the country stand up to the powerful nations, and helped the nation as a whole to regain self-respect.

The reality that the rule of morality was replaced by the KMT "military dictatorship" and later by the communist "proletarian dictatorship" shows that economic liberty and political equality were hardly issues in China's twentieth-century revolutions. The top concern was social "mobilization" for "modernity." Modernization entails three main tasks, namely, nation building, market building, and state building. The first would achieve for China a mechanical solidarity; the second, an organic solidarity; and the last would achieve an advanced form of government that would replace the dominance of traditional patron–client ties with "legal-rational" authority. According to Weber and mainstream "modernization" theorists, the emergence of a legal-rational authority indicates the completion of modernization. Thus, a country could become "modern" without necessarily being democratic. China under Mao accomplished the first task, and under Deng, the second. Then came the issue of "state building." The communist "dictatorship" has now become outdated, and China is in need of a modern polity, so as to institutionally guarantee social justice under a market system. The "total" control by the party, and particularly by its Politburo in education, media, ideology, and the executive, judicial, and legislative branches of government, no longer suits the state-building task. The concentration of power leads to the systemic abuse of power. So come the two current options of political reform: democracy or rule of law.

For the following reasons, I see rule of law as a more promising option in China.

1. China is not a hotbed for large sociopolitical groups. The social basis of the traditional Chinese society was free, scattered, undifferentiated, self-sufficient farmer families, and the country was a loosely structured "big family" of stagnant communities/villages. China is a country of equal families, not a country of social classes or large interest groups. Otherwise, the "rule by moral principle" would not hold. Mao's "class struggle," which was imported from the West, was extremely hard to carry out, and was easily given up. Once imposed on the Chinese society, it led to bloody Hobbesian wars of "all against all." In contrast, through the 2,500-year dynastic history, there were so few large-scale, government-threatening farmer rebellions that counting them on one's fingers would be more than enough. Most dynasties collapsed from external invasions. In today's industrial markets, the small-farmer society has naturally evolved into a society of family-based small and medium enterprises, which are becoming the backbone of the Chinese economy today. They enjoy high vitality and are just as competitive as the family-based firms in Hong Kong, Taiwan, and Singapore. Their interests are as scattered as the small-farmer families in the past, and due to the lack of a consciousness of power politics, the entrepreneurs do not feel the need to form large interest groups to protect or promote their interests. Scattered socioeconomic interests can be obstacles to social solidarity, but they can also be a sound precondition for a highly unified will under the law. Laws in China can be the incarnation of universal justice, neutral and acceptable to all. It is not necessary to make laws favoring politically influential groups or civic organizations, and there are no obvious signs in China of strong civic organizations like those in the West.

Many in the West expect a rapid growth of civil society in China. The presence of civil society was once widely believed to be the driving force and social basis for democratization in Eastern Europe. Nevertheless, the current development of civil society in Eastern Europe is disappointing, which leads to a second thinking about the collapse of the communist regimes there, and casts a shadow over the promise of its growth in China.[21] If political opposition groups are considered civic organizations, then China has had a long history of that. Particularly in the modern era, mass movements against the government have emerged one after another. Was the Communist Party a "civic organization" during the Republican era, or are only organizations against the Communist Party "civic"? Those who expect independent civic society to check Chinese government power would surely be very disappointed. China does not have that kind of civilization. The so-called nongovernmental organizations (NGOs) in China are mostly state sponsored, and I would call them "official civic organizations." In fact, even crime syndicates—known as "underground societies" in China—have little room for survival without connections to certain key officials. NGOs without any connection to government officials are rare and of little influence. This is not to say that there is no room for opposition in China. Even a faction of the Communist Party could turn against the Communist Party, as in the case of Tiananmen in 1989. The collapse of the Soviet Union was not due to civil societies, but to a split within the Communist Party. Taiwan's democratization was not due to the emergence of "civil society," but to the split in the KMT.

It is a fallacy to believe that plural economic interests in today's China must naturally lead to political pluralism. It is the case in the West, but not in China. The Hong Kong and Singapore markets are way more "plural" than most Western economies, but they have not led to pluralistic politics. Democratization in Taiwan had little to do with plural interests in the economy—it came from "subethnic" (by provincial origin) politics and international politics as well. The key is not just how "plural" the economic interests are, but whether the scattered and divided economic interests can be integrated into powerful political groups. That has to do with two things—cultural tradition and the size of the economic units. The entrepreneurs in the context of Chinese tradition do not appear to believe in the strength of such political grouping. The lack of that belief has to do with the size of economic units: mobilizing and organizing the small and scattered firms into large and politically powerful groups incurs high "transaction" costs. Anyone who tries it has plenty of chances to suffer from the state's instinctive response to "divide and rule," and from the constant pressure of betrayal among fellow firms. This is most obvious in the case of today's Taiwan. The selective "tax check" is already enough to silence even the strongest business leaders. Thus, the "politically correct" idea of group politics or class politics has not taken root even today.

2. Due to the lack of powerful social groups or clear-cut social cleavages, Chinese people have a natural difficulty identifying with power politics. Rather than resorting to competition for government power, they tend to place their hopes in the justice of the government. They expect that government will act in accordance with the basic principles of social norms. In the West, interest groups make the government represent their interests by winning a (relative) majority of votes, and this is considered fair game. In China, however, the game is not considered that fair or legitimate; the admired virtue is *jun zi bu dang*—a decent person should not join any clique. Partisan politics—the key to the democratic politics of balance of power—has no natural legitimacy in the Chinese tradition. The people do not admire politicians who hanker after politicizing the existing social cleavages. And the principle of "social harmony" disapproves of stirring up people against people by exploiting potential cleavages. For the average people, fair law enforcement by a neutral civil service, or *gong zheng lian ming* in Chinese, is what justice means. Although the democratic principle of the majority can be indoctrinated, and the ideology has overwhelmed a considerable part of intellectual society in China, more often than not the people who claim to be democrats do not respect election procedures, often abuse the procedures, and often disdain the authority of the winners with the excuse of "unfair procedures." Indicative of this are those U.S.-based Chinese organizations for democracy, which are constantly suffering from splits, betrayal, corruption, personal slander, and scandal, and one after another "coup d'etat." The most effective ones, as it turns out, are those organized after the principle of Leninist parties, or simply mafia. In the Taiwan presidential election of 2000, James Soong, an independent without the support of a party machine, put forward a platform centered on the concept of "supra-party and all people's government." As runner-up, he lost by only 2 percentage points of the vote (37 percent vs. 39 percent). All three candidates had little difference in their platforms of socioeconomic policies. Having won the election, President Chen

Shui-bian picked the KMT defense minister to be his prime minister, in charge of forming his cabinet, and claimed that he had turned a "supra-party and all people's government" into a reality. The point is, a "supra-party and all people's government" is hardly a democratic one; there cannot be a democracy without partisan politics. Today's Taiwan seems to be in deep social strife, and that is out of a very primitive kind of partisan politics—that of subethnic groups, which has made nearly all politicians notorious.

3. As in traditional times, there is little popular pressure for more liberty in today's China; the strongest pressure comes from the demand for "fair terms" of liberty. People and firms compete wildly to win a niche in markets, and there is always a way to ignore or bypass the concerned regulations. The lack of fair rules and of effective rule enforcement is astonishing. Winners are often, if not always, those who are capable of and willing to bribe the concerned authorities. Due to the need for building a market economy, the power of the ruling party is "feudalized" in the process of decentralization. Each party secretary has become a monarch of a locality or sector. As the success in competition becomes the essential means of subsistence, neither moral principles nor the communist ideology can effectively regulate party officials. The traditional moral pillars of governance have collapsed, and officials are "commercialized." The feudalized and commercialized government system is endangering the newly created and vulnerable market order, and the market system remains in the rudimentary stage of unfair competition—competition for government connections rather than competition among firms. Therefore, the corruption problem has become the top concern in China. The mainstream Chinese political culture is not necessarily more tolerant of corruption than others. In China, corruption is the most legitimate reason to overthrow a government. The KMT government on the mainland was overthrown on charges of rampant corruption instead of for representing certain social classes or foreign forces.

Democracy by way of periodically electing leaders is not the right medicine for the lack of fair terms of competition. Pleasing certain social groups is not much better than pleasing party secretaries. If the democracy in Taiwan has not increased corruption, it has not reduced it. It has solved the problem of who should control government power instead of how government power should be controlled. Taiwan's corruption problem might be brought under control later, but it will be done by more rule of law instead of more democracy. The problem in China today is not about liberty, but liberty under what terms. It is not about who should run the government, but how the government should be run. Strictly enforcing laws is to increase the cost of firms' "government connections," making immoral competition "inefficient," and creating fair and just conditions for market competition. To make strict law enforcement possible, a decisive political move in the direction of rule of law is required. The government powers must be separated so as to build an effective mechanism of checks and balances, and make the law above any one person or any one party in power. In other words, it is a solution similar to the polity in Hong Kong and Singapore. It is a practical solution for China, although it may not be a "politically (i.e., ideologically) correct" solution in the eyes of many in the United States.

4. The Chinese social setting and the tradition of rule by moral principle are com-

patible with an essentially rule of law regime. First, moral principles are the very basis of the Law. There is no insurmountable barrier between rule of moral principles and rule of law. The spirit of the law is the spirit of justice found in basic social norms. From the Natural Law and the Ten Commandments, to British Common Law and the U.S. Constitution, the law was "found" according to the moral principles of the time instead of "made" according to the will of the majority. Take the U.S. Constitution: it was "agreed" to by only a tiny number of self-proclaimed "representatives" of the people more than two hundred years ago; no plebiscite or referendum has been held ever since. Take the U.S. Declaration of Independence: "the Laws of Nature and of Nature's God" was mentioned in the very first sentence to justify American independence. Of course, laws about concrete details of life should be those agreed upon by the people or the people's representatives. Yet man-made laws of the time must derive from the Basic Law, and should not be contradictory to the basic moral principles of the time. They should not violate the spirit of the constitution, so to speak.

Second, rule of law directly answers the most urgent need of the Chinese society —curbing corruption in a market economy. Electoral competition for government office is not an effective way of curbing corruption; it could well lead to the concentration of power in the hands of elected leaders. During the fifty-five years after World War II, the Italian government changed hands fifty-eight times, but it was always very corrupt, at least until the mid-1990s. India has had a stable democracy already for half a century, but it is no less corrupt than before. In East Asia, no country is more democratic than the Philippines, but its corruption is as bad as any authoritarian regime could be. The least corrupt regimes in East Asia are found in the two essentially Chinese societies, Singapore and Hong Kong, and their governments are not only similar, but also nondemocratic. China today needs a government in which officials should neither be party secretaries' pets nor the instruments of civic organizations. It needs a system to institutionally check and balance government power, replacing the authority of leaders with the authority of the law.

Third, the "consultative rule of law" regime suggested in the next section represents an attempt to revitalize a unique tradition of Chinese political civilization. China itself had a legalist tradition: the "Law School of Thought" was started by Guan Zhong (?– 645 B.C.E.), a prime minister of the State of Qi. That school of thought dominated China until Liu Che's time in the Han Dynasty when it was replaced by Confucianism around 130 B.C.E., more than 2,000 years ago. Like the polity in Hong Kong and Singapore, the proposed regime inherits the tradition of civil service and consultative gentry support, but it refuses the ultimate power of a top leader and abstract moral principles as the pillar of governance. Like the polity in Hong Kong and Singapore, the proposed regime borrows legalism from the West, checks and balances in particular, to force government to be law abiding, but it refuses the democratic principle as the only source of legitimacy. Elections are no more legitimate than examinations and independent evaluations. People and people's representatives should be intensively consulted, but the regime would not be the rule of people's representatives, it would be rule of law supplemented by representative democracy. The proposed regime is made accountable to the people's demands by effective and impartial law enforcement, by the representatives' right to approve laws, by extensive social consultation arrangements, and by the freedoms of speech, press, assembly and association.

Elections and examinations are two competitive forms of political participation. In the real world, the two approaches coexist in all regimes, but it is impossible to make the two equally important—one has to be the core institution in the political machine. A parliament by election is the core institution in a democratic regime, and a civil service by examination is the core institution in a rule of law regime. "Liberal" democracies are based on the rule of both law and people's representatives, with the balance tilting toward the latter. The "consultative rule of law" regime is also a mixed regime of rule of law and democracy, but with the balance tilting toward the former. It allows less room for the rule of political leaders.

Toward a Consultative Rule of Law Regime

As is pointed out in the beginning of Part I, rule of law is not so much about regulating those who are ruled than regulating government power and behavior. How can the authority of the law be built in China? Inspired by the polities in British Hong Kong and Singapore, this section proposes a "consultative rule of law regime" consisting of a six-pillar structure.

A Six-Pillar Structure

Unlike any democracy where a parliament is the core institution, the civil service is the core institution in the proposed six-pillar regime. The legislature, whether selected or elected, is essentially a consultative institution to the executive branch. The six pillars of a consultative rule of law regime consist of the following.

1. A neutral civil service system. This system has two functions: the primary one is to strictly and impartially enforce laws, and the secondary function is to propose legislative bills. Compared to democratic regimes wherein the parliament is the core institution of the polity, the civil service is a much more neutral instrument of governance due to its source of power—open examinations, comprehensive evaluations, and life employment. Examination is the only way to enter the civil service, and promotion to each higher level requires a certain length of time in service and passing a higher level of examination. Internal and external evaluations also play a large part in promotions within the system. Examinations, performance evaluations, seniority, and life employment are the four basic elements that internally sanction career professionals. All people have equal opportunity to take the open entrance exams of the civil service, which represents the principle of political equality based on meritocracy instead of the majority. There is no short cut to the top level within the bureaucracy. Civil servants can only follow the legally designated system of promotion, demotion, reward, punishment, transfer, and retirement. Although the system of civil service is sophisticated, knowledge of its mechanism is not beyond

China's current political civilization. More importantly, Chinese culture generally accepts that examination is a fairer approach than elections. China's civil examination system started 1,400 years ago, and lasted until the beginning of the 20th century. Once again, most Chinese people still consider examination to be the fairest thing in modern Chinese society.

   2. An autonomous judicial system. The civil service must be checked and balanced. This is accomplished, above all else, by autonomous judicial power. The judicial system also plays two functions. First, it has independent and final authority to settle any legal disputes between the society and the civil service, within the society and within the civil service. Second, the Supreme Court has the authority of judicial review, so as to serve as the Constitution's final gatekeeper. There must be laws that protect the judicial system's autonomy from the civil service and from social influences, such as separating the administrative districts from the judicial ones. Judges must be neutral career professionals, guaranteed by life employment and a sophisticated internal system of promotion, demotion, reward, punishment, transfer, and retirement. This is to say, meritocracy is also the principle of the elite selection process. The judiciary is the weakest branch of government among all, and therefore its power is allowed to be more autonomous than the others. Nevertheless, to prevent power abuse within the judicial area, transparency, public evaluation, and an internal mechanism of checks and balances must make up a critical part of its institutional arrangement.

   3. Extensive social consultation institutions. The civil service would also be checked and balanced by an extensive system of social consultation. At the national and provincial levels, China's People's Congress could be the institutional basis of this system, which is supplemented by a wider system of social consultation. It also serves two functions. First, it has the final authority to approve, reject, or shelve legislative bills proposed by the civil service. The civil service has the authority to propose laws, the People's Congress has the authority to approve or reject laws, and the Supreme Court enjoys the authority to review laws. The law-making procedure is thus made difficult. Second, it has a legally designated power to make executive suggestions, regularly hold hearings, and carry out investigations in administrative affairs, forcing the civil service to perform its functions transparently. Moreover, as is the practice in Hong Kong, each level of every governmental department must build its own social consultation committee (SCC), which should consist of retired civil servants, concerned citizen representatives, and concerned entrepreneurs/specialists.[22] By law, the civil service has the duty to report periodically to the People's Congress and SCCs, hear their suggestions, and submit to their investigations by providing necessary government files. By law, the civil service must answer their inquiries, and within a legally designated time limit they must openly accept, reject, or partially reject the suggestions made by the People's Congress and SCCs. The suggestions from the people, the decisions made by the civil service, and the administrative results must, by law, be put on file with higher levels of the civil service and made available to the public media, so as to provide a basis for openly evaluating the performance of the concerned executives. By China's Constitution today, the National

People's Congress is the institution with "the supreme power." Everyone knows that it cannot possess that power without free elections. The legislative power is actually in the hands of the Communist Party, and the People's Congress is at best a consultative institution. Although China's provincial people's congresses enjoy a partial right to make local laws, just as the National People's Congress enjoys a partial right to make national laws, they are also mainly consultative institutions, serving the dual-executive system of the party and government. The people's congresses at the county and township levels have performed only consultative functions. Hong Kong's Legislative Council, nevertheless, is also merely a consultative institution to the Executive Council, as is Singapore's Parliament. Instead of a revolutionary change to a democracy, this design cancels their authority on paper, but strengthens and institutionalizes their consultation functions, so as to make the regime accountable to various social demands, though not to surrender to those demands. In so doing, a pure rule of law regime is turned into a "consultative rule of law" regime.

4. An independent anti-corruption system. As historical experience shows, the critical danger of the civil service is not whether it can maintain neutrality, but corruption. The civil service must be checked by an independent anti-corruption system, specializing in investigating corruption among public servants. Singapore invented such an institution in the late 1960s and Hong Kong imitated it in the early 1970s. While Singapore's Corrupt Practices Investigation Bureau (CPIB) has been acting like a secret police, Hong Kong's Independent Commission Against Corruption (ICAC) has been highly visible and has maintained good public relations. These independent institutions have played a decisive role in curbing corruption among public servants in both Singapore and Hong Kong. Promotion inside the system depends solely on achievement in uncovering corruption among civil servants. By virtue of its single duty, it is a very lean institution, and its own internal corruption has very little social impact. Its single function plus its small size make the work of checking the system's internal corruption simple—an internal disciplinary commission will do the job. In both Hong Kong and Singapore, the wild corruption of the 1960s was effectively controlled within three years of the institution's establishment. By the early 1980s, Hong Kong's ICAC even extended its mandate to finding "corruption" within the private sector, for corruption in the civil service had become extremely rare. The ICAC is widely trusted and respected in Hong Kong society. The key to its success is the system's complete independence from the civil service and its partial independence from the judicial system.

5. An independent auditing system. The civil service should also be monitored and checked by an independent auditing system. Public office is most often abused by officials misusing government finances. The financial power of the civil service is easily concentrated, for the general public, as well as the people's representatives, can hardly understand the sophisticated arrangement of government spending. Therefore, an institution of professional auditors, which is independent from the civil service, would serve the function of preventing civil service from abusing taxpayers' money as well as other government income. Social criticism and evaluations will help

make government income and spending effectively transparent. However, for the working of an independent auditing system, the reform of China's budgetary system is an absolute precondition. All the budgets of all levels and branches of government should be counted from zero, and thus funds can be allocated with transparent needs and explanations for later auditing. The degree of transparency and discipline in government spending indicate how well a government is regulated by law.

6. The freedoms of speech, press, assembly and association. These "rights" of civil liberty do not constitute government institutions, but they do constitute a standard and critical principle that all government branches must observe, hence a pillar in the political system. The civil service is also checked and made accountable to the general public by constitutional provisions that guarantee the freedoms of speech, press, assembly, and association. While these freedoms are an indispensable part of any modern and civilized society, they are particularly important for a rule of law regime. These freedoms represent major channels for the expression of people's demands, and major approaches to monitoring and evaluating the performance of the civil service. Although people's rights to freedoms of speech, press, assembly, and association appear to be a basic criterion for modern civilization, these freedoms are often feared by governments of developing countries, and their people are often deprived of them. The lack of self-command among the media and political associations is only part of the reason, which comes from the lack of a strong middle class or "mainstream" class. The major reason, however, comes from the tendency that the four freedoms are often used as a major political tool for obtaining state power. Under a rule of law regime in which the civil service is the backbone and the doorway to government power through partisan politics is narrow, that tendency is minimized, hence there are many fewer reasons on the part of the government to fear the people's right to those freedoms. Moreover, the four freedoms are guaranteed and regulated by law, and under a rule of law regime wherein strictly enforcing laws is vital to its survival, the freedoms are more secure and healthier than under a democratic structure of power competition.

The above-proposed political system represents an attempt at institutional innovation, with the hope of a fine regime for China. It is a practical combination of Chinese and Western political systems, proposed for the purpose of solving China's current problem of power concentration and abuse. It derives from China's tradition of a civil service–based structure that includes consultative co-governance with the gentry, while discarding the emperor's absolute power at the very top, as well as the tradition of rule by abstract moral principles. It also derives from the Western tradition of legalism, but reduces the current Western emphasis on the legitimacy of power competition among social classes and groups. It is innovative because it is a rule of law regime supplemented by democracy instead of a democracy supplemented by rule of law.

What Is to Be Done?

If China's political reforms are set to take the direction of consultative rule of law instead of democratization, the following five steps should be taken.

1. Mobilize an open discussion on the rule of law, particularly the need for power separation and checks and balances, just like the discussion on the "criterion of truth" in the late 1970s, so as to exert political pressure on corrupt officials and generate support and consensus in the society, clearing the way for further action.

2. Announce that the "central work" has been shifted from "economic construction" to "building rule of law." The declaration of a new "central work" has utmost significance in China's political life under the Communist Party, for it decides the promotion of new government officials. In Mao's time, "class struggle" was the designated "central work," and the most important criterion for promoting cadres was how active and capable they were in carrying out class struggle. In Deng's time, "economic construction" was designated the "central work," and the indices of economic growth were the basic criteria in promoting cadres. In the new era of "building rule of law as the central work," effective law enforcement along with the government's strict observance of laws at each level and in each department should be the criteria in promoting cadres. Deng decisively changed the party's "central work" in 1979 from class struggle to economic construction, which marked a new era in China. The post-Deng regime could do a similar thing to open an era of political reform.

3. Separate the duty of the party from that of the government. "Separating the party and government work" was a decision made in 1978 by the Third Plenary Session of the 11th Party Congress, but it has never been implemented. In other words, the dual-administrative arrangement of the party and government should be changed, so that the party leads through its members inside the government, and the government should be reformed to observe the regulations of a civil service system. It is a "rule by law stage," the purpose of which is that the party would no longer control and administer personnel affairs inside the government, and would not interfere in the government's routine work of law enforcement.

4. Build an institutional system of checks and balances. This would allow the genuine independence of the judicial system, anti-corruption system, and auditing system, and the building of laws based on the relationships between the civil service and the social consultation institutions. This would be a primary stage of "rule of law," the purpose of which is to provide the legal basis for the relationship between the regime's six pillars.

5. Make the four freedoms the basic principle of governance. Officials of all government branches and institutions must be told to observe this principle.

With the five steps taken, the "consultative rule of law regime" would be established, and the law instead of the party would represent the supreme authority in China. The Communist Party would only nominally lead via its members inside a neutral, honest, and law-abiding civil service, which would appear like Singapore's People's Action Party. The Communist Party leader would become a symbol of neutrality and social unity.

Although our Western friends would be reluctant to accept even the nominal leadership of the Communist Party in China, the party, if it could make a rule of law regime possible, would enjoy very high prestige among the Chinese people, for it would have accomplished all of the three tasks of China's modernization: mechanic solidarity in nation building, organic solidarity in market building, and sustainable justice in state building. Attaining modernity, instead of democracy, has been the dominant theme in China's modern history. And that has been the source of legitimacy of communist rule in China.

Is a Consultative Rule of Law Regime Feasible?

Compared to a democratic option, the proposed regime might be feasible for the following reasons: (1) It is a direct and effective approach to deal with the corruption problem; and a decisive move in that direction could earn the Communist Party its badly needed legitimacy. (2) It provides for reliable social stability since the linkage between law and order has endured the test of time. (3) It does not eliminate one-party rule in form; it merely reduces the role of the party. And it requires that the party, especially its top leaders, carry out political reforms. (4) The proposed regime is not very far from the current political structure, although some major changes must be made to allow the genuine independence of all six pillars. (5) Rule of law is the surest indicator of modernity and has long been cherished by the Chinese people. (6) The polities of Hong Kong and Singapore, both essentially Chinese societies, have provided rich experiences for building such a regime.

Nevertheless, the construction of any new political system depends on heroic leader(s). There is no exception in the entire history of humankind, be it the creation of a democratic or a communist system. The feasibility of *building* a new polity in China depends decisively on the will and capacity of the Chinese leaders of our time. And, compared to a democratic option, it is obviously less difficult for China's top leaders to accept the proposed regime. For example, they, particularly the late paramount leader Deng Xiaoping, often admired the polities in Hong Kong and Singapore.

Deng openly signaled his political support for the Hong Kong system. He said a number of times, "We need to build a few more Hong Kongs inside China." He stubbornly resisted the British attempt to democratize Hong Kong on the eve of the handover, and declared: "Hong Kong's system must be preserved for 50 years, and afterwards we will no longer have any need to change it." And he added, "I've said that many times—I am serious, not talking irresponsibly."[23] He might have assumed it would take half a century for China to build a system similar to Hong Kong's. He dared not say that he supported the Hong Kong political system, just as he dared not say, during his economic reforms, that the other side of the river in his famous "Crossing the river by searching for stones" was the capitalist market economy. Nevertheless, this outstanding statesman clearly showed his political preference and his expectation for China's political future "in 50 years" (from 1988). Under Deng, so came Jiang Zemin's famous support for the city of Zhangjiagang, a medium-sized city in southern Jiangsu Province, which boasted an official goal of building a city that was like a daytime Singapore and a nighttime Hong Kong.

The skepticism to a rule of law regime in China often comes from the following five challenges, to which I cannot agree.

1. *The legal system and the tradition of legalism in both Hong Kong and Singapore were imposed by British colonial rule. Could China adopt such a system without a similar experience?* There is no doubt that the legal system and the tradition of legalism in both Hong Kong and Singapore were imported from Great Britain, and it attests to the great success of the exchanges between the Chinese and Western civilizations. However, British colonies were all over the globe, so why did a polity of "rule of law short of democracy" only take root in Hong Kong and Singapore and not anywhere else? The answer is that Chinese civilization has the capacity to imitate and absorb the Western tradition of legalism because it fits well into the need for managing a modern Chinese society. For both Hong Kong and Singapore, fair laws make "foreigners," or "racial" and "ethnic" minorities, live together fairly harmoniously, as in traditional China, where even a large number of Jews "melted" into Chinese society. Playing the power politics of democracy would enlarge the cleavage, and it would be very hard to organize the scattered families, lineages, underground societies, and ethnic minorities. The British enjoy the longest tradition of democratic institutions in the world, but did not make any attempt to democratize Hong Kong until the early 1980s when China and the U.K. signed the Joint Communiqué on Hong Kong's return; and Governor Patten, the last British governor in Hong Kong, only tried seriously to democratize the territory on the very eve of its reversion. As rulers of Hong Kong, the British understood that democracy could only create chaos, and their attempt to build a mature rule of law was easy and successful. The policy would not have been very different had the United States ruled the two cities and seriously wanted to maintain its rule there. If the Chinese people in Hong Kong and Singapore could imitate and accept the rule of law, there is no reason that the Chinese on the mainland should not be able to do the same. It would only take a longer time due to the country's size. Although the difference between the common law system and the continental law system is obvious, and Hong Kong and Singapore inherited British common law while China has adopted continental law, the difference is not large enough to hinder the building of rule of law. While China's judicial practice has been to import many of the elements of the common law system, both Hong Kong and Singapore have been revising the common law system toward continental law, and the jury trial has been rare in both cities. In short, the consultative rule of law originated under British colonial rule, but British colonial rule is not a precondition for building a consultative rule of law. China could imitate it—just as China had the capacity to import the Russian communist system, which did fit the Chinese needs of the time. In fact, the rule of law without democracy was not just a British invention. It has existed nowhere else, including in Great Britain. The system was created with the joint efforts of the British and the Chinese; and it was created in essentially Chinese societies.

2. *Since the rule of law in Hong Kong was guaranteed by the democracy of the U.K., how could China build and maintain it without democracy?* Rule of law was not built by democracy—nowhere was this the case. The spirit of rule of law in America

was built before American settlers crossed the Atlantic. The earliest settlers went to Virginia by *patent* and *charter.* When by mistake the pilot of the *Mayflower* sailed to Cape Cod instead of Virginia, the Pilgrims knew that they needed a *compact* before pulling in to the shore of Massachusetts. The American respect for law came from Europe, and the European respect for law came long before democracy. Japanese rule of law, which was also imported long before democracy, is another case. Was rule of law in Hong Kong built and maintained by democracy? Saying so is a mistake. The British took Hong Kong with gunboats. The respect for law among Hong Kong's citizens was imposed by the authoritarian power of the British governors who ruled Hong Kong like emperors. If the rule of law in Hong Kong was "guaranteed" by British democracy, whose democracy has guaranteed the rule of law in Singapore since its independence in 1960? Moreover, Hong Kong had been a place of wild corruption before the early 1970s, when most rank and file officials came from the U.K., Australia, and New Zealand. The Hong Kong government became an honest government only after imitating the independent anti-corruption institution of Singapore in the early 1970s and after the Hong Kong government started "localization." Singapore invented its anti-corruption institution by the end of the 1960s, well after its independence from Great Britain. The likely scenario is that Hong Kong's rule of law would have been destroyed and replaced by personal rule had Deng not firmly refused the last British governor's attempt at democratization. Rule of law in Hong Kong and Singapore is not guaranteed and maintained by the British democracy, nor by democracy of any kind. Rule of law is easier to maintain without democracy. It is maintained by rule of law itself, by separation of government powers to establish checks and balances.

3. *Since Taiwan has successfully adopted democracy, why cannot China do the same?* The Taiwan model is unlikely to spread to China for four major reasons. First, Taiwanese democracy is based on a "natural political cleavage" that does not exist or is not allowed to exist in Communist China. For the forty years after World War II, the KMT from the mainland monopolized the political resources while the native-born Taiwanese had few chances to participate in the government. Provincial origin thus became a "natural cleavage," allowing the formation of an effective opposition party. Second, democracy has split Taiwanese society into political factions, more than just provincial origins. For Mainland China, however, no leader would allow provincial or ethnic cleavages to enlarge and become political, because that would mean splitting China into a dozen or more countries, killing the very existence of "China." Third, Taiwanese democracy is also based on the Taiwanese independence movement, which would not have been possible without the security guarantee of the United States. Democracy could not take root in either Taiwan or China without a separatist movement and its context of international politics. Fourth, compared to the performance of the Hong Kong and Singapore polities, the performance of the Taiwanese democracy has not been attractive. Corruption, underground criminal societies, separatism, dependence on American strategic checks on China, and so forth further reduce its attractiveness in China.

4. *Hong Kong and Singapore are just two small cities. How could their experiences fit into the reality of the largest country in the world by population?* Democracy originated in Athens, so how could a country as large as the United States adopt democracy? The size of a country has to do with the degree of a political system—American democracy is far less democratic than the Athenian democracy. However, American democracy, or Western liberal democracy in general, has far fewer flaws than Athenian democracy, and it is much more mature. There is no doubt that the degree of rule of law in China cannot match that in Hong Kong and Singapore, but it will become a well known and mature type of polity once adopted by one-fifth of the world's population. Important for China is that both Hong Kong and Singapore are essentially Chinese societies, and the two metropolitan cities represent a very likely image of China's future—a highly urbanized China. China has no other way to economic prosperity but by building many more huge cities to accommodate its farmers, who consist of 60 percent of the population.

5. *How could the Communist Party—an institution that wields nearly absolute power and is as corrupt as it currently is—build a rule of law regime?* I can never be sure that the party will build rule of law. Yet, if any top Chinese leader intends to build rule of law, it is likely that the Communist Party will be the right instrument with which to do so. While it is not a certain thing, I see quite a number of supporting factors: a popular demand for controlling corruption, an urgent necessity for a substantial political reform, the impossibility of real democratic reform short of a sudden regime collapse, a very receptive socioeconomic setting for implementing rule of law, the popular expectation of "modernity," an existing polity whose structure is not too far away from my proposed six-pillar regime, and a Politburo in which a few members could make the decisive decision to embark on a substantial political reform like what they did in pursuing the market-oriented economic reforms. In short, I do not see much room for an alternative other than a rule of law regime, with the possible exception that the decision makers may not want substantial political reform at all, which is hardly an "alternative." A "pure" democracy may rise as the result of inaction—a general collapse, followed by a popular dictatorship.

I want to end this long essay with a short, simple, and unreliable prediction. China's political option in the future could be so unique that it might again surprise the world. China has surprised the world with a unique traditional polity, with the Communist takeover, with the Cultural Revolution, with the result of Tiananmen, and with a huge economic miracle amid the economic collapse of nearly all of the other formerly communist countries. The Bible says, "Many are called, but few will be chosen." This largest country by population can hardly be "converted," for its people are hopelessly nonreligious and pragmatic, indifferent to "universal" political values. The Chinese have clearly heard the call of democracy, but are unlikely to be chosen for its "irresistible and universal spread." That may be just another surprise to come.

2

Political Liberalization Without Democratization

Pan Wei's Proposal for Political Reform

Suisheng Zhao

After the three great waves of democratization in the world during the nineteenth and twentieth centuries,[1] observers eager to see the termination of the Chinese Communist Party's (CCP) monopoly of power have been frustrated by China's slow progress toward a Western-style multiparty democratization. The pressure for political reform has, indeed, been increasing inside China. However, the direction political reform has taken and the way it is discussed in China is rather different from the democratization that has been pushed by many outside pro-democracy activists. In fact, many Chinese government officials and some Chinese intellectuals do not believe that the Western style of democracy is a feasible or, for that matter, desirable option for China, at least in the foreseeable future. Instead, they have looked upon political liberalization without democratization as an alternative solution to many of China's problems related to the extant authoritarian system. Pan Wei's argument for building a rule-of-law regime is a representative work of this group of Chinese intellectuals.

Pan's Proposal for Political Reform to Improve Single-Party Rule

Pan Wei's answer to the debate about whether or not China's political reform should advance toward democratization is "not now," because the pressure for political reform is not derived from any democratic ideals but from pragmatic concerns over corruption and other troublesome social-economic problems for which democratization may not be an immediate solution.

Pan is not alone among Chinese intellectuals in expressing doubt about whether China can or should adopt a Western-style democracy anytime soon. Pan's premise regarding the lack of popular pressure for democratization has been substantiated by some field research conducted in China by both Western and Chinese scholars in recent years. One survey of Beijing residents in the mid-1990s that attempted to determine if the climate of public opinion was favorable to a transition toward democracy in Beijing supports the thesis that although the future is likely to bring pressure for a more liberal society, there is little apparent public opinion pressure for democracy in the immediate future, especially in comparison to other values.[2] A Hong Kong scholar investigating the political orientation of Chinese university students found that after the 1989 crackdown on the democratic movement, students' political stance changed from democratic idealism to a nonideological kind of technocratic pragmatism: a let's-just-solve-the-problem approach to concrete quotidian frustrations. Utility, efficiency, and feasibility were the major concerns of the pragmatic attitude. Skepticism, experimentation, and reform were seen as the pragmatic keys to social progress. Whether or not reality fit with normative political principles was no longer the ultimate consideration. Rather, whether or not the principles could solve existing problems became the main concern.[3]

These findings call into question the extent to which Chinese people now place a high value on democracy and the prospect for democratic transition. Pan Wei's argument, therefore, became feasible to many Chinese intellectuals as they assessed democracy in terms of its capacity to serve as an instrument for ameliorating the problems of corruption and facilitating successful economic development, rather than as a good in itself. This attitude toward democracy has been held by many Chinese elites in the country's modern history, as democracy was rarely regarded as an end in itself in the Chinese search for democracy during the twentieth century. It was instead regarded as merely a means for gaining national power and wealth under wise and enlightened rulers. Chinese intellectuals looked around the world to find modern political means to promote the end of making China rich and strong. It did not matter whether the most efficient means was liberal democracy or Marxist communism. In this narrow prism, some Chinese intellectuals opted for democracy only in the belief that it had brought power and prosperity to Western countries. Others turned to communism because they saw it as the wellspring of Soviet power and industrialization.[4]

Since Pan does not see democratization as a desirable option for China today, he proposes a consultative rule-of-law regime, which, he believes, is "a new form of polity" even though it does not change the single-party rule of the CCP. Pan argues that this type of political reform is not only feasible, but is also necessary to complete China's process of modernization, because it would be more practical in solving China's immediate problems, including the wild corruption of cadres who use public office for private gain. Pan calls for reform without democratization for a number of other reasons as well. The crucial one among them is that it has a far better chance for acceptance by the CCP because this reform would not threaten one-party rule. Pan makes explicit that rule of law does not eliminate one-party rule in form, but merely reduces the role of the party. He further asserts that a decisive move in that direction could gain the Communist Party badly needed popularity.

For those who have called for democratization through multiparty competition in China, neither Pan's proposal nor his bases for defending it would be appealing as the CCP's detractors do not believe that the CCP could carry out any fundamental political reform. They also do not want to see the CCP retaining power any longer, even if it is not directly engaged in the daily lives of most Chinese people. Indeed, from the perspective of the democratic ideal, governance should be rotated among different political parties through regular and competitive elections. This ideal is realized in many countries and has given birth to democratic movements in many single- or no-party states and has transformed a large number of them into competitive political systems. Riding this wave of democratization, political reform in China should break the monopoly of the CCP over state power and give other parties the legal and equal opportunity to compete with the CCP. If one concludes that the central moral and instrumental political problem in China is the monopoly of political power, then reform without democratization does not appear fundamental.

To understand China's present government and its capacity for change, however, one must appreciate that there has often been a huge gap between practice and ideals in the PRC. The CCP has repeatedly shown a penchant for altering its practices while claiming to maintain the same ideals, or it has reformulated ideals while practice lagged behind them. As a result, the party has not only survived the collapse of communism in other parts of the world, but also initiated and implemented some significant social-political changes to meet the challenges of economic modernization during the reform decades. Although these changes have been incremental and often piecemeal, their continuation has not only generated political liberalization and openness, but also laid a foundation upon which democracy may one day be built. In addition, the CCP has started a process of transforming itself from a Leninist revolutionary mass party to a pragmatic, system-maintaining ruling party and, arguably, a latent type of social-democratic party. Many observers, particularly those who want to see immediate democratization in China, have gravely underestimated the significance of the reforms initiated by the CCP and the consequent political development toward openness and liberalization. From this perspective, Pan Wei's political reform without democratization is a pragmatic concept rooted in his understanding of the complicated political reality in China.

The Trajectory of Political Liberalization

Indeed, China's political reform without democratization is successful insofar as it has resulted in significant liberalization and other positive changes in China's political life in recent decades. While some observers do not want to believe that the CCP could play a positive role for change in China's political life, many other observers have taken a positive view of the CCP's initiation of political liberalization. It is true that political liberalization is different from democratization, which entails building democratic institutions, including holding regular relatively free and fair elections for political offices. However, political liberalization is a necessary precondition for democratization because it involves expanding basic freedoms of expression, association, and the rights of individuals.

Political liberalization started in response to the legitimacy crisis that the CCP suffered in the wake of Deng Xiaoping's economic reform in the late 1970s, which relaxed Mao's totalitarian control over Chinese society. Deng's original intention was to eradicate all ideological and psychological obstacles to economic reform. Unexpectedly, it resulted in the demise of the communist ideology and the profound "three belief crises" (*sanxin weiji*): the crisis of faith in socialism (*xinxin weiji*), the crisis of belief in Marxism (*xinyang weiji*), and the crisis of trust in the party (*xinren weiji*).[5]

In response, the party launched political reform in the 1980s, which redefined the content and role of the official ideology with the aim of creating a new basis for its authority. Deng Xiaoping's famous speech on the reform of the party and state leadership system in 1980 was the first call from the CCP's top echelon for political reform. Deng set three major objectives of the reform:

> (1) In the economic sphere, to rapidly develop the productive forces and gradually improve the people's material and cultural life. (2) In the political sphere, to practice people's democracy to the full, ensuring that through various effective reforms, all the people truly enjoy the right to manage state affairs and particularly state organs at the grassroots level and to run enterprises and institutions, and that they truly enjoy all the other rights of citizens. . . . (3) In the organizational sphere, if we are to achieve these objectives, there is an urgent need to discover, train, employ, and promote a large number of younger cadres for socialist modernization, cadres who adhere to the four cardinal principles and have professional knowledge.[6]

Following Deng's call, political reform was carried out and has resulted in political liberalization in at least the following three broad aspects of social life: First, the interference of the state in the daily life of Chinese people has been reduced. Second, the opportunities for popular participation at grassroots levels have been expanded. Third, popular participation at the national level has expanded along with the changing role of China's people's congress system. Together, the reforms have greatly relaxed the degree of political control over Chinese society, albeit without fundamentally altering one-party dominance.

Reducing the Scope and Arbitrariness of Political Intervention in Daily Life

Since the inception of reform, the CCP has tried to promote reconciliation between state and society by reducing the scope and the arbitrariness of political intervention in daily life. To accomplish this objective, the party repudiated many of the ideological concepts associated with Mao's later years. The main task of politics was declared to be promoting modernization and reform rather than undertaking continuous struggle and revolution. Moreover, the party began to imply that the responsibility of the state was to expand socialist democracy rather than exercise dictatorship, although it never defined democracy in Western terms. The party also admitted that many intellectual, scientific, and technical questions can and should be addressed on their merits, without regard to ideological considerations. This attitude presented a stark contrast to Mao's era, when all decisions were supposedly taken only after a consideration of the relevant doctrinal principles.

As a result, ordinary citizens began to enjoy much greater freedom of belief, expression, and consumption than under Mao's dictatorship. They have been able to buy and sell shares of stock freely, and have access to almost any consumer goods on the domestic as well as world market. Such choice has been accompanied by a significant loosening of government control over employment and residence choices.

Of course, the scope of change in the communist state's intrusions on personal choice has many limitations. In particular, Deng Xiaoping's four fundamental principles —Marxism-Leninism/Maoist thought, party leadership, socialism, and proletarian dictatorship—implied the limits of relaxation of political life. These principles found echoes in traditional Chinese values that give the state the right and obligation to promote moral conduct by educating citizens in an official doctrine believed to be morally valid. The four principles, however, have become increasingly rhetorical. Only one principle, the party's leadership, has been vigorously defended. Ren Zhongyi, former party secretary of Guangdong province and former CCP Central Committee member, in an article with the provocative title "Upholding the Four Cardinal Principles Reconsidered," argued that "Deng Xiaoping enunciated the Four Principles in March 1979—twenty-one years ago. China has changed a lot since then. We can't be dogmatic about them. Their meaning changes as the situation changes and is made richer by their constant development through practice. They should be given new meaning and content with opening and reform. If we don't, we will be stuck in ideological rigidity."[7]

Although the four principles have not been formally abolished, the scope for personal expression has been greatly expanded. In very sensitive artistic and intellectual matters, for example, artists and writers have moved into various previously banned areas, reviving traditional styles and experimenting with modern techniques. Popular tabloids, widely available in major cities, have carried articles and pictures on subjects ranging from crime to romance. Foreign music, drama, literature, and films can be seen everywhere in China. Although the state and the party continue to promote socialist morality, religion is no longer condemned outright as superstition. Many churches and temples in urban areas have attracted more and more believers, although "foreign-sponsored" religious activities are still banned. As an American sociologist Richard Madsen discovered in his study of Catholic churches in China, a large "wave of religious revival" has been sweeping across the country as "one of many responses to a spiritual crisis" facing post-Mao China.[8] In addition to foreign cultures and religions, there has been a revival of folk customs and local religious practice in the countryside.

Expanding Grassroots Political Participation

Political liberalization has, arguably, laid the foundations of a democratic culture and politics. Opportunities for voluntary participation in politics have been increased at both the grassroots and national levels as multiple candidates and secret ballots have been introduced for elections to people's congresses at the local and county levels and for village committees.

The village committee election is one of the most important developments to expand grassroots political participation. It started in the late 1980s, although the first post-Mao Constitution of the PRC in 1982 already stated that villages should practice self-government through village committees whose members are to be elected by villagers. The National People's Congress (NPC) drafted a set of regulations governing village committees in 1986 and passed a trial Organic Law of Village Committees in November 1987. Direct elections of village committees were first held on a trial basis in selected areas in the winter of 1988–89. The Tiananmen incident in 1989 did not stop such elections from being extended to other areas in the early 1990s. Almost all of China's one million villages have held at least one round of elections since then. The elected village committees are responsible for all administrative affairs in the villages, including education, infrastructure and housing, dispute resolution, and financial management.

According to one study, "an important reason for granting villagers self-government is the impracticability of doing otherwise in post-Mao China." In Mao's days, the commune system enabled the central government to shift its very burdensome responsibilities of administration and provision of services in the vast rural areas to the communes. After the abolition of the commune system in the early 1980s, the township government (the replacement of the commune) no longer controlled the resources to perform these functions. Even if township governments were able to do so, providing more or less the same level of services to many villages with different levels of income would contravene the anti-egalitarian thrust of reform policies and would be opposed by villagers. As a result, most administration and provision of services have to be delegated to the village level. Such delegation of responsibilities cannot but be accompanied by a corresponding delegation of power. To introduce direct elections at the village level, "the regime hopes that democratic election would make office-holders more accountable to their electorates, thereby ameliorating problems of corruption, nepotism and inefficiency."[9]

Village elections have been enhanced by economic development. As one Chinese scholar indicates, "With economic development, village committees will control more collective revenues, thus increasing the stakes villagers have in elections. This will result in greater participation by villagers in elections, and in more competitive elections. Increased competitiveness of elections will facilitate changes in the institutions regarding village committee elections."[10] The key question, however, is whether genuine self-government in the villages is possible when one-party rule continues. One answer is that it is possible for the Chinese Communist Party to introduce some reforms and expand the people's democratic rights while maintaining its hold on power. The cumulative effect of these piecemeal reforms is changing the very nature of the Communist Party itself and its rule. The introduction of village self-government is, or has the potential to be, one such reform.[11]

Village committee elections have attracted extensive attention from Western scholars. Both the Republican and Democratic institutes in the United States, operating under the congressionally funded National Endowment for Democracy, have provided technical assistance to these elections. The Carter Center in Atlanta has sent delegations on a regular basis to observe them and has published generally favorable reports from the field in its working paper series since the mid-1990s. These Western organizations have concluded that village elections have become a training ground for democracy in China as more and more village residents become aware of the elections and their benefits. Villagers are voting more responsive and talented leaders into office. Many of them are young entrepreneurs who may or may not be members of the Communist Party. The elections have thus made a difference in China since party organizations in the rural areas have generally been weakened. As a matter of fact, many party branches have ceased to function and those that are still influential maintain their influence mainly through their role in the rural economy. To resolve the problem, there has been a tendency for mergers between the party branches and village committees at the village level in recent years as party secretaries have been obligated to run for positions on village committees in order to establish their "acceptability to the villagers." As a result, the party organizations' vertical relations with other levels of party organizations and their horizontal relations with the government and with society have all changed accordingly. The party members sitting on village committees no longer constantly think of upholding party interests, because there is no longer a uniform perception of what party interests are among party members who have to win elections in order to sit on the village committees. As one study indicates, "party secretaries cannot simply be appointed from above and must win popular support in regular elections. In principle, this is a step forward in terms of the goal of democratization of holding officials accountable."[12]

Although it is perhaps too soon to tell whether village elections are a foundation for further democratization, one Western observer indicates that "democratic elections are being entrenched at the village level and sincere efforts are being made to establish the necessary electoral institutions to support them."[13] A study of village elections by a careful Chinese-American scholar also indicates that "a fundamental change has occurred in rural China. . . . As occurred in other developing countries, changes brought about by economic development not only significantly influenced the attitudes of elements of the political elite toward political reform but also increased the peasants' resources and skills and enhanced their desire to get involved in the decision-making processes in their villages."[14]

Expanding Participation at the National Level

In addition to the expansion of political participation at the grassroots level political liberalization has also been accompanied by changes in the role of the people's congresses, which were rubber stamps during the Maoist period as they held short and infrequent meetings in which laws, policy documents, and personnel appointments were approved by acclamation. The elections of deputies were known as "elections without choice" as they were highly ritualized affairs in which deputies were nominated and selected by the Communist Party and served only to legitimize party decisions.[15]

Post-Mao reform has brought changes in China's people's congress system. As a change to the practice by which the CCP nominated only as many candidates as there were vacancies to be filled, a new Electoral Law requires that the number of candidates exceed the number of vacancies (*chaer xuanju*). It also prescribes that deputies at the township level (*xiang-zhen*) and the county level (*qu-shi-xian*) be elected by universal direct suffrage, and deputies at the prefectural (*di*), provincial (*sheng*), and national levels be indirectly elected, with deputies at one level electing deputies at the next. Although Communist cadres still tried to manipulate the elections, gradual implementation of the electoral law has produced significant changes in the role of the people's congress. Even the *Washington Times,* known for its hawkish position in the U.S. China policy debate, admits that, "Long derided as rubber-stamp legislatures filled with nothing but hand-raising delegates, the various levels of congresses from townships and counties up to the National People's Congress (NPC) are getting some teeth. As Chinese society becomes more sophisticated and people's awareness of their rights increases, this change is reflected in the congresses, whose delegates gradually are becoming more assertive and increasingly dare to go against Communist Party dictates."[16]

At the national level, the role of the National People's Congress has been notably expanded. Although it has not yet become an independent legislature that can routinely initiate legislation, veto state proposals, or impose accountability on government or party officials, the NPC, as documented by Tanner and O'Brien, is no longer merely a rubber stamp and has gradually asserted itself.[17] It holds an annual plenary session, and its standing committee meets five or six times a year. The NPC has established functional committees that specialize in particular aspects of foreign and domestic policy and that have played a more active role in drafting legislation. Some members of these committees come from the small "democratic parties," which are primarily associations of intellectuals, scientists, and former capitalists and have resumed the recruitment of new members. Although they are not considered opposition parties and are treated merely as advisory organizations that can offer suggestions to the CCP, some of them have exercised considerable influence on certain technical decisions in NPC sessions. Whether members of "democratic parties" or not, NPC deputies actually debate issues, and sizable blocs of deputies have voted against officially approved candidates and causes. About 40 percent of the deputies rejected the work reports of the Supreme People's Procurator and Supreme People's Court in an unprecedented display of dissatisfaction with rising crime four years in a row at plenary sessions between 1997 and 2001. One-third of the NPC delegates cast opposing or abstaining votes on legislation to begin the $25 billion Three Gorges Dam project in 1992. While these actions hardly constitute a political revolution, they do indicate a trend toward increased assertiveness in the highest organ of political power prescribed by the Constitution.

This trend is reinforced by the NPC's efforts to expand its professional capacity to draft laws in-house and engage in serious debate during the drafting and promulgation process. Efforts to build a stronger judiciary are the result of small but systematic steps to facilitate economic reform. Chinese officials and scholars often claim that a market economy should be governed by law, which provides rules like those in athletic games, although, as Stanley Lubman indicates, neither the game nor its rules "seem to be free from ambiguity" in China.[18] As a result, the economic boom has necessitated the development of a viable legal infrastructure comprised of transparent laws and courts and professional, informed judges capable of understanding and adjudicating matters involving those laws. It is striking that the NPC and its standing committee passed more than 332 laws in the twenty years between 1978 and 1998.[19] The promulgation of new laws by the NPC has helped highlight the need for the Chinese to address deficiencies in their traditionally weak judiciary system. The efforts to recruit and train lawyers and judges and increase public awareness about the law and its applications are all indications of a commitment by the party to reduce the role of the state and correspondingly increase the autonomy of the individual to make life choices within the framework of known rules predictably interpreted and applied. Incrementally, the NPC is changing from a hollow political symbol to a more and more active political institution.

While local people's congresses in general are less active than the NPC, some of them have become very assertive in voting down personnel appointments and work reports submitted to them by local government, the court, and the prosecutor's office. One Western journalist reported the "unthinkable" action of the municipal congress in Shenyang, China's fifth largest city with 6.8 million people, in March 2001. Angered by massive layoffs at struggling state enterprises and a huge corruption scandal that implicated the mayor and dozens of other top government and court officials, the Shenyang congress rejected the work report of the Intermediate People's Court, with only 46 percent of the 474 delegates voting for it. The vote stunned Chinese legal experts, who say it is the first time a work report, which is a summary of the previous year's work, has been voted down by a congress of any level. The work report of the prosecutor's office in Shenyang also came close to being rejected, passing by just 57 percent, a far cry from the unanimous votes of a decade or so ago.[20]

Reform of the CCP's Single-Party Rule

Although political liberalization at the grassroots and national levels has resulted in the weakening capacity of party and state control over Chinese society, it has not aimed at abolishing the one-party rule but reforming it and making it more efficient in meeting the challenges of economic modernization. The reform was introduced by Zhao Ziyang in the late 1980s to separate the party from the government. After Jiang Zemin came to power, the party attempted to redefine its role by repackaging itself as the repository of "advanced social forces" and the standard-bearer of national interests. The primary goal of this effort was to re-brand the Communist Party and make it more *inclusive* and less *intrusive*. Since Hu Jintao took over the leadership position in 2002, he has focused efforts on what he has called "strengthening the party's ability to govern." In practice, that means a sustained campaign aimed at curbing the abuse of power, strengthening the party's internal discipline and auditing agencies, and issuing new rules governing the behavior of party members.

A first step to reform single-party rule was taken at the CCP's 13th National Congress in 1987 with a number of measures to prevent the party from intervening in government and economic institutions and to concern itself with political supervision and coordination. The rationale was to reduce the cost of the party's involvement in overseeing the government and to give governmental officials and other administrative personnel more autonomy and greater incentive to be both efficient and willing to take action in light of economics rather than political rationality. Economic efficiency was the essential motivation in institutionalizing this reform. Although Jiang Zemin reverted to the merging of party and state at the top levels, partial implementation of the reform has resulted in a de facto dual structure of party leadership. The CCP has retained its ultimate authoritative control over state institutions, but largely relinquished its traditional role as the vehicle for mobilizing and inciting the masses at the grassroots levels of economic and social institutions.[21] The party has retreated from many parts of the countryside, making way for clans and secret societies. In urban areas, its role is increasingly perfunctory. Many grassroots party committees and branches in state-owned enterprises could not, or did not even bother to, collect membership dues for months or years. The relative demise of the state-owned economy further caused the party to lose its grip over the day-to-day management of economic enterprises.

The weakening of the party's capacity to intervene in China's social and economic life does not mean that single-party rule is about to collapse. Although the party has lost some of its capacity to inspire or mobilize the Chinese people, it retains effective control over the military, government agencies, and some strategic sectors of the economy. With its ultimate authority over the state, the party remains a ticket that must be punched and the main avenue of upward mobility for many politically ambitious elites. Most of these elites still want to join the party in order to advance their careers. No longer seeking to penetrate society, the CCP has become a network of bureaucratic elite committed to retaining a large reservoir of power translatable into personal status and affluence. These elites are no longer concerned with ideological correctness or even disciplined grassroots-level organizations.

The Third Road: A Social Democratic Party in China?

Reform of one-party rule is aimed at reclaiming CCP legitimacy based on improving the Chinese people's standard of living rather than on ideological correctness and mass mobilization. How can the political legitimacy of the party be reclaimed based on its economic performance? This is a question that some Chinese intellectuals have tried to help the party answer. Far from being detached, scholars observing sociopolitical change from the sidelines and many Chinese intellectuals have been active participants in the process. In promulgating his paradigm of a consultative rule-of-law regime, Pan Wei takes his place among them. More specifically, he implicitly associates himself with those who have urged top-down reform and have tried to find a middle road between the collapse of the CCP and evolution toward Western-style democracy. Members of the Chinese elite have presented this top-down approach to reform along two lines of thought. One is the proposal to transform the CCP from a revolutionary mass party into a conservative ruling party. The second proposal would change the vanguard nature of the CCP into a more inclusive social democratic party. A group of intellectuals and official think-tank analysts presented the first proposal in the early 1990s. Former party general secretary Jiang Zemin advocated the second.

From a Revolutionary Mass Party to a Conservative Ruling Party

As early as 1992, a group of intellectuals and think-tank analysts in Beijing proposed the transformation of the CCP from a revolutionary mass party to a system-maintaining "ruling party" (*zhizheng dang*) in a well-known internal circulation article, "Sulian Jubian Zhihou Zhongguo de Xianshi Yingdui yu Zhanlue Xuanze" (China's Realistic Counter-Measures and Strategic Choices After the Drastic Change in the Soviet Union). These authors asserted that "an important issue that our party faces is the shift from a revolutionary party to a ruling party. This shift becomes urgent after the change in the Soviet Union."[22] To carry out the shift, they suggested a number of policy changes. Among the ideas for facilitating such transition was to abandon the communist mass mobilization and revolutionary social transformation goals and to adopt nationalistic and patriotic goals.

In light of the notion of transforming the CCP into a conservative ruling party, there were proposals to redefine single-party rule within the legal framework of the state. In March 1994, an article in *Faxue Yanjiu* (Law studies) explored the legal status of the CCP as a ruling party. It stated that "the CCP cannot be superior to the National People's Congress (NPC) because the CCP does not have the sovereignty to rule the country even in a socialist setting." The author directly refuted the notion that since the CCP is the "leading party" it is naturally the "ruling party," and went on to argue that the idea that "the party is above the law" is preposterous in theory and unacceptable in practice. The author suggested that the CCP leadership should come from its prestige, power of persuasion and informal influence, should not be deemed equal to the state in authority, and should not exercise coercive power. The CCP leadership, he argued, should not constitute "one-party dictatorship," and cannot exceed the people's sovereignty. The author claimed that the CCP is not a sovereign entity and cannot treat the exercise of state power as a natural right. He criticized the view that "the government should accept the CCP's organizational leadership," and suggested that the CCP is only a "leading party" and cannot take its current "ruling party" status for granted.[23]

Pan Wei's is one of the proposals to reform the party's rule within the legal framework of the state. Pan thus became a member of the substantial faction of Chinese intellectuals who believe that the party elite can be the principal agents of constitutional reform. He urges CCP leaders to share his belief in the necessity for substantial political reform, which may meet the popular demand for controlling corruption and the internal/external challenges of the country's social unity. To make his proposal more attractive, he tells CCP leaders that the structure of the existing polity is not too far away from his proposed rule-of-law regime and, therefore, there is no need to take revolutionary steps to destroy the existing system.

The Third Road of Democratic Socialism

It is hard to know whether or not the CCP leadership took these proposals from Chinese intellectuals into serious consideration when they made up their own minds about reform. However, it is interesting to note the development of the so-called Three Represents (*sange daibiao*) campaign that took place shortly after Pan Wei first circulated his proposal. This campaign was derived from a speech that Jiang Zemin gave during his inspection tour of the south in February 2000. Its key theme was that the CCP should no longer just represent workers but should be "a faithful representative of the requirements in the development of advanced productive forces in China, the orientation of advanced culture in China, and the fundamental interests of the broadest masses of the people in China." In effect, the party's responsibility was to represent these forces and lead China toward the wealth and power that give the party the right to rule. As a Western reporter in Beijing interpreted, "That is, the party can be all things to all people, promoting the interests not just of workers and farmers but of wealthy entrepreneurs as well."[24] This new thesis of the Three Represents was disseminated at meetings across the country and through official propaganda mouthpieces, such as the Xinhua News Agency, *Renmin Ribao, Qiushi,* CCTV, and other major official media later. Three Represents were hailed as an "inheritance and development of Marxism" and a major guideline for the CCP's development in the new period. This thesis was reiterated in Jiang Zemin's landmark speech celebrating the eightieth anniversary of the CCP's birth on July 1, 2001, and was written into the party constitution at the 16th Party Congress in November 2002 to serve as a compass to guide the party in the new century.

Although many pro-democracy activists have looked at this Three Represents rationale for party leadership with either skepticism or outright dismissal as just another communist propaganda campaign, the Three Represents do represent an attempt to reform one-party rule by making it more inclusive. This attempt is obviously a departure from the orthodox Leninist party doctrine written in the party constitution that the CCP is "the vanguard of the proletariat" and an organization of workers and peasants whose mission is to ensure the "dictatorship of the proletariat" over rival elements such as capitalists. As Jiang, in his famous July 1, 2001, speech, openly advocated, the CCP should try to recruit not only workers and peasants but also private entrepreneurs (capitalists) into the party.

The Three Represents certainly has provoked serious discussion and debate within China's political elite, which is one reason why it is myopic to dismiss it as mere propaganda. Critics have come from two directions. Orthodox conservatives have dogged the campaign from the start. They indicted what they believed to be an intent to change the nature of the vanguard party to a catch-all social democratic party, and saw as much logic in inviting entrepreneurs to join the Communist Party as in welcoming steak eaters into a vegetarian society. Their opposition was aired in China's state-run media in the summer of 2001 and prompted a crackdown on dissent by Jiang, who ordered the shutdown of a high-profile leftist journal, *Zhenli de Zhuiqiu* (Search for Truth), after it criticized the speech Jiang gave on July 1, 2001, which paved the way for entrepreneurs to enlist in the cause.

Liberals also criticized the Three Represents as they saw it impossible for the CCP to represent all social interests. They called for open party competition. Bao Tong, in his criticism, holds that the CCP no longer represents workers because it "tramples on the workers' right to organize unions, suffocates the voice of workers, and is prepared to crush any economic and political demands of workers." It no longer represents peasants or students. "Extending an olive branch to red capitalists does not in the slightest way imply relaxing the principle of one-party rule. On the contrary, it implies that it is now time for the party to admit the unspoken truth and formally declare that it has become China's party for the rich and the powerful."[25]

Indeed, the conservatives are correct when they claim to see in the Three Represents rationales for a major revision of Communist Party doctrine. This revision attempts to make the CCP a party for all Chinese people, including the working class, the rising middle class, and even the newly rich. This re-branding implies policy and structural change within the party. A Hong Kong journalist reported that this revision to the party doctrine has resulted in one of the hottest fads in Chinese elite circles: studying the structure and philosophy of European social democratic parties. Apart from the economic advantages of facilitating growth and social stability, one frequently perceived political advantage of the transformation would be that, having shed the "Communist" label, a Chinese-style, at least nominally social democratic party could become less of a target for Western criticism and political sabotage. According to the reporter, aides and think-tank members associated with Jiang and other top leaders conducted research into this controversial topic after the Three Represents theory was disseminated. Politburo Standing Committee member Wei Jianxing visited Europe in October 2000 and one of the top items on his agenda during the visit was to observe the ideals and operations of such groups as Germany's Social Democratic Party.[26]

Of course, this attempt to tinker with orthodox party dogma and emulate social democratic parties does not signify any intention to abolish single-party rule in China anytime soon. Although some CCP leaders have considered the feasibility of transforming the CCP into a social democratic party, they certainly are not ready to see, coincident with the transformation, a lifting of the ban on forming new political parties. What they have wanted to find is the so-called "Third Road" for the transformation of the CCP. The "First Road" is to become a "classic" social democratic party such as those found in Western Europe, which have evolved over the past century through parliamentary and electoral systems. The "Second Road" is a reference to the road taken by members of the former Soviet bloc, which have since the early 1990s embraced social democratic ideals through the so-called "shock therapy" of rapid change, including overthrowing communist party rule.[27] Countries following the Second Road have suddenly adopted Western-style democratic norms such as one-person-one-vote elections and competitive party politics. In the eyes of the CCP elite, the result has been turmoil and instability. The elite and sympathetic intellectuals argue, sincerely in many cases, that China's different political history and culture require a third way if China is to evolve in a unified and peaceful manner. The CCP wants to transform itself into a Third Road social democratic party by establishing democratic socialism in which single-party rule prevails despite changes in other areas. It is believed that the Third Road of transformation could spur both social stability and economic growth while not compromising the party's authority to rule China.

The Uncertain Future of Political Liberalization without Democratization

Pan Wei's rule-of-law regime, as well as all other proposals, debates, and actions to reform and liberalize China's one-party system, should be welcomed. The CCP leadership should be encouraged to co-opt the creative ideas of Chinese intellectuals regardless of whether they are friendly or unfriendly to the CCP. The political changes in China have been substantial, even dramatic, and have been the catalyst for greater individual freedom. Although China's history reminds us that the course of change is never certain, the changes that have already occurred may have slowly laid down a foundation for eventual democratization. However remote, it is possible that the ruling Communist Party will begin a transition toward democracy by gradually opening up elections above the village and county levels and eventually lifting the ban on opposition parties.

Democracy is not, however, an inevitable result of political liberalization. The transition toward democracy will occur only if the ruling elite, or a substantial section within it, perceive that the potential advantages of a shift from liberalization to fundamental democratization outweigh the risks of trying to sustain authoritarian one-party rule. If Pan Wei were correct in believing, as he seems to be, that the regime is not under such pressure to make the ultimate choice of whether or not to open political competition, China's transition toward democracy will still be uncertain and the change will continue to be gradual and incremental. Although the Third Road of transformation of the CCP has been explored, the likelihood that the CCP will change into a Chinese-style social democratic party anytime soon is remote.

It is likely that single-party rule will remain for the foreseeable future because there is no other organized political force in China powerful enough to replace the Communist Party in the near future. The CCP and its army still have controlling power and have enormous vested interests in single-party rule. The struggles within the CCP have been over the distribution of power, not over the nature of the system in which power is exercised.

The forces of democrats in exile are very fragile and divided. Moreover, it is debatable whether, if the exiled elite were to miraculously secure control of the state, it would necessarily rule democratically. As one study indicates, many students involved in the 1989 pro-democracy demonstrations did not seem to have very sophisticated ideas about what democracy was, and they certainly did not do the best job of practicing democracy in their movement, which was "much more explicit in terms of what it opposed than what it supported."[28] Under these circumstances, there seems to be little likelihood that democratization could take hold in China simply with the replacement of the CCP by the exiled democratic forces. Rather, the transition to democracy would be more likely to come from above, namely, from the CCP itself. The process could be difficult, prolonged, complex, and inconclusive.

Looking beyond the immediate future, prolonged political and economic liberalization without democratization will prove to be more and more difficult to sustain, in part because it will only become harder for the CCP to justify its monopoly over political power as society and the economy become increasingly pluralistic. As indicated by Bao Tong, a senior architect of China's reforms until 1989, when he opposed the crackdown in Tiananmen Square, "China's economy and society have grown too complex to be directed even by a modernizing party."[29] Dissonance between ideology and reality and between a pluralistic economy and one-party politics could render the rule of the Communist Party increasingly ineffective. Political liberalization without democratization has not addressed the root of China's political problems: the crisis of legitimacy. This type of crisis is related to the demise of the official ideology and a profound crisis of confidence in communism. To find an alternative to the declining communist ideology, some liberal intellectuals turned to Western democratic ideas and called for Western-style democratic reform. The confidence crisis thus evolved into a pro-democracy movement, which produced large-scale anti-government demonstrations in the spring of 1989. After the crackdown on pro-democracy demonstrations, the CCP was determined to substitute for obsolete Marxism-Leninism a legitimacy based upon the success of China's surging economy and a nationalist legitimacy provided by the invocation of distinctive characteristics of Chinese culture. Economic performance has indeed, in practice, helped the CCP to reclaim its legitimacy to a certain extent.

However, it is hard to maintain a high rate of economic growth forever. Economic growth has come in cycles in China as in many other countries, which means the inevitability of a downturn. An economic downturn, together with rising unemployment and growing corruption, can be a powerful indictment of single-party rule and a potential cause of opposition. Many observers have pointed to the fact that the CCP has encountered widespread antipathy and more and more organized opposition to its rule even though it has achieved remarkable success overall in economic reform and has initiated from above a certain measure of political reform.

This is evident in the fact that the party has faced challenges not only from China's isolated dissident community, but also from much larger groups who subscribe to noncommunist belief systems, such as the banned Falun Gong. In addition, political liberalization has given rise to many quasi-independent social organizations, which have inhabited some public spaces created by the party's withdrawal from many areas of society. Moreover, with the rise of a middle class including entrepreneurs and professionals, it would appear to be just a matter of time before these upwardly mobile sectors start clamoring for greater political representation. With a sense of vulnerability, the fourth generation of CCP leadership under Hu Jintao has sensed an urgency about the need to improve the party's capacity to govern the economy and society since it assumed power in 2002.

The Third Road of democratic socialism has been designed to neutralize the potential of such social groupings by presenting the Communist Party in a more inclusive light, providing it with a more progressive image, boosting its popularity, and strengthening its rule. However, the party remains exclusive rather than inclusive to these social groups because it cannot tolerate any organized opposition or subject itself entirely to the rule of law. It has been very hard for the CCP to follow the rule of law and incorporate increasingly diverse social groups into the constitutional framework because it is unwilling to subject itself to genuine political competition. Even the most open-minded reform leaders have great difficulty in accepting the Western concept of check and balances. An interesting exchange between then Premier Zhu Rongji and a non-Communist member of the NPC in early 2001 says much about the nature of political reform and the maintenance of single-party rule. At a briefing for members of China's eight "democratic parties" on the governmental program for developing the western provinces before the annual NPC plenary session, the premier was taken aback by a question from a democratic-party stalwart and NPC deputy: "Shouldn't the party and government first seek the approval of the legislature before going ahead with the Go-West Program? At present, many aspects of the Go-West scheme are based on government regulations and fiats, not laws." According to a Hong Kong reporter, the premier was angry because he considered the query a challenge to his authority as head of the government, although out of politeness he said that he would give the issue fair consideration. The reporter observed that "this episode showed that even for a liberal cadre such as Zhu, the concept of a 'Western-style' legislature—and checks and balances among different arms of the government—remains quite an alien concept."[30]

The CCP has justified its monopoly of political power in terms of its indispensability to China's political life and the claim that loosening its grip would precipitate chaos. Political stability, defined as the preservation of single-party rule, must therefore be maintained at all costs. However, the problem for the CCP is that economic reform and political liberalization have created increasingly diverse social groups that would inevitably make demands on the Communist regime. There are two ways of handling these demands in order to maintain the so-called stability. One is to repress them. The other is to allow the expression of those interests and channel them into newly constructed political and legal institutions. Obviously, the CCP cannot rely only on repression to maintain its one-party rule in today's China. Therefore, the biggest challenge for the CCP is to find a way to gradually incorporate increasingly diverse social groups into a constitutional framework that would eventually include allowing genuine political competition. The CCP has to completely separate the party step by step from the state and from economic activities, open its ranks to critical discussion, and allow the local grassroots electoral process to percolate to the top. Movement along these lines would not necessarily lead to the CCP's loss of power in the foreseeable future. To make the transition smooth, multiparty competition can be avoided for some time until the CCP has completely transformed itself into an efficient and fully functioning social democratic party that is experienced and confident in running elections. Uninterrupted long-term political stability, administrative efficiency, and economic development in China, however, ultimately depend on the emergence of a genuinely representative government chosen by the people through regularly conducted competitive elections.

3

A Government of Laws

Democracy, Rule of Law, and Administrative Law Reform in China

Randall Peerenboom

Pan Wei is to be congratulated on a bold attempt to chart a feasible path of political reform for China. Resisting the temptation to throw his hands up in the air and declare all is lost unless and until single-party socialism is consigned to the grave alongside Marx and Engels, he dares incur the wrath of both Party leaders and more liberal reformers by suggesting that political reform without democracy is possible even within a single-party system, albeit a system with a considerably different role for the Party. The six pillars of his new political order, which he refers to as *consultative rule of law,* are a neutral civil service; an autonomous judiciary; extensive social consultative institutions; an anti-corruption body similar to Hong Kong's Independent Commission Against Corruption (ICAC); an independent auditing system; and more extensive, but still limited, freedoms of speech, press, assembly, and association.

Pan commendably provides a concrete agenda and clear timetable for realizing the new polity. The process is divided into three stages. During the first five-year phase, which he refers to as the rule *by* law period, the emphasis is on education, propaganda, and initial institutional reforms. The first step is to mount a campaign to explain the virtues of a law-based order, and to shift the emphasis from economic construction to establishing rule of law. The next step is to separate the Party from government, and to dismantle the nomenklatura system whereby the Party continues to appoint key personnel in all government organs.

The focus of the second five-year phase is institutional development, including the creation of a system of checks and balances and the establishment of an independent judiciary, an anti-corruption commission, and social consultative committees. This phase constitutes the primary stage of rule of law. The centerpiece of the following ten years, which culminates in a consultative rule of law, is the expansion of freedoms of speech, press, assembly, and association and the adjustment of the relations between state and society. In the end, the Party's role will be reduced to one of nominal leadership. Although the Party could still from time to time offer some basic policy guidance, its policies would have to be transformed into laws and regulations by the legislature and executive to have any legal effect, and the legislature and executive would be free to disregard the Party's suggestions.

Pan's plan, particularly the earlier stages, has a prima facie plausibility. The Party has endorsed a socialist version of rule of law, and has even gone so far as to amend the Constitution to incorporate the new *tifa* (official policy formulation). Moreover, there are many reasons why rule of law is attractive at this juncture. Initially, the impetus for post-Mao legal reforms came from a visceral and personal reaction to the arbitrariness of the Cultural Revolution on the part of many senior Party leaders who had been victimized by Mao's mercurial rule. The main engine for rule of law, however, has been and will continue to be the need to ensure economic growth and attract foreign investment. The movement has gained additional support from the regime's aspiration for legitimacy at home and abroad, as well as the central government's desire to rationalize governance, enhance administrative efficiency, and rein in local governments that increasingly ignore central policies and laws in their hell-bent pursuit of economic growth.

Support for rule of law is not limited to the Party-state, of course. Foreign investors are among the most vocal champions, with the voices of international human rights agencies equally as loud if somewhat shriller. There is also a rising domestic demand by citizens who increasingly expect the legal system to protect their rights, particularly their increasingly valuable property rights.

Further, the Party announced as far back as the historic 11th Party Congress in 1978 that it intended to separate the Party from government. In the last twenty years, the Party has in fact turned many of the day-to-day operations of governance over to the usual state organs: the legislature, executive, and judiciary. The National People's Congress (NPC) is unquestionably stronger, even if still a pale shadow of its counterparts in Western liberal democracies. CCP influence on administrative rule and decision making is also breaking down, and agencies are increasingly assertive in pursuing their own agendas. The Party has even allowed the courts to decide most cases on their own. To be sure, the process is far from complete. In particular, the Party maintains control over the various state organs through the nomenklatura system, and remains wary of major institutional reforms such as creation of a truly independent judiciary.

Although I will return to the feasibility issue later, it should be noted that Pan appreciates that there are many challenges to realizing the new order. Indeed, having chosen to wage battle on two fronts simultaneously, Pan may well have met his Waterloo. His proposal may fall under the joint attacks of the Party on one side, and of reformers who think the emphasis should be on democracy on the other. Personally, I agree that the most likely path to political reform is to establish rule of law without democracy. Democracy is not a feasible political option, and even if it were, now is not the right time. Accordingly, rule of law is a desirable alternative in that it allows for political reforms without democracy and holds out the promise of a limited government and perhaps some relief from the pervasive corruption that is threatening to destabilize China.

While sympathetic, then, to Pan's basic approach,[1] I would nevertheless like to comment in passing on Pan's view of democracy and then raise two sets of concerns about his proposal, in the hope that the observations and queries may be of use in implementing what in my view is an exciting and promising reform agenda. In the first section, I note how Pan's ideas about democracy reflect traditional beliefs. Like many intellectuals, Pan remains an elitist, and like many Chinese of all stripes, he rejects three basic assumptions that underwrite Western liberal democracy: that to treat another with respect and equality requires that one refrain from imposing one's views on that person (the normative equality premise); that one knows what is best for oneself, and individuals reasonably disagree about what constitutes the good (the epistemic equality premise); and that the interests of the individual, social groups, and the state are not reconcilable (the fact of pluralism or the utopianism of harmony premise). Given these beliefs, it is unclear whether Pan sees consultative rule of law as a sustainable, stable equilibrium or just a stage on the way to democracy, and if the latter, whether Pan would embrace or regret the ultimate establishment of democracy.

In the second part, I turn to the main issue of Pan's conception of rule of law. First, I suggest that Pan's understanding of rule of law is somewhat simplistic and rather optimistic, and that his faith in the miraculous power of rule of law to put an end to corruption, resolve pluralistic conflicts, and produce a just and harmonious society is wildly unrealistic. Law is a more limited tool than Pan imagines, and cannot by itself deliver all that Pan hopes. Second, and related, Pan is correct to focus on administrative law reforms as the heart of China's efforts to establish rule of law. But he over-states the neutrality of the administrative agencies and has a much too mechanical and formalistic view of how law is made, interpreted, and implemented. The notion of civil servants as neutral technocrats who serve the public by deciding technical issues based on special expertise is hard to sustain nowadays. Although critical legal scholars have challenged the neutrality and expertise of administrative agencies by arguing for the pervasiveness of politics, Pan valiantly but vainly tries to keep politics out of the policy-making and implementation processes in his imaginary administrative law regime.[2] Similarly, even though philosophers have questioned the value-neutrality of science, Pan proceeds as if every administrative decision were not about value-laden resource allocation and policy choices but rather simply technical issues with a clear-cut, scientific, singularly correct answer. Meanwhile, Pan pays little heed to the warning of public choice proponents who have demonstrated that agencies time and again put their own institutional interests ahead of the public's interests and are susceptible to capture by special interests.[3]

Pan also underestimates the problems in establishing a modern administrative law regime. It will take more than an independent corruption commission and consultative bodies to cure all of the maladies of China's administrative law system. The biggest obstacles to a law-based administrative system in China are institutional and systemic in nature: a legislative system in disarray; a weak judiciary; a number of poorly trained judges and lawyers, themselves prone to corruption and professional responsibility violations; a low level of legal consciousness among the populace; the persistent influence of paternalistic traditions and a culture of deference to government authority; and the fallout from the unfinished transition from a centrally planned to a market economy, which has exacerbated central–local tensions and resulted in fragmentation of authority.[4]

In the third section, I reconsider the relation between rule of law and democracy. Although rule of law is possible without democracy, the lack of democracy creates certain obstacles to its implementation and raises accountability issues. Accordingly, I suggest that in the long run China will most likely become democratic, though probably not a *liberal* democracy. In the fourth and concluding section, I expand the scope of Pan's proposal to explore various possible administrative law reforms and legal reforms more generally required to realize rule of law in China, while suggesting that ultimately their success turns on issues of power that exceed the limits of the law.

Democracy

Chinese philosophical thinking has always been elitist. Few Chinese intellectuals would accept the liberal assumption (the epistemic equality premise) that people reasonably disagree about what constitutes the good for society. From the prehistoric mythical ancestors Yao and Shun to the Confucian sage-ruler of the Warring States period to Mao Zedong, Deng Xiaoping, and the leaders today, Chinese rulers have been credited with an uncanny ability to fathom what is in the best interests of society. Indeed, much of their authority to rule is predicated on their claim to special ethical insight and unique political knowledge of the way of rulership. Pan too believes that elites should rule based on their superior insights. Just as the Confucian literati of old who passed the imperial examinations thought the ruler should entrust day-to-day governance to them, Pan believes that China's socialist leaders should turn over day-to-day governance to technocrats who have demonstrated their intellectual superiority by passing the civil service exam. The only difference is that whereas the Confucian literati claimed the right to rule on the basis of superior moral wisdom, modern-day civil servants would claim the right to rule on the basis of superior technical knowledge.

The rejection of the epistemic equality premise calls into question the normative equality premise (for liberals, the latter also follows as the conclusion of the former): that is, that to treat another with respect is to refrain from imposing one's normative views on the other. Western democracy is based on the notion of a neutral state and the social contractarian myth that individuals precede the state and have the right to choose the normative agenda for society. Because people reasonably disagree about the good for society, a procedural mechanism is needed. Elections provide that mechanism by allowing the majority to decide through ostensibly fair procedures the goals for society and the means to achieve them, subject to certain limits in the form of anti-majoritarian rights that trump the electoral process and safeguard the basic liberties of individuals and minorities against the tyranny of the majority.

In contrast, in China the government has always pursued a substantive moral agenda defined in large part by the particular normative vision of the ruler. Chinese governments have been and continue to be paternalistic. The image of the father dominates the political rhetoric of China, though the specifics of the image vary by school. In the past, the Confucian father-ruler was kind and compassionate and more of a facilitator of order than a dictator, whereas the legalist father-ruler was a tough disciplinarian who well understood that to spare the rod is to spoil the child. In the socialist era, the Party combined tolerance for the people with harsh attacks against the enemy who dared oppose the scientifically correct Party line. Now Pan would turn matters over to an impartial and neutral civil service. Nevertheless, the image remains the same: the father, knowing what is best, takes care of his children. Justice, this time dressed up not as the Party line but in the new clothes of a technocratic and public-minded civil service, once again trumps democracy and choice. But as in all previous regimes, what remains most important is social order, which trumps liberty and the demands for a greater voice for citizens in choosing their own individual ends and the ends for society. To be sure, Pan realizes that liberty has been excessively slighted in the past. Accordingly, there must be some balance between the need for order and freedom. To draw that balance, however, requires better elites—not Party hacks, but civil servants above the fray of the political conflicts that have distorted the decision-making process in the past and led to needlessly tight restrictions on freedom.

Pan is also traditional in holding out hope that the increasingly pluralistic interests of the diverse sectors of society can ultimately be reconciled harmoniously. At times, he seems obsessively intent on denying that there are any deep cleavages in contemporary society. At other times, he seems to acknowledge growing pluralism but to claim that the various diverse interests can be melded into a highly unified will under the law. In law lies the power to ensure that everyone lives together harmoniously; law is universal justice, neutral and acceptable to all. Accordingly, politics is not needed. There is no need for citizens to form political groups and contest for power because civil servants will work out what is best for everyone. Indeed, the role of the legislature will be merely to approve laws drafted by administrative agencies.

As Pan eloquently and persuasively argues, democracy has its flaws. It does not necessarily go hand in hand with economic development, and may even inhibit development in some cases, contributing to heightened social tensions and possible social chaos. All too many third-wave democracies have failed to generate economic growth, implement rule of law, invest in human capital, or to deliver on human rights promises. Disenchanted with democracy, citizens in some states have opted to return dictators to power or have become apathetic, relinquishing their hard-won right to vote.[5] Indeed, as Pinkney notes in his survey of democracy in developing countries, "what is remarkable is that almost all third world countries have had at least nominally pluralist political systems at some time in their history, yet the majority did not (or could not) build on these to establish durable forms of democracy."[6] Even where electoral democracy remains in place, the governments exist in a limbo state variously described as soft authoritarianism, semi-dictatorship, semi-democracy, or nonliberal electoral democracy.

On the other hand, despite its flaws, democracy has its advantages. Democracy does provide a procedural mechanism for regulating interest group conflicts and for smoothing over social cleavages; it arguably allows for more open debate and greater expression of diverse viewpoints, thus facilitating better decision making, and provides a more accurate feedback mechanism, as evidenced, for instance, by fewer famines in democratic states;[7] and it provides for more, albeit still limited, government accountability because citizens can vote out those in office if they so choose.

But there is little to be gained by debating once again the pros and cons of democracy in the abstract. Democracy in China is not a viable option at present.[8] The Party opposes it. There is little support among intellectuals for genuine elections, as Pan notes. Nor is there a hankering for democracy on the part of the general populace. Indeed, poll after poll shows most people are more concerned about stability and economic growth than democracy and civil and political liberties.[9] Moreover, even if the Party were willing to endorse democracy and the people did want it, China currently lacks the institutions, including rule of law, to make democracy work. Pan is right, then, to look elsewhere for possible solutions to the serious corruption problems and the growing dislocation between a repressive and nontransparent Party barricaded in Zhongnanhai and a developing market economy and evolving society. Rule of law offers the possibility of political reform without democracy, although that depends on what one means by rule of law.

Rule of Law

Pan suggests that unlike democracy, rule of law is a much simpler concept and easy to define: it means ruling in accordance with established legal requirements. Were it only so simple. Rule of law is in fact a much contested concept both in China and elsewhere. Many legal scholars in particular share Judith Shklar's fear that rule of law "may well have become just another one of those self-congratulatory rhetorical devices that grace the public utterances of Anglo-American politicians."[10] Debates about the meaning of rule of law should not blind us, however, to a broad consensus as to its core meaning and essential elements. At its most basic, rule of law refers to a system in which law imposes meaningful limits on the state and individual members of the ruling elite, as captured in the notions of a government of laws, supremacy of the law, and equality of all before the law.

Generally, rule of law theories can be divided into two types, thick and thin. A thin theory emphasizes the formal or instrumental aspects of rule of law—those features that any legal system allegedly must possess to function effectively as a system of laws, regardless of whether the legal system is part of a democratic or nondemocratic, capitalist or socialist, liberal or theocratic society.[11] These features typically include the following requirements: there must be procedural rules for law making and laws must be made by an entity with the authority to make laws in accordance with such rules to be valid; transparency—laws must be made public and readily accessible; laws must be prospective, relatively clear, consistent, stable; laws must be enforced fairly and impartially, with the gap between the law on the books and law in practice narrow; and laws must be reasonably acceptable to a majority of the populace or people affected (or at least the key groups affected) by the laws.[12]

A variety of institutions are also required. The promulgation of laws assumes a legislature and the government machinery necessary to make the laws publicly available. It also assumes rules for making laws. Congruence of laws on the books and actual practice assumes institutions for implementing and enforcing laws. The fair application of laws implies normative and practical limits on the decision makers who interpret and apply the laws and principles of due process, such as access to impartial tribunals, a chance to present evidence, and rules of evidence.

In contrast to thin theories, thick theories incorporate into rule of law elements of political morality such as particular economic arrangements (free-market capitalism, central planning), forms of government (democracy, single-party socialism), or conceptions of human rights (liberal, communitarian, "Asian Values," Islamic).[13] Thick theories of rule of law can be further subdivided according to the particular substantive elements that are favored.[14]

Thus, one could distinguish between a liberal and a socialist rule of law. Liberals would incorporate free-market capitalism (subject to qualifications that would allow various degrees of "legitimate" government regulation of the market), multiparty democracy in which citizens may choose their representatives at all levels of government, and a liberal interpretation of human rights that gives priority to first-generation civil and political rights over second- and third-generation economic, social, cultural, and collective or group rights.

The socialist rule of law favored by the current administration in China incorporates a socialist form of economy, today an increasingly market-based economy but one in which public ownership still plays a somewhat larger role than in other such economies; a nondemocratic political system in which the Party plays a leading role; and an interpretation of rights that emphasizes stability, collective rights over individual rights, and subsistence as the basic right rather than civil and political rights.

The first point to be noted about Pan's conception of rule of law is that it is underdeveloped and incompletely theorized even compared to thin conceptions of the rule of law. It amounts to a sketch or outline of a rule of law system with many details apparently to be filled in later. Pan need not present a fully developed theory of rule of law, of course, and as a political scientist rather than a legal scholar he is perhaps wise to allow others to supply the missing details. However, his seeming lack of familiarity with the legal literature or China's efforts to carry out legal reforms in the last twenty years and the obstacles encountered along the way may explain his untempered exuberance for the benefits of a civil service–based consultative rule of law and his excessive optimism as to the ease with which it might be implemented.[15] Any credible version of rule of law will surely require more than changes in the civil service, which by itself would be no mean feat.

Second, there is a tension between Pan's notion of rule of law as acting in accordance with the law and his assertion that rule of law will deliver justice. This tension is reflected in the difference between thin theories of the rule of law, which promise predictability and certainty but are consistent with great injustice, and thick theories of rule of law that reject thin theories precisely because they do not rule out the possibility of evil empires such as Nazi Germany or apartheid South Africa. Thus, some scholars, both in the PRC and abroad, have suggested that rule of law requires "good laws." Harold Berman, for instance, claims that rule of law requires laws that are based on some normative foundation that transcends the legal system itself. In the past, divine law or natural law provided the moral ground; today, a more secular notion of democracy and human rights provides the normative underpinning.[16] Similarly, others distinguish between a *Rechtsstaat* and rule of law. Whereas a *Rechtsstaat* could be a morally bankrupt state properly governed in accordance with positive law, rule of law entails some moral limits on laws.[17]

The fear is that in the absence of a sufficiently robust normative basis, law may be used instrumentally by authoritarian or fascist regimes for their own ends. There is no gainsaying the fact that the instrumental aspects of rule of law may enhance the efficiency of authoritarian governments and reinforce their legitimacy. As Zhu Suli, one of China's leading legal scholars, has argued, rule of law will promote economic development, which in turn will strengthen the government fiscally and bolster its legitimacy. A stronger, more legitimate government may be better positioned to resist meaningful political reforms.[18] More concretely, given China's currently repressive laws, which require the registration of all social groups and allow for the punishment of dissidents under broadly defined state secrets regulations and laws against endangering the state, it is doubtful whether justice is possible even if laws are faithfully followed.

Setting aside justice in politically sensitive cases that threaten the survival of the ruling party, whether Pan's civil service would produce just laws in more mundane policy areas is also debatable, particularly given the limited channels for public participation and relatively weak constraints on the power of the civil service. Pan seems to think that neutral civil servants could simply deduce laws from certain "generally accepted moral principles of the time," and hence the public would accept such laws as just. But growing pluralism implies increasing diversity over fundamental moral issues; and in any event, the path from general moral principles to particular legislative outcomes is hardly straightforward.

I am not suggesting that China must either adopt a liberal democratic version of rule of law or forgo rule of law completely because of the risks. As the former would be a nonstarter, I think China should focus on creating the institutions and establishing a legal system that at minimum meets the standards of a thin rule of law.[19] Although there are dangers of an authoritarian regime misusing law for its own despicable ends, they should not be overstated. Even a thin rule of law differs from instrumentalist rule *by* law in that rule *of* law imposes meaningful restraints on state and government officials. In a rule of law state, law is not just a tool to be used by the ruling regime to control the people or promote the interests of the privileged few. Law also binds government leaders and officials. One of the main purposes of rule of law is to limit the arbitrary acts of the government and impose meaningful constraints on the ruling elite. Thus the potential positive value of even a thin rule of law should not be discounted. Rule of law imposes restraints on the state and provides the basis for challenges by citizens of government arbitrariness.

In the long run, establishing a thin rule of law usually will alter the balance of power between the state, society, and individuals regardless of the thicker social and political context in which the legal system is embedded, and which gives rise to competing thick conceptions of rule of law both domestically and internationally. The establishment of a legal system with some degree of autonomy acts as a counterweight to political power. While a strong civil society is not inevitable, it is more likely in a state that implements rule of law than one that does not. A strong civil society is arguably more likely to seek and more likely to obtain political reforms aimed at further limiting the power of the authoritarian state and increasing the power of society, even though we should not assume "civil society" in China will be of the same nature or political orientation as in liberal democracies.[20] Thus, even if the goal is democracy and the protection of human rights, it makes sense to ensure at minimum that a thin rule of law is realized. The more probable result of implementing rule of law in China is not a stronger authoritarian government able to resist reforms but greater pressure for liberalization and democracy as in Taiwan and South Korea.

Pan contemplates precisely such a shift in power from the Party-state to society in the third stage of reform in which the citizens will come to enjoy greater civil and political freedoms and power will be allocated among, and checked by, newly created institutions, including the anti-corruption commission, social consultative groups, and a more independent judiciary. But in the absence of democracy, opportunities for public participation in the law-making, interpretation, and implementation processes remain limited. As a result, the possibility that law will serve the interests of the few rather than the many continues to exist. Traditionally, administrative law has played a central role in holding officials accountable and diminishing the risk that officials will use their position to benefit themselves rather than the public.

Rule of Law and Administrative Law Reform

Pan sees administrative law reform, and in particular the establishment of a neutral civil service, as central to the realization of rule of law. Here he is on firm ground. Because administrative law plays a key role in limiting the arbitrary acts of government, the centrality of administrative law (administration in accordance with law— *yifa xingzheng*) to rule of law is well accepted both in China and abroad. He is skating on thinner ice, however, when he suggests that a professional civil service can be readily established, and that it will not only be able to solve the problem of corruption but to resolve conflicting social interests in an impartial and neutral way. Although the civil service has been a force against corruption in Hong Kong and Singapore, in many other Asian states, including China, government officials are a leading source of corruption.

Indeed, China's administrative officials are themselves one of the major obstacles to rule of law. They regularly abuse their authority, ignore central laws, and pass inconsistent administrative regulations that promote their own institutional interests. Accordingly, one of the biggest challenges facing administrative law reformers has been to overcome the traditional attitudes of government officials and create a culture of legality.

In the past, government officials were considered parental authority figures and of-ten referred to as *fumu guan* (father and mother officials). The Confucian emphasis on hierarchical social roles reinforced the idea that lay people were supposed to defer to the superior judgment of government officials who knew best what was in their interest and the interest of society as a whole. The CCP's victory did nothing to challenge these fundamental beliefs about the nature of governance or the relations between govern-ment officials and the people. Leninist ideology assumed that because the Party had no other interest than what was in the best interest of the people (and knows what that interest is), there was little need for external restraints on the Party or the government that carried out Party policy. If a mistake was made or people felt the need to point out that their interests had been overlooked, they could simply bring the issue to the atten-tion of government officials. Thus, the primary means of challenging an administrative decision was by complaining to the agency or to the procuratorate. For the most part, however, people were expected to defer to the judgment of government officials. Backed up by the awesome power of the Party, bureaucrats were used to giving orders and having them obeyed. Moreover, given the low status of formal law during much of the Mao period, officials regularly ignored the law when it was inconvenient.

Today, the Party has realized the need for external restraints on administrative officials. Accordingly, a number of institutions and mechanisms have been estab-lished for reining in the bureaucracy, including legislative oversight committees, ombudsmen-like supervision committees, Party discipline committees, internal ad-ministration reconsideration procedures, a system of letters and visits, and judicial review. Given the traditional views of the role and status of government officials vis-à-vis the people, however, it is not surprising that many officials have been slow to accept the notion that rule of law requires that government officials themselves act in accordance with, and be subject to, the law. According to one survey, almost half of the officials surveyed thought at the time of the implementation of the Administrative Litigation Law that it would decrease administrative efficiency.[21] Many feared that it would decrease the authority of government officials. The idea of officials being hauled into courts to account for their actions was both threatening and demeaning.

Officials have responded by developing various techniques to avoid litigation. Sometimes they issue decisions in the name of the CCP. Or else they pressure the plaintiff to withdraw the suit or pressure courts to reject the case or find in favor of the defendant. Once the case is accepted, many officials refuse to cooperate with the courts. They refuse to accept the summons, appear in court, respond to the complaint, provide evidence, or comply with the court's decision. Some even fabricate or de-stroy evidence.

Conversely, it has taken some time for Chinese citizens to get used to the idea that an average person could challenge the decision of a government official. Thus, although the number of administrative cases has reached 100,000 per year, there are still many fewer cases than one might expect. For instance, in 1996, there were 20,000 driver's license confiscation cases in Guangxi but not one was challenged through either administrative reconsideration or litigation.[22] Similarly, there were 1,600 cases of reeducation through labor in 1996 but only 35 requests (2.2 percent) for administrative reconsideration.[23]

To be sure, culture is not determinative, as indicated by the success of Hong Kong and Singapore in establishing modern administrative law systems. Indeed, attitudes are changing in China. But the process will take time, and will be influenced by a variety of factors. Economic reforms, for instance, have both contributed to and hindered administrative law reforms. The transition to a market economy has necessitated a new form of government and style of regulation. Government officials used to the patterns and practices of a centrally planned economy have had to change their ways. The transition has not always been a smooth one. Getting entrenched bureaucrats to abide by the law when in the past they *were* the law has not been easy.

More fundamentally, the basic paradox of economic reforms is that strong administrators are needed in a period of rapid economic transition, and yet the administration itself is responsible for market distortions. In the current transition state, there is often either no market or only an imperfectly functioning one. Many industries are still state monopolies or dominated by state-owned entities. In such a system, the administrative agencies have a greater role as regulators. Inadequate information resulting from market imperfections also suggests a larger role for the administration than in a well-functioning market. Similarly, agencies are needed to deal with a variety of externalities that are not found in more market-oriented economies. For the moment then, as in other East Asian developmental states during their period of rapid economic growth and restructuring, a strong government and administration with considerable discretion is necessary to respond to the needs of reform.[24]

At the same time, the administration is itself often a cause of market failure. In the absence of a well-functioning legal system and mature markets, companies have found it advantageous to establish close relationships with the government officials that control access to valuable inputs such as technology, capital, and raw materials, and who can assist in resolving disputes with third parties. Thus, the unfinished transition to a market economy has fostered the growth of clientelism and corporatism. As a result, local government officials frequently interfere in the operation of businesses and in the process of judicial review of administrative decisions in an effort to protect local companies in which they have a direct or indirect interest.

Economic reforms have also created new incentives for officials and exposed them to new pressures. The combination of more economic activity and weak control mechanisms provides agency officials ample opportunities for corruption and rent seeking. This is particularly problematic because agencies now face additional financial pressure. Cut off from state subsidies, salaries and bonuses of employees are funded in part by the revenue of the agency, which provides a strong incentive to agencies to impose random and arbitrary fees.

In light of the costs of corporatism and clientelism and the sharp rise in administrative corruption and rent seeking, the role of administrative agencies is currently being redefined. In keeping with the policy of separation of government and business, agencies are supposed to become regulators rather than market players. Corporatist and clientelist ties between government agencies and businesses are being severed and the nature of the relationship between government and private businesses is becoming more limited, voluntary, and symmetrical. In the future, companies that prefer to forgo government assistance in exchange for greater autonomy should find it easier to go their own way without incurring the wrath of government officials or being subject to discrimination and harassment. Over time, the withdrawal of the administration from business should result in fewer conflicts of interest; administrative agencies will be regulators but not competitors. And as the market develops, the role of administrative agencies may diminish as there will be less need for regulation. The State Council has embarked in recent years on a major overhaul of the approval and licensing system. As the result, the number of approvals and licenses required to do business has decreased, and become more a matter of formal, rather than substantive, review.

Nevertheless, business activities remain heavily regulated. Administrative agencies continue to resist reforms aimed at decreasing their control over enterprises and the economy. Accordingly, the separation between government and enterprises is far from complete.

Agencies are also responsible for a variety of law-making problems. Despite the promulgation of the Law on Legislation, China's legislative system continues to be characterized by a high incidence of inconsistency between lower- and higher-level legislation. One reason for the high degree of inconsistency is that the lines of lawmaking authority are not clear. Administrative agencies, for instance, have vaguely delineated inherent authority to pass certain types of regulations. In addition, agencies frequently receive broad delegations to issue legislation. Far from the neutral public servants envisioned by Pan, agencies regularly use their authority to pass legislation that protects their institutional interests. Often, such regulations are at odds with central laws and regulations. Moreover, the transition to a market economy has exacerbated interagency conflicts. The struggle for turf among administrative departments leads to a variety of departments claiming jurisdictional authority over the same area and issuing conflicting rules to protect their institutional interests.

China's administrative law woes are also due to a weak judiciary. Granted, the importance of judicial review is easily overstated.[25] In fact, experienced lawyers often note that one wins the lawsuit at the agency rather than in court. Moreover, judicial review is only one means of ensuring that administrative officials act in accordance with law. Nevertheless, independent courts are still necessary, if not sufficient, for a modern administrative law regime in that they serve as a final backstop against government arbitrariness and oppression and structure agency behavior and institutional politics. The lack of independence and authority of PRC courts undermines their ability to discipline wayward administrative agencies.

Particularly damaging to the autonomy of courts is their dependence on local government. There are four levels of courts in China: the Supreme People's Court, High People's Courts, Intermediate People's Courts, and Basic Level People's Courts. Each is responsible to the people's congress at the equivalent level, which supervises its work and appoints and removes judges. Moreover, courts are financially dependent on the corresponding level of government for salaries, housing, benefits, and so forth. The lack of security of tenure combined with financial dependence leaves judges beholden to their government counterparts. Contact between government officials and judges, many of whom have known each other for years, is a regular event. Not surprisingly, local protectionism is an issue in some cases as courts refuse to enforce judgments against local entities with strong government support. Moreover, given the weak stature of the courts and their dependence on the local government, courts naturally are reluctant at times to challenge administrative agencies.

Pan of course realizes that a more independent judiciary is required. He is also aware that China's administrative law problems cannot be solved overnight, and hence suggests a twenty-year process. In light of the many problems and the size of the country, the creation of a modern administrative law system in China will inevitably take considerably longer than in Singapore or Hong Kong. Perhaps twenty years may be enough. But even assuming Pan's six-pronged reform agenda is implemented, it will not be sufficient by itself. A wide range of other administrative and legal reforms is required, and legal reforms must be complemented by changes in the political, social, and economic realms.

Rule of Law and Corruption

Pan places great weight on corruption as one of the main problems, if not the central problem, confronting the government today, and proposes a new anti-corruption agency, civil service reforms, a more independent judiciary, more public scrutiny, and a social consultative system as the answer. Corruption is undoubtedly a major issue, though whether it is as threatening to the government as Pan suggests is debatable. But assuming it is, will Pan's reform package provide the cure? Corruption is a multifaceted problem, with many causes. As Pan observes, economic reforms have provided more opportunities for those lower down the ladder to take advantage of their position to extort rents. The government's intensive regulation of economic and social activities creates ample occasions for officials to extract benefits. The emergence of a private economy has given rise to new sources of wealth to be exploited by government agencies needing to bolster their revenues in light of cutbacks in funding from the central government. A general crisis in values, combined with a get-rich-quick mentality and resentment over the excessive wealth flaunted by the offspring of high-placed government officials, exacerbates the problem.

Legal reforms cannot alter some of the underlying causes of corruption. Accordingly, corruption is likely to continue until economic reforms are completed and the government adopts a less interventionist approach to regulation that deprives government officials of the opportunity to extract rents, as the State Council has recognized in embarking on the overhaul of the approval and licensing system. Furthermore, as we have seen, the administration itself is responsible for much of the corruption. In the end, an administrative system is only as good as the administrators who run it. Ultimately, the success of administrative reforms requires the establishment of a culture of legality and the development of internal norms of behavior that ensure honest officials. Pan appreciates the need to establish a corps of honest officials. To achieve that end, he suggests a combination of old-style campaigns aimed at changing the character and attitudes of officials and newly established external mechanisms for dealing with corrupt officials.

Moral campaigns to instill honesty in government officials are not likely to have much impact in the jaded and materialistic contemporary world. To change the behavior of officials requires changing their incentive structure. One way to do that would be to increase the costs of corruption through better external mechanisms for detecting and punishing improper behavior. To date, however, legislative oversight, the letters and visits system, administrative supervision bodies, Party discipline committees, administrative reconsideration, judicial review, and scrutiny by the media and public have all been of limited effectiveness in dealing with corruption for a variety of reasons, including the institutional and systemic weaknesses discussed previously, doctrinal shortcomings in some cases, and problems unique to each mechanism.[26]

Why expect that Pan's proposals, even if implemented, will be any more effective? To be sure, Pan's proposals do address some of the problems by strengthening the judiciary and enhancing the ability of the public and media to monitor agencies by bolstering the freedom of the press and other civil liberties. Yet judicial review is no panacea, and neither greater public scrutiny nor Pan's consultative committees are likely to have a major impact. Pan's consultative committees have no real powers. They can require agencies to submit reports to them, to listen and respond to their suggestions, and to make a public record of the responses. In that sense they are somewhat similar to notice and comment requirements in the United States, which are notoriously weak. All too often, agencies, captured by special interest groups or out to further their own interests, simply consign the comments of the public to the dustbin. In the absence of democracy, Pan's government officials are immune from the threat of removal from office, and remain free to pursue their own agendas.

In the end then, Pan puts most of his chips on the anti-corruption commission, which he hopes will be able to replicate the results of agencies in Hong Kong and Singapore that brought corruption to heal within three years. Unlike existing supervision bodies, which are organized under the State Council and responsible to local governments, Pan's commission would be independent of the State Council and even insulated to some extent from judicial review. But to whom would it be responsible? The NPC? The Party? How will its members be appointed? Who will approve its budget? Most important, what is the source of its authority? To date, the Party has been unwilling, and perhaps unable, to curb corruption at higher levels. Without Party support, none of the other mechanisms have the political clout to bring high-level officials to heal. Apart from a few scapegoats sacrificed to appease the public (and who may have lost out in internal political power struggles), those brought up on corruption charges have been small fish. Yet if the Party were willing to deal with corruption, an independent agency arguably would not be needed. It is hard to imagine at present an agency more powerful than the CCP discipline committees. Why would the Party tolerate such an entity?

Twenty years is a long time, of course. Although at present it seems unlikely that the Party would tolerate a truly independent anti-corruption agency with sufficient authority to attack corruption even within the Party, it is possible that the CCP will be compelled to accept further limitations on its power to stave off a fateful day of reckoning when it must either concede its privileged position or risk an uprising.

Rule of Law Without Democracy

Ultimately, the key to the future realization of rule of law in China is power. How is power to be controlled and allocated in a single-party socialist state? To the extent that law is to limit the Party, how does the legal system obtain sufficient authority to control a Party that has been above the law? In a democracy, the final check on government power is the ability of people to throw the government out and elect a new one. In the absence of multiparty democracy, an authoritarian government must either voluntarily relinquish some of its power or else have it taken away by force. Naturally, Party leaders will resist giving up power so readily. They may therefore be disinclined to support reforms that would strengthen rule of law but also allow institutions to become so powerful that they could provide the basis for challenging Party rule. The result may be that at least on those issues that threaten the survival of the Party, the needs of the Party may continue to trump rule of law for some time. To be sure, there are numerous ways in which the legal system can be improved and strengthened that do not rise to the level of a threat to the Party. But some reforms, such as those aimed at promoting a more independent judiciary, a robust civil society, or a powerful anti-corruption commission, could put the Party at risk.

Nevertheless, there is some reason to believe that the issue of power can be resolved in favor of rule of law and that law will come to impose meaningful restraints on Party and government leaders. As Jiang Jingguo's deathbed support for greater democracy in Taiwan and the experience of South Korea and the Soviet Union show, authoritarian leaders are capable of relinquishing power given the right circumstances. The endorsement by Party leaders of the principle of ruling the country according to law and a socialist rule of law state, with its subsequent incorporation into the Constitution, suggest that the Party is willing to accept limitations on its power.

Although Party leaders may be wary about rule of law, they appreciate its advantages. In his speech at the 15th Party Congress, Jiang Zemin portrayed rule of law as central to economic development, national stability, and Party legitimacy.[27] Not surprisingly, much of the initiative for legal reforms has come from the center. For the Party to achieve its goals of stability, implementation of central policies, economic development, and legitimacy, further legal reforms are required, including a stronger administrative law regime and a more independent judiciary. Currently, widespread discontent over judicial corruption, bias, and incompetence is deterring investors, undermining the legitimacy and effectiveness of the legal system, and ultimately hurting the Party.

To be sure, from the Party's perspective, a stronger legal system with a more independent judiciary has both advantages and disadvantages. While the Party has for years acknowledged that local protectionism is undermining the independence of the judiciary, it has refused to address the institutional causes of the problem, presumably because it fears that an authoritative and independent judiciary able to decide commercial and administrative cases on their merits would also be able to decide politically sensitive cases on their merits. Thus the dilemma facing the Party is how to strengthen the judiciary without allowing it to become too strong. In deciding whether to support further reforms, the Party must determine whether the benefits outweigh the costs. That calculus, however, is influenced by factors beyond the Party's control.

The need to sustain economic growth will continue to put pressure on China's leaders to carry out reforms, even if that means further erosion of the Party's power. Economic reforms have resulted in a devolution of authority to lower-level governments and also shifted the base of power in some measure from the Party-state to society. Although the extent to which reforms have weakened the Party and diminished central control is hotly debated, clearly the Party-state is much less dominant than in the past.[28] As reforms continue, the balance of power will continue to shift.

Moreover, rule of law is a function of institution building and the creation of a culture of legality. Progress has been made and continues to be made on both fronts. Now that the genie is out of the bottle, legal reformers will continue to push for more independent and authoritative courts, as will members of the judiciary, if for no other reason than path-dependent institutional self-interest. Political and legal reforms tend to take on a life of their own, with institutions bursting out of the cages in which they were meant to be confined.[29] In Taiwan, for instance, the Council of Grand Justices assumed a much greater role in curbing administrative discretion and limiting government as legal and political reforms progressed, thereby contributing to further reforms.[30] In Indonesia, the Suharto government's desire to obtain legitimacy abroad and to deal with corruption and patrimonial practices that were adversely affecting business confidence led to the establishment of administrative courts. But then the courts turned on Suharto, pursuing key allies on corruption charges and defiantly striking down the government's decision to ban a popular weekly news magazine. In response to a groundswell of public support, the judiciary became increasingly aggressive in challenging the government, to the point where Suharto was brought up on charges of corruption.[31]

Further, although much of the impetus for legal reforms in China has come from the center, the demand for rule of law has increasingly come from citizens, domestic businesses, academics, members of the judiciary, and legal reformers in state organs such as the NPC. Even local governments have begun to appreciate the advantages of a law-based order. For instance, notwithstanding Guangdong's reputation for flex-ibility and finding ways to circumvent the rules, Guangdong officials were among the first to jump on the rule of law bandwagon because they felt a flexible approach left them vulnerable to a predatory central government and that implementing rule of law would help them maintain their competitive edge over other provinces.[32]

In short, the development of the legal system hinges on more than the ideas of the top leadership. Legal reforms will continue to be driven to a considerable extent by objective forces, including the needs of a market economy; the demands of foreign investors and domestic businesses; international pressure, as evidenced in the amend-ment of the Criminal Law and Criminal Procedure Law and China's accession to various human rights treaties; the World Trade Organization (WTO); and the ruling regime's desire for legitimacy, both at home and abroad.

Assuming, then, that a consultative rule of law is feasible, is it sustainable, and if so, is a consultative rule of law without democracy a normatively attractive alterna-tive? Both the sustainability and normative appeal of a consultative rule of law turn to a large extent on the degree to which the new elite can be held accountable.

Pan places a great deal of faith in the civil service to pass fair laws. Most laws would be drafted by administrative agencies. The NPC would simply approve them. Pan seems to think that the NPC's approval function would make law-making more difficult. However, in modern parliamentary systems, the ruling party is generally able to push through whatever bills it wants due to its control of the executive branch. In the absence of greater public participation in the law- and regulation-making pro-cesses, the accountability of civil servants will remain an issue. By controlling the law-making process, agencies are able to legalize corruption by passing laws to favor the elite few. For instance, state assets may be siphoned off and end up in the hands of private parties under the guise of various privatization schemes. The courts, consulta-tive committees, and an anti-corruption agency are impotent to challenge such legal-ized corruption.

Even if China's law-making civil servants really were simply public-minded offi-cials who always put the interests of society first, the lack of accountability would still threaten the legitimacy of the system and lead to greater calls for more participa-tion by groups that felt their interests have been slighted. A political regime's legiti-macy may be performance or consent based. Without democracy, a consultative rule of law order would derive its legitimacy from performance and the opinion of citizens that the system is fair and just and produces good results. In a pluralistic society, however, individuals inevitably will disagree about what is fair and just and judge laws in terms of their own interests—hence the need for politics to work out the conflicts. Yet Pan would forgo politics in favor of technocratic civil servants and rule of law. Unfortunately, he greatly overstates the ability of law to mediate conflict, in part because he thinks there are no deep cleavages in contemporary China, and in part because he sees law making, interpretation, and implementation as simply a technical process rather than a value-laden one. Neither assumption withstands close scrutiny.

Social cleavages exist in China and are likely to increase over time. One major fault line runs along the rural-urban divide. Huge differences in wealth between eastern coastal and inner regions have already led to sharp conflicts and political infighting. The issue of Taiwan looms ever larger, and will eventually require a political solution. The future of Hong Kong and Macau, not to mention Tibet and Xinjiang, also pose potentially thorny resource allocation, legal, and political issues. Generational conflicts are likely to become more acute as the effects of the one-child policy force later generations to devote more of their income to supporting the elderly. State-owned enterprise reform and the need to honor the implicit social contract between the Party and soon-to-be unemployed and unemployable elderly state workers will exacerbate tensions. A viable social welfare system has yet to be established. But whatever the final form, any such system will inevitably produce winners and losers. China's legal system cannot by itself sort out such problems. Similarly, although there are environmental laws on the books, they go unenforced, in part because of the lack of political will to enforce them if that means slowing down economic growth. Yet the failure to deal with pollution now simply means that the unavoidably higher costs of cleaning up the environment later are passed on to future generations. The most divisive cleavage of all, however, is between the haves and the have-nots. Economic reforms have increased income inequality.

Reforms have also produced different economic interest groups, including a rising middle class. Individuals have had more exposure to the West as a result of doing business with Westerners or working in foreign companies, studying or traveling abroad, surfing the Web, or just watching television shows and movies. In short, Chinese society is becoming more diverse and pluralistic. Yet Pan denies that Chinese will form political interest groups. But Chinese entrepreneurs, like their counterparts in Singapore and Hong Kong, already are a formidable interest group. They may not yet dominate the political process as much as the great hongs and the business community more generally do in Hong Kong, but they are a force to reckon with.

Pan seems to think that the ruling regime will be able to hold off the demands for democracy in the face of greater social diversity and increased interest-group conflicts by implementing rule of law and cleaning up the government. But that is not likely to be sufficient. At minimum, the ruling regime must also be able to sustain economic growth and continue to raise everybody's living standards, even if at somewhat different rates. Indeed, Hong Kong and Singapore are illustrative in this regard. The Hong Kong government in the 1960s and 1970s was able to overcome growing popular discontent and a challenge to its legitimacy without introducing democratic reforms by promising to implement rule of law *and* by buying off the populace through a series of welfare reforms.[33] Similarly, in Singapore people arguably accept limitations on civil and political freedoms because of their rising living standards and considerable benefits such as subsidized housing. China, however, is much less wealthy than Singapore and Hong Kong, and the country is much larger. Accordingly, its ability to buy off the populace is more limited.

In the long run, disputes over how to divide the pie, even assuming the pie continues to grow, are likely to lead to greater demands for democracy. Of course, China could become democratic without becoming a liberal democracy: a democratic system plus rule of law. Although the third wave of democratization has brought majoritarian democracy to many nations, it has not necessarily made them more liberal, particularly with respect to civil and political rights.[34] Thus, even if China becomes more democratic, there is no guarantee that Chinese citizens will endorse a liberal view of human rights that gives priority to civil and political rights over economic rights and collective interests, or interpret civil and political rights in the same way as liberals, or strike a similar balance between concern for the individual and concern for the interests of society and the nation.

In allowing for greater but still limited civil and political rights, Pan may have predicted how the balance will ultimately be drawn. But whether he is right or not, what is notable about Pan's position is his instrumental view of rights. Certain civil and political freedoms are necessary to provide checks and balances. Nevertheless, such rights are subject to limits, including the need for social order. The conception of rights as one type of interest to be weighed against other interests, including the good of society as a whole, differs significantly from the deontological conception of rights as anti-majoritarian devices that differ in kind from interests and precede and trump the good and the interests of society.[35]

Whither China? An Expanded Reform Agenda

Establishing rule of law is one way to achieve political reforms without democracy. However, realization of rule of law will require numerous changes not only in the legal realm but in the social, economic, and political realms as well. Such changes will inevitably alter the nature of Chinese society and the current balance of power between state and society, Party and government, the central government and local governments, and among the three branches of government.

Market reforms have already shifted the balance of power away from the state toward society. The balance will continue to shift with the further separation of government and enterprises, the elimination of administrative monopolies, and the creation of a professional civil service in which government officials serve the public as regulators rather than extracting rents or competing with private companies in the marketplace. For instance, at present, the government continues to subject many economic and social activities to licensing requirements. Although the decision as to what needs to be regulated is ultimately a political one, the Administrative Licensing Law has helped delineate the boundaries of individual autonomy and freedom. Holding government officials to clearly defined substantive and procedural standards will ensure that citizens are able to take full advantage of whatever freedoms they are granted.

Administrative law reforms have empowered society by giving citizens the right to challenge state actors through administrative litigation and other channels. The next step is to increase public participation in the rule- and decision-making processes. The Law on Legislation opens the door slightly for greater public participation in the making of national laws. Pan's consultative committees would open the door a little more. The Administrative Procedure Law, currently being drafted, may go even farther in giving the public access to administrative rule- and decision-making.

A more robust civil society, a freer media, and greater reliance on private actors would all benefit the cause of administrative law reform but would require a further shift in power toward society. Judging by its harsh crackdown on Falun Gong and other social organizations with even the hint of a political agenda that could threaten the Party, it may well take two decades for a more robust civil society to develop.

Establishment of rule of law will also require a change in the balance of power among the branches of government, particularly the judiciary and executive. The courts are simply too weak. The independence of the judiciary needs to be increased by changing the way courts are funded and judges are appointed. In addition, the authority of the courts must be enhanced by increasing their powers. For instance, courts should be given greater authority to interpret laws and regulations and to overturn lower-level rules, including administrative regulations, that are inconsistent with higher-level legislation.

The existing mechanisms for holding government and agency officials accountable all need to be strengthened. Administrative supervision, reconsideration, and litigation could all benefit from doctrinal changes as well as other more institutional reforms. Pan's consultative committees and anti-corruption agency are worth trying. The government might even consider creating a separate control branch as envisioned by Sun Yat-sen.

Another possibility might be to explore more direct ways to change the incentive structure for government officials. Currently, officials are evaluated in accordance with a cadre responsibility system that emphasizes quantifiable targets over qualitative ones.[36] Officials who meet their targets are rewarded financially with bonuses and larger allocations of discretionary funds and in other ways, such as promotions or honorary awards. Perhaps a quantifiable rule of law index could be created. Officials would be evaluated based on indices such as the percentage of local regulations that are inconsistent with superior legislation, court judgments and arbitral awards that are unenforced at year's end, administrative cases in which the administrative agency decision is reversed in whole or in part, local court judgments that are reversed on appeal, local judges subject to discipline for corruption, and so on.[37]

Although various external checks can reduce administrative abuse of discretion, there are limits to what the law can achieve. In the end, no legal system can rely primarily on compulsory enforcement to ensure compliance. The core of any administrative law regime is government officials who respect the law. Citizens and officials alike must internalize norms of respect for law that render compulsory enforcement unnecessary in most cases. It is essential, therefore, that efforts to establish rule of law and internal norms of legality continue.

As it has so far, the Party will need to take the lead in promoting rule of law. Economic reforms are not as far along as Pan suggests. State-owned enterprises, the banking system, and the finance system are all still in need of major reform, to cite just a few problem areas. Nevertheless, Pan's suggestion that rule of law be made one of the main focuses of the next decade is laudable.

Equally as important, Party leaders must make good on their promise to separate the Party from government, and on their own commitment to act in accordance with law. Party organizations must make known their displeasure with interference in court affairs by Party members or government officials, take corruption seriously, and subject Party members to the courts or an anti-corruption agency. And they must provide government officials with more legal training, encourage them to change their attitudes, and subject them to stricter discipline.

Unfortunately, however, senior Party leaders and legal reformers cannot simply legislate a culture of legality. It will take time to overcome the lingering influence of culture and tradition, weak institutions, and the challenges presented by the still incomplete economic transition. Ultimately, Party leaders will need to sign off on deeper institutional reforms that could come back to haunt the Party. While the Party may be forced to risk such reforms to stay in power, whether it will do so is a matter of realpolitik and power and exceeds the limited reach of the law. If the Party does decide to continue to retreat from day-to-day governance and turn over certain functions to other state actors, these other actors can be expected to contest for power. The State Council and administrative agencies have shown themselves to be effective gladiators in the struggle for power among the other branches.

The establishment of rule of law is a long-term, multi-front effort. Pan has provided some useful proposals, which, combined with other reforms, could fundamentally change the nature of the Chinese polity.

4

The Rule of Law as Transition to Democracy in China

Larry Diamond

Over the past decade, there has been mounting evidence in China of what Pan Wei terms in the first chapter of this book, "the urgent necessity for substantial political reform." It is not merely the dramatic rise in political and bureaucratic corruption, to which Pan Wei repeatedly alludes. Several factors combine to threaten the viability of the entire political system of Communist Party rule. Corruption and abuse of power are pervasive throughout China, breeding resentment and anger among Chinese in communities (large and small) that feel they have no institutional means of voicing or redressing their grievances or defending themselves against predation. Because of the paucity of legitimate channels for challenging unfair policies and expelling corrupt leaders from office, distressed people in China's countryside and towns have increasingly turned to illegal and even violent protests. Expectations that competitive elections would move up from the (relatively inconsequential) level of the village committee at least to China's townships and municipalities, and even before long to the county level, have essentially gone unfulfilled, deepening disenchantment with the political sclerosis.

As a result of both the rapid emergence of the market economy and the absence of a rule of law, the politically connected (which is to say, the Communist Party–connected) have reaped a vastly disproportionate share of the benefits from China's economic boom. Inequality in urban areas in particular has become much wider and more visible. Overall, inequality in China has worsened dramatically in the past two decades, with the Gini index rising from 28.8 in 1981 to 40.3 in 1998—the largest increase among nations in this period.[1] By 2001, the index had deteriorated further to 44.7; by comparative standards, income distribution in China is now worse than in Turkey and about as bad as in the Philippines and Bolivia, two countries known historically for extreme inequalities and steep class divisions.[2] In China (as last measured in 2001), the top fifth of income earners capture half of all income, while the bottom fifth earn less than 5 percent—a far cry from the Communist vision of social equality.[3] A recent (1999–2001) nationwide survey shows that ordinary Chinese attribute this growing income gap not to the neutral functioning of the market but to "political corruption and the prevalence of business cheating," and thus consider it unjust, unfair, and illegitimate.[4] Further stoking anger and resentment to explosive levels are rising levels of urban unemployment—estimated at 15–20 percent nation-wide[5]—generated largely by the closing or restructuring of state-owned enterprises (SOEs) and by the difficulty laid-off workers have often encountered in obtaining the benefits promised them.

The most difficult steps in this wrenching social and economic transition may still lie ahead. A few years ago, economist Nicholas Lardy warned that China faces "the possibility of a domestic banking crisis. The central precondition for a crisis, a largely insolvent banking system, already exists." While the total amount of bank lending had exploded during the 1980s and 1990s, the quality of bank assets had "declined sharply." As a result, at least a quarter of China's outstanding bank loans, net of provisions, were nonperforming, a proportion "far higher than reported by financial institutions in Thailand and Korea prior to the onset of the Asian financial crisis in 1997." Compounding the fragility of the system was the relatively low (and declining) capitalization of the large state-owned banks. If, in the wake of a growth slowdown or political crisis, domestic savers lose confidence and attempt to withdraw their deposits, China could, warned Lardy, face "a financial meltdown."[6]

Underlying the acute vulnerability in the banking sector has been the problem of highly overleveraged firms. "Chinese firms now have debt to equity ratios that are among the highest in the world," higher even than the highly leveraged Korean chaebol.[7] Most of the largest SOEs (which are chronically over-leveraged and often unprofitable) remain to be privatized, rationalized, or closed. If this challenge is not finally tackled (after years of procrastination), economic growth will slow and China will become even more exposed to a chain-reaction financial crisis. Yet reform of the largest SOEs will generate substantially increased unemployment in the short term, with the danger of massive labor unrest. In addition, liberalization of imports, under the terms of China's entry into the World Trade Organization (WTO), and other pressures for economic change associated with globalization, will also generate enormous and very painful dislocations. Unless China can manage these escalating social and economic disruptions in a transparent, efficient, and fair manner—controlling political corruption and favoritism, while providing a viable social safety net for the poor and unemployed—social frustration and outrage may reach convulsive proportions.

A number of experts have recently argued that the Chinese authorities have relieved some of these pressures in a way that will make for a "soft landing" for the overheated economy. However, more recently, Lardy and Morris Goldstein have argued that China's investment boom is unsustainable and that the country is likely headed for a sharp decline in economic growth, possibly by half of its annual 9 percent rate of recent years. Moreover, bank lending continued to mushroom to an all-time high of 25 percent of GDP in 2003, driving bank credit growth "out of control" and leaving China with the prospect (from previous experience) of nonperforming loans that could amount to as much as 15 percent of GDP.[8] The combination of an undervalued renminbi and very low real interest rates heightens the structural problem of the Chinese economy.

There is a growing consensus among academic observers that China must accelerate the pace of economic reform while making governance more accountable and responsive if it is to preserve political stability. Along with China's socialist legacy of state responsibility for the individual, there is still a cultural tendency "for the state to be either credited or blamed for what happens in people's lives."[9] Should the banking sector sink into crisis or the state prove unable to provide minimal, promised benefits to a broad new swathe of unemployed workers, blame would likely be openly pinned on the Chinese Communist Party itself. Even if frustration and anger remain focused at the factory or local level, "China's reality at present is one in which procedures for dealing with popular grievances remain weak and ad hoc. And as Samuel Huntington observed long ago, political systems which arouse high popular expectations without developing effective institutional mechanisms for handling such feelings within the system are asking for trouble."[10] In reflecting on the potential for disaffected workers to form system-challenging alliances with reformist intellectuals, Merle Goldman comes to a similar conclusion:

> If China's leaders have learned any lesson from June 4, . . . it should be that gradual movement toward building political institutions, such as a genuine legislature, independent unions, rule of law, and a free press, will give disaffected elements such as laid-off workers, their former Red Guard associates and politically-concerned intellectuals and students a way to express their views so that they will not have to resort to destabilizing demonstrations and mass protests in order to air their grievances and get redress.[11]

With an acute appreciation of what is at stake, Pan Wei has proposed a sweeping and in many ways visionary agenda for political change in China, not to democracy but to a "consultative rule of law regime," with Hong Kong and Singapore as models. Yet there are a number of serious problems with his approach. His rejection of democracy as fundamentally (and perhaps—although he is not clear on this—permanently) inappropriate for China is, in my view, based on a number of naïve assumptions and theoretical and empirical flaws. In particular, Pan finds democracy in the developing and postcommunist worlds lacking because he holds it up to unrealistic standards of immediate performance and generalizes on the basis of a highly biased sample of illiberal and pseudo democracies. At the same time, he idealizes the Singapore and Hong Kong experiences while largely dismissing questions about the transferability of these city-state models to a nearly continental country of 1.3 billion people. Thus, he assumes that an attempt to develop democracy in China would wind up looking like the former Soviet Union or the former Yugoslavia, rather than, say, Poland or Hungary, but he is confident that an attempt to build an authoritarian "rule of law" system will wind up looking like Singapore, not Egypt or Kazakhstan. Later in this commentary, I will further address some fallacies in his argument.

These logical and empirical flaws notwithstanding, I believe the proposed "rule of law" system—even though it would be less orderly than Singapore—would represent considerable political progress for China and might well preserve (by substantially reforming) a political system that is otherwise headed toward crisis and collapse. Many in the West welcome the prospect of this collapse, precisely so as to clear the way for the emergence of democracy in China. Yet, while I wish for democracy in China—and believe, unlike Pan, that it is both possible and desirable for China—I do share some of his skepticism about its possibility in the near future. In the next decade, the alternative to rule by a restrained, reformed (and quite possibly renamed) Communist Party is more likely to be a right-wing nationalist dictatorship than an electoral democracy at the national level. On the basis of democratic theory and comparative experience, one could argue that democracy is more likely to emerge and take root if China passes through some transitional period of more restrained, "consultative," and law-based rule than if a completely authoritarian communist regime suddenly collapses.[12]

Pan Wei's proposal, I therefore argue, is best viewed as a transitional system for China, albeit with a more rapid transition than he envisions. Moreover, to work, it must make use of competitive elections (even, as is now the case at the village level, on a nonparty basis) in order to provide a vital additional instrument for holding leaders accountable at the local level.

The remainder of this chapter will assess the specific elements of Pan Wei's proposed "consultative rule of law regime" and the gaps in his thinking. I focus first on the architecture and appointment of a system of horizontal accountability; next on the role of the Communist Party (or its successor hegemon) in the proposed system; then on the timing and phasing of the transition to a rule of law system; followed by discussion of the neglected role of elections in fostering more accountable and lawful rule. I conclude by highlighting some additional empirical and conceptual flaws in Pan's argument, which underscore China's need not simply for the rule of law, but for democracy as well.

A "Consultative Rule of Law Regime"?

Pan Wei proposes, in essence, a liberal autocracy as the answer to China's mounting crisis of political performance and legitimacy. Democratic elections, he maintains, would only increase corruption and reify and politicize social cleavages. However, a regime that separated politics from government—through a truly independent civil service, judiciary, and counter-corruption apparatus—could, in his view, deliver good government, check the abuse of power, respond to the needs and grievances of society, and thereby reestablish political stability and legitimacy without the dirty, polarizing effects of elections. Crucial to such a "consultative rule of law regime," he argues, are basic civil freedoms of speech, press, assembly, and association, which the rule of law would guarantee. Leaving aside (for the moment) the fact that there exist virtually no such liberal autocracies—certainly not Singapore[13]—would such a political system be feasible and desirable for China?

My answer is yes. Anything that would reduce the overweening political power of the Communist Party, subject it and other political actors to a rule of law, and enhance government accountability and personal freedom would represent very considerable and badly needed political reform in China.

Although he does not use the term, what Pan Wei proposes in part is a much stronger system of horizontal accountability. "Horizontal accountability" is the means by which some agencies of government hold other governmental actors, particularly the executive branch of government, accountable to the law and the public interest.[14] The judiciary at all levels is an indispensable actor here, and as Pan notes, a true rule of law would require not only an independent, professional judiciary in general but also a constitutional court with supreme authority to interpret and enforce the Constitution. (This would represent a political transformation, even short of democracy, because it would put the court's authority above that of the Party.) Also vital is a counter-corruption body like Hong Kong's Independent Commission Against Corruption (ICAC). It is important to underscore, however, that in a country as large as China, an independent counter-corruption apparatus would have to operate not only at the national level, to scrutinize the decisions and functioning of national-level government bodies, but also would need a substantial organizational presence as well in every province and probably every county. In fact, China is so large that every province, at a minimum, would need a very substantial and autonomous counter-corruption commission, with a large staff of auditors, investigators, and prosecutors to back up the work of commissioners. Like the judges, prosecutors, and court clerks (as well as police and investigators) who compose the judicial system, the leadership and staff of the counter-corruption apparatus would need to be recruited through an independent, meritocratic process insulated from political control. This is a major element in the challenge—vital for the "rule of law" system—of separating the Party from the state, as discussed below.

An effective system of horizontal accountability requires as well other agencies to investigate wrongdoing and hear public complaints, such as an ombudsman's office and an independent audit agency. These again would have to be independent of Party control, and thus of executive-branch control. In the financial sector, new systems of regulation and prudential oversight would be needed, such as a Securities and Exchange Commission and a fully independent central bank that would not only regulate the money supply but oversee and vigorously regulate the entire banking industry. These bodies would reinforce, but also themselves scrutinize, the work of the judiciary and the counter-corruption commissions. Only when there are overlapping, reinforcing agencies is a truly effective system of *horizontal accountability* possible.[15]

Real accountability also requires transparency. Pan Wei mentions the general (eventual) importance of freedoms for the rule of law, but there is a specific reason why civil freedom is so important for accountability. Unless there is some degree of *vertical accountability*—unless the public has access to information and the press has freedom to investigate and expose—it is impossible to know if the agencies of horizontal accountability are doing their jobs seriously. Neither is it possible to correct them if they become compromised. Transparency of information (including, ultimately, a legal provision for citizens to sue for access to government information) and public involvement in the process of accountability provide an additional check on wrongdoing. Such transparency and participation deter corruption and favoritism within the agencies of horizontal accountability while assisting them to acquire the information they need to perform their tasks.

If China could somehow develop such an elaborate and truly autonomous system of horizontal accountability, it would greatly improve the quality of governance. But can that be done under Communist Party rule?

What Role for the Chinese Communist Party?

One of the weaknesses of Pan Wei's formula is that it offers no clear idea of what role the Communist Party (or its successor) will play in the new system, and of how a crucial condition for the implementation of the rule of law system—separation of Party from government—is to be achieved. The proposed system is viable in the near term as a reform agenda for China precisely because it does not require the Communist Party to surrender power, or to put itself at risk in free and fair multiparty elections. It is also emphatic about the need to separate Party and government in the first stage of an envisioned three-stage (twenty-year) reform process. But the proposal is vague about the powers the Party would retain. Clearly, recruitment into and functioning of the civil service and "routine" law enforcement must be professionalized and depoliticized. But if the systems of state administration and accountability (the civil service, judiciary, and so on) are to be filled through some modern, Weberian version of the examination system, how would this work? Who would administer recruitment into these agencies of governance, oversight, and regulation? How would these various agencies be insulated from interference and intimidation by the Communist Party elite, many of whom they would wind up investigating and putting behind bars if they took their responsibility seriously? This is a piece of the reform puzzle that is striking for its absence in Pan Wei's proposal. Eventually, senior leaders of these various administrative and regulatory agencies might rise from the lower ranks through meritocratic processes (more or less), but initially, leaders must somehow be recruited or appointed (in some cases, replacing existing officials who are not adequately independent or competent). These officials would include constitutional court judges, members of the counter-corruption commission (at the national and provincial levels), ombudsmen, heads of other regulatory agencies, and so on. So long as top officials of the Communist Party appoint these leading figures, there will be an irresistible temptation to choose individuals who are familiar and pliant. Those individuals will, to some degree, owe their jobs to the Party, even if they are not—as they must not be—Party members themselves.

If the Communist Party truly intends to build a rule of law, it must tie its own hands in an irretrievable way. This means giving up the power to appoint these various officials and entrusting the appointment and supervision of these bodies to some source of authority that is truly independent of politics. Only in that circumstance could a "rule of law" system be credible in China. How could such a supervising authority be assembled in China today, in the absence of democracy and of any traditions of autonomous control in China over the past century? This is one of the great institutional questions that advocates of a rule of law system for China must confront.

To work in anything like the way intended by Pan Wei, such a system must truly separate Party from government. The Communist Party would then reign and guide, but in some important respects, it would no longer rule, certainly not without considerable constraints that it could no longer ignore or reverse. Presumably, the Party would still appoint government ministers, junior ministers, and heads of executive (not regulatory) agencies, but their power would be limited by the civil service, the law, and the Constitution. Only by tying its own hands in this irreversible way will the Party survive and continue a more limited form of rule. But which Party leaders will have the courage and skill to bind the entire structure in this way?

Timing and Phasing the Transition to a "Rule of Law System"

Pan Wei envisions a three-stage, twenty-year process of transformation to a consultative rule of law system. In the first five years, Party and state would be separated, somehow. In the next five years, a system of genuine horizontal accountability would be constructed, with an independent judiciary, anti-corruption system, and presumably other autonomous regulatory agencies. Only in the next ten years would freedoms of speech, press, assembly, and association be emphasized, and the state–society relationship would be further tested and adjusted. This phasing assumes that enlightened, benevolent leaders of the Communist Party will be the engine of political system transformation in the first decade, since society will still be too repressed, cowed, and co-opted to generate the necessary pressure from below.

This process may work well in theory, but it is highly dubious in practice. Rarely in history do state officials act purely on their own—from a conception of the public good—to bind their own hands; Singapore is truly an exception here (in Hong Kong, horizontal accountability was imposed by a colonial state). To the extent that state officials do move from above to institutionalize horizontal accountability, they are motivated at least in part by the incentives of *electoral accountability* (the fear of being defeated in the next election if they do not improve governance), and/or by other pressure from below, in civil society. The story of how systems of horizontal accountability get constructed simply cannot be told without reference to the roles of civic organizations, interest groups, mass media, and public opinion in denouncing the ills and inequities of the current system and pressing for specific institutional reforms.[16]

If civil society organizations and the mass media are going to become agents of reform and allies of reformers within the state and Party, and if these civil society actors are going to educate and mobilize the public to seek *institutional* reforms for better governance (rather than simply protesting individual acts of bad governance), they will need considerably more freedom. Unless sociopolitical life is liberalized in the first decade of Pan Wei's reform program—so that there is greater freedom to speak, write, publish, and organize independently of the state—reformers from above will be hard-pressed to overcome the powerful political resistance to good-governance reforms. Greater civil freedom is thus not simply some self-contained piece of a reform puzzle that can be deferred and put in place at the pleasure of an abstract timetable. It is absolutely vital to cleanse and invigorate a political system that has become deeply corrupt and elitist.

There is also the question of whether China can wait twenty years to put a "consultative rule of law system" fully in place. This returns us to the question of "urgency" addressed briefly at the outset of this essay. The Chinese Communist Party faces a growing crisis of legitimacy as more and more of the poor see the Party and the newly rich joining in a corrupt alliance.[17] In both rural and urban areas, grievances are multiplying as the quality of governance and the provision of public goods deteriorate while predation becomes more intense and decentralized, sometimes intersecting with the criminalization of the local state.[18] While it is often assumed that competitive village elections have revived accountability in rural governance, the extent of local conformance with national standards for these elections is unknown and clearly uneven. There is growing documentation of township and village Party officials hijacking the elections or marginalizing and victimizing independent elected officials precisely in order to circumvent scrutiny and accountability. In the Qixia area of Shandong Province, for example, fifty-seven village chairmen resigned en masse over their inability to rein in the corruption of local Party officials or have their petitions heard by provincial and national officials.[19] The rot in the foundations of the system is deepening, rendering the country all the more vulnerable to political turmoil in the wake of a global economic shock or a domestic financial crisis. As one member of a Party research institute recently observed, "People are asking what will happen when the economy has severe difficulties or even a major crisis. What can the party leaders offer?"[20]

What the Party leaders can offer is real institutional reform to improve governance and allow for the peaceful airing and redress of grievances. But the longer the country takes to institutionalize accountability and a rule of law, the more it risks a rupture of political stability if economic stability unravels. I do not think that China—with its multifold signs of accelerating political and moral decay—has twenty years to realize the type of system Pan Wei proposes, especially given that it will likely only be a transitional system.

What Place for Elections?

One of the boldest elements of Pan Wei's proposal is its rejection of democratic elections at any level as a tool for improving governance. In Pan's view, democracy is not linked to any cure for corruption, but rather will only increase corruption as well as social divisiveness. Certainly in an immediate and superficial sense, competitive elections do structure or crystallize and make manifest certain types of cleavages in society (though the impact of elections in structuring cleavages depends greatly on the nature of the electoral system). However, interests and cleavages are bound to take shape eventually in any society, particularly as development proceeds, social differentiation and class formation intensify, and social injustices go unaddressed. Competitive elections perform several positive functions: They provide a means for frustrated interests and classes to air their grievances and have them addressed. They offer different groups some share of political power and thus a stake in the system. They enable people to remove venal, exploitative, unresponsive leaders. They therefore provide an incentive for leaders to rule in a responsible way, to restrain their rent-seeking behavior and produce public rather than private goods. Thus, if competitive elections work in a transparent way—if they are free and fair—they are more likely to temper social divisions than aggravate them, and thus to breed over the long run a belief in the legitimacy of the larger political system.

Pan Wei looks to Singapore and Hong Kong as models for China's political future. But a different Chinese society, Taiwan—with its own history of quasi-Leninist, one-party rule—may provide a more realistic set of lessons. There a decadent political party, the Kuomintang (KMT). which had lost political legitimacy and suffered the traumatic loss of the mainland in 1949, began to reconstruct its rule on the foundation of more limited government (what Thomas Metzger has called an "inhibited center"[21]), with local electoral competition taking place under the overall control of the single ruling party. In Taiwan, elections gradually became more competitive over time, drawing in local elites to the ruling party and refurbishing its legitimacy, as the ruling party gained in self-confidence and political capacity. Over time, independent candidates gradually cohered into an opposition network, the *dangwai,* and then, more than three decades after the inception of limited elections, into an officially tolerated opposition party, the Democratic Progressive Party (DPP). Gradually, the Republic of China evolved from a failed state to an inhibited and increasingly pluralistic (albeit still autocratic) political center, or what Robert Scalapino has called an "authoritarian pluralist" system. In such a system, "political life remains under the unchallenged control of a dominant-party or single-party regime; strict limits are placed on liberty . . . ; and military or national security organs keep a close eye on things," but there exists a civil society with some autonomy from the state and some capacity to express diverse interests, as well as a mixed or increasingly market-oriented economy.[22]

This bears a strong kinship with the system Pan Wei recommends for China. It is worth pondering the positive role that limited elections played in Taiwan in promoting political learning by citizens and elites, ruling party adaptation, and peaceful political change, while generating more responsive, accountable government and some public identification with the political system.[23] One can also point to the persistent vitality, and the fluidity, of electoral politics in Hong Kong after its transition in 1997 to Special Administrative Region (SAR) status, and to the enthusiasm and skill with which people in Mainland China have participated in the village election process.[24] Further suggesting a latent capacity for *democratic* citizenship among Chinese is the survey evidence of Tianjian Shi showing that political interest, efficacy, and participation appear to increase with education among Chinese, and therefore seem likely to continue to grow over time.[25]

Scholarship on the impact of village elections does not support Pan Wei's cynicism about democracy. One of the most systematic lines of research on China's village elections has been undertaken by Lianjiang Li and Kevin O'Brien. They note that "Rural residents have been quick to recognize that grass-roots elections give them a way to dislodge corrupt, partial, and incompetent cadres," while township officials have generally been willing to tolerate even very unpopular village leaders as long as they met their quotas. Li and O'Brien conclude:

> Grass-roots elections have been welcomed by many villagers and tolerated by a growing number of local leaders. It is true that in some places "local bullies" (*eba*) have bought elections or coerced villagers to vote for them, while electoral competition has also, at times, intensified lineage conflict. . . . Nevertheless, village self-government has often made cadres more accountable to villagers. Where elections are the norm, village cadres live in a different world than [unelected] officials above them.[26]

Moreover, Li and O'Brien do not find evidence of the irresponsible populism that Pan Wei fears. Villagers have not been so naïve as to opt for candidates who threaten blatantly to defy higher-level authority, and elected village heads have generally been scrupulous about carrying out tasks that are assigned by the townships, even taking the lead in state policy compliance. They have not made wild and unsustainable promises, but have often delivered on their pledges, including the frequent promise of greater transparency. In general, it appears that the better relations with villagers generated by electoral accountability have worked to smooth policy implementation. Vertical conflict is visible primarily when higher-level authorities violate the rules. Elected village officials have been "more willing, in the name of their constituents' lawful interests, to confront township officials who concoct unauthorized 'local policies' (*tu zhengce*)" and to stand "up to grasping township officials."[27] This portrait of how competitive elections are actually functioning in China—albeit at a very micro level of extremely limited political authority—simply does not coincide with Pan Wei's demonization of the process.

I do not suggest that China can or will transform itself overnight into an electoral democracy at the national level. But the comparative experiences of Hong Kong and especially Taiwan, and the experience with village elections in Mainland China, all testify to the role that competitive elections can play in making government officials more accountable and responsive. Limited elections for local offices—and crucially, extending the scale of electoral authority from the village committee (which has very little real governing power) to the township level—are likely to reinforce rather than undermine the effort to construct a "rule of law" regime. It is possible to imagine for some time competitive elections proceeding on the mainland, as they did in Taiwan, on a one-party or nonparty basis, without the presence of any formal opposition party. Such elections would not challenge the political hegemony of the CCP, but they would provide real incentives for officials to govern with the public good more firmly in mind. It is just not conceivable that a meritocratic civil service is going to solve the problem of venal, abusive, and even criminal governance at the local level, in a country with close to a million villages and tens of thousands of townships. Political and economic life in China today is simply too vast, complex, and decentralized to allow for the kind of comprehensive and standardized administration that exists in Singapore. At the local level, only truly competitive elections—with standards of conduct monitored and enforced from above—can provide the antidote and corrective to bad governance.

Why China Needs Democracy

In applauding Pan Wei's call for the rule of law in China, I have also identified some flaws and misconceptions in his analysis. Others need to be noted. His dismissal of Taiwan's democratization as simply an ethnic (provincial origin) movement trivializes a protracted popular struggle that was based in part on a growing normative commitment to personal and civic freedom, human rights, and popular rule, and a desire for integration into the democratic West.[28] Democratization in Taiwan was about much more than the assertion of Taiwanese identity. And the quest to deepen democracy in Taiwan and improve the rule of law has been a consistent theme of DPP election campaigns, featuring prominently in Chen Shui-bian's 2000 presidential election campaign and in the embrace of that insurgent campaign by a number of key societal and business leaders in Taiwan.[29] It has also been a goal of the DPP government since it came to power in May 2000, as evidenced in the vigorous crackdown on organized crime and its infiltration into electoral politics. Pan Wei's flat assertion that corruption has increased with democracy in Taiwan is both unscientific (how can we measure the extent of corruption in the opaque years of authoritarian rule under the KMT?) and, in any case, outdated. Taiwan's experience shows that democracy may not only provide new incentives and vehicles for corruption (in the electoral process), it may also provide the incentives and means to control and punish corruption. It is thus wrong to assert, as Pan Wei does, that there is no cure for money politics. There is. And it involves the same principles of horizontal accountability that I have outlined above: independent institutions of scrutiny and justice that rein in fraudulent and corrupt practices. The crackdown on vote-buying in Taiwan during the past few years is precisely a case in point.

It is possible that Pan Wei's skepticism about democracy derives partly from intellectual confusion. He asserts that definitions of democracy are vague and cumbersome, hardly usable to differentiate democracies from nondemocracies as they focus on ends rather than means. But he cites no definitional literature in support of this broad assertion. While it is true that the conceptual literature on democracy is voluminous, and we are a long way from pure consensus on definitions, there is in fact broad agreement among political scientists today that democracy is a political system defined precisely by *means* rather than ends. At its core, democracy is a system for choosing political leaders through regular, free, fair, and competitive elections. This requires some degree of political and civil freedom to permit elections to be truly free, fair, and meaningful. Debate then ensues about how many other procedural requirements are necessary for a country to be considered a democracy, but the debate remains largely fixed on political procedures.[30]

A mature democracy is not just about elections, however, and the goal for political development is not simply to institutionalize competitive elections. Rather, political development and good governance are best served by a liberal democracy that combines the pure democratic element of electoral choice with the liberal elements of protection of individual rights and limitation of state power and with the republican element of commitment to the public good.[31] It is in part the system of horizontal accountability, with its separation of powers and checks and balances, that produces this uniquely successful governing model. The consultative rule of law system that Pan Wei proposes will take China some of the distance down the road to this combination of governing virtues. But China will not achieve a truly vigorous rule of law, and bridge the widening chasm between the people and the ruling elite, unless it also develops, however gradually, democracy.

5

A Comparative Politics of Democratization in China

Edward Friedman

In intercultural exchange, it is important for all parties to learn from each other, especially about themselves. A model is how Americans still ponder the insights in the Frenchman Tocqueville's great study, *Democracy in America.* In like manner, Pan Wei explores China's political prospects partly in terms of the experiences and achievements of other countries, especially Asian success stories. Insights into Chinese political dynamics may be won by grappling with this able Beijing University scholar's broadly informed perspective. It is refreshing to read a work which ridicules the Marxist nonsense that pre-modern China was a multi-millennia feudal system. Professor Pan is worth taking seriously.

First, Pan Wei illuminates some conundrums of Chinese politics. He finds that largely because of pervasive and gross regime corruption, the ruling party is losing legitimacy. Many Chinese intellectuals see democracy as a way to bring this corruption under control. But the ruling party of the People's Republic of China so far will not permit a democratic opening. In fact, the Communist Party regime was upset to see the nearby ruling party in the Republic of China on Taiwan, the Nationalists (KMT), lose the presidency in a free and fair election in 2000. In his chapter, Pan notes that because of the fear of a Taiwan-like result, even China's propaganda on village democracy has disappeared. So far, China's dictators intend either to co-opt democrats with minimalist reforms that preserve the authoritarian system or to crush democrats.

The regime's public rationale for monopolizing power and precluding an opening to democracy is that democracy causes chaos. Professor Pan reflects the views of a broad array of politically conscious Chinese who accept the rulers' contention that the terrorist vigilante chaos of Mao's Cultural Revolution was the outcome of too much democracy, that Russia's reform-era chaos was also a result of democracy, that ethnic strife in democracies such as India and Yugoslavia is also a consequence of a democratic political system. Over and over, Pan asserts that democracies enlarge and sharpen identity cleavages and communalist strife. Most Chinese, entering the twenty-first century, and equating democracy with chaos, readily abjure democracy, seeing it as a nonsolution to China's de-legitimating and hated corruption, and as a source of yet worse disasters.

Although Pan's argument against democracy really is popular in China, what flourishes in China is public sentiment and not public opinion. Such sentiment is volatile. One day the Cultural Revolution seems great; the next day it is a catastrophe. This negation of the momentarily popular could also happen in an instant to the notion that democracy brings chaos. After all, empirical studies of democracy in comparative perspective by numerous social scientists establish that democracy is the most stable political system in the world. In fact, democracy tends to be a harbinger of stability.

There is little point in spending space on some of Pan's attributions of chaos to democracy, on the Cultural Revolution as democracy (actually it was an intensification of despotic terror), on Russia (where the party apparatus was so entrenched that it resisted all economic reform, forcing dictator Gorbachev to shake it up politically), on Yugoslavia (whose ethnic strife is the fruit of the Communist era and the demagogic policies of Beijing's friend, Milosovic), and India (where democracy actually has helped to meet communalist claims and thereby hold the complex nation together). What matters is confronting the real Chinese conundrum, which Pan wonderfully illuminates. Massive and brutal corruption is ruining China, and democracy, Pan informs us, is not a likely solution in the near future because of the attitudes of both weapon-wielding ruling elites and a chaos-fearing citizenry. So what are Chinese to do? To do nothing and allow corruption to de-legitimate and disintegrate the regime would block China's rise to modern greatness. The danger must be dealt with.

Professor Pan believes that China's ruling-party elite, or a significant segment thereof, will be forced by the objective situation to open itself to political reform because the alternative is a continuing decline into political decay. This is what happened in 1997–98 to the Suharto kleptocracy in Indonesia, which, like the leadership in Beijing, had previously imagined itself a successful "Asian developmental despotism," only to find that unaccountable power was absolutely corrupting, a point made long ago by Lord Acton in discussing papal history. Indeed, China's ruling caste was so worried by what happened to its mirror image in kleptocratic Indonesia that it stepped up its anti-corruption campaign after 1997. Yet that intensified little campaign, because of the sharp, deep, and systemic nature of the problem, does not impress most Chinese. People in Xiamen are typical in describing the supposed crackdown on corruption in their city as actually a cover-up. Something more than an empty campaign is demanded. Pan wisely tries to address this demand.

Asian Alternatives

Pan Wei finds an alternative to both the unacceptable status quo and an impossible transition to democracy in the political institutions of East Asian civil service lawfulness. But Chinese critics ask if Pan offers an actual alternative or merely a cultural spin on the now discredited concept of "Asian developmental despotism." To Chinese who see Professor Pan as a neoconservative—that is, a defender of authoritarianism and of Chinese virtues—his solution, synthesizing the ancient wisdom of Chinese Confucianism and legalism, understood by Chinese analysts as a foundation for China's long-enduring arbitrary despotism, does not seem a way to attain the liberties and lawfulness that Pan seeks to achieve. Rather, the synthesis of ancient Chinese practices is likely to produce a despotic rule by the law, the coercive imposition of authoritarian rules on a populace whose unaccountable rulers will still remain above the law.

At first blush, Pan's stress on goals of liberties, lawfulness, and the market seems quintessentially liberal. But in the context of the political discourse in China, his overall stance seems more neoconservative or New Left, that is, an opponent of market openness and a proponent of Mao-era policies to prevent income polarization. He rejects democracy, stigmatizing it as "Western" (even denouncing ancient Athens), because he finds solutions only in Chinese culture (its civil service and ancient notions of lawfulness), and because he blames China's pervasive corruption on the policies of openness and reform rather than on the inherited political-economic system of Leninist socialism or of a continuation of ancient despotism, as, in contrast, did Mao's former executive secretary, Li Shenzhi, who by 2000 was a leading voice for democracy in China.

Personally, I am not sure that these critical Chinese readings of Pan Wei are always fair to his complex arguments. After all, he treats China's Communist Party as an alien entity whose power should be checked. He even seeks a solution that would eventually, albeit peacefully and gradually, deprive the corrupt CCP of power. Therefore, it is unhelpful to dismiss Professor Pan's quest for useful lessons for China in the successes of East Asian polities.

Pan Wei invites Chinese leaders to end corruption with what the Asian authoritarian model takes to be the proven tools of a purportedly nondemocratic Japan (until the ruling conservative party, the Liberal Democratic Party [LDP], lost power in 1993), of a nondemocratic Singapore, and of a nondemocratic Hong Kong. One should applaud Professor Pan's rethinking of comparative politics so that political knowledge is not defined in a way that privileges and idealizes "the West" as the only model of successful modernity. Too often in comparative politics, analysts focus on the political systems of Germany, France, Britain, and the United States, and contrast a good West with a bad rest of the world, an authoritarian other—the egregious ploy of prominent scholars such as Samuel Huntington who will not probe the experience of the 1.5 billion citizens in democratic Asia for lessons about democracy.

Asia actually is most of the human race. It is inconceivable that its politics are not creative, rich, and diverse. It is inconceivable that the institutional innovations of Asia's great historic civilizations not be worthy of study and emulation. In fact, the civil service exam, a glorious Chinese invention, a central factor in Professor Pan's analysis, did, of course, greatly impress Voltaire and most French philosophers of the eighteenth century. That borrowed Chinese innovation was central to America's late-nineteenth- and early-twentieth-century movement to limit corruption and replace it with good government. In rejecting "Asian developmental despotism," the example of Suharto's failed kleptocracy led many American analysts myopically to conclude that there was nothing to learn from Asian governance, that it was all merely crony capitalism. Pan is an excellent corrective to that error.

Pan Wei has studied European history and political theory. He is right that in many empires where a divine monarch's legitimacy was absolute and unchallengeable, much political space could, at times, be provided for religious minorities, for markets and money earning, for physical movement, and for a rich, autonomous cultural life. Authoritarian rule need not annihilate all liberties. There was more liberty in some ancient empires than in many modern chauvinistic and intolerant despotisms.

Yet, one should not idealize ancient despotism. Pan implies that authoritarian liberty automatically guaranteed ethnic harmony. The Chinese empire actually slaughtered millions of Muslims in the nineteenth century. Previously, Manchus slaughtered Han. The eighteenth-century Qing Dynasty murdered Zunghar Mongols. Pan's claim that premodern China lacked ethnic strife is simply not true.

Whatever yesterday's monarchical complexities, is it true that today is quite different —that modern China can emulate the good of ancient empires? Ancient liberty in premodern empires actually is structurally and ideologically a world apart from the institutional basis of liberty in a modern nation-state. Ruling groups in China, Pan informs us, lack legitimacy of the ancient type. Yet it is that unchallengeable legitimacy from sacral rulership which permitted authoritarian monarchies to allow some space for liberty without having to fear for their own survival.

In contrast, rulers in Beijing, entering the twenty-first century, lacking such legitimacy or confidence, cruelly try to nip all opposition in the bud. Indeed, Professor Pan informs us that China's Communist Party rulers would not tolerate organized representation for China's diverse and ever more important regional cleavages. Leaving no safety valve, the repression that ensues in today's politically unreformed China could be a pressure cooker for an eventual explosion of intensifying tensions. Here is yet another reason to prefer democracy—the importance of stability.

As with ancient empires, Professor Pan claims, liberties happily thrive in modern postwar Asia in numerous nondemocratic societies. He then examines governance in Japan, Singapore, and Hong Kong, and finds something important in the shared political practice of these purportedly nondemocratic systems that should attract China's ruling despotic party to reform itself in order both to save the party and also to save China.

Pan Wei is looking for nondemocratic institutional mechanisms that will check corruption yet not directly challenge the ruling party with competitive party democracy. It is difficult to wish his project ill since, living standards aside, life for the Chinese people would be much better if they could enjoy the daily blessings of the people of pre-1993 Japan or even of today's Singapore or Hong Kong. So is Pan right that in Japan, Singapore, and Hong Kong a better life is the result of Confucian nondemocratic lawfulness?

Actually, Japan is a democracy. It has been democratic since the end of World War II, not merely since the fall of the dominant party, the LDP, in 1993, as Pan claims. From Sweden to Israel, there are many democracies with long-term, one-party hegemony. Japan's Social Democratic Party already held Japan's prime-ministership in the late 1940s. Indeed, it was the left opposition that, at first, preserved Japan's democracy. The massive, and at times violent, democratic struggles of Japan's left, its parties, unions, and citizenry prevented the emperor Hirohito, as well as the conservative party's as yet unreformed elements and reactionary parts of the old bureaucracy, from reversing Japan's democratic breakthrough in the years after World War II. This successful popular mobilization helped keep elites, especially Prime Minister Kishi, from stealing the people's democratic liberties. Japan's democratic stability was made possible by left-wing strength sufficient to prevent an amending of the democratic constitution. This struggle culminated with the forced resignation in 1960 of Prime Minister Kishi, a former war criminal. He was the last threat to Japan's postwar democratic achievement.

If Chinese are serious about opposing Japan's remilitarization, they should be celebrating the achievement of Japanese democracy since 1945, which defeated the revanchist forces of the old order that Pan wrongheadedly celebrates in praising a purportedly nondemocratic Japan. It is a nontrivial lesson that a robust democracy can defeat the challenge of chauvinistic militarism. This is so not only in Japan. Since these dangerous forces have been on the rise in China, democracy would be a practical way to grapple with China's most pressing problems. It would help institutionalize a region of peace, prosperity, and tolerant pluralism.

All quantitative studies comparing how democratic and authoritarian regimes survive in bad economic times establish that democracies are far more stable, while authoritarian regimes are far more likely to decay into chaos. If the top priority of China's rulers really were stability through the difficult times ahead of remaining economic reforms, they then would already be working assiduously to democratize China. Pan's insistence that democracy brings chaos may appeal to uninformed popular prejudice in China, but it disregards all the solid research that incontrovertibly establishes as fact the superiority of a democratic system for preserving an enduring social stability, especially in times of great economic pain.

Yet Pan is surely correct that most leaders and politically conscious people in China believe that democracy brings chaos. This Chinese illusion may be hastening the decay of the system. Chinese remain Ah Q's in embracing what actually threatens their survival. Objectively, the top priority of rulers in China is not stability but rather the survival of their privileged positions through a system that, Pan informs us, produces China's debilitating corruption.

Whatever one should learn from Japanese institutional practice, it cannot be because Japan embodies uniquely peculiar Asian ways that contrast with allegedly irrelevant, so-called "Western" institutions. Japan's administrative centralized state, Pan's unique Asian model for Chinese emulation, is, overall, very similar to France's.[1] It has no peculiarly decisive Asian flavor in its institutional arrangements. It also has little in common with nondemocratic Hong Kong or with Singapore. Japan's Meiji-era constitutionalism, Taisho-era party governance, and postwar democratic practices all were premised on Japan's learning from and borrowing non-Asian institutional practices, especially from Germany (e.g., voc-tech education), Britain (postal savings banks), and America (post–World War II Ministry of International Trade and Industry). The reason why Japan's conservative party, the LDP, like Italy's Christian Democrats after World War II, would long remain the dominant party of governance was because conservative factions united while the left remained split and weakened by internecine strife. Japan's persistent, conservative, single-party predominance is readily explained without resort to fictions about unique Asian ways. Misleadingly, Pan treats very different regimes—democratic Japan and nondemocracies in Asia—as similar, and then ignores democratic Japan's real similarities with democratic France and Italy, something that cannot be explained in culturalist terms.

Still, Professor Pan is importantly right that the central bureaucracies in Japan have exercised great weight in the political system. But are they a model of good government? Corruption in Japan's powerful Ministry of Finance is notorious. I have heard Japanese wax eloquent about how even corrupt Italy did better in dealing with its corrupt political system than did Japan. How, then, can Japan serve as a model for ending corruption in China?

In addition, Japan's decade-plus inability, starting in 1991, to make the tough decisions needed to get its economy moving again is also no model for a China still in need of difficult decisions on behalf of economic reform. Without an ability to throw the "ins" out, without an alternative party with a different agenda that could a serious challenge for national power, Japan stagnated, albeit at just about the world's highest level of per capita income.

Since Japan's post–World War II democratic political system clearly is no solution for China's corruption, then Hong Kong's political system should have even less appeal to China's ruling-party elite. There is no dominant party in Hong Kong for China's Communist Party to copy. The major party in Hong Kong has been an opposition party working for democracy. Hong Kong's administrative authoritarianism therefore offers no way out for China's ruling Communist Party, whose top priority is a means to preserve its own institutional power and privileges. While it is true that the pro-government party in Hong Kong is gaining strength, so is corruption.

That leaves Singapore. Can its experience be emulated by China? Singapore is a mere wisp of a city-state. Also, in contrast to China, Singapore never suffered the pains of an economically irrational command economy or a Leninist party dictatorship. It had no corrupt institutions similar to China's to clean up. It therefore is hard to imagine that China has much to learn from this extraordinarily different Singapore. Yet, I in no way reject Pan Wei's basic argument that, although China cannot copy Singapore's institutional arrangements, perhaps, in some unique way, given the narrowly constrained political possibilities in China in the short run, trying to move in Singapore's direction would be wonderful for most Chinese people.

However, as with liberal divine monarchical empires, the legitimacy of Singapore's government cannot easily be transferred to China. Singapore, often described as a Chinese pea in a Muslim sea, began life in 1965 as a democracy. Its predominantly Chinese cultural population was expelled from the Republic of Malaya to guarantee that Muslims, not Confucians or Buddhists, would rule the new Malaysia. Singapore had to survive, in the era of Communist Vietnam's successful war, worried about militarily active, much more populous Muslim neighbors, and worried about home-grown Communist subversives in Singapore. In a fragile, new, and threatened Singapore, the new nation's leader, Lee Kuan Yew, could move in a popular authoritarianism direction, not wishing to upset authoritarian Indonesia or Malaysia, because the city-state's citizens shared Lee's trepidations about their threatening international environment. China, in contrast, is a strong, secure, and rising power. No one is going to invade China or challenge its sovereign existence. Fears to the contrary are worrisome paranoid fantasies.

What will happen to Singapore's political system now that its environment has changed? Communism is no longer a threat. Also, the fledgling democracy of over 200 million people in neighboring Indonesia, the regional giant, could stabilize and institutionalize a democracy. In such a changed environment, it is not unlikely, some analysts find, especially after Singapore's prestigious founding leader, Lee Kuan Yew, is no longer among the living, it distinctly possible that Singapore too will democratize.[2] Even Lee himself has expressed doubts about the future of his system. As with the democracies of Japan, Taiwan, and South Korea, all of which Lee once misleadingly treated as stable instances of an authoritarian development state model, Singapore too could democratize. Stable Asian developmental despotism is therefore a theoretical chimera. Except for China, most of the people of Asia, from the Korean peninsula to the Indian subcontinent, enjoy the blessings of democracy.

Yet Pan is surely right that, with the exception of democratic Denmark and a few other democratic nations, Singapore is uniquely noncorrupt (although political insiders do unusually well economically). It surely is worth inquiring why. Similarly, Pan is also correct that Hong Kong did an excellent job of reining in its earlier corruption. Most importantly, Pan is right again that this controlling of corruption is a major political achievement and that the Chinese government is threatened by an inability to greatly reduce corruption. Pan is a reliable guide to key features of the Chinese and other Asian polities.

Since Pan is well-read in American political science, as shown by his incisive distinction between liberty and democracy, why does he not then build on solid political science literature that explores how a once venal France eventually limited its corruption in comparison, say, to similar successes in Asia, or at different times, in Britain and the United States, each of which once was famously—or infamously—corrupt? The sad answer is that no such solid political science literature exists. There is no insightful study comparing successes in constraining corruption in Singapore, Hong Kong, South Korea, Britain, France, and America.

Pan Wei's sharp questions, which subvert Eurocentrism, can offer an agenda for important future research in comparative politics. I am completely at one with him in deriding the parochialness of too much of "Western" political science in not looking more to the rich political reality of successful Asian nations seen in true comparative perspective.

Pan is importantly right yet again that "Taiwanese democracy is not based on economic cleavages." He is right that, in general, Asian democratization contrasts with

Western Europe in not having a competitive party system pitting one left party based on labor against a right party based on big business. The cleavages of late-twentieth-century democratizations in Asia seem to have little in common with the cleavages of late-nineteenth-century and later attempts in Europe to democratize. I have seen this point made earlier by political scientists in democratic Korea. Their conclusion is that the lack of such sharp and destabilizing cleavages in Asia is a major reason why, in contrast to, say, France, Italy, Spain, and Germany in Europe, democratic breakthroughs in Asia have been easier to institutionalize with great stability. Democratization in Asia does not produce chaos. That is, in direct contrast to Pan's anxieties, a stable transition to democracy may be easier in an Asian context. Pan's claim that a democratic China "would require a bottom-up rebellion" is a case of inventing terrifying dragons to scare people. Surely revolution from below was not the path to democracy in South Korea or Taiwan. On this one issue of the stability of a democratic transition, the truth seems far from the specter of chaos that is imagined by Professor Pan.

A more general hypothesis that flows from Pan's insights is that it is dangerously misleading to premise a comparative politics on the very special early modern Western European experience. Struggles for democracy in the nineteenth century focused on who could vote, with old elites excluding workers for as long as possible. Labor and socialist parties won their backers among workers by struggling to include them in the political nation. After World War II, however, everyone assumed that all adult nationals should be voting citizens. The left–right split is therefore very differently constituted after World War II, and not only in Asia. Europe's party politics of class conflict may have little resonance in an Asia democratizing in a very different era.

Sympathizing with Pan's rejection of West Europe's historically peculiar comparative politics as a generalizeable norm, I hoped for in-depth analysis from him on Asian democracies—Japan, India, Mongolia, South Korea, the Philippines, Thailand, and Taiwan. They, each and all, produce great scholarly literatures. If Pan were better acquainted with democratic South Korea, he would never claim that Chinese are uniquely fixated on exam-taking. In fact, the commitment, the mania, of democratic Koreans to exams is so strong as to make Chinese in comparison look like small time players. The wealth invested in preparatory courses for the SAT and LSAT exams in America suggest that China is far from unique.

So why isn't South Korea a model for Professor Pan or Chinese leaders? South Korea, after all, is the one and only instance from 1965 to 1988 of an Asian dictatorship creating a professional civil service and reining in corruption as part of state-leveraged industrialization. The Park Chung Hee military dictatorship in the 1960s greatly reduced Korea's political corruption, which had been rife in the era of the patriotic tyrant Syngman Rhee. But to students, union members, and religious groups, Korea's arbitrary and unaccountable authoritarian system became unacceptable. Perhaps one reason Korea is not attractive to the Communist Party leaders of China is that Korea is democratic and that Korean democrats, after coming to power in 1988, put the leaders of the previous brutal military despotism on trial. The dictators were found guilty and sentenced to prison.

That experience is not something Chinese dictators wish to emulate. Chinese dictators intensified a political crackdown on pro-democracy forces when the kleptocratic Suharto regime fell in Indonesia and efforts began in Indonesia's fledgling democracy to bring the deposed despot Suharto to trial for corruption. China's leaders and their families, who chose, after the Soviet systems of Eastern and Central Europe democratized, to present China as similar to other supposedly successful Asian developmental dictatorships, the largest of which was Indonesia, know how similar corrupt China is to Suharto-era Indonesia. Pan is an excellent guide to the sensitivity and sharpness of the legitimation crisis in China, which turns Indonesia or South Korea or Russia from a positive to a negative model when the authoritarian system falls and corrupt or hated leaders are prosecuted or toppled.

Another reason democratic Korea may not be attractive to China's corrupt dictatorship is that the Korean government has been trying to reduce the power of the nation's gargantuan economic conglomerates, the *chaebol,* while the Chinese regime has long refused to abandon control of their money-losing state-owned enterprises, which serve as power networks and milch cows for China's greedy ruling-party networks. The most brutal corruption occurs at local levels in China, where officials rip off property, tax money, and semi-privatized enterprises. Still, given the commitment of China's leaders to making China a world leader in information technology, and given the fate of foreign CCP friends, from Ceausescu to Milosovic, Beijing may yet look for models in nations really facing up to the imperatives of the new economy.

If Asian nations like South Korea and Indonesia have lost their attractiveness to rulers in Beijing, where should one look for models and ways to solve China's problems? I think Pan Wei not unwise in not taking Western European politics as a unique standard and looking instead, indeed first, for relevant comparative experiences in Asia.

India and Russia: Distorting Mirror Images

Surely it is by putting China in comparative perspective with great powers with similar problems, nations such as India and Russia, rather than by looking to minuscule, market-oriented Singapore and Hong Kong, which, in contrast to China, have no large, impoverished countryside, that one will get a more realistic perspective on Chinese possibilities in dealing with corruption and other problems inherited from a Leninist command economy. India and Russia are large and populous neighbors trying to grapple with and reform, as China, the persistent evils of irrational command-economy institutions. Yet Pan dismisses both India (alleging that ethnic strife results from democracy) and Russia (alleging that chaos results from democracy), instead fixating on Singapore and Hong Kong, which never had a Leninist command economy. In contrast, India, which began economic reform in 1991 and which still has a lot of reforming to do, is, like China, dealing with the detritus of a failed command economy. Already India's information technology (IT) sector greatly outperforms China's, a significant matter since China has moved from a 1978 policy of modernization to a postmodern project entering the twenty-first century where IT and biotechnology are top priorities. It seems a bit premature to be certain that China is a success and India a failure in these crucial sectors.[3] In fact, China has sent teams to learn from India's IT success, although India's world-class achievements with generic drugs also merit close attention.

China's IT development seems hampered by a lack of political freedom, by great Beijing government fear that IT just might be put to anti-regime uses. Arrests have already occurred. Restrictions multiply. Since the liberties Pan seeks do not include such political freedoms, it is not obvious that his solution removes this undemocratic political obstacle to China's better economic future. It is worth asking which economy has a better future when, already at the turn into the twenty-first century, India grew at just about the same rate as China with only a fraction of the foreign investment and with reform having hardly scratched the surface. The corrupt waste of the Chinese economy that Pan inveighs against is indeed a disaster for the Chinese people. He is an excellent guide to key issues.

This is not to gainsay China's economic prospects. In another new economy sector, biotechnology, India seems somewhat hampered by its political culture. As in America, environmental and religious fundamentalists limit biogenetic development in India. Not so in China, which is already making large advances in genetically modified crops that can feed China's large population on far less land while using far less water or pesticides. Anti-scientific religious fundamentalism does not hamper Chinese growth.

As with India, Pan's comments on Russia also seem strange. There seems to be a hidden message, a narrow nationalism obscured by liberal words. Pan contrasts Russian chaos with Chinese order. Yet, in fact, disorder, criminality, and gangs are spreading in China too. In both countries, the government was at first only able to garner about 13 percent of gross domestic product (GNP) in tax revenues, one-third or one-fourth of what advanced economies manage, although Beijing is doing much better more recently in taking a bigger share of revenue from the regions.

In both Russia and China, during economic reform, members of the nomenklatura in the party-state apparatus grabbed state-owned enterprises for themselves. But the CCP has grabbed this wealth down to the most local levels, making China far more unequal than a very unequal Russia. China, like Russia, still does not have a prestigious, professional, technically competent civil service. It is even possible that, as an overcentralized China fights the consequences of regional decentralization and local autonomy, it will falter in its economic rise, whereas a Russia that is now more a nation than an empire, the former prisonhouse of nationalities having been liberated, will get through its difficulties better than China. It is far too soon to claim that China is a success and Russia or India a failure. That Chinese nationalistic perspective misleads.

Yet Pan is right that Chinese tend to agree that Russia is a failure. They also agree on why. They readily regurgitate early 1990s party propaganda. Russia, in this Chinese perspective, reformed too quickly (big bang, shock therapy), while China, correctly, moved gradually. Russia wrongly began with political reform, while China wisely began with economic reform. And Russia's sequence of reform was wrong. Russia began with property reform, privatizing state-owned enterprises, while China supposedly rightly began with rural reform.

Despite the Chinese consensus, in fact, popular Chinese perceptions about Russia are wrong. This is dangerous because it gives way to misleading lessons for China, especially not seeing the reasons for the democratic opening in Russia. When Deng Xiaoping began reform in 1978, the Soviet Union still stagnated and declined under Brezhnev's corrupt rule. Gorbachev came to power only in 1985, a time when China had already decollectivized agriculture and begun to open to foreign investment. Gorbachev wasted time with nostrums, believing in discipline as a solution, hoping that a campaign to end vodka consumption could save the economy. When Gorbachev finally attempted serious economic reform in 1988, China was already a decade into its reform project, uniquely benefiting from contingent factors such as the 1985 Plaza Accords, which made low-end Asian products from Japan, Taiwan, Hong Kong, and other places too expensive to export to America, leading to huge investments in low-wage China. In contrast to Beijing's official story, in fact, Russia was slow. It was China that was fast.[4]

China's success also depended on contingent factors. When the USSR's entrenched apparatus, made fat and happy by stagnant Brezhnev-era corruption, successfully resisted Gorbachev's economic reforms from 1988 to 1991, he was forced to shake up the political system in order to make a little space for economic reform. In contrast, the Chinese Communist Party had recently suffered greatly in Mao's Cultural Revolution. While Brezhnev's greedy CP became ever more entrenched and opposed to economic reforms that threatened its perks, much of China's CP uniquely welcomed reform. Different historical experiences made it most difficult for Russia to follow the path that China took. It was not a matter of policy wisdom, but of historical path dependency.

In like manner, Russia could not return land to peasants because the Soviet Union, since launching war communism in 1918, had declared war on the peasantry and, over two generations, had destroyed the Russian peasantry. In contrast, China only collectized agriculture in 1955–56 and began decollectiziation already in 1978–79. In China, when reform began, the original generation of peasants was still alive and knew how to make money with market opportunities. All of this was literally impossible in Russia. Much of long-devastated rural Russia still remains unreformed.

Russia implemented economic reform in 1993, only after Yeltsin was consolidating his power. At that late moment, uniquely confronted by hyperinflation and government bankruptcy, Yeltsin began to privatize state-owned enterprises, thereby entrenching a somewhat criminal oligarchy. Contrary to the official Chinese view where Yeltsin's error was to act on political reform first, in fact, he prevented free and fair elections even while freeing up the media and allowing new political parties. He entrenched his power to stop opponents of his painful reforms from taking power. Yeltsin erred because he did not see that "the first order of business should have been democratic restructuring of the state so as to create structures of democratic power."[5] By achieving a democratic consensus on how to share the pain of economic reform, stable progress becomes possible. Russia's small democratic opening may now be closing.

Not only is it untrue that Russia went too fast or wrongly put political reform first, as the misleading, self-congratulatory Chinese consensus has it, but there is also nothing wonderful in Chinese sequencing. MIT Sloan School professor Huang Yasheng has found that it is best to begin economic reform with the financial sector. This decreases a need for foreign investment and increases funds available for successful private firms, which maximize employment. Instead, Chinese banks waste their money subsidizing money-losing, unprofitable state-owned enterprise dinosaurs and force China's entrepreneurs to look elsewhere for capital. Analysts worry that when the Chinese business cycle turns down, as some day it must, a dependency on foreign capital, investments, firms, and markets could ignite a chauvinistic explosion in China that would threaten the completion of China's reform project. A hint of such nativistic passions was revealed in the 1999 trashing of American businesses after the Chinese embassy in Belgrade was bombed by a plane from the United States, and again in China's 2005 Japan-bashing.

Clearly, it is premature to dub China's reform a success. Reform out of Leninist trammels is a painfully long process. It is difficult to escape command economy irrationalities. So why do Chinese agree that Russia has failed when only five years after serious reform began in 1993 in Russia, the Russian economy began growing at a healthy rate? Just as China benefited in 1985 by how the Plaza Accords raised the price of other Asian currencies and brought investment into China, Russia benefited from a spike in petroleum prices. What matters is that both seized a good opportunity.

But when people in China judge Russia, they ignore the complex facts about Russia's economic reforms and look mainly at Chinese great-power aspirations. In that regard, Chinese say they do not want to end up like Russia. Chinese feel the Russian outcome is a failure. They see that failure in the numerous Russian prostitutes in China. Yet China too is rife with Chinese prostitutes. Misleading feelings aside, what specifically is it that Chinese fear for themselves that sadly they find in Russia since, in fact, it is much too early to conclude that Russia failed or that China succeeded?

The Russian flaw is not the bloody war in Chechneya. Beijing admires and supports that effort and would like to take the autonomous island of a democratic Taiwan as Russia incorporates Chechneya. The passionate issue in Chinese politics is national greatness. To Chinese, Russia seems a failure as a superpower. Russia seems in free fall from its prior military superpower status, the antithesis of the ambitions of a great-power China seeking predominance in Asia.

Han Chinese want to take multiethnic Taiwan and hold onto Buddhist Tibet and Muslim Xinjiang. They do not celebrate the liberation of Eastern Europe or the independence of Latvia, Lithuania, Estonia, and the previously subordinated nations incorporated by the czars to suffer in Russia's "prisonhouse of nationalities." While the deceased despot Mao Zedong thought such ethnic-nationalist liberations from Russia's czarist type imperialism would be a human triumph, today's Chinese chauvinists do not. Communist China intends to maintain and enhance the empire it inherited from the militarily expansionist Qing-era gunpowder empire.[6] Russia's imperialist decline makes Russia seem, to superpatriotic Chinese, a failure, chaos. But Russia's imperial decline was not caused by some purported democratization of Russia that has not yet happened.

Chinese feel that this is the moment for a large China, far and away the most populous nation on the planet, to return to global greatness. A Russia of weakness is no model to Chinese. A Russia with a humiliated military is not a model for patriotic Chinese. While Russia is played up by Chinese chauvinists looking for a strategic partner to join with to challenge the United States, many Chinese liberals, promoters of markets, limited government, and societal liberties, tend not to want their government to waste the nation's wealth, as Brezhnev did in the USSR, in an unwinnable arms race with the United States. Given the Brezhnev-like corruption pervading China, Beijing, by abjuring political reform, actually may be taking a debilitating Russian path, entrenching selfish interests similar to prereform Russia.

In short, China's portrayal of Russia as a failure has almost nothing to do with the real Russia's economic path or its painful closing of a democratic opening and almost everything to do with Chinese beliefs that Chinese greatness requires the military power to stand up strongly in Asia. Actually, an ever more powerful China, whose willingness to use weapons worries its neighbors,[7] falsely portrays itself to itself as a potential victim of invented international slights and foreign threats, a potential declining nation like Russia, unless it takes as a priority making itself militarily strong and assertive.

Nationalism: Seduction and Self-Destruction

So where does Pan Wei stand on the issue of China's imperial chauvinism? Although he has no section of his essay devoted to nationalism, the present superpatriotic atmosphere in China can not help but infect virtually all Chinese. They tend to seek to prove themselves more patriotic than their rulers. This produces a dangerously expansive chauvinism. That nationalism pervades Professor Pan's paper and is worth exploring. Pan denigrates and caricatures so-called Western democracy, equating it with genocidal acts in ancient Athens and the rise of Hitler's Nazis. This is just plain absurd. Chauvinism blinds.

Next, Pan equates alien "Western" democracy with "political agitation, money politics and personal slander." In contrast, Chinese civilization is claimed to have a core of fairness that allegedly contrasts with the unfairness of majoritarianism. Evenhandedly, Pan also dismisses China's party dictatorship as alien, an "imitation of Russian communism." Consequently, Pan appears to offer a solution of supposedly politically neutral universal justice premised on alleged virtues of inherited Chinese civilizational ethics. His message: stay Chinese and all will be well.

Pan Wei's solution of returning to alleged historic virtues, of ending corruption by "strictly enforcing laws" (which sounds a bit like Gorbachev's failed reform of "discipline") implemented by a merit civil service, presumes an apolitical Chinese uniqueness. It is a solution, however, that can appeal to Chinese chauvinists even though it solves nothing. That is, it ignores the real world of politics and economics, such as what kind of state leveraging will best aid China's IT sector or how to handle the burden on reformed regions of subsidizing the nonreformed.

Pan also is never clear as to why people in the apparatus who live high on the hog and have obligations to kin, allies, patrons, and clients will welcome his solution, which denies them all the advantages that they hold dear. He argues that, given his solution, political leaders become irrelevant, as supposedly was the case in postwar Japan.

Such a portrayal of democratic Japan is wrong. Yoshida Shigeru's postwar premiership was crucial to Japan's democratic success in economic growth. Maintaining that path required removing Premier Kishi, the war criminal, in 1960. And Kishi's successor, Premier Ikeda, was crucial in his leadership away from the old divisions of Japanese society and toward a stable, mass-middle democracy. Pan's political prescription forgets the centrality of politics. There is no solution to China's complex contemporary problems in revitalizing ancient practices. This neoconservatism is mixed, as is explained below, with the old leftism of the so-called New Left.

Thinking within the categories of traditional Communist Party nationalism, Pan asks why China lost the Opium War, why 400 million Chinese could be defeated by a few thousand British with a handful of ships from halfway around the world. A useful answer was given by post-Mao reform leader Deng Xiaoping. Since the Ming Dynasty, China had closed itself off from the advanced science and technology of the world such that by 1840 China's military, for a millennium a world leader, could not match Britain's.

But Pan's answer is that the Qing Dynasty lost the Opium War and then was toppled "because it failed to mobilize farmers to effectively resist . . . imperialism." Pan's stress on mass mobilization and fighting imperialism, even as Chinese standards of living rise from integration with the world market, has a Mao-era ring to it. This is part of what makes Pan seem to some Chinese a New Left thinker, someone who sees the West and democracy as evil and locates all solutions in a combination of Mao-era ways plus traditional Chinese virtues. Chinese see this as a combination of populism and traditionalism, a virtual red–brown alliance.

In addition, this neoconservative nationalism misses a key point about the Manchu invaders who conquered China in the seventeenth century, slaughtering thousands of times more people than ancient Athens ever did. The aggressive Manchus, who established the Qing Dynasty in China, were actually builders of one of the most successful imperialist empires in the history of the human race. They used their military might and diplomatic wiles to double the size of the territory ruled by the prior, Sinicized Ming Dynasty, incorporating Taiwan, Tibet, Mongolia, Xinjiang, the northeastern region that was the base of the Manchus, and regions to the southwest.[8] To portray the successfully imperialist Qing as merely weak in resisting nineteenth-century British imperialism misses how much the tensions in Chinese politics today, both domestic and foreign, stem from a Han nationalist attempt to digest everything the expansively imperialist Qing swallowed, from Taiwan to Xinjiang to Tibet. Such expansive nationalism is presuppositional to Chinese patriotism. Pan accurately reflects what most Chinese feel.

Pan's entire perspective makes almost invisible the superpatriotic passion that permeates China and worries China's neighbors. This expansive chauvinism is virtually invisible in both Pan's chapter and in China's patriotic imagining of a glorious Chinese future contrasted with a present in which others supposedly threaten China. Russia is seen as chaos and a failure because it surrendered a multicentury imperial expansion which most Chinese heirs of Manchu imperialism have absolutely no intention of abandoning. Indeed, for Chinese patriots, it is virtually inconceivable. They are the unquestioning, proud heirs of Qing Dynasty expansionism.

Taiwan: A Democratic Imperative

Pan Wei discusses Taiwan mainly to claim that democracy is unsuitable to China. If democracy is a disaster among Chinese elsewhere, he contends, how can democracy be good for Chinese in China? Pan argues that brutal factionalism among China's émigré dissidents reveals their true essence. It is sadly true that exile politics breeds mistrust and backstabbing in virtually all exile communities, not just the Chinese one. It is also true that authoritarian China's intellectual scene today is so pervaded by nasty, factionalized back-stabbing ambitions that, in contrast, the democratic exile community almost seems a model of harmony.

Given that disorder and crime are already spreading in China because of a decaying and politically unreformed Chinese authoritarianism, a chaos that most Chinese already worrisomely see intensifying over the horizon, it seems a bit disingenuous for Pan Wei to claim that, uniquely, "a real democracy may create social chaos." Pan perversely argues that democratic "liberty . . . means people . . . do what they want to do." He forgets that democracy is, to cite the catch phrases of democratic theorists, "coexistence in diversity," "ordered liberty," "majority rule with minority rights." Democracy is a stable proceduralism.

For Pan, however, if not for a uniquely strong European inheritance of lawfulness, democracy would bring chaos, political agitations, money politics, and personal slanders in the West, too.[9] Consequently, Chinese prefer universal justice. Pan's description of democratic politics, a description that has no place for things such as the rise of the social welfare state or religious tolerance or communalist coalitions, is, to say the least, not balanced.

It also seems odd that Pan treats the rich debates of traditional Chinese in diverse schools—of which Confucianism was but one—as some singular, harmonious, agreed-upon "universal justice." In reality, Confucianism's heritage includes a complex and ever-changing philosophy that spawned at least as many rich divisions as the entire European intellectual tradition. Yet in his claim, Pan Wei undermines his argument for liberties, which means tolerance of pluralities in a world where people with incommensurable ultimate life ends—Tibetan Buddhists, Uighur Muslims, Hakka Christians, and perhaps one day, multiethnic Taiwanese—might live in civil peace.

Imagining a singular universal justice as embodied in Chinese culture again hides the nasty real world of Chinese politics. Pan's glorification of Chinese civilization as "nonreligious and pragmatic" omits the frenzied Boxers, Mao's Cultural Revolution madness, and today's chauvinistic zealotry. In reality, all cultures contain all human possibilities, from the best to the worst. That is why, everywhere, democracy helps check arbitrary power and civilize conflict, facilitating a logic of broad, inclusive coalition building.

Imagining some unspecified universal fairness as a criterion for political action in China, Pan Wei also gets village elections all wrong. He writes, "It is common sense in rural China that villagers often do not respect the authority of the elected leader, for the majority principle is 'unfair.'" Actually, majoritarianism is not the essence of democracy— no person or crucial decision is chosen in the U.S. federal government by a simple majority, not one. More importantly, the problem with village elections in China is not majoritarianism. There is an ongoing struggle between villagers hoping to use elections to rid themselves of useless and corrupt rulers, and the local CP despots are trying to hold onto unaccountable power. While I wish the villagers well, it is the party bosses who are winning. They are further entrenching massive corruption, as in the USSR during the Brezhnev era. Merely focusing on China's economic rise hides the pains of brutish political stagnation. Pan would do more to help long-suffering Chinese villagers by promoting villager self-government (*cun min zizhi*) rather than denigrating it.

The alleged failure of democracy in China is Pan's trump card in supposedly proving that democracy will not work for Chinese. Again, Pan is a good guide to political sentiments in China. Many Chinese do indeed believe that the democratic struggle of 1989 is dead-end ancient history and not a tragic, lost opportunity. They feel that post-1989 economic growth proves that the 1989 democracy movement was irrelevant to China's real problems. Yet Pan's comparative politics is not persuasive. Democracy actually flourishes on the island of Taiwan, which Chinese in the PRC see as a Chinese cultural location. And democracy was incipient in Chinese Hong Kong until Beijing reversed that democratic progress.

Pan's portrayal of politics in the Republic of China, which fled to the island of Taiwan to escape Mao's red armies in the late 1940s, does not capture Taiwanese reality. Pan claims that "Taiwan's electoral politics, underwritten by illegal money, organized crime, and widespread corruption, has little appeal" for people on the other side of the Taiwan Strait in the People's Republic of China. Whereas the Democratic Progressive Party's Chen Shui-bian actually won the presidency in Taiwan in 2000 on a platform of cleaning up corruption, Pan argues that democracy intensifies corruption. Comparative politics data show that, while corruption can indeed flourish in a democratic polity, democracy's liberties make it far more likely that corruption will be constrained than is the case with arbitrary tyrannies whose power-holders cannot be held accountable for their misdeeds. It would be great progress if corruption in China were reduced to the level of Taiwan. And it is not good in Taiwan.

Yet the nub of Pan's argument against democracy is his claim that democracy would bring chaos for China and power for the United States. He argues that "provincial origin was the key political cleavage" in Taiwan and that Taiwan's democracy is premised on native Taiwanese and not the mainlanders who arrived in Taiwan after losing to Mao's armies in the 1940s. Democracy in Taiwan, Pan contends, is actually an independence movement, a splittist effort.

In contrast, traditional China is said to be without ethnic cleavages, a claim, as shown earlier in discussions of Muslims, Tibetans, Uighurs, and Manchus, that is palpably not so. For Pan, democracy is both alien to Chinese culture and the enemy of Chinese national unity. This is an appealing argument to many Chinese confronted by both overcentralization and growing localism. But this play to real anxieties ignores all the ways that good democratic political crafting (e.g., federalism and religious freedom) best accommodates diverse communities and maintains a strong, united nation. The alternative to political reform for China is endless corruption combined with authoritarian repression.

Finally, for Pan, Taiwanese democracy is simply unpalatable to patriotic Chinese: "Corruption, underground criminal societies, separatism, and dependence on American strategic checks on China, further reduce its [Taiwan democracy's] reputation in China." This mention of the nationalist feeling is probably central to Chinese chauvinist passions. Again, Pan is no doubt right about Chinese sentiments. Of course, as with Finland and the Soviet Union, were the big entity, China, not to threaten the smaller one, Taiwan, then no outside military aid need be sought by Taiwan. After all, though, Beijing does threaten Taiwan.

Professor Pan's description of Taiwanese politics misconstrues the experience of the Taiwanese themselves. Taiwan is an island just south of Japan's Okinawan islands, just north of the Philippines and 100 miles distant from China's southeast coast. It is about as large as Massachusetts and Rhode Island combined, and more populous than two-thirds of the member nations of the UN. Far from having "always" been Chinese, as Beijing propaganda has it, a deep, sudden drop in the ocean floor between Taiwan and the Asian continent, a barrier of dangerous roiling waters, called a "black water gap" in Chinese, long kept settlers from continental Asia to Taiwan's west to a minimum. When Ming stalwarts fled to Taiwan, there may have been more Japanese there than Chinese.

As Taiwanese tend to experience their democratization, the island was settled many centuries ago by people of the Austronesian civilization from the south. Then, in the late Ming, Chinese settlers crossed the Taiwan Strait. Tributary relations were still maintained with Japan and the Ryukyu Islands by the Austronesians. The settlers on Taiwan were conquered by the Dutch. The name Taiwan is a Chinese transliteration of a Dutch corruption of an Austronesian place name. Then, in the seventeenth century, the alien Manchu, who had cruelly conquered China, also took the western coastal region of Taiwan. They were replaced by the Japanese at the end of the nineteenth century, and then by Chiang Kaishek's defeated Nationalist army after World War II. The corrupt brutality of Chiang's conquest led Taiwanese to begin to imagine themselves as a long-suffering people, conquered by one group of nonislanders after another, a people who could enjoy a decent life only by ruling themselves, thereby ending a multicentury history of victimization by numerous invaders. That goal was finally achieved after Taiwan began to democratize in 1988.

Taiwanese experience their glorious democratic autonomy as the happy negation of 300 or so years of rule by a long series of conquerors. In fact, it is democracy that has allowed the diverse ethnic communities of Taiwan to reconcile, live in peace with each other, and forge ahead toward a common destiny. Professor Pan's claims to the contrary are far from the truth. This is not to gainsay the reality that in Taiwan, as everywhere else on the planet, there are politicians who appeal to and mobilize mistrustful and hate-filled communalist identities.

Politics on Taiwan, Pan to the contrary not withstanding, does not pit a mainlander Nationalist Party (KMT), that is, post–World War II arrivals, against a native Taiwanese party (DPP), that is, pre-1945 arrivals. The recent arrivals are only about 13 percent of the people. Yet the DPP has not been able to get more than 40 percent of the vote for parliamentary seats. Since democratization, the 15 percent who were Hakka and did not speak the major local language, Min-Nan, sometimes called Taiwanese, tended to vote for the KMT. So did Austronesians. So did a little less than half of Taiwanese speakers. Taiwan's flourishing democracy incorporates all its people in a common democratic quest which, contrary to Pan, palpably is not a matter of one province of people against all others.

Beijing's perception of Taiwanese politics, infused by Chinese superpatriotic passions and anxieties, has little to do with Taiwanese reality. In contrast, millions of Taiwanese have visited China as tourists, relatives, investors, and traders. Taiwanese understand China. But the government in Beijing does not want to understand a Taiwan seeking to continue a peaceful situation that will preserve the autonomy and democracy Taiwanese have long struggled for, while enhancing mutually beneficial economic ties with China. Instead, China's Communist Party portrays Taiwan's democratically elected presidents as troublemakers.

Chinese fantastically imagine this peaceful Taiwan as a threat to China. Yet it is Chinese chauvinistic fantasies that endanger peace in the region. To superpatriotic Chinese, Taiwan is felt to be a humiliation, a continuation of a divided China from the age of colonialism, an era when Japan ruled Taiwan. In addition, an autonomous Taiwan is imagined in China as an inspiration and instigation to separatists in Buddhist Tibet and Muslim Xinjiang. Taiwan is seen as a threat to the rise of the Chinese race, whatever that is, because of the Taiwanese embrace of a multiethnic, open identity, a self-conception that is not narrow Han nationalism, China's surging, dangerous national identity. In China, Taiwanese also pose a threat because of their appreciation of Austronesian, Japanese, and American culture, as well as Chinese culture. Han Chinese on the mainland of China hate internationally open Taiwanese multiculturalists as blood polluters. Patriotic Chinese on the China mainland curse the weakness of their government for not yet attacking Taiwan. The chauvinism that the Beijing government uses to legitimate itself threatens not only Taiwan but also everything China has won in the age of reform, as well as peace in the Asia-Pacific region. Pan does not even mention the danger.

In short, an unstable, rising, and anxious China—a volatile political mixture that rejects democratic legitimacy and promotes chauvinistic legitimation of a purist and monist sort—has engendered a war-prone politics that threatens the peace, security, and prosperity of the peoples on both sides of the Taiwan Strait and in the Asia-Pacific region. The Chinese people, ignorant of Taiwan realities, are competing among themselves in patriotic demagoguery. The Beijing regime, not wanting war, tries to rein in a force unleashed by its superpatriotic opposition to democratic legitimation. The contradictions of Chinese political dynamics include explosive elements.

Pan Wei's analysis feeds these nasty passions in China, as he describes Taiwan as a corrupt, splittist, American dependency. He offers not a word on how Taiwan's economic engagement with the PRC is beneficial to China. In general, Professor Pan has little to say about how much the Chinese people have gained from an unbelievably rapid economic rise which, whatever its flaws, requires the priority attention of the Chinese government to the remaining reforms if the Chinese people are to continue to rise.

A democratic China would be far more attractive to Taiwanese, economically as well as politically. Why should a prospering, democratic Taiwan wish to surrender its hard-earned gains by becoming the subordinate part of a very centralized, relatively poor, Beijing-run dictatorship? China's threats alienate Taiwanese and strengthen a separate Taiwanese identity. The joke in Taiwan during its 2000 presidential election campaign was that the best way Beijing could have blocked the opposition DPP candidate Chen Shui-bian from victory would have been to come out strongly in his favor. Of course, Beijing did the opposite, and did so with threatening language.

A lack of democracy in China even kept Beijing leaders optimistically misinformed about Taiwan's presidential race. Advisors in Beijing dared not inform China's leaders that their favorites, the KMT candidate or a third-party mainlander candidate, could easily lose. Similarly, in the 2001 Taiwan legislative elections, Beijing embraced Taiwan's New Party, which died for a lack of any popular support. China was unprepared for a DPP victory in 2001, and unprepared for a Chen Shui-bian presidency in 2000 and 2004. Actually, President Chen has been conciliatory to Beijing in ways the KMT had never been. While momentarily continuing the peace and increasing economic ties, Beijing propaganda barrages the Chinese people with inflammatory lies about Chen's presidency, making it seem that he is insincere and provocative.

China is caught between a rock and a hard place. Introducing us to China's conundrums on democracy, comparative Asian politics, and Taiwan is Professor Pan's brilliance. Being silent about the chauvinist alternative, which his essay cannot help but reinforce, obscures why democracy, which offers Chinese a promising opportunity to grapple with its pervasive corruption, is the best solution. Democracy is a way to have Chinese agree on how to share the pain of continuing reform both so that reform can be successful and so that China can remain stable. Democracy is an imperative for China, that is, if the people of China seek peace, prosperity, and stability.

Conclusion: The Dangers Ahead

In general, Pan Wei's chapter is an important reminder of how much is at stake for the people of China, of the Asia-Pacific region, and of the world in China's tortuous and painful reform project and in U.S.–China relations. There is so much unfairness and suffering concomitant to escaping the trammels of a Leninist command economy. Passions in China are running high. Chauvinism intensifies. Chinese patriotism has defeated Chinese forces of democracy and liberty ever since the late 1930s. It therefore would be naïve to believe that democracy can easily win in China. That sad truth is the premise of Pan's complex argument and his profound struggle with so many crucial topics.

However, Pan is wrong that democracy would hurt China. But he could be right that democracy is off the agenda for China in any short run. My belief, based on conversations in China, however, is that there is a deep yearning among the Chinese people, often just below the surface, for the blessings of democracy. Political sentiment in China remains as volatile as ever. A successful democratic project requires China's political leaders to move in that stabilizing direction as soon as possible. It would win them great popular support and help defuse tensions with both Taiwan and the United States. It would make it so much easier for China to maintain stability and enhance its global stature while solving the remaining conundrums of economic reform. That someone as informed and wise as Pan rejects that democratic path makes me worry about our shared destiny.

6

Pan Wei's Consultative Rule of Law Regime

Reforming Authoritarianism in China

Gunter Schubert

Assessing Political System Reform in the PRC

As the PRC heads toward more world market integration and internal economic restructuring after its entry into the World Trade Organization (WTO) in late 2001, rampant corruption and deepening social and political cleavages force the Communist leadership to engage in new initiatives to stabilize one-party rule and consolidate overall regime legitimacy. On the welfare front, this has led to efforts to build a nationwide social security network,[1] to ameliorate the living conditions of migrant workers,[2] and to alleviate the tax burden of the peasants.[3] Apart from these new policies, political reforms are officially deemed necessary to enhance accountability at all levels of the system. As a matter of fact, they have been regarded as critical for the eventual success of Chinese socialism since the early reform era. Besides separating the Party from the state by giving more political autonomy to government organs[4] and bestowing more independent decision-making authority to the management of state-owned enterprises (SOEs), the Communist leadership embarked on a policy of introducing direct village elections in the late 1980s, initiated new methods of candidate nomination for the elections of the PRC's national, provincial, and local people's congresses, along with reform efforts to strengthen their supervisory functions in the 1990s, and—more recently—began experimenting with new modes of internal competition to install Party secretaries and other leading cadres at the local level.[5] As for China's leaders, most important in the area of political system reform is the professionalization of the cadre management system, which aims at upgrading the civil and Party bureaucracy's efficiency and impartiality, and the gradual institutionalization of a rule of law system to which all political and legal decision-making power should be subjected.[6]

For many observers, these reforms are profoundly flawed, because they are not embedded in a concept of political change that does away with one-party rule. By this logic, any effort to achieve democratic accountability without institutionalizing political participation (up to the national level) and multiparty competition—albeit temporarily successful—is eventually doomed to failure. However, many scholars now focus on the possibility that such a verdict carries the danger of ignoring the different degrees of accountability and regime legitimacy that may have been generated by political system reform in the PRC in the recent past, probably permitting the Communist leadership to preserve one-party rule and authoritarianism much longer than previously predicted.[7] Consequently, scholars have dealt more cautiously with China's political and legal reforms, measuring them in terms of relative gains and losses concerning regime legitimacy and stability before turning to their "democratic (non-) potential" *à la longue*.[8] The criteria for assessing those reforms usually focus on their success in reining in corruption and bureaucratic malfeasance; enhancing elite professionalism; and establishing a sound rule of law system, that is, giving the people genuine power to sue for their rights and to bring corrupt cadres to justice. Most scholars, it seems, concede that the reforms initiated by the Chinese Communist Party (CCP) regime in the post-Tiananmen era have instilled new practices of contestation into the system and have made it more accountable by administrative streamlining, cadre professionalization, the co-optation of new (non-Party) social and economic elites, and the growing "legal bind" of political and bureaucratic decision making.[9] However, quite a number of experts contradict such an analysis by contending that the political reforms have actually failed their objectives and that the CCP regime has indeed become more unstable and authoritarian in recent years.[10] To put it differently: On the one hand, there seems to be a major consensus among most observers that political system reform *actually takes place* in the PRC and that it affects the internal dynamics, accountability, and legitimacy of the CCP regime. On the other hand, there is also a consensus that the net effects of these reforms are not sufficient to provide for long-term stability and legitimacy of the system, as they do not touch upon one-party rule. At the same time, there are different opinions as to the degrees of stability and accountability that have been generated by the reforms up to the present. Many scholars—perhaps the majority—claim that the CCP regime has gained new legitimacy (and "state capacity"). However, there is also a substantial number of experts who think that the reforms have actually deepened the current regime crisis by strengthening the Party's autonomy from the people, resulting in an insufficient response to the participation crisis that plagues the Chinese polity.

Turning to the Chinese domestic debate on political system reform among both intellectuals and Party officials, much effort has been spent in recent years on the attempt to reconcile non-negotiable one-party rule with more (democratic) accountability of the regime and a controlled decentralization of political power.[11] Because the Western model of liberal democracy or any democratic system based on multiparty competition is a nonoption for obvious political (or normative) reasons, China's reformers must come to terms with the concept of "socialist democracy"[12] pursued by the Communist leadership—at least rhetorically—since the 1980s. "Socialist democracy," for its part, has been linked to a reform agenda that broadly contains the following objectives: rejuvenating cooperation with the other "democratic parties," rationalizing the division of labor among government agencies, developing a modern cadre management system, establishing new inspection mechanisms to oversee cadre performance, introducing grass-roots self-government, and developing a modern legal system.[13] In this context, Suisheng Zhao has noted in his chapter that:

> [T]he direction of political reform has taken and the way it is discussed inside China is rather different from the democratization that has been pushed by many outside pro-democracy activists. In fact, many Chinese government officials and some Chinese intellectuals do not believe that the Western style of democracy is a feasible or, for that matter, desirable option for China, at least in the foreseeable future. Instead, they have looked upon political liberalization without democratization as an alternative solution to many of China's problems related to the extant authoritarian system.[14]

Partaking in this seemingly more pragmatic political thinking, Pan's proposal of implementing a "consultative rule of law regime" is of special concern.[15] This author, who has been branded a "neoconservative thinker" by Western China scholars, gained both domestic and international attention in recent years for his outspoken and provocative views on the inadequacy of liberal democracy for present-day China and the future of political reform in the PRC. A U.S.-trained political scientist with a Ph.D. from the University of California in Berkeley, Pan became alienated from much Western thinking on China and finally returned to his country to take up a position as professor at Beijing University's prestigious School of International Studies.

Pan's reform approach does not speak of "socialist democracy" at all, nor does it unspecifically claim the necessity of political reforms along the official line. Much more, he provides us with a democratic theory translated into a concept of one-party rule that combines elements of the Western liberal tradition with—as he says—the Chinese tradition of meritocracy. His vision of erecting an institutional framework based on limited participation and the absolute authority of the law is indeed noteworthy. It transcends to some extent the official understanding of "socialist democracy" by theorizing on one of its most prominent aspects—the implementation of a sound legal system. At first sight, this seems to be the essence of what the Communist leadership promises nowadays in terms of reforming Chinese authoritarianism and establishing a socialist rule of law regime. Pan Wei's ideas therefore deserve more attention than usually accorded to reform proposals by academics who do not straightforwardly question one-party rule and, hence, are quickly discredited as political opportunists in the West.[16]

This chapter reconstructs the basic line of Pan Wei's argument, scrutinizes the theoretical underpinnings of his approach to democracy and the rule of law, and—with this backdrop—examines the conceptual consistency of his consultative rule of law regime. A critique of Pan's negative political comments and judgments on democracy and democratization in other countries (such as Russia, India, and Taiwan) is of minor importance here.[17] It is held that Pan's proposal might work given certain preconditions. However, there is considerable space for the CCP regime to gain new legitimacy for quite some time if only some elements of Pan Wei's concept are rigorously implemented. Most importantly, these elements are the introduction of new modes of direct political participation and the further development of the legal system to contain the power of the cadre bureaucracy. Pan Wei's consultative rule of law regime might indeed be the most realistic variant of democracy in China that one can hope for in the near future.

The Argument

The blunt statement that the current pressure in China is not derived from an eagerness to speed up marketization, but rather from strong resentment against widespread corruption, is the point of departure from which Pan Wei develops his concept of "consultative rule of law," set against the unspecific official terminology of "communist leadership," "democracy," and "rule of law" in order to explain what political reform in today's China precisely is and *should be* about. Pan Wei starts by distinguishing democracy from the rule of law. Democracy is understood by him in accordance with the Schumpeterian definition of the term as "a polity featuring *periodic elections of top leaders by electorates.*" He concedes that this is a narrow definition that excludes many "good things," for instance, additional normative elements such as the rule of law, the respect for human rights, freedom of speech, and so forth. However, Pan is certainly not the only one to see sense in a focus on the core characteristic of democracy that makes it distinguishable from autocracy—regular elections. He claims that all the "good things" of democracy can be obtained without the elections of top leaders.

The "rule of law," therefore, according to Pan, must be distinguished from the "rule of the people," as one could potentially exist without the other. The ensuing enumeration of differences between democracy (as defined by Pan Wei) and the rule of law is most telling concerning the second of five points mentioned: While "democracy is to authorize a few elected with the power to rule," the rule of law regulates a government and operates through the institutionalization of checks and balances within the political system that "reduce the leaders' accountability to the electorate and increase their accountability to the law." Clearly, the subjection of the government to the law is more important to the author than the election of a few to govern. Also, as he adds, democracy is about majority while the rule of law is about meritocracy. This implies another important distinction: whereas democracy is based on elected lawmaking bodies, rule of law is grounded on "nonelected law enforcement offices, mainly civil service and the judiciary." Most of the ensuing arguments that the author presents in favor of the rule of law centered on his observation that all essentials of so-called liberal democracy—freedoms of election, speech, press, assembly, and association— are ultimately based on the correct application of the law, which depends on an impartial civil service and an independent judiciary. In that sense, he feels that those rights can be protected without periodic elections of leaders.

According to Pan Wei, only the rule of law can solve the core problem of China's political system—corruption. Institutionalizing the necessary checks and balances within the government structure, recruiting officials with higher moral standards, and restraining public officials from misusing their authority for private gain do not require *electoral* democracy. However, they certainly require *liberal* democracy, with liberty obtained through the authority of the Basic Law, so as not to impose the will of the "majority" on the minority. Consequently, the rule of law stands as the core ingredient of liberal democracy, which, for its part, is a mixed regime combining the rule of law and elections by the many. It is argued that such a regime could be a parliamentary democracy supplemented by rule of law, or a rule of law supplemented by parliamentary democracy. For Pan Wei, it is the second option, already installed in Hong Kong and Singapore, that should also be implemented in China. To put it differently, Pan asserts that the rule of law could be created with little democracy (though this would still be a liberal democracy).

As Pan claims, such an arrangement corresponds to the Chinese social and cultural context (closely linked to Chinese history, which he sketches skillfully to make his point) in which conflict and a concept of justice, derived from the institutionalized counterbalancing of powerful groups within society, are not valued the same way as in the West. He feels that in China the nonelected officials tend to enjoy more respect than the elected ones, if they govern according to the principle of justice. To average people, fair law enforcement by a neutral civil service, or *gong zheng lian ming* in Chinese, is all that justice means. It is important to note here that Pan Wei explicitly— and rather offensively—criticizes the Chinese government's ideology of centralizing power, which is legitimized by the notion of democracy in a "pure" sense (socialist democracy), that is, a democracy that does not provide for the rule of law via an *institutionalized* separation of powers. To the contrary, "the government power must be separated, so as to build an effective mechanism of checks and balances, and make the law above any one person or any one party in power." Although elections may take place in Pan Wei's rule of law system, they would be no more legitimate than examinations and independent evaluations.

With his theory explained, Pan Wei then turns to the institutional set-up of his rule of law-*cum*-democracy. Such a regime should be based on six pillars:

- *a neutral civil service system* grounded on the principles of examination, performance evaluation, seniority, and lifetime employment;
- *an autonomous judicial system* that checks the civil service, but is also subjected to public evaluation and "an internal mechanism of checks and balances" to avoid abuse of judicial power;
- *extensive social consultation institutions,* especially the people's congresses at the national and provincial levels, supplemented by a wider system of social consultation with the objective being to approve or disapprove laws proposed by the civil service (and reviewed by a Supreme Court);
- *an independent anti-corruption system* modeled along the lines of Hong Kong's and Singapore's anti-corruption agencies;
- *an independent auditing system* to control the civil service; and
- *the freedoms of speech, press, assembly, and association,* which "do not constitute government institutions, but [. .] constitute a standard and critical principle that all government branches must observe."

Figure 6.1 **Pan Wei's "Conservative Rule of Law Regime"**

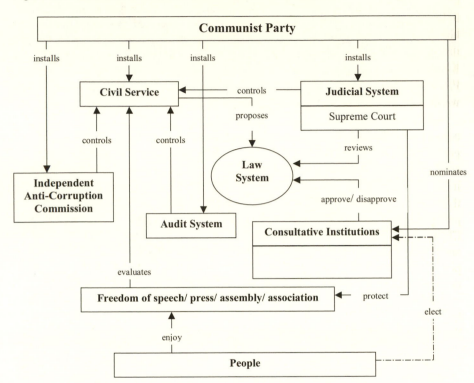

For Pan, a rule of law regime based on these pillars combines most fruitfully both Chinese and Western elements, as it receives from China the tradition of a civil service–based structure with the consultative co-governance with gentries, while discarding the emperor's absolute power at the very top, as well as the tradition of abstract moral principles. It also receives from the Western tradition legalism, but reduces the current Western emphasis on the legitimacy of power competition among social classes and groups. It is innovative because it is a rule of law regime supplemented by democracy instead of a democracy supplemented by rule of law.

Pan advises the implementation of his regime in five consecutive steps: (1) a campaign to mobilize more discussion on the rule of law; followed by (2) an official announcement that the Party's "central work" has shifted from "economic construction" to "building rule of law"; (3) rigorously separating the Party from the government; before (4) building the institutions of checks and balances; and (5) obliging all public officials to observe and respect the four freedoms of speech, press, assembly, and association. According to Pan, such an arrangement ensures for the first time that the Party would no longer control personnel affairs inside the government, and would not interfere in law enforcement (see Figure 6.1). It would only nominally lead via its members inside a neutral, honest, and law-abiding civil service, as is (allegedly) the case of Singapore's People's Action Party. The fact that one-party rule is not abolished but just reduced in scope and intensity is one of the main reasons why Pan Wei deems his "consultative rule of law regime" feasible in present-day China. The Party would be "the right instrument" to build the rule of law, although Pan admits that he is not sure that it will turn out this way. However, as the people demand effective corruption control and a modern polity, political system reform will be necessary. While "real democratic reform" (terminating one-party rule) is impossible—and because the socioeconomic circumstances are receptive—Pan sees "quite a number of chances" that the Party will eventually engage in establishing what he calls a consultative rule of law regime.

Problems of Consistency and Practicability

The backbone of Pan Wei's concept is his law-abiding and impartial civil service. The Party is assigned the important task of installing both highly qualified civil servants dedicated to the uninterested application (and ongoing development) of the law, and professional auditors and an efficient anti-corruption system to check the civil service, as well as establishing independent courts that control the cadre bureaucracy and review all laws. The Party provides and guarantees, therefore, all institutions necessary to maintain a transparent and rule-bound system of mutual linkages. Laws are approved (or disapproved) by the people's congresses at their respective levels, while it is the civil service that proposes these laws. The people come into play by evaluating the performance of the civil service via constitutionally guaranteed rights of free speech, press, assembly, and association. They may elect a set of consultative institutions, which approve or disapprove laws (but do not initiate them). However, Pan Wei makes it very clear that contrary to the PRC Constitution, which claims that the NPC has "supreme power" within the political system, "legislative power is actually in the hands of the Communist Party, and the People's Congress is at best a consultation institution."[18] This implies that the Communist Party dominates the election process of those institutions, especially by controlling or "supervising" the nomination of candidates. As a matter of fact, this interference guarantees the consultation functions of the People's Congress, which otherwise would make an unwanted "revolutionary change to democracy."

How sustainable is such a system, as much in theoretical as in practical terms? Compared to Western liberal democracy, it is first of all striking that in Pan Wei's system the *demos* is subjected to the Party, which—after the latest ideological twist spelled out in the "Three Represents" (*sange daibiao*)—now de facto represents the whole Chinese nation.[19] In fact, there is no theoretical inconsistency in giving the Party such a prominent role if it simply executes the people's will while the people can still give input by substantial consultation. Certainly, though, this is quite a paternalistic and idealistic approach to modern politics. It takes for granted that the Party knows what is "good" for the people. It also (intentionally) ignores much historical evidence of the failure of one-party states to keep the people's interest apace with the party line. It sounds strange in the context of Western concepts of government that Pan Wei believes in the impartiality of a civil service installed by the government in a one-party state. This seems to reflect a deep but empirically ungrounded belief in technocratic expertise as politically "de-contextualized." No administrative decision, however, is taken impartially in the sense that it can be set free from the necessity to decide on resource allocation and specific policies in very normative terms, thereby automatically touching upon divergent interests in society which have to be mediated. Divergence of interests, for its part, is not generated by democracy in the first place, as Pan Wei underlines in various passages of his text, but by socioeconomic modernization that is strongly affecting China's political system.

Pan Wei seems to have factored in these objections by bestowing the right of evaluation to the people who are free to express their views and (maybe) even to launch protests against civil servants failing in their jobs. Moreover, the people can turn to the judiciary, which controls the civil service by subjecting it to the law. This could work as long as the civil service then reformulates the laws to make them more "representative" and acceptable. But what happens if not? The system might still work if the Party resolutely replaces "bad cadres" with new ones and does not exempt any civil servant from punishment because of "superior political considerations." It is obvious that only then could it prove that it represents the people's interests and that it does everything to fill in the gaps of regime legitimacy that might occur in the process of making laws and governing the country. But once again, what happens if the Party does not act upon the results of consultation with the people?

Most thrilling in Pan Wei's thinking is his analytical distinction between the rule of law and democracy, which he supports by introducing a narrow definition of democracy and a very positivist rule of law theory. Law is assigned the highest authority. By way of definition, it must be enforced impartially and according to fixed procedures, "with the gap between the law on books and law in practice narrow."[20] It remains doubtful, however, whether law enforcement can deliver justice in Pan Wei's system. In Western liberalism, this is achieved—at least at the theoretical level—by the democratic accountability of those institutions that are exclusively accorded the authority to make laws: the parliament or legislative assembly. For Pan Wei, however, justice is delivered by an independent civil service drafting and submitting laws to be "fine tuned" by the consultation process in the NPC, which must approve (and can disapprove) those laws. While the *demos,* consequently, cannot make laws itself, it still participates in the process of making "good laws" introduced by the civil service. If everything goes fine, this might work out quite well. But the circumvention of the *demos* as the originator of the law can (and often enough did) come down as a heavy burden on the whole system, which fully depends on the quality of its civil service, its judges, and on the foresight of the Communist Party to choose among the best of the cadres to assume government responsibility—while dismissing those who are not up to their jobs. It is against the logic of (Western) democracy and ignorant of much historical experience if those

making the laws are not structurally restrained by the people and their representative institutions. Pan Wei's consultative regime may be able to avoid "bad laws," but
it lacks the teeth to do so as compared to those systems in which the powerful face
the people in regular elections.

At this point, it should be clear that Pan Wei's consultative rule of law regime can
be called both theoretically consistent or flawed, depending on the perspective that
one takes regarding the paternalist role of the Communist Party. If one subscribes to
the idea that the Party eventually "knows best" and, hence, one trusts in the mode of
self-correction within a system of one-party rule, there is no reason to doubt the practicability of Pan Wei's consultative rule of law regime. However, the Party then
assumes exclusive responsibility for providing all pillars of such a system and at the
same time must guarantee the functionality of those mutual checks and balances that
make the system operate. Moreover, the Party must continuously generate a big pool
of professional, highly qualified cadres and ensure the organizational and financial
independence of China's judges. The current degree of corruption rampant throughout all cadre ranks, and the continuing dependence of the courts on the governments
at their respective administrative levels (concerning the nomination of judges, their
salaries and social benefits, and their job security), do not leave one overly optimistic
that the Party can manage all this.[21] Besides this, the fact that "bad cadres" can only
be removed by the Party's will cannot be trusted as an adequate means to bring about
good laws and good government.

The same is true with respect to necessary "quality controls" of the anti-corruption
agency and the auditing system proposed by Pan Wei. As the officials working in
these institutions are Party members, will they be able (or willing) to confront their
fellow Party members in the civil service in case of conflict? This all comes down
to the most challenging question to Pan Wei's ideas: Can his checks and balances
work properly if the corresponding institutions are "stocked" with cadres whose
interest is in the minimization of frictions within the political system. For only
when the authority of the Party is unquestioned can such cadres maintain their
privileged positions.

It becomes clear that Pan Wei's understanding of the rule of law is rather simplistic
and certainly instrumental. Law does *not* rule if those who govern are not subjected to
meaningful constraints. As Pan Wei's civil service enjoys far-reaching autonomy from
the *demos,* it is still the Party that dominates the system and guarantees its functionality. Certainly the Party's official terminology to promote a concept of *yifa zhiguo*—to
govern the country *by* law—has never permitted any doubt as to where the ultimate
authority of political (and legal) power lies and should lie in the PRC. Pan Wei does
not and cannot challenge this premise. Therefore, it may be of limited relevance to
point at the theoretical inconsistencies of Pan's consultative rule of law regime—
albeit it is quite necessary to correct his sometimes weird understanding of democracy at work in Russia, India, or Taiwan. Most importantly, drawing on the Hong
Kong and Singapore cases as the two most prominent and telling examples to prove
that the rule of law—as understood by Pan Wei—is possible without democracy, ig-

nores the very particular circumstances of those two entities. It is certainly challenging to point at Hong Kong's and Singapore's civil services, which still enjoy an international reputation for high efficiency and impartiality. But politicians in each of
these entities are aware that the public acquiescence in the absense of democracy not
only depends on the requirement that civil servants perform well but also that Hong
Kong and Singapore manage to maintain their prosperity in an ever more volatile
international economy. It remains debatable whether Hong Kong can continue without more electoral democracy in the future, given the obvious dissatisfaction of the
public with the postcolonial government's handling of the economy and whether Singapore's People's Action Party will be able to preserve its elitist approach to government once the socioeconomic divide in the city-state, confirmed occasionally by
observers, becomes more salient. Finally, it is at least courageous to suggest that
China, a country with continental dimensions, could be administered in the same way
as two urban metropolises. The phenomenon of corruption and bureaucratic
intransparency plaguing the PRC has much to do with administrative complexity,
which is certainly easier to tackle in a city-state environment.

Outlook: Rule of Law vs. Democracy

How do we make sense of Pan Wei's consultative rule of law regime? Is it merely an
apologetic effort to legitimize one-party rule in a modern world where democracy
still enjoys discursive supremacy when political reform is at stake? Does it grasp and
conceptualize political change in the PRC that is actually taking place and might one
day evolve into liberal-democratic rule along the Western model? Do we face a concept of government here that is sustainable, at least in the Chinese context? And how
do we qualify the current degree of legal reform in the PRC in terms of establishing
the rule of law as postulated by the Communist leadership? Concerning this last point,
Guo Sujian—along with others—has refuted the idea that Chinese legal and political
reform has approached the rule of law so far:

> The government has relaxed its leash to a certain degree on the legal profession and prac-
> tices in civil and business laws with an increased number of law offices, legal advisors,
> and legal practices. Post-Mao legislative reform has rationalized the people's congress in
> many regards and has brought about some organizational changes, including the expanded
> role of the people's congress, the strengthened NPC Standing Committee and its expanded
> scope of action, increased specialization, more procedural regularity, full-time staff, and
> improved internal organization. However, all these changes or adjustments of action means
> are functional—they maintain the hard core of the communist totalitarian regime and
> serve the purpose of policy change defined by the party line.[22]

Although the Chinese political system can hardly be called totalitarian without
devaluating totalitarianism's analytical usefulness, Guo Sujian's uncompromising
verdict may also be valid for the rule of law regime promoted by Pan. However, even
critical analysts like Randall Peerenboom can come to a different conclusion when

the significance of China's legal reforms for long-term political development and the rise of genuine rule of law in the PRC are under consideration:

> [R]ule of law is a function of institution building and the creation of a culture of legality. Progress has been made and continues to be made on both fronts. Now that the genie is out of the bottle, legal reformers will continue to push for more independent and authoritative courts, as will members of the judiciary, if for no other reason than path-dependent institutional self-interest. Political and legal reforms tend to take on a life of their own, with institutions bursting out of the cages in which they were meant to be confined.[23]

Hence, Chinese legal reforms, as we see them today, contribute to a gradual and meaningful change of political awareness and behavior within the cadre elite and the broader population. If these reforms are judged against the background of other modifications of the Chinese political system initiated by the Party—that is, strengthening the supervisory functions of people's congresses, implementing direct elections at the village and (maybe) township levels, introducing new mechanisms of intra-Party participation to enhance transparency and cadre accountability—there is much reason not to be too pessimistic about the prospect of more "voice" and even democratization in the PRC. As becomes very clear in Pan Wei's ambitious endeavor to conceptualize a politico-legal system that allegedly suits China better than the Western model of liberal democracy, this process still empowers the people and will inevitably lead to the bordergate of one-party rule some day. It is hardly imaginable that the development of a legal system can be sustained without the concurrent rise of interest groups that address the rule of law to fight for their political emancipation.[24] The Communist Party will then be confronted with the question of who knows best what is good for the people—the Party or the people themselves. Arranging for a legal system and more political consultation, as is suggested by Pan Wei's proposal, might indeed give more legitimacy to Communist one-party rule for some time. In that sense, "consultative rule of law" is feasible. However, this is borrowed time that should be well used by the Party to learn how to make the *demos* the ultimate source and authorizer of the law—instead of being forced to such acknowledgment by the people one day.

7

Toward the Rule of Law
Why China's Path Will Be Different from the West

Baohui Zhang

Pan Wei argues that what China needs first is the rule of law, not democracy. According to Pan, there are four kinds of relationships between democracy and the rule of law: democratic government without the rule of law (mostly third world countries); nondemocratic government with the rule of law (Hong Kong and Singapore); democratic government with the rule of law (mostly Western countries); and nondemocratic government without the rule of law (again mostly third world countries). According to Pan, the first combination is actually the worst outcome since a democracy without the rule of law is likely to result in chaos, corruption, and general governance problems. This is why most third world democracies are not successful in terms of political stability and sustainable development. According to Pan, the second pattern, nondemocratic government with the rule of law, has been proven to be a viable political option, especially for countries without democratic traditions. Hong Kong and Singapore are well-governed societies with efficient and clean government. Therefore Pan concludes that at least in the mid-term future, China should focus its political reform on building up the rule of law, since that can best ensure the emergence of successful democracies as in the West. Moreover, Pan even suggests that due to its history and culture, the Singapore option of rule of law without democracy may also suit China in the long run. As a result, Pan prescribes a future polity that embodies the rule of law, but shuns competitive democracy.

Although I agree in this chapter with Pan Wei's emphasis on the importance of the rule of law for effective democracy and its general role in successful governance, I question Pan's optimistic view that the rule of law can emerge from the present political system characterized by single-party rule. This chapter argues that it is unrealistic to expect the current ruling party to successfully carry out a profound political reform for the purpose of creating the rule of law, since it is fundamentally inconsistent with single-party rule.

Political Requisites for the Rule of Law

According to Randall Peerenboom, the rule of law "means a system in which law imposes meaningful limits on the rulers."[1] Law serves to constrain the power of the state and its rulers. A political regime based on the rule of law can only emerge out of political checks and balances, and appropriate historical, cultural, and ideological contexts. Unique medieval political and ideological conditions in Western Europe gave rise to the so-called "medieval constitutionalism" that served as the foundation of the rule of law in the West. In China, a political legacy of highly centralized rule makes the emergence of the rule of law difficult, especially if the current political system of single-party rule continues. While the development of the rule of law preceded democracy in the West, only democratization offers a reasonable chance to advance the rule of law in China, since only democracy has the necessary ideology, political checks and balances, autonomous civil society, and a free media that can together constrain the power of the state and its rulers.

The rule of law requires supporting institutional and ideational conditions that establish the supremacy of law. As British legal scholar Joseph Raz observes, "Taken in its broadest sense this means that people should obey the law and be ruled by it. But in political and legal theory it has come to be read in a narrower sense, that the government shall be ruled by law and subject to it."[2] Harold J. Berman, in his classic study of the formation of the Western legal tradition, argues that what distinguished the West from the rest of the world was the supremacy of law over the state and its rulers. In the West, "the historicity of law is linked with the concept of its supremacy over the political authorities. . . . Since the twelfth century in all countries of the West, even under absolute monarchies, it has been widely said and often accepted that in some important respects law transcends politics."[3]

In a recent study of the relationship between law and revolution in the West, Berman once again comments on the Western notion of law's autonomy and its supremacy over political rulers: "The supreme political authority, the king, and pope himself, may make law, it was said, but he may not make it arbitrarily, and until he has remade it—lawfully—he is bound by it."[4]

Berman argues that the rule of law in the West was critically embedded with Western history, politics, and ideas. Its supremacy was the result of Western political pluralism and Western legal philosophy, in particular the impacts of natural law and divine law. Basically, Berman suggests that ideological constraints on rulers due to natural law, and divine law's conception that men are subject to law, and political checks and balances, all of which were the result of pluralism, are the key conditions for the rise of the rule of law.

As he observes, in the West the belief of the law's supremacy was rooted first "in the theological conviction that the universe itself was subject to law." Next, he asserts:

> The belief in the supremacy of law was rooted in the pluralism of secular authorities within each kingdom, and especially in the dialectical tension among royal, feudal, and urban polities. . . . The pluralism of secular authorities within each kingdom was, of course, not only a concept but also an overriding political, economic, and social reality. The cities of Europe were built on the foundation of communal self-government and the liberties of citizens. Feudal authorities, too, continually resisted before royal encroachment on their privileges.[5]

Why are these two conditions—ideological constraints on the rulers by natural law and divine law, and political checks and balances—vital for the rise of the rule of law? Simply put, they serve to prevent anybody from possessing all the power and being above the law. Political fragmentation in medieval Europe, a decentralized military system, a strong civil society, and representative institutions such as parliament all served to constrain the power of the kings. Most importantly, these conditions forced the kings to use law to define mutual rights and obligations with their feudal lords and their subjects in general. As a result, Western monarchs in the medieval era were already bound by law in many significant ways. This legal constraint on European rulers was also complemented by the natural law and divine law conception that although the king was above everyone else, he was nonetheless beneath God and law.

As the case of England shows, establishing the rule of law requires lengthy struggle between the absolutist tendency, represented by the kings on the one hand, and counter forces on the other hand. This prolonged and bloody struggle was made possible only by the political and social pluralism of the West at the time. For example, powerful noble lords controlled significant military forces and autonomous cities and towns that often allied with each other in their resistance to the royal power. As Ralph V. Turner's recent study of the Magna Carta indicates, from its inception in 1215 to the English revolution in the early seventeenth century, the configuration of political power in England enabled a broad coalition of forces to resist the royal tendency for absolutist rule.[6] The most important institutional check on the absolutist tendency was the Parliament, where English lords and gentries eventually foiled the kings' efforts to defy the rule of law. During this final stage of the emergence of the rule of law in the seventeenth century, English philosophers and legal scholars such as Matthew Hales and Thomas Hobbes also developed views, based on medieval natural law and divine law traditions, that rulers, like everyone else, were subject to law, since the universe itself must be governed by reason.[7]

This is where the West and China profoundly differed. Historically, China had neither the political checks and balances nor the ideological conception that rulers were subject to law and that law was supreme and autonomous. Instead, Chinese political history was marked by highly centralized rule by absolutist emperors. The dominant political philosophy of Confucianism emphasized rule by virtues and virtuous men, not rule by law. In one of the few Chinese comparative studies of the rule of law in the West and China, Chinese legal scholar Xia Yong emphasizes the importance of political checks and balances as a precondition for the rule of law. He points out that while China's political system emphasized the importance of virtuous men as rulers, "the West emphasized the vital role of mutual checks and balances between men."[8]

The emergence of the rule of law requires both a certain configuration of political power, in specific checks and balances, and political ideologies that subject rulers to the supremacy of law. Differences between China and the West on these two conditions explain why China could not develop the rule of law in the past and why China's future transition toward the rule of law has to be complemented by political democratization. Only democracy champions the ideological notion that rulers must be subjected to law. Moreover, only democracy provides the necessary political checks and balances through institutional separations of power, judicial independence, free media, and autonomous civil society that prevent anyone from being above the law. Therefore Pan Wei's suggestion that China could develop the rule of law without democracy is unrealistic. The emergence of the rule of law in China has to proceed hand in hand with political democratization.

The following sections will use these two critical factors—political pluralism and checks and balances on the one hand, and the ideological conception that men are subjected to law on the other hand—to examine why China could not develop the rule of law while the West succeeded. China's failure may be attributed to its historical legacy of highly centralized rule and its political-philosophical emphasis on rule by virtues and virtuous men. In the West, political pluralism in the medieval era resulted in checks and balances that forced kings to use law to define rights and obligations with both their feudal lords and their subjects in general. The supremacy of law was also rooted in the Western notions of natural law and divine law, under which men were subjected to the rule of fundamental values, reasons, and virtues of the universe, which formed the basis of law.

Rule of Law in China's History

According to the standard interpretation of Chinese political tradition, the configuration of political power in China's history was against the development of rule of law, since the Chinese central state power, as embodied by the emperors, was not counterbalanced due to a lack of political pluralism that marked the West. Moreover, besides Taoist tradition, which never became a powerful ideology for political rulers in China, there was no equivalent of the Western natural and divine law traditions that saw rulers as subjected to the fundamental reasons of the universe, which constituted the basis of law in a civilized society. The two political philosophies that were systematically practiced by Chinese rulers, the legalist tradition and the Confucian tradition, as elaborated later in this section, were both anti–rule of law.

According to Jacques Gernet's study of Chinese history, in the later part of the Warring States Era, which lasted from the end of the fifth century B.C.E. until 221 B.C.E., China went through a state revolution. A highly centralized form of state emerged first in the kingdom of Qin, largely due to the influence of the legalist tradition. Prominent legalist statesmen such as Shang Yang and Han Fei proposed a centralized political system maintained by a strong code of law. This system was put into place by the last king of the Qin kingdom, who eventually unified China and became its first emperor. Gernet observes that this can best be described as a revolution "since it provided the basis of the imperial power and continued to inspire the most fundamental political conceptions of the Chinese world."[9]

After China was unified in 221 B.C.E. by Qin, the political system was further centralized. As observed by Yu-chuan Wang, "With the creation of the title 'Emperor' there was instituted for the first time in China a centralized imperial government, which through its provincial and local administrative agencies directly controlled the whole empire. The local governments and the people looked to the central government for directives in all important political, military, and legal matters."[10]

This imperial rule by the emperor was exercised through a highly elaborate administrative system, which became increasingly centralized under the Ming and Qing dynasties. Miller argues that by the time of the Qing, the totality of imperial Chinese state control over the population, economy, and military far exceeded that of the embryonic modern European state. The imperial state was administered by functionally defined and highly specialized civil and military bureaucracies, stretching vertically from the capital to localities.[11]

As a result of this highly centralized political system, historically China lacked the political pluralism and centrifugal forces that defined medieval Europe. First, China never developed a feudal system in which powerful nobles controlled regions of the country and served as a counter-force to central rulers. According to Gernet, at the beginning of the Han Dynasty, Han emperors made deliberate efforts to weaken the power of princes and nobles, who then controlled sizable fiefs and independent militaries. This led to a rebellion by seven royal princes which was subsequently defeated in the year 154 B.C.E. After this failed attempt, "the princes had lost all territorial power; the only advantage which they still enjoyed was the right to levy taxes in grain on a certain number of peasant families."[12]

Charles O. Hucker also noted that in the Ming Dynasty, princes and nobles had little practical power. Although many were awarded large tracts of land as estates, unlike feudal lords in medieval Europe, "the princes were not feudatories in any normal sense. They did not have any administrative or judicial functions. . . . On the whole, the princes were salaried dignitaries and no more."[13]

China also lacked the other aspects of political pluralism that characterized medieval Europe, such as autonomous cities and towns and civil society. As elaborated in the next section, many medieval European commercial towns and cities were largely autonomous from royal rule. They were granted charters by the kings to exercise self-governance. Cities often allied with nobles who also feared the expansion of the king's power. In China, on the other hand, cities were the center of imperial power. They were the seats of imperial administration and control.

The Chinese imperial state did not directly rule the vast rural region of the country. It depended on the collaboration of local elites, who assisted county magistrates, the lowest level of imperial reach, to implement policies of the state. This local gentry class, however, was hardly an organized counter-force to imperial power. In fact, most members of the class were easily co-opted by the state through its exam-based career advancement system.[14]

China did not develop the Western equivalent of a civil society either, which can serve as a societal check against state power. In fact, the Chinese state developed various systems of societal control, such as the infamous secret police system in the Ming Dynasty. During the Qing era, a harsh *bao jia* system, which involved group punishment, was instituted to deter any organized activities against the state.

In short, the Chinese political system was highly centralized and there was a lack of any significant checks and balances against imperial power. Inevitably, this system was incapable of fomenting the rise of the rule of law, in the sense that the state and its rulers should be restrained by law. The only challenges to the system were either foreign invasions or peasant rebellions. However, successful foreign invaders and peasant rebels merely reinstituted the same highly centralized imperial system, modeled after the one that they just overthrew.

Beside the lack of political checks and balances that helped constrain the power of absolutist rulers, Chinese ancient political and legal philosophies also contradicted the concept that law was autonomous and supreme and that rulers must be subjected to the rule of law. Randall Peerenboom offers a comprehensive study of the subject. According to him, there were two prominent ancient Chinese political doctrines that contradicted the spirit of the rule of law. One was the Confucian doctrine of *lizhi,* which was predicated on and achieved political order primarily by reference to the *li* or rites, that is, traditional customs, mores, and norms. The other was the competing *fazhi,* which "refers to political order attained primarily through reliance on *fa,* or laws, that is, publicly promulgated, codified standards of general applicability backed up by the coercive power of the state." According to Peerenboom, both political doctrines run against the spirit of the rule of law. Confucius rejected using law to achieve political order. Even if the threat of harsh punishment could force people to obey political orders at the time, it would not turn them into better human beings. Rather, people needed to be educated and led through *li* so that they understood what is morally right and what is wrong. Through this, Confucius believed that rule by *li* could "achieve a harmonious social order in which each person is able to realize his or her full potential as a human being through mutually beneficial relations with others." Although Confucius did not advocate the complete abandonment of laws, he believed that by inspiring and teaching people correct conduct and values, they would all aspire to do the moral things and this would lead to a harmonious society. Thus, Confucius rejected law as a means for attaining social order because it focuses on external compliance only, not the internal betterment of human characters. Confucian *lizhi* gave a prominent role to the ruler. As Peerenboom characterizes it, "The ruler was to lead by example. His virtue was to sweep over the people and transform them just as the wind blowing over long grass bends them as it passes." In contrast to Confucius, the legalist doctrine believed that humans were self-interested. To avoid conflict and achieve order, they must be manipulated through a system of rewards and punishments. Clear, codified, public law lets every person know the consequences of one's actions. As Peerenboom emphasizes, *fazhi* in this sense had little to do with the rule of law, which means legal constraint over the ruler. Instead, *fazhi* means the rule by law to help the state maintain political control and social order.[15]

In fact, legalists were fervent promoters of strong centralized rule. They saw strong absolutist rulers as key to national unity, security, and prosperity. Law was conceived as the means to achieve such goals. As Suzanne Ogden sees it, "Indeed, it was because of the tenants of Legalism that law in China became equated with punishment, with criminal law, and with rule by one man, the emperor."[16]

Therefore, both *lizhi* and *fazhi* doctrines in ancient China contradicted the spirit of the rule of law. *Lizhi* emphasized the role of moral leadership by a virtuous ruler and thus justified rule by man. *Fazhi,* on the other hand, only sought to use law to enhance the state's control over society. Neither emphasized external checks against the state and rulers and their subjection to law.

Indeed, Confucian tradition was not in support of despotic rule. In fact, it argued that rulers must be just and fair and be governed by virtues. However, by emphasizing the roles of virtues and virtuous rulers it devalued the importance of law in society and state. Recent Chinese studies therefore blame Confucianism for China's lack of tradition in the use of law as an organizing principle of state and society.

For example, Yang Hefu, a professor of the history of law at the Chinese University of Politics and Law, criticizes the Confucian emphasis on virtues. He claims that *lizhi,* or rule by virtue, retarded the development of a legal culture in China for two thousand years, since it "omitted the importance of using law to regulate society and the state."[17] Xia Yong, who is director of the Institute of Law, Chinese Academy of Social Sciences, particularly criticizes Confucianism for equating the role of virtues with that of law and thus creating the problem of lack of separation between law and virtues in traditional Chinese legal thinking.[18]

Legalist and Confucian political philosophies profoundly influenced the way China has been governed in the last two thousand years. Confucian ideology became the de facto official ideology of successive Chinese dynasties while the legalist influence led to the wide use of punishment to help rulers achieve control over society. In effect, they both contributed to the autocratic nature of Chinese political history.

However, it must be mentioned that there was a third philosophical tradition, Taoism, that once competed with Confucianism and legalism for prominence, and it contained natural law elements that saw the universe, including political rulers, as governed by fundamental reason and morals. At the same time, however, Taoists opposed efforts to use man-made rules, including law, to organize society.[19] Because of its distain for politics, Taoism never achieved political significance in ancient China.

The Rise of the Rule of Law in Western Europe

While China lacked political checks and balances against absolutist tendencies and lacked powerful ideologies that see men, including rulers, as subject to the supremacy of law, these conditions were the causes of the emergence of the rule of law in the West.

This chapter argues that its emergence in Western Europe was not accidental but decided by the unique political, social, and religious conditions in the medieval and early modern periods. These conditions include the following: political fragmentation and pluralism with its consequent checks and balances, Christianity's view of law, and the peculiar nature of the feudal system. These conditions together gave rise to the so-called Western constitutionalism that included representative bodies, personal liberties, and the sanctity of law that together formed the basis of the rule of law and set the West apart from the rest of the world.

Political Checks and Balances, Natural and Divine Laws, and the Emergence of Constitutionalism

Medieval Europe was decidedly different from China in that its political landscape was characterized by decentralized power, multiple power centers, and thus fragmentation. This was very different from the centralized political structures that defined China's dynastic empires. The main reason for the European situation was the collapse of the last European empire before the medieval era. The Carolingian Empire was created in the eighth century C.E. by the Franks, who emigrated from today's Germany to France. The Carolingian Empire culminated when Charlemagne was crowned by the pope as its emperor on Christmas Day in 800 C.E. However, as Brian Downing points out, the governing system of the Carolingian Empire was not as centralized as the Roman Empire that preceded it. The development of institutions for administration, taxation, and justice were at best rudimentary. Thus, as Downing claims, "Such an empire had more pulling it apart than holding it together."[20]

Therefore, after Charlemagne's death the empire quickly collapsed. It was divided among his three sons by the Treaty of Verdun in the year 843. The three kingdoms corresponded roughly to today's France, Germany, and upper Italy. This signaled the end of centralized governance in Western Europe for many centuries to come. In the various kingdoms that emerged in the European political landscape the new central authorities were weak at best, since it took time to rebuild centralized rule out of empire collapse. The most important consequence of the collapse of centralized authority was political fragmentation. The states that started to reemerge in today's France and Germany in the eleventh century were characterized by weak kings who were constrained by a variety of other political forces. In the words of Henry Spruyt, the state at this time was not even sovereign since it faced competition from other political forces.[21] These forces include powerful nobles who controlled sizable private militaries, a universalistic church that claimed supremacy over secular rulers, towns that possessed wealth and remained relatively independent from both the kings and nobles, and strong, well-organized corporate bodies in society, such as guilds and lawyers.

Powerful nobility derived its influence from the decentralized military system of the feudal era. In fact, this decentralized military system defined the very nature of feudalism. Lacking centralized resources to conduct war, the king decentralized the military into the hands of his lords. In return for a fief or land from the king, which provided financial support for the lords, the latter had the obligation of raising a private military to support the king in times of need. This reciprocal relationship could also be extended between a lord and his knights, who had the duty of coming to the aid of the lord when needed. This private and decentralized military system defined the nature of feudalism and created a balance of power between the kings and nobility, since the latter in fact controlled the bulk of a country's military.

The second political force that contributed to the political fragmentation of medieval Europe was the Christian Church with its universalistic claims. According to Finer, before the eleventh century the church's, and, in particular, the pope's power were not at all that significant, since they could not control the appointment of bishops and archbishops, who were selected by the kings and powerful nobles. In the eleventh century, the church's power began to ascend under Pope Gregory III, who was elected in the year of 1073. Under Gregory III, the papacy embarked on a far-reaching program to strengthen church power by claiming supremacy over all the lay rulers. The chief elements of the program were embodied in the *Dictatus Papae* of 1075, which claimed (1) that the pope was the sovereign head of the church, establishing its laws and deposing and translating its bishops, and (2) that he was the superior to the emperors and kings, able to depose them and release their subjects from their oaths of allegiance. Thus the church did not recognize territorial boundaries to its authority and this brought it into conflicts with kings of states, which lasted for many centuries in Europe.

Because of the Gregorian reform, the church became a powerful political force in medieval Europe. It possessed vast resources in the form of land holdings and was also immune from taxation by secular kings. Secular laws were also not applicable to the personnel of the church, since they were subject only to the Canon law of the church.

A third political force that contributed to European political fragmentation came from the many independent towns that began to resurface in Europe in the Middle Ages. In the Dark Ages that followed the collapse of the Roman Empire, cities of significant size disappeared. However, according to Finer, by the fourteenth century towns were once again "the most vital part of Western Europe's economic life and a quickening presence in it polities." They were trading and manufacturing centers of the time and thus possessed wealth and economic resources. Most important, however, was that many of them were relatively independent from the kings or nearby lords. As Samuel Finer points out, most of the cities in the Middle East and China were seats of imperial power. "By contrast, the European towns were communities of free citizens who, at the least, administered and controlled their own internal affairs by charter from their overlords or king and, at the most, owed allegiance to nobody at all except themselves."[22]

Throughout medieval Europe, according to Downing, these towns often played nobles and kings against each other, siding with whomever could promise them greater independence. They often used alliances with one side or the other in exchange for fundamental rights, freedoms, and immunities, which were often stipulated in written charters.[23]

The last source of political fragmentation in medieval Europe was the existence of strong corporate bodies that resided in the society at the time. As Samuel Huntington observes, medieval Europe saw the rise and persistence of diverse autonomous groups based not on blood relationships but on commonly shared corporate interests. They ranged from monasteries and monastic orders to guilds and professional groups, such as lawyers.[24] These groups essentially constitute what we call today a civil society that was autonomous from state control. Moreover, they possessed organizational ability to resist state actions that they perceived as threatening to their corporate interests or privileges.

Together, powerful nobles with their private militaries that could rival that of the king, a universalistic church that claimed supremacy over lay rulers, autonomous towns that exercised self-rule, and a dense network of corporate societal organizations led historian Joseph Strayer to make the following observation: "To sum up, the basic characteristics of feudalism in Western Europe are fragmentation of political authority, public power in private hands, and a military system in which an essential part of the armed forces is secured through private contracts."[25]

Finer also comments that the feudal characteristics gave the political system "a highly peculiar texture: at once decentralized, polyarchical, and cellular. Government was an activity shared between the king and his vassal-tenants, his barons. The king did not, at least did not in many or even most significant aspects, govern his subjects directly, but through his barons, indirectly." As Finer further points out, "Here the king is not absolute at all."[26]

This decentralized system, in particular the balance of power between kings and nobles, according to Downing, gave rise to so-called Western constitutionalism. Precisely because nobody possessed all the power, a system of mutual constraint was adopted to accommodate all the political forces. It included first and foremost the rise of representative or parliamentary bodies in which monarch, aristocracy, burghers from the cities, and clerics determined basic matters, including fundamental ones of taxation and war.[27] The power of the representative bodies included a wide range of activities such as deciding taxation, legislating new laws, government oversight, and serving as the highest judicial body of the land.[28]

Second, it included the use of charters and legal norms, agreed upon by both kings and nobility to define their mutual rights and obligations. The best example was, of course, the Magna Carta, which was forced upon the English king by his barons in the year of 1215. It defined the legal basis of crown–noble relations. For example, the king had to summon his lords to a parliament to discuss policies for taxation and war.

Berman comments that "feudal law gave the West its first secular experience of mutuality of legal obligations between persons of superior and inferior rank."[29] Thus the contractual, mutually binding nature of feudal laws contributed to the sanctity of law in medieval Europe. Finer also notes the importance of law for the system of limited government in medieval Europe. According to him, "What is arresting and profoundly original about medieval European feudalism is that the relationships of dependency and service which began as expedients should end up as a legal system of rights and duties, the framework of a lawful political order."[30]

Besides the necessity of law for political checks and balances, and the unique need for law in guiding feudal relationships, the natural law tradition of Europe also contributed to the sanctity of law in the medieval political system. According to Berman, natural law believes that "human law derived ultimately from, and was to be tested ultimately by, reason and conscience. . . . This theory had its basis in Christian theology as well as in Aristotelian philosophy."[31] Thus natural law incorporates elements of divine law, which is the will of God that is reflected in biblical precepts such as the Ten Commandments.

In the Christian view, as contained in the Old Testament, divine law ruled over the king. According to Finer, it portrayed heroic Jewish kings, who, by arms, upheld the divine law. Through and through, it made the single point: there was a divine order, a divine law, and kings were both its defenders and its subjects. By the early Middle Ages, Christian scholars began to equate divine law with natural law. For example, in the middle of the twelfth century, a learned lawyer and monk named Gratian claimed: "Mankind is ruled by two laws: Natural Law and Custom. Natural Law is what is contained in the Scriptures (i.e., the Old Testament) and the Gospel." According to this Christian view, kings were thus subject to natural or divine law, since "It was God given, not made by man at all. Christian monarchs were to be seen simply as chief executives circumscribed and regulated by Natural Law." Hence, in medieval Europe there was the concept of "king not under man but under God and the law."[32]

Entering the modern era, the influence of natural law and divine law led prominent English philosopher John Locke to claim that "The law of Nature stands as an Eternal Rule to all Men, legislators as well as others. The Rules that they make for other Mens Actions, must, as well as their own and other Mens Actions, be conformable to the Law of Nature, *i.e.* to the Will of God."[33]

As a result of representative bodies where nobles, clerics, and representatives from the towns met to discuss national issues, and the sanctity of law that codified the king's power and his relationship with his lords, basic conditions of rule of law were created in medieval Western Europe since the king's power was constrained. Basically there were institutionalized external checks against the power of the state and its king. As a result, in two particular areas the king's power was severely restricted. The first was the legislative. The use of representative institutions made law making at least a shared authority between parliament and the king. In the English case, there was even the fundamental idea of Crown-in-Parliament, which means that no laws could be enacted without the consent of Parliament.

The second constraint on the king was fiscal. Since most of the country was not directly governed by the king but by his lords or magnates, the king's taxation power was limited. In practice, no medieval monarch was ever fiscally absolute. Indeed, precisely the reverse. This is a central feature of the medieval kingship. Of particular importance for fiscal restraint on the king was the sanctity of property rights in medieval Europe. The resurrection of Roman law in this era rejected imperial claims over subjects' property. Neither pope nor lay rulers had claim over any individual's property. Therefore, only in medieval Europe did the following concept emerge: taxation without consent was simply robbery. As a result of the king's fiscal dependency on his lords and towns and the medieval concept of property rights, taxation by the king had to be approved by representative bodies such as Parliament in England and the Estates-General in France. The nobles and burghers had to agree to the king's request for additional taxation.

To summarize, the unique conditions of political fragmentation and checks and balances in medieval Europe gave rise to the emergence of institutions that began to lay the foundation for the rule of law. Representative bodies and the sanctity of law served as constraints on the king's power.

The Case of England: A Long Road to Constitutional Rule

The specifics of each country differed. In some, such as France, there was a long tug of war between the king and the nobles who opposed him. At times, the nobles had the upper hand and forced the French king to pursue governance with his lords. This was shown by the extensive use of the Estates-General, especially during the thirteenth to fourteenth centuries when France and England fought for almost a hundred years. The kings during this period needed revenue for the war effort and collaboration with their lords became crucial.

By the mid-fifteenth century, however, the royal power began to centralize and the role of the Estates-General declined. A main reason was that by this time French nobles had gained the right of tax exemption, so they no longer had the same motive to constrain the king's power. Nonetheless, even in the seventeenth century French kings were still "impeded strenuously" by nobles, estates, and local governments. This took the form of a series of nobles' rebellions, often joined by localities and municipalities, in the sixteenth to seventeenth centuries. Even the Sun King, Louis XIV, did not abolish the institutions and corporate bodies that had thwarted his predecessors.[34]

The English alternative was gradual evolution toward constitutional government, and this section thus focuses mostly on the English experience. The Magna Carta, or Great Charter, was the beginning of constitutional constraint on the king's power. In 1214, a group of nobles defeated King John, who wanted to unilaterally impose taxes without their consent. In the following year, these nobles forced John to sign the Magna Carta, which imposed limits on the king's power. Fundamentally, the charter forced the king to consult with representatives of the "community of the realm" to discuss issues like taxation and war.[35] The institution that represented this community was Parliament, which included both nobles and representatives from the town.

Moreover, the Magna Carta demanded due process of law. In Clause 39, it was stated: "No freeman shall be arrested, or detained in prison, or deprived of his freehold, or outlawed, or banished or in anyway molested; and we will not set forth against him, nor send against him, unless by the lawful judgment of his peers or by the law of the land." As Finer notes, this clause defined the sanctity of rule of law and "the application of nothing but the law."[36] Even more dramatic was Clause 41. The rebellious lords were so distrustful of the king that this clause provided for a committee of twenty-five nobles with the right to seize the king's property and lands and seek justice in whatever way possible, saving only the persons of the king, the queen, and their children.

According to Thomas Eartman, the Magna Carta Parliament gradually achieved the position of shared rule with the king. Not only did it possess veto power over new taxation, it also developed co-legislative rights in that no laws could be enacted without its consent. The English common law tradition saw law as the custom of the community, not a body of mandates from the emperor, like Roman law. Therefore, law could only be enacted with the common counsel of the community, which means the consent of the representative institution of the community—Parliament. So by the mid-1300s, it was universally accepted that law could only be promulgated with the consent of Parliament.[37] Finer refers to this power as the idea of Crown-in-Parliament, which means that Parliament represented the highest authority of the land.[38]

Beside fiscal and legislative power, Parliament over time also extended its role to administrative oversight. Starting in the 1370s, Parliament created many "commissions of reform" with wide authority to remove incompetent officials and correct mismanagement. Parliament also attempted scrutiny of royal finances during the war with France. Thus, as Eartman concludes, by the early 1400s, "Parliament had come to occupy an important role as an agency of administrative and financial oversight and a source of reforms."[39]

However, after the conclusion of the Hundred Years' War between England and France, Parliament in England saw a decline in its influence, since the king no longer needed extraordinary taxation to finance his war and thus no longer needed to call parliaments. During this period, up to the Civil War, royal power expanded and was increasingly centralized.

The Civil War once again resurrected the power of Parliament. The autocratic rule of Charles I brought him into conflict with Parliament and caused the Civil War of the 1640s. In the end, the king was defeated and ordered beheaded by Parliament in 1649. A parliamentary republic, the Commonwealth, was proclaimed.

After the Civil War, the Tudor dynasty was restored under King Charles II. The tug-of-war between monarch and Parliament resumed. This long conflict between the king and Parliament came to an end during the reign of King James II, brother of Charles II. When the Catholic James II attempted absolutist rule during his short reign from 1685 to 1688, he caused sufficient fear among the largely Protestant nobles of England that in 1688 they invited the Protestant Dutch Prince William of Orange to invade England. He did and James II fled, after most of his military defected. This ended the long battle between Parliament and English kings, since the new era of constitutional government was about to begin. As Finer observes, the so-called Glorious Revolution of 1688 transformed "Parliament into a permanent and central organ of the constitution." After 1688 Britain became the first constitutional monarchy of Europe, "in that the Parliament could certainly stop the king from doing what he wanted to do but was unable to compel him to do what it wanted done." Therefore, "without the slightest doubt, this was a *limited* monarchy."[40]

Legalism as Foundation of the Rule of Law

Finer observes that the foundation of the emerging rule of law in Europe was legalism. In this kind of state: (1) law had a particular, indeed a paramount sanctity; (2) the individual was not a mere subject but a citizen entitled to the certain inherent rights to life, liberty, and above all, property; (3) particular respect was shown for the principle of private property; this principle and the related "No taxation without consent" thwarted the absolutist attempts of kings for many centuries; (4) lawboundedness, respect for private property, and passive citizenship together implied that rulership was in some sense limited; (5) despite the monarchs' unceasing efforts to abolish these restrictions, they were upheld by the power of numerous corporate bodies into which the society had formed itself, such as the guilds, representative institutions, and even the Church. Although these principles were nowhere implemented fully, and many were more honored in breach than observance, Finer argues that they were the necessary preconditions for the later constitutional monarchy, which was characterized by the rule of law. Nowhere else were these principles practiced. As Finer points out, "Neither China nor Japan entertained any but the haziest and most moralizing notion of limitations upon the ruler's absolutism. . . . His power—and this was true of all Asian states—was reinforced in so far as none of them developed the concept of legal personality. No distinction could be made between the person of the ruler and the state." Therefore, as Finer concludes, "This central notion that the relationship of the government to the individual must be based on law, that the individual possessed certain inherent rights, and that consequently he could be deprived of these only by due process, marked the essential difference between these arisen European states and those of Asia."[41]

The Rule of Law and Democracy in China

The rise of the rule of law needs certain political conditions. In the West, the rule of law emerged out of the context of political fragmentation and checks and balances of the medieval era. Mutual balancing between the king and his nobles and towns required representative institutions that served to constrain the king's power, as did codified laws that defined the rights and duties of both the king and his lords and subjects. Thus the rise of the rule of law in the West was not accidental. Political checks and balances are almost a precondition for the limited state.

Therefore, Pan Wei's prescription for rule of law in China under a system of single-party rule is unlikely to succeed, since the limits set by law run counter to the unlimited power of single-party rule. It is hard to imagine that the ruling party will give up its dominance in state and society, since it will no longer be a single-party-dominant system. Thus, how to reconcile the conflict between single-party rule and the rule of law is never successfully answered by Pan Wei.

Pan suggests that a future rule of law–oriented political system in China should incorporate several institutional elements: an independent bureaucracy, an autonomous judicial system, an effective anti-corruption agency, a consultation system centered around the People's Congress at both the national and provincial levels, and finally a free media.[42] This system essentially tries to incorporate political checks and balances among several institutions. The only element left out by Pan is the chief executive of the country—how it is selected and the nature of its relationship with other institutions. And this is not a small omission, since it is precisely the relationship between the king and other institutions in medieval Europe that provided the foundation of constitutional rule in that the king's power was restrained by these institutions.

Moreover, every one of these institutional elements begs the question of the institution's relationship with the ruling party: How can they become truly independent or autonomous or free from the ruling party? It is hard to imagine that operationally this future rule of law–oriented system can successfully be implemented in substance, and not just in name.

Only democracy offers institutional and political checks and balances, autonomous civil society, and a free media that can together restrain the power of the state and its officials. Therefore, the rule of law can only emerge out of democracy. Although a democracy may not succeed in establishing effective rule of law, just as most of the third world democracies have failed to do so, it nonetheless provides a much better opportunity than a single-party-dominant system, which is fundamentally inconsistent with the rule of law. Drawing from the experience with development of rule of law in East Asia, Randall Peerenboom concurs that, "Despite considerable institutional reforms, the limited ability of the legal system to check political power in South Korea, Taiwan and Indonesia suggests that ultimately the lack of democracy imposed limits on the implementation of rule of law."[43]

Thus, this chapter disagrees with Pan's assertion that democracy is not necessarily good for China since it has not led to the rule of law in many third world countries and the results have been political chaos, corruption, and instability. The point here is that no other system offers a better chance than democracy for establishing the rule of law, certainly not a single-party-dominant system.

Pan points to the experiences of Singapore and Hong Kong as examples of successful societies with the rule of law but without democracy. However, both Singapore and Hong Kong share one unique legacy: they used to be British colonies. As historian Niall Ferguson argues in an important study, the rule of law marks one of the greatest legacies of the British Empire of the nineteenth century.[44] The legacy of Britain as the world's first government based on rule of law and the birthplace of the Magna Carta certainly contributed to the strong tradition of law in Singapore and Hong Kong.

Pan discounts the British legacy in Singapore and Hong Kong's tradition with law. He asks why only these two out of many former British colonies developed a strong tradition of law. There are three answers to this question. First, studies have shown that indeed democracies with the British legacy, almost all of them parliamentary democracies, do survive longer than democracies without the British legacy.[45] They are less likely to see democratic breakdown precisely because they tend to have a better system of rule of law.

Second, Singapore is a country of rule by law, not rule of law. It has a one-party-dominant regime, which imposes severe restrictions on liberties and attempts wide-ranging control over the society. Therefore, as Singapore political scientist Lam Peng Er argues, the system does not have an independent civil society and media, nor, as a result, a viable opposition.[46] Many characterize Singapore as soft-authoritarian rule, not a democracy. Its strict laws are designed for state control over society. Therefore, this is a political system of rule by law, not rule of law.

Third, Hong Kong's judicial system is very British and this is why law and its enforcement are effective. In fact, many of the current judges in Hong Kong are still of British descent. They were appointed to their positions during the colonial era. It is thus not a surprise that the British rule of law tradition can flourish in Hong Kong.

Therefore, this chapter argues that Singapore and Hong Kong will not and cannot become models for China's future development with the rule of law. Their British legacy, high level of affluence, and minute size have given them unique advantages in developing strong traditions with law in both governance and society. China cannot replicate the British legacy and so cannot copy the experiences of Singapore and Hong Kong.

In conclusion, China's path toward the rule of law will be different from that of the West. As Fareed Zakaria argues in an influential article, in the West the emergence of constitutional liberalism preceded the emergence of democracy. This is what sets the West apart from the rest of the world. As Zakaria defines it, "It is liberal because it draws on the philosophical strain, beginning from the Greeks, that emphasizes individual liberty. It is constitutional because it rests on the tradition, beginning with the Romans, of the rule of law."[47] China's political system of single-party rule is irreconcilable with the basic tenets of rule of law. Thus, while the development of the rule of law in the West preceded democracy, China's chance for establishing effective rule of law lies with democratization. A democracy does not guarantee the rule of law. But it does stand a better chance than any other political system to achieve the rule of law. Only democracy offers the necessary ideology, political checks and balances, autonomous civil society, and free media that can together limit the power of the state and its rulers.

8

The People's Court in Transition
The Prospects for Chinese Judicial Reform

Qianfan Zhang

This chapter examines the limits of China's judicial reform in order to illuminate the constraints of Pan Wei's proposal for rule of law in China. Observers generally agree on two aspects about the development of rule of law in China. On the one hand, since its first experiment with "reform and opening" in 1978, China has made a "great leap forward" on the road toward rule of law; on the other hand, China still has a long way to go before it becomes a state truly governed by rule of law. In the span of two decades recovering from the trauma of the Cultural Revolution, the National People's Congress (NPC) and its Standing Committee have made over 160 laws, the State Council has issued some 770 administrative decrees, and the local authorities have made over 5,200 local decrees.[1] The judicial system did not remain stagnant. The courts and the procurators' offices were reorganized in 1979 to better serve the new economic reform. By 1997, the number of persons employed in the various courts and the procurators' offices exceeded 290,000 and 210,000, respectively. In the meantime, the number of lawyers has grown to 100,000, a public registry has been established all over the country, and legal aid centers had begun to emerge in the cities.[2] Both the legislation and legal framework seem to have served their functions to buttress a burgeoning market economy, so far the major driving force of the Chinese reform. In 1999, the constitutional amendments explicitly avow, for the first time in the constitutional history of the People's Republic, to "govern the state according to law" (*yifa zhiguo*) and "establish the socialist state of rule of law." Yet observable marks, including seemingly solid ones like statistical data, can be deceptive and misleading; the quantity of achievements normally fails to relay the quality. In fact, the remarkable Chinese achievements in contributing to the rising expectation for steady progress in rule of law only make the deficiencies all the more conspicuous. Although China can now claim that the laws necessary for sustaining a stable flourishing society are by and large in place, these laws have yet to be obeyed and effectively enforced, hopefully before the common people become so disappointed as to treat them as pure sham. Writing the words on paper is, after all, only the first and comparatively easy step in a hitherto lawless society; making them count in daily life is a much tougher task, but its fulfillment is the very touchstone for rule of law. This task now confronts the Chinese government, particularly its judiciary—the very focus of this chapter, as it is commonly believed that the court is the last place that makes the laws count.[3]

The Chinese courts are loaded with tasks that are difficult to accomplish even from the view of their Western counterparts: they are to strike reasonable balances in civil disputes arising from ever more complex economic relationships; they are to keep in check crimes of all sorts that come with mobilizing a society in which the previous constraints on human behavior are dissolving, while paying due regard to the basic rights of criminal suspects; they are also to contain the operations of the hitherto omnipotent administrative powers within the orbits of law, at the same time ensuring that their own judgments are consistent with the guidance and political imperatives of the Chinese Communist Party (CCP). Is the Chinese judiciary up to the task? Even a cursory examination of the current conditions would point to a dismal answer. Plagued by too many long-standing problems, the Chinese judiciary is clearly not in good shape. The courts face a serious shortage of funding; the judges are poorly paid and professional quality is low compared to their Western counterparts; relying on the local government for finance and appointments, the "people's court" has come close to being the "lieutenant of its local government" for protecting its territorial interests; the trial process is inefficient and has lent itself to biases and the personal influence of litigants; the enforcement of judicial judgments has long suffered from low rates of success, making a significant portion of the legal decisions unfulfilled promises of the state; and judicial corruption has been rising in proportion to economic growth: trading the power of law for personal favors and material benefits has been a promi- nent phenomenon among Chinese judges, and private dealings between judges and lawyers at the expense of the litigants are becoming commonplace.[4] The list could go on. The consensus of the Chinese legal community is that the problems of the Chi- nese judicial system have grown to such a critical extent that it *must* be reformed.

As a result, judicial reform has become a hot topic among Chinese legal scholars as well as judicial officials, all of whom seek to remedy what I call the Chinese "judi- cial syndrome." In October 1999, the Chinese Supreme People's Court (SPC) pub- lished, for the first time in its fifty-year history, a blueprint for legal reform entitled "The Outline of a Five-Year Reform of the People's Court" (hereafter "Outline"). The Outline vowed to improve the existing judicial structure in China, to enhance the power and autonomy of individual judges, and to guarantee judicial efficiency as well as fairness. Judges, whose qualifications are yet to be precisely defined, would be carefully selected from the existing stock of judicial tribunals and lawyers who had established records of good performance, and would become "judges in the real sense."[5] In the meantime, those judicial personnel unable to meet the standard would be put off the post (*xiagang*). Apparently, the institutional reform carried out in ordinary government agencies has also entered the Chinese courts.

The Outline created much hope for the prospect of the badly needed judicial re- form. Now the first five-year experiment has just ended and a second reform plan just surfaced after long delay. Has the first Outline achieved its purposes? Are future re- forms likely to achieve the intended effects in the given political framework? Divided into four parts, this chapter is essentially an analysis of the current judicial problems in China and their proposed solutions. First, it presents a preliminary theoretical model for analyzing a judicial system. Next, it categorizes the problems that constitute the judicial syndrome in China. It then outlines solutions that have been put forward by the author to cure the syndrome. The chapter ends with a brief discussion of the likelihood that these solutions will actually work. Although much of this chapter is limited to the judicial system, it does indicate that the political hurdles encountered in the process of judicial reform suggest that rule of law can hardly coexist with one-party monopoly.

A Preliminary Theoretical Model

Every practical inquiry begins with a normative aim, and the aim for the Chinese judicial reform is very clear: a working judicial system, that is, a system of courts that can decide legal disputes fairly and efficiently. The next step, which is to be dealt with by the rest of this chapter, is about the means: What does it take to build such a system? Here we need to integrate the macro (statistical) and micro (rational choice) models to analyze the judicial behavior. A judge sitting in the court hears a case and decides. To reach a "fair" or "impartial" decision means that the judge decides by properly applying the law to the facts, without being influenced by "irrelevant factors" in the eyes of the law, such as personal opinion or interest. She or he must have the right education and training to acquire the professional ability of understanding and applying the law and relevant facts, and in some way must acquire the moral integrity to steer clear of various interferences. These interferences come from multifarious sources that can potentially find an infinite number of connections with the person sitting on the judicial bench. The most obvious source is the government authority from the other departments or a dominant political party, especially if these entities control some of the goods that the judge regards as personally important. Powerful social groups may also influence the judge's decision; indeed, the fear of bad publicity may deter a judge from deciding in the way that the law dictates. The other common source of interference, especially familiar in China, is the influence of relatives and friends in the broadest sense, who may impose a pervasive pressure upon the judge's daily life. Even a litigant may succeed in influencing the judge's decision simply by bribery. Of course, if the judge's integrity is impregnable before all sorts of pressures, threats, and temptations, then he/she in theory does not need any shield from outside interference; in the real world, however, such a person is hard to find. Although the judge's professional and moral quality is indispensable, institutional guarantees are provided precisely to make judicial independence possible for judges who share both the virtues and weaknesses with common, fallible human beings.

Even though this study is not meant to be quantitative, a more definitive model may help to make clear the mechanism for achieving judicial impartiality. Such a model should, as the foregoing discussion shows, contain the "dependent variable" (labeled as Y_j), which measures judicial fairness, and a number of "independent variables" that affect the judicial functioning. Variables are designated since they are quite numerous. There are two types of independent variables: internal (subjective) and external (objective), both of which are explained below.

Internal Variables

The internal variables refer to the judge's personal quality, including the professional ability (X_{prof}) and moral integrity (X_{mi}) to decide cases in the right way. Variables of a subjective nature are difficult to measure, however, and can be usefully reduced to objective variables if possible. Since the professional ability is acquired through legal education and training, we can decompose X_{prof} into objective variables X_{edu} and X_{train}, which may be expressed in turn by the years and the level of education and training. On the other hand, it is difficult to decompose moral integrity into totally objective variables. The tendency and tenacity to resist judicial corruption are partly encouraged by the four institutional variables explained below, but they do not take into account personal differences. Without a clear understanding of the objective causes for moral integrity or the lack thereof, we cannot properly objectify this variable. So the residual term X_{mi} is kept to indicate the subjective difference. Although it is difficult to measure this term, its presence seems to be necessary to make the model complete.

External Variables

The external variables refer to those environmental factors that would affect judges' decisions. They mainly include (but are not necessarily limited to) the terms of appointment and removal (X_{apr}), the judges' remuneration and working conditions, including funds for judicial operations (generally labeled as X_{wc}), and the judges' personal responsibility for individual case decisions (X_{ind}). High values for the external variables will lead to an independent judiciary, as they indicate that the judges are more entrenched in their positions, that the courts have sufficient financial capacity for independent operation and are less likely to succumb to the administrative power in exchange for funds, and that the judicial decisions are less likely to be replaced or modified by a superior external power. High values for both internal and external variables will lead to a working judicial system in the sense that it can decide cases fairly and efficiently.

Judicial Corruption

Finally, there is the problem of judicial corruption. In a way, it is the opposite of judicial fairness as it occurs when the internal and external variables take low values, but it also serves as a constraint to judicial reform, especially regarding judicial independence. Since no judicial system in the real world can achieve perfect conditions for the independent variables, the tension between judicial independence and corruption is always there. Obviously, judicial corruption will be deterred to some extent by the penal law that punishes such devious behavior, and the effects of deterrence are designated by X_{cor}.

Judicial corruption complicates the way in which the independent variables interact. If the overall level of the judges' moral integrity (X_{mi}) is high, for example, then improving judicial independence $(X_{apr}, X_{wc}, \text{and } X_{ind})$ will truly improve judicial fairness; if the moral integrity level is low, however, improving judicial independence may actually reduce judicial fairness (since the corrupted judiciary would be running without external control), unless various penal laws can effectively keep judicial corruption in check (that is, X_{cor} is high). In this way, moral integrity and penal laws against corruption complement each other. To achieve judicial fairness, mere independence is not enough; rather, judicial independence, moral integrity, and a legal environment that checks judicial corruption interact in a complicated, nonlinear fashion.

To sum up, a fair and just judicial system will result (1) from a highly educated and well-trained body of individual judges distinguished by high moral integrity; (2) from the effectiveness of the penal law in controlling judicial corruption; and (3) from judicial independence as a result of the judicial appointments and dismissals made strictly according to law, a high socioeconomic status and sufficient operational funding as guaranteed by law, and the individual responsibility of the judges for delivering judicial opinions without political, administrative, and social interference. Improvement of a judicial system toward judicial fairness requires improvements in all the independent variables discussed above, and the breakdown of any conditions listed above is likely to result in failures in the judicial system.

Viewed according to this model, what is the current condition of the Chinese judiciary?

The Judicial Syndrome in China

China has been a country of many ironies that continue to perplex a thoughtful outsider. Particularly perplexing is the disparity between words and reality. Historically, China has purported to be a unified state under the control of a centralized government, which in effect admits no limit in its power, yet a closer look reveals a picture of a terribly fragmented governing structure, particularly in the administration of justice. The current regime also purports to be a socialist state in which social justice is supposedly the primary goal, yet its court system, commonly supposed to be the vanguard of justice, has been woefully inadequate for rectifying and deterring any injustices. Although the judicial system bears the name of the "people," whom it is supposed to serve, the problems as outlined here have long prevented the courts from effectively serving the public interest. A Chinese judge is supposed to enjoy many rights, including an independent institutional status,[6] but in practice he/she is far from independent. These problems interact to form what I call the Chinese "judicial syndrome," which includes four related aspects: the low professional quality and entrance requirements for Chinese judges (X_{prof}), the lack of adequate funding from the central government and the reliance on the local government (X_{wc}), which has led to blatant local protectionism (related to X_{apr}), the inefficient structural settings within the courts that emphasize administrative control at the expense of the judicial independence of individual judges (X_{ind}), and the receptivity of the Chinese judiciary to various forms of corruption (X_{mi} and X_{cor}). The present chapter cannot quantitatively measure the relevant judicial variables, but it will present the qualitative conditions of the Chinese judiciary below.

The Professional Quality Problem: The Condition of Chinese Judges

Rule of law means that power is carried out without arbitrary personal influences, but it does not mean to neglect the personal and professional qualities (X_{prof}) of those who occupy the positions of making, interpreting, and executing laws. Indeed, it would be almost a truism to state that the prerequisite for bringing rule of law as a particular social and political ideal to reality is the willingness and ability of the public power holders to submit to such an ideal.[7] Thus, before talking about China's judicial reform, we must have some idea about the people who make up the judicial system. Here we see the first symptom of the Chinese judicial syndrome, a necessary result of the combining influences of the history, the tradition, and the institutions at the personal level.

For most of Chinese history, the judiciary has been a neglected branch of government, subordinate to and often directly overseen by the executive. At the level of local government, the "judge" was the very executive head of the county; whenever his authority was in question, he was the judge of his own cause (subject, of course, to review by his superiors). Such an institutional arrangement, in which the same person executed and judged the law, has been regarded in the West as anathema to liberty and justice since Montesquieu. At the highest level in the central government, the Chinese judiciary, with various names in different dynasties, was maintained as a separate function, and was subordinate to the highest executive officer. In either case, judicial independence was next to nonexistent.

This situation remained unchanged for most of the current regime. The revolution, claimed to be unprecedented in history, did turn many things on their heads, but the shadow of tradition was most conspicuous in the judicial model of the new China. Indeed, it is fair to say that revolution brought retrogression rather than progression to the judicial integrity of the Chinese courts. In the various versions of the People's Republic constitutions, the judiciary has been a separate branch, but it is consistently treated as an ordinary state functionary fulfilling the role of "proletarian dictatorship," in parallel to the other functionaries that are primarily executive in nature, notably the public security bureau and the procurator's office. A directive of the central government in 1950 stated, "The people's judicial work is just like the people's army and the people's police; it is one of the important tools of the people's government."[8] Thus, for a long time, the Chinese judiciary was expected to fulfill the same function as the police and the armies—the "knife's handle" (*daobazi*) of the proletarian dictatorship.[9] It was hardly surprising that, until very recently, a Chinese judge looked quite similar to a policeman or a military officer, wearing an army uniform with starred epaulets. The judicial reform in 1952 further consolidated the party leadership over the judiciary. By 1957, party control came under serious attack within Chinese judicial circles. The result was not the reduction of political control, but the purge of 6,000 "old law personnel" who had constituted the pool of extremely scarce Chinese judicial resources. In the civil division of the Shanghai second middle-level court, for example, eight among twenty judges were declared "rightists."[10] The vacancies were filled by the revolutionary activists, who had rarely acquired legal or, as a matter of fact, any academic training.

Since a "judge" in China is hardly different from an ordinary cadre in the bureaucratic echelon under the party leadership, he is supposed to perform a variety of public functions: he might be executing a court order, in which case he is equivalent to an American sheriff, except that the order is often made by the very judge executing it; he might be gathering evidence on his own initiative for a criminal prosecution, in which case he is acting as a civil law magistrate; he might be actively engaging in settlements of civil disputes or administrative compensations, where he plays the role of an arbitrator; he might even be traveling in the countryside during an episode of "popularizing legal education," explaining to peasants the party policy in a particular legal area and earnestly seeking cases for summary judgment. Thus, sitting in court, hearing cases, and delivering legal decisions comprise only one of the many roles—and perhaps not even an important role—a Chinese judge is supposed to play.

So who are the "judges" in China? This question implies two related questions: First, how is the judge (or the judicial function) defined? Second, who may become a judge in China? A judge in the West holds a specialized and privileged position requiring special knowledge and qualifications for deciding a legal dispute. In comparison, a Chinese judge has a much broader definition. Someone who decides cases is of course called a judge, but so are those who merely execute the court orders or manage internal court affairs. The trial function is commonly exercised by the "trial chief" and "trial members" under the guidance of the presidents of the entire court and its particular divisions. The latter's function is to assure that every legal judgment is politically "correct" and socially acceptable. A Chinese "chief judge" (that is, the head of the court) may never try a single case by himself, yet he is still respectfully called a judge. In fact, anyone who works in a court and deals with some paperwork might be referred to as a judge. As a result, China has a large body of "judges" (over 290,000, a number that greatly exceeds the number of lawyers—indeed a peculiar Chinese phenomenon),[11] but only a portion of them really *judges* any cases.

Consistent with the broad definition, the entry qualifications (say, X_{edu}) for becoming a judge are abnormally low. It used to be the case that almost anyone could get into a court and become a "judge." The current judicial body is the result of rapid expansion after 1979, in response to the need for regulating the rising social conflicts during the economic reform. The judicial personnel were largely "borrowed" from social and political organizations previously having little to do with works of a judicial nature. A significant portion of the judges was made up of army veterans who were assigned political and legal work at the time of retirement from the service, without any prior legal training. Some of them have become the court presidents or the division chiefs—the real power holders controlling the judicial decision making. The appointments were made by the party leaders mainly according to their political loyalty rather than professional qualification, and anyone deemed suitable to work in the "party and political institutions" is thought to fit judicial work as well. Likewise, factory workers and high school graduates can be assigned to the court and become "judges." Court secretaries can also become judges within a few years after they are promoted to "assistant judge," without having to go through formal academic training and extensive legal practice. Many appointments of court personnel are still made on the basis of personal friendship or family kinship; if the direct appointment of one's own relative seems too obviously inadequate, then two friendly courts can exchange their desired appointees.

Measured against the professional yardstick, then, the quality of the large Chinese judiciary is low. According to a recent survey, only 5 percent of the judges nationwide have earned undergraduate degrees, and only twenty-five among a thousand judges have earned graduate degrees.[12] It was reported that in Beijing, where the education level of the judges is among the highest in the nation, 75 percent of its 45,000 judges have obtained degrees from "specialized colleges," but 60 percent of these degrees were issued from televised education and nonprofessional colleges; among the small 10 percent of the judges who have obtained undergraduate degrees, it was unclear what percentage of them were formally educated in law.[13] Nor is the Chinese court an attractive place for people with integrity. Few graduates from the schools specialized in law and politics are willing to work in the courts or the procurator's office: between 1984 and 1998, the judicial organizations absorbed only 20 percent of the almost 2,000 graduates from these colleges; for the graduates holding advanced degrees, the court is simply *not* the place to be.[14] And recent attempts by the SPC at open recruitment have failed to attract lawyers and legal scholars to this supposedly highest echelon of legal practice.[15]

Although definitions alone seldom make a substantive difference, the general nature of Chinese judges does have practical consequences. For one thing, it is difficult to formally distinguish between the judges who exercise different functions and to treat them differently in terms of status and salaries. Given the limited financial resources available, and the necessity of dividing them among a large number of "judges," the average per capita remuneration of judges is necessarily low. Large numbers in the profession, low remuneration, and low professional quality have created a stable equilibrium in Chinese judicial circles. The first step toward a more effective judicial system should be to break the vicious cycle by reducing the scope (and thus the number) of Chinese judges and improving the social and economic status of this more select group. The key to the success of judicial reform will be to make the courts a more attractive place for young talent. As an editor points out sharply, a good institution is perhaps the necessary condition for judicial reform, but it is certainly not sufficient; indeed, before institutional reforms can take effect, the personal quality problem must be resolved.[16] As this chapter seeks to show, problems at the personal and institutional levels are inextricably linked to each other, and neither can be resolved without the simultaneous resolution of the other.

Three Related Problems: Money, Institutional Dependence, and Local Protectionism

It is not hard to imagine from the above that, in general, the Chinese courts are relatively poor, partly reflected in low X_{wc}. Not only are judges poorly rewarded, but the working conditions in many courts are truly primitive. In some remote areas, the court can hardly maintain an outer image dignified enough to be called a "court." The presidents of the courts have been nicknamed "Mr. Public Relations," or, more scathingly, "beggars carrying the scales [of justice]."[17] The funding problem is exacerbated from the perspective of the functions that Chinese judges are expected to perform. Following the continental model, a Chinese judge is supposed to undertake an independent investigation, often in areas outside his jurisdiction, if he finds the available evidence insufficient to reach a justified decision. Maintaining this type of inquisitive court is naturally more expensive than the American or British courts, where judges strike the evidential balances without having to leave the courtroom. In China, however, the limited funds allocated for the judiciary often prevent the judges from fulfilling their official functions, and force them to get the job done by using mechanisms that are both legally and morally dubious, thus contributing in significant part to judicial corruption (more below). It is common for Chinese courts to solicit various types of financial endorsements not defined by law and for judges to commingle with the litigants on their field trips, during which the litigants pay for the judges' personal expenses. The scarcity of judicial funds has also made a substantial proportion of court decisions essentially empty pronouncements, since Chinese courts are responsible for enforcing their own orders, some of which involve other jurisdictions and imply the incurring of additional expenses that the courts cannot afford. By the end of 1997, there were over 2 million court decisions awaiting enforcement. The lack of judicial resources has seriously threatened judicial independence, undermined the effectiveness of the law, and cast doubts on the quality of justice.

A more direct threat to judicial independence is the way in which judicial funds are distributed. Ironically, the People's Republic purports to be a unified central state, but at least in one important respect it is terribly fragmented, and the situation is made even worse by the ongoing economic reform. Following national implementation of the financial self-responsibility (*chengbao*) system in the rural areas, the scheme of "eating from separate stoves" (*fenzao chifan*) has also been promulgated among the over 3,000 Chinese courts. Until very recently all local courts, from the lowest "basic-level courts" in counties and city districts to the high courts located in the provincial capitals, were financially dependent on their local bosses, the parallel local governments. The judges' salaries and the funds for court operations came mostly from the local government budgets and were subject to the threat of reduction whenever the court decisions adversely affected the local interest. Just like the case of American school taxes, where leaving the public school finances entirely up to the local property tax created significant regional inequality, leaving court finance to local governments has also created regional disparity among judges of the same rank as far as salary, working conditions, housing and welfare, and funds for carrying out judicial investigations. In particular, courts in the poor areas are obliged to seek income and funding through a variety of means, which can seriously compromise their independent status. Thus, although devolution of power to the local level did bring vitality to economic reform, in judicial administration it seems to have created more serious problems than it has solved.

More directly, the local people's congress (LPC) and government control the selection and promotion of the court personnel (low X_{apr}). According to Article 11 of the Judges Law, the presidents of the various levels of local courts are elected and dismissed by the LPC at the same level, and the vice presidents, presidents of the divisions, and ordinary judges are appointed and dismissed by the corresponding standing committee of the LPC upon recommendation of the court president. It seems that these provisions will stay valid for an indefinite period of time despite judicial reform, as they highlight the "Chinese character" of the political structure centered (theoretically) on the people's congresses. As a result, a judge failing to carry out instructions of the local leaders can be reprimanded or even removed. The local congress may even summon the leaders of a court to discuss specific cases together with the litigants and hand down the decision, for which the court is to be held responsible. In Anyue county of Sichuan Province, for example, the standing committee of the LPC "sat together" with the vice president of the court, the chief of the division, and the local defendant to figure out how to "draft the judicial decision."[18] An LPC might not always be able to assert its own independence against the party or the executive departments of the government, but it can be quite effective in interfering with the judicial process.

Therefore, unable to shield judges from material pressures exerted by the local government, China's current institutional arrangement has failed to protect the most basic aspects of judicial independence. The problem is most obvious in administrative litigations, where the defendants are administrative agencies that are likely to be holding pieces of the judicial pork; an unfriendly decision may very well trigger the denial of salary raise and funding, housing and welfare, means of transportation, and other personal or institutional benefits. Partly for this reason the administrative cases are few on the whole (only 1.5 percent of the total number of cases in 1996, a small amount compared to the civil and economic cases), and the rate of "voluntary withdrawal" has been consistently high. A controlled judiciary can hardly be expected to be independent and act impartially in the interest of the law. Indeed, the supposedly unified judicial system in China has become the "court of local governments" in the sense that courts are naturally inclined to act on behalf of local interests at the expense of the uniform application of law. It is not uncommon that, in a dispute involving litigants of different localities, the judge should distort the obvious interpretation of the law or ignore the preponderant evidence in order to decide in favor of the litigant in her own jurisdiction. The following case, which has aroused national attention, is but a typical illustration of such a phenomenon.

In Beihai of Guangdong Province, a woman fell from her motorcycle at a sharp left turn and was found bleeding and unconscious on the ground. Liu Qiuhai, a representative of the LPC in a neighboring city, happened to pass by and see the scene. Liu, the driver of his van, and a few pedestrians helped to carry the injured woman to a local hospital, where she received treatment until she recovered. Liu left before her recovery without asking for reward, but he was surprised to find an array of penalties waiting for him. A month later, when he passed by the same spot with the same van, he was stopped by a traffic policeman and a friend of the woman's brother-in-law who informed him that he had been charged with committing a hit-and-run and confiscated his vehicle. The police action apparently violated the administrative procedure. But when Liu and his driver initiated administrative litigation in the city court against the police action, the charge was summarily dismissed and the legality of the police action upheld. Liu and the driver of the van were then sued by the self-claimed "victim" in Beihai for criminal and civil liabilities. In a curious opinion, the district court dismissed the charge against the individual parties, but found the driver's employer liable for the plaintiff's losses. When an outspoken Guangzhou-based newspaper, *Southern Weekend News* (*Nanfang zhoumo*), reported the event, it was sued for libel by four parties: the injured woman and her brother-in-law involved in the event, the policeman, and the transportation police branch of the city public security bureau, all seeking enormous sums of damages because the report allegedly harmed their reputation. The city court found the press liable for all charges. The decision was sharply contested by many legal scholars and practitioners, and the case has been appealed to the higher courts. While the final decision is pending, the Beihai example makes it obvious that the local courts cannot be trusted to administer impartial justice whenever "outsiders" are involved.

The Structural Problems of the Courts: Lack of Personal Independence and Responsibility

As already discussed, the Chinese court used to be viewed as an organization akin to other administrative organizations; the "judicial system," including the courts and the procurator's offices, was seen as a part of the "party and political organs," similar to a party committee or a local executive office. And so was the style of its administration, indicating a low X_{ind}. Once a case was opened in the court, it would be circulated among half a dozen internal sections, each giving a summary decision (which has to be *summary* since each section is to go through all cases). Partly owing to the low professional quality of the judges and the need to reduce judicial errors, the final decision was not made by individual judges, but by a "trial committee." The hearing judges would report the facts of the case and their tentative decision to this committee to get its approval. And to guarantee "political correctness," the decision of the committee also had to be approved by the head of the division and then the president of the court. A common decision would be discussed by people at many different levels: a panel of judges who actually tried the case, the trial committee (which usually did *not* try the case), the committee of the division to which the case belonged, and the administrative heads of the court, who had (and still have) the power to remand the case to the trial committee if they disagreed with the conclusion. The majority of the decision makers involved in this formidable process neither saw the litigants nor heard their arguments, and had at best an indirect knowledge of the facts. Hence the "separation of trial and decision," in the sense that those who tried the case could not decide it; the real decision maker did not try the case. Such a procedure has not only reduced judicial efficiency and resources, but has also made it more likely that the litigants can succeed in affecting the judicial decision somewhere in the chain process through the "back door"—via their personal relationships with someone inside the court.

Of course, the most pernicious effect of this style of judicial administration is that it removes personal responsibility from the judges. A judge became little more than a bureaucratic clerk whose decision depends on layers of approval within the power pyramid in order to take legal effect. And a dependent judge is surely an irresponsible judge. It has been common for an ordinary Chinese judge to avoid sensitive problems and refer them instead to the "leaders"—the heads of the court and its particular divisions, who are in a sense "the judge of the judges"[19]—or if the latter cannot decide, to the higher courts. As is commonly said, "whoever has a higher authority, that's whose words count." The result is that the judge—if she can still be called as such—is obliged by self-interest to obey rank and status rather than the voice of reason and law; otherwise she merely puts her career at risk and must be prepared to suffer the penalties for disobedience. Conversely, the pre-reform would enable a shrewd judge to use the trial committee as a shield for his own invidious judgments; through misleading and biased reporting of facts (which are rarely, if ever, published), he could successfully foist a biased decision upon the committee as the formal decision maker, and stay away from any culpability. Last but not least, although the LPC appoints and removes the judges, the head of the court has the power, pursuant to Article 11 of the Judges Law, to appoint and remove assistant judges, who actually perform the judge's functions.[20] Owing a favor to the head, these people are usually the "president's men" who tend to pay more heed to the order of their patron than the command of the law.

Judicial Corruption: Constraints to Judicial Reform

It has been easy to blame the Chinese judiciary for its lack of independence. Yet judicial independence presupposes a minimum degree of professional and moral integrity on the part of the judiciary itself, for independence necessarily implies abolition of some forms of external control that might otherwise be used to deter the self-seeking behavior. To be sure, despite the institutional handicaps, China does not lack upright and competent judges. But worldwide experience suggests that, although a society may tolerate occasional corruption in an ordinary bureaucracy, the standard for probity is especially high for the judicial office. The long-standing neglect of the need for this special requirement has left the Chinese judiciary as a whole far below the world standard. As many have sensibly argued, the Chinese courts seem to be corrupt enough even when they are supposedly under close scrutiny; further independence could only make things worse. Can Chinese society afford an independent judiciary and trust it to run by itself?

This brings us back to the initial problem: every operating institution implies the prerequisite that the people making up this institution respect and follow the basic "rules of the game" that the institution openly purports to uphold. Pursuit of individual self-interest in violation of these basic norms undermines institutional effectiveness, and is commonly called corruption if the institution to which the power holder belongs happens to be a public office. Ever since the market reform inaugurated in 1978, the corruption of public officials rose sharply in both variety and quantity. Unfortunately, the Chinese judiciary is no exception. Reports of judicial corruption, which may appear stunning by Western standards, have become commonplace in China; partiality and exchange of favors between the judges and litigants have seriously undermined the fairness of judicial outcomes that is central to the legitimacy of any judicial system. Judicial corruption takes a variety of forms, in which the judge(s) enter illicit relationships with the interested party for mutual benefit. Bribery is the most common, taking the form of an exchange of court favor and material benefits, most frequently money and sex. Benefits can also be intangible, to be paid off by a long-term relationship with the beneficiary of an unduly favorable decision, usually a powerful figure in the government or party organ directly or indirectly involved in the case. Sometimes a corruption case might begin with plain judicial errors, and develop as the courts and other government departments collude in a grand concealment project. Even in Jiangsu Province, where the judicial system is relatively clean and the quality of judges regarded as high compared to an average inland province, sixty judges were punished for engaging in various forms of unlawful activities.[21] Between 1993 and 1997, a total of 376 judges and 370 procurators were found to have committed crimes.[22] And these do not include the major infringements yet to be uncovered and countless minor ones that few would bother to take seriously. The Judges Law, for example, explicitly prohibits judges from "privately meeting the litigants and their representatives, or accepting their invitations and gifts" (Article 30). Owing to the lack of institutional guarantees, however, it has been common for the judges to commingle with the litigants and for the litigants to seek to establish or improve a personal relationship with the deciding judges of their cases. Indeed, corruption has become so pervasive among the Chinese judiciary that anyone can hardly stay "clean" in judicial circles. Compared to courts worldwide, it is no exaggeration to say that Chinese courts are among the most corrupt. This harsh fact places Chinese judicial reform in an uncomfortable dilemma as it constantly triggers debate as to how much autonomy should be given to the Chinese judiciary.

To summarize, the Chinese judicial syndrome has been the combination of personal and institutional problems that have reinforced each other into a stable equilibrium. On the institutional level, Chinese judges, too many in number, are poorly paid and lack proper funding to carry out the judicial functions (X_{wc}); the local controls of judicial finance and appointments have made the Chinese courts overly responsive to the local demands (X_{apr} and X_{wc}) at the expense of their judicial independence and the national uniformity of law; the administrative control model of the internal court structure further depresses the independent spirit of Chinese judges (X_{ind}), making them reliant on administrative leaders in judicial judgments. These poor institutional arrangements have made the Chinese court an unattractive place for judicial elites. Thus, it is not hard to understand seemingly contradictory demands: on the one hand, the body of Chinese judicial personnel has grown to such a large size that it has absorbed a significant portion of resources and constituted a serious burden for society; on the other hand, China is acutely short of talent specialized in law. Many who acquired the title of judge lack the ability to really try and decide cases; and even among the competent judges, those graduating from extension programs of various sorts greatly exceed the formal graduates in law (low X_{edu}). The overall low quality of judges and their poor working conditions have jointly made the Chinese court an easily corruptible place (low X_{mi}), imposing further constraints on judicial reform and reinforcing the stability of the existing system.

Is it still possible, then, to resolve the Chinese judicial syndrome? The Chinese legal community answers affirmatively with an ambitious blueprint for fundamental reform.

Reforming the Judiciary Within the Existing Political Framework

"The Outline of a Five-Year Reform of the People's Court" came into being as a result of academic discussions, criticisms, and reform experiments that have lasted for the last several years. Consistent with the analysis above, the Outline recognizes that judicial independence and impartiality in China have been impeded by four types of problems: (1) local protectionism that has seriously undermined the uniformity of law; (2) the overall low professional and moral quality of Chinese judges, which makes them prone to corruption and unfit for impartial administration of justice; (3) the bureaucratic management model at odds with judicial independence and efficiency; and (4) the lack of material provisions (e.g., funding and working conditions) necessary for the effective functioning of the courts, especially of the basic-level courts. To cure the judicial syndrome, the Chinese government has come up with a systematic plan. Aiming to resolve these problems, the Outline sought to achieve the following reform measures in the span of five years between 1999 and 2003. The program will be summarized below as a response to the four types of problems outlined above.

Curing the Professional Quality Problem

The professional quality of judges is probably the most extensively discussed problem in China. Here, the Outline has focused mainly on improving the quality of the existing judges, without extensively modifying the academic requirements (X_{edu}) for existing and new judges as already provided by the Judges Law. To improve judicial quality, the SPC is going to offer comprehensive legal training in the next three years to the presidents and divisional chiefs of courts above the middle level, and the provincial high courts are to offer similar training to the basic-level courts within their jurisdictions. In a teleconference, Xiao Yang, the president of the SPC, vowed to establish a modern court system according to the Outline and the Judges Law. In July 2000, the SPC published a tentative method for selecting chief trial judges. The new selection method was intended to reduce the number of judges qualified to sit on the bench and actually try cases. Over half of the basic-level courts were to implement the judge selection system in the year 2000, and the task was supposed to finish nationwide by the end of 2001. In some experimental areas, the judges would then be fixed in ranks (*dingbian*) and provided with judicial assistants.[23]

The reform also called for improvement of the rules for selecting future judges and court clerks, so as to accomplish an "elitist transition" of the judicial team. According to the Outline, every court would establish a limited number of posts for judges, whose performances would be evaluated periodically by a special committee; supposedly, only those who scored high enough would be given the positions. Articles 16 and 17 of the Judges Law state that Chinese judges are to be divided into twelve levels, and a judge's level is to be determined according to "his/her occupation, virtues and talents, the level of professional fitness, the performance of trial work and the years of service." According to Articles 46 and 47 of the Judges Law, the judges' performance is to be assessed by an Examination and Evaluation Committee composed of the president of the court and several judges. These provisions are meant to introduce a merit-based system providing rewards for competent judges, but in practice they have been reduced to a mechanism of internal balance of interests, and amount to little more than bonuses for administrative positions and seniority. The administrative features of the Chinese courts are reinforced by differentiating the judges' levels and status. The Outline by and large leaves the bureaucratic structure of the court untouched, and adds more selection criteria and tests. As discussed later, such a scheme may actually exacerbate rather than ameliorate judicial reliance on the administrative leaders and further complicate the personal relationships among the judges.

The reform also aims to improve the low quality of reasoning in current judicial opinions. So far Chinese judicial decisions have been notoriously brief on legal reasoning, and in many opinions the "reasoning" part is really a pretext for predetermined conclusions. Following a fixed format, most written decisions used to fit within a single page, and their cryptic written style helped to hide personal bias. The situation is made worse by the fact that in China the judicial decision of a particular case is normally available only to relevant parties, not to society at large. Thus, it is essentially a "private opinion" without public supervision. To rectify this deficiency in criminal trials, the SPC drafted in 1999 the "Model Format for Judicial Opinions in Criminal Trials," and laid emphasis on legal reasoning in all types of judicial decisions. Consistent with the national reform in judicial opinions as a part of judicial reform, several provincial high courts have organized competitions that award high-quality opinions. Judicial decisions will also be gradually made open to the public. From the middle of June 2000, the SPC began to selectively publish judicial opinions of "especially important and typical" cases in the *SPC Gazette,* the *People's Court Daily,* and even on the Internet. The publication is currently limited to the legal opinions of the SPC, and it is uncertain when the lower courts' opinions will also be made open to the general public.

The Outline leaves untouched, however, the low educational level of the existing judges. The Judges Law, promulgated in 1995, aimed to solve this problem, but it has achieved very limited success in this area. Article 9 in Chapter 4 (The Judges' Conditions) requires that a judge must "graduate from a high-level college specialized in law" and have worked for two years, but it also allows those who graduated from colleges not specialized in law, yet nevertheless possessing "specialized legal knowledge," to become judges. Without a clear definition, the term "specialized legal knowledge" leaves a loophole in judicial recruitments. It was thought that the first assessment of judicial levels should be carried out according to personal ability and educational background. In practice, however, neither matters more than administrative rank and the length of tenure. According to a recent report, the Judges Law is about to be revised, yet the proposed revisions fail to clarify the vague terms. It is doubtful that the revisions can effectively improve China's practices in selecting its judges and deciding their status. Still, some progress has been made in certain areas. For example, the high court of Jiangsu Province will no longer recruit judges without a graduate degree, and the basic-level courts will abolish the past practice of recruiting graduates of middle-level specialized schools except as speed typists.

Curtailing Local Protectionism

Local protectionism has led to the strongest outcry against the existing judicial system, and the Chinese government has long grappled with this problem in vain. To be sure, sinister as it is, local protectionism is present to a degree in any sizable political unit. The state courts in the United States are known for their local biases. The problem is effectively solved by the federal system, especially the mechanism of diversity jurisdiction provided by the Constitution of the United States. Traditionally China was a centralized state, but in judicial administration, it appears to be insufficiently centralized, and local protectionism has been rampant owing partly to China's vast geographical span and great disparity in economic development, and partly to the unreasonable financial structure of the judicial institution. Ironically, while decentralization and devolution carry the day for the general reform of the Chinese economic, political, and social structure, recentralization seems to be an indispensable remedy for judicial reform. An obvious approach is to break the current horizontal structure (*kuai,* or block) and establish a vertical structure (*tiao,* or slat), which would enable the central government to directly finance the local courts, thus removing the local pressures over the latter. In 1999, some of the city courts reportedly no longer lived on the "mixed food" (*zaliang*) supplied mainly by their local governments and began to receive the "imperial supply" (*huangliang*) flowing directly from the central treasury.[24] In the meantime, the leadership of the lower courts will be frequently switched to other locations to reduce the establishment of personal ties with the local governments. It remains to be seen whether these mechanisms effectively reduce local protectionism in judicial behavior.

A major aspect of local protectionism is evident in the "enforcement difficulty." This problem has a broader scope than local protectionism (even a native resident may find it hard to enforce an unfavorable judgment, say, against an official in the same jurisdiction), but it is particularly difficult for a court to enforce its judgment in another jurisdiction (especially in another province). Judicial enforcement received heightened attention in 1999, "the year of enforcement." Recently, the SPC fashioned an institutional mechanism that establishes a special "enforcement bureau" in each provincial high court. The mechanism is expected to not only streamline the overall enforcement process within a jurisdiction, but also reduce local protectionism in enforcing a favorable judgment obtained by a party outside the jurisdiction. Instead of having the deciding court to directly enforce its judgment in another province, the task will be delegated to the enforcement bureau of the latter province. The mechanism, which has now been promulgated in a dozen provinces, will hopefully enhance the efficiency and reduce the cost in the enforcement process.

Improving the Internal Structure and Processes

The reform of the internal court structure is probably the most ambitious and potentially most far-reaching program that the SPC has ever launched in its history. The Outline explicitly aims to accomplish several goals. First, the reform is to modernize the trial process through the "three separations" (*not* the separation of three powers!), that is, the separation between the filing and the trial of the case, the separation between the trial and the enforcement of the court order, and the separation between the trial and supervision of the judicial decision. The goal of the three separations is to make sure that the trial process follows cases, not judges, in order to thus prevent the litigants from consulting the judges' opinions on the cases and to eliminate the "three together" during the investigation (in which judges and litigants travel, eat, and lodge together).[25] This mechanism might have some limited impact on checking judicial corruption. Second, to improve the efficiency of trial processes, the courts will limit the amount of lag between the filing and hearing of cases, and adopt streamlined management to track the cases. The reform is also to touch the rule of evidence, especially the guarantee of the rights and duties of the key witnesses and their due appearance in court. To improve the quality of judicial opinions, the SPC is to publish "typical cases" as "references" (*cankao*) for the lower courts in judicial decision making, though the binding nature of these "references" remains dubious.

Third and most significant, the Outline seeks to enhance the personal independence of judges (not simply of the court as an institution) in limited ways. Judicial reform is to modify the internal court structure by establishing rules for selecting judges that will either try the cases alone or lead the panels of judges. The panels or individual judges are to make the final decisions, which cannot be changed by the administrative leaders of the court, except in those "important and difficult cases, which the panel may petition the president of the court to refer to the trial committee for discussion and decision" ("Outline," Para. 20). In this way the Outline preserves the trial committee system, though limiting its role to "studying the problems with fundamental and systematic impact on the trial work and providing authoritative guidance" (Para. 22).

A prominent problem with the Chinese judicial structure has been the heavy administrative control of the courts, as reflected in the high proportion of administrative personnel. Recently, the administrative proportion has been reduced in the SPC, and the percentage of judicial personnel rose from 59 to 72 percent.[26] The same structural reform was to be carried out in the lower courts and completed at the end of 2001, aiming to reduce total court personnel by 10 percent nationwide.

Curbing Judicial Corruption?

Like local protectionism, judicial corruption has been much talked about in China, but effective solutions remain elusive. Judicial corruption may be curbed by a number of mechanisms. The existing system, in which the committees of judges monitor themselves, will be gradually transformed into a new system containing single judges or panels of judges. In the reformed system the role of individual judges will be enhanced, and the monitoring function of the old system will thus be curtailed. The traditional remedy, which has deep historical roots in Chinese history, is to use China's "fourth branch"—the People's Procurator—to challenge suspicious judicial decisions at the higher courts. Although this mechanism raises questions about the relationship between the procurator and the court, and is likely to impinge on judicial independence and the finality of legal decisions, it will continue to be employed as a mechanism of judicial checks and balances. It has also been proposed that the LPCs or their standing committees should have the power to engage in supervision of individual cases, by which the representatives can supposedly correct the errors in specific judicial judgments.[27] In some cities (e.g., Dalian in Liaoning Province), the LPCs actually review the performance of individual judges and vote on their qualification. Finally, just like judges in the West, Chinese judges are also restrained to a degree by the party's disciplinary measures (mainly through the Jilü Jiancha Weiyuanhui) and social pressure in general, particularly through the mass media. Although the latter mechanism is informal and its effect depends on the willingness and ability of Chinese journalists to ferret out the dirty details, it can become quite effective if freedom of expression is reasonably guaranteed.

The mechanism of judicial supervision is a hotly contested topic among different views because it impinges on the heart of judicial independence. According to the conservative view, Chinese judges must be watched closely in order to reduce the chance for corruption. Tight supervision by other organs is expected to help prevent an unreliable judiciary from plainly disregarding the law. On the other hand, the liberal voice tends to undermine the extent of troubles that judicial liberalization might cause and is determined to break the vicious cycle of low judicial quality and extensive administrative control. Liberals also point out the problems inherent in the conservative solution. A particularly controversial issue is the power of the NPC to supervise judicial decisions upon appeal or complaint, since it directly undermines the separation of the legislative and judicial functions. In terms of legal knowledge and experience, the representatives are below the average level of the judges, and they are usually not familiar with the facts of the cases. It has occurred in the past that the interested parties have taken advantage of the representatives' lack of knowledge to foster local protectionism by goading them to pass a bill of supervision for relevant cases. Thus it does not seem to be suitable for the NPC to directly exercise the judicial function and decide cases for the courts. Largely owing to the liberal opposition, the bill for legislative supervision failed to pass the NPC to become law, yet a few provinces implemented various versions of a legislative supervisory mechanism.

In this respect, the Outline remains ambiguous as to the specific mechanism for correcting judicial wrongdoings. It calls for establishing both internal and external mechanisms of checks and balances; enforcing the authority of the supervision of the high courts over the lower courts and discipline for illegal judicial behavior; preventing collusion among the judges, the litigants, and their legal representatives, and; enabling supervision of the representatives of the people's congresses and the procurators over judicial behavior, without spelling out the details. Perhaps the most concrete plan is to establish a personal responsibility system for erroneous decisions, largely to be implemented within the Chinese judicial system—the courts and procurators. Beijing, for example, has promulgated a tough guideline, the violation of which may result in revoking the qualifications of an offending judge. Judges can also be held personally liable for damage done to the victims of their wrongful judgments in litigation. Yet, in practice, it might be difficult to distinguish intentional or reckless judicial errors from those ordinary mistakes of facts or law, which any human court can make and thus should not, in the interest of judicial independence, be imputed to the individual judges. The performance review mechanism might work well for other departments of the government, but not necessarily for the judiciary; it could indeed be used for curbing judicial corruption, but it might also be used by the administrative power to suppress those upright and competent judges who are bold enough to ignore personal will or the political order of a superior.

Now, given the blueprint for Chinese judicial reform, how likely is it to succeed?

The Unresolved Problems: Tensions and Constraints

Ongoing Achievements and Precautions

Since the SPC set the pace of reform in the Outline, the courts nationwide are reported to have responded positively. A change that has touched almost every court is
the selection and testing of the judges; every candidate is to pass a series of selective
processes, including self-introduction, qualification review, campaign speech, peer
review, and written examinations, in order to demonstrate his political, moral, and
professional fitness for the judicial position. Some of the courts have also begun to
reform their technical procedures: the filing of cases is made easier and is no longer
dependent on personal relationships with court personnel, "sunshine projects" are
initiated to make the trial process more transparent, and the judicial appraisal of
crucial facts is no longer an opaque process that provides occasion for judicial partiality and corruption. The presidents of the courts and the divisions, previously
mainly responsible for internal administration, have begun to sit in the courtrooms,
hearing and deciding cases as full-time judges do. In certain areas, the courts have
begun to depart from the established control model in which an effective judicial
decision requires many levels of administrative approval. Now a single judge or a
panel of judges reportedly has the authority to pronounce the final judgment. With
the exception of so-called "important, difficult, and complicated" cases, a judicial
opinion no longer needs approval of the presidents of the court and the relevant
division—a measure, if faithfully carried out, that would significantly enhance the
judge's personal independence. Finally, the courts in various areas have also moved
to rectify the rampant judicial corruption. In Sichuan Province, for example, the
courts are to spend two years to clean up those judicial personnel who have caused
strong discontent by their "distortion of law for pursuing private interest, embezzlement and reception of bribery, and rude working style." The Sichuan courts will also
implement mandatory uniform judicial examinations and dismiss those who fail to
pass them. In Tianjin municipality, about a quarter of the judges in the basic-level
courts failed to pass the judicial tests and were removed from the responsibility of
adjudicating legal cases.

This is good news, but these situations need to be taken with a grain of salt. At least
since the Great Leap Forward in the late 1950s, which struck the high pitch of the
"wind of flamboyance and exaggeration," China has been beset by one campaign
after another initiated from the top for a variety of purposes. Impractical goals meet
with exaggerated reports that make everyone happy, only to leave the real issues
unresolved. It is disturbing to see that the same spirit is making its way into the current judicial reform, from the top to the root level. As an example, the president of the
SPC claimed recently that China was planning to significantly improve overall judicial quality and to effectively cut judicial corruption within a mere two years. This is
an astonishingly short time for solving a historical problem with which the Chinese
have long been grappling in vain. It is difficult to think of any expedient measure that

can so quickly remove this long-standing impediment to judicial reform. In one favorable report about the effects of judicial reform, the litigants of a case wanted to invite the judges to dinner, but failed to do so because they could not find out the identity of the specific person in charge of trying the case.[28] Hiding the names of judges may fool an inept party or his attorney, but it would be simply futile to attempt to reduce judicial bias and corruption by this type of "cheap shot." The general human tendency is to find quick and easy fixes, but they rarely solve hard and real problems like judicial corruption. As one expert points out, at least in criminal litigations, judicial reform of the trial process has already turned out to be a failure.[29] The lesson seems to be worth learning for the greater project of judicial reform as a whole. To genuinely reduce judicial bias and the "personal relationship cases," Chinese judges and society in general must cultivate a legal culture and an instinct for rule of law that discourage ex parte contacts between judges and litigants. Of course, this will take much more effort and a much longer time to achieve.

The academic community also shares part of the responsibility for providing shoddy recommendations. Recently, some Chinese scholars proposed that announcements of judicial decisions should take place in court, right before the litigants at the end of arguments, as an effective means of both curbing judicial corruption (since it reduces the chance that the litigants can influence the judges' decisions by bribery and personal relationships behind the scenes) and improving trial efficiency (since it saves time for deliberation). The press reports were quick to applaud the clean dockets of some courts by the end of each year. Of course, the judicial efficiency of the Chinese courts needs to be greatly enhanced, but that does not simply mean an increase in the number of cases that a judge tries per day. Chinese scholars were quick to learn the English idiom "justice delayed is justice denied," but they seem to have forgotten that mistaken justice is no justice either! The emphasis on the speed of judicial decisions is itself dangerous since it could seriously undermine the quality of the decisions, which is by no means high as it currently stands. It is well recognized in the West that equity and speedy justice have always been self-contradictory, but China has yet to overcome the "hopeless worldly optimism" that Max Weber associates with the Chinese culture, which has in the recent decades created human tragedies of great scale. Although parts of the current Chinese judicial process might be cut short without undermining equity, the emphasis on numbers at best misunderstands the Western system and at worst could lead the ongoing reform astray. Scholarly articles often cite how many cases an average American judge decides every year, but fail to note that the numbers are greatly inflated by an overwhelming amount of small-claims cases such as parking violations and rent payment disputes, and that the Chinese counterparts can easily "get the numbers right" once similar courts are established there (and indeed, a few such courts are being set up in major cities like Beijing). But that would simply miss the key aspect of judicial reform.

Despite the apparent successes, then, a neutral prognosis is still indicated for Chinese judicial reform.

Success or Failure? A Tentative Prognosis

Chinese judicial reform contains many components that are likely to meet with different degrees of success. Although almost all areas of judicial reform are expected to encounter difficulties of various kinds, some reform measures are more easily implemented than others. Here I distinguish three types of measures, designated by the variables discussed in Part I; the measures taken by Chinese judicial reform may fall into any one of the categories or a combination of them. The first category is the *material* variables, referring to physical conditions, such as X_{wc}. Material variables are perhaps the easiest to improve if it is technically feasible, since this is unlikely to offend, and thus invite opposition from, any particular block of power holders. They will be improved immediately as long as the government is able and willing to do so. The second category is the *personal* variables, referring to relatively pure personal quality of the judiciary, for example, those as measured by X_{edu} and X_{train}. This respect of judicial reform is likely to illicit social consensus, but improving the variables could be difficult owing to their nature. The third and most important category encompasses the *institutional* and *cultural* variables. For our purposes they include the most significant group of variables identified in this paper, such as X_{ind} and X_{apr}. They are also the most difficult to change because the improvement is likely to be resisted by some dominant political forces, which perceive change in the current institutional setting as adversely affecting their interests. Of course, these categories are by no means clear cut, but rather interact with each other (for example, one way to improve the professional quality of the judiciary is to make the court institutionally attractive to college graduates trained in law). And a few variables may defy single classification: X_{mi} and X_{cor}, for example, are as much personal as institutional or cultural. Nevertheless, the simple characterization offered here will still be helpful to the analysis of different aspects of judicial reform.

First, the material measures are technically feasible and are unlikely to encounter significant human resistance. Increasing the judges' salaries and the funding necessary for carrying out investigations, improving their working conditions, and providing them with trained assistants—these measures can be accomplished as long as the material (particularly financial) conditions are satisfied. Yet, although progress in this respect might come surely, it turns out to be exceedingly slow for a large number of courts located in the poor areas, which are seriously handicapped in providing judicial finance. The situation in some areas might be aggravated owing to the economic reform, which has resulted in the shutting down of many state-owned enterprises, severely reducing the local tax income. Since even the Outline for judicial reform does not mention a word about the central government's helping out these local courts, we can expect to see that the disparity in judicial quality will continue (or even enlarge) on the national scale. And, of course, money is obviously not the only issue. A higher salary and better working conditions do not necessarily improve the quality of judicial judgments; they may not even be effective in curtailing judicial corruption. So other aspects of the reform must follow simultaneously, yet their success is even less guaranteed than the material improvements.

Second, the personal variable can be slow to change because some aspects of human endeavor are set by the laws of nature, and it simply takes time to modify the current situation, no matter how strongly people wish to change. Improving the quality of the judicial personnel, for example, is bound to be a long-term project, and cannot be accomplished solely by a government-initiated movement; it is often the case that the "software" develops much more slowly than the "hardware." As the old Chinese proverb says, "It takes ten years to grow a tree, a hundred years to establish a person"; it will take the efforts of several generations for the Chinese judiciary to reach a level of professional competence comparable to its Western counterparts, provided that everything else goes smoothly. The Chinese government has attempted to speed up the change by introducing competition to the courtrooms, but, as discussed above, the measures taken here seem to be ill-conceived in the first place and the effects are at best mixed. Probably the most malleable variable that reform can tamper with is that of judicial training, to which the government has already devoted much effort. Yet post hoc training may have some inherent limits that simply cannot be transcended; to be a qualified judge one need not begin preparation in kindergarten, but it will be too late after one has grown up without the right kind of education.

Finally, there are aspects of the judicial reform that will follow even less certain paths since they depend on the interactions of various sectors of human interests and the ability to dissolve or circumvent the major forces of resistance. Of course, some technical (and in a sense "material") reforms might be easier to accomplish, such as streamlining the judicial process and opening up bottlenecks, but these are also rather trivial and insignificant to the main purpose of judicial reform. The core tasks are much harder to accomplish. Switching to vertical management style, with the central government controlling the purses of all courts nationwide, is likely to be resisted by local governments and, even if it is fully implemented, it is still difficult to predict how much impact the measure will have on reducing local protectionism. One must remember that judges still depend on the local people's congresses for their reappointments and promotions, and on administrative power for funds and benefits. And even though judges are made independent in name, they will still be subject to administrative and political control. The tangible incentive for good judicial performance provided by Articles 27 and 28 of the Judges Law reminds one of the traditional reward–punishment scheme designed for an ordinary bureaucracy. Indeed, the competition mechanism introduced by the Outline might further reduce rather than enhance judicial independence. It is likely to instigate political battles among the judges, facilitate the Party's paramount control over the judicial process, and pave the way toward building a new patron–client network within the courts. For one thing, in the examination of judicial performances, the evaluation of the party committee would count for 40 percent of the total score.[30] Politics still holds overwhelming discretionary power over the supposedly neutral tribunals of justice.

Inherent Limits to Judicial Independence: Party Politics
versus Courts and Rule of Law

The most direct and fundamental limit to Chinese judicial reform is still China's political system. Political control of the judiciary has been a perennial feature of CCP history; the working style of authorizing the party committee and secretary to approve judicial decisions, and the Political and Legal Committee to settle disputes, was established as early as during the Yan'an period. The current Constitution, enacted in 1982, formally recognizes in its Preamble the leading role of the CCP; as the party is not mentioned elsewhere in the Constitution, the limit of its power remains undefined. On the other hand, the 1982 Constitution explicitly stipulates that "The People's Courts independently exercise judicial power according to the provisions of law, and are not to be interfered with by administrative agencies, social organizations, and individuals." It seems that, to avoid logical contradiction, any judicial independence is to be interpreted within the contours of the political power of the party; that is, the courts are "independent" only insofar as they deal with cases without adverse effects on the party, and they are obliged to accept the party's command as soon as the party's interest is implicated. The latter is true whenever the case deals with any "political question," as in the judgment on the appeal of former Beijing mayor, Chen Xitong, who was sentenced to sixteen years' imprisonment for embezzlement. Although the SPC offered some legal reasoning, it was correctly expected that the judgments of the lower courts were simply to be upheld since Chen's sentence was already politically decided. The same can be said about the case against the former vice chairman of the NPC Standing Committee, Cheng Kejie, who was sentenced to death for alleged embezzlement. In this type of political judgment, the Chinese court has no alternative but to formally confirm what the party has already decided. In fact, the Outline itself requires that judicial reform follow the principle of party leadership, along with principles of "democratic dictatorship" as the form of the state and the political institutions represented by the NPC (Para. 4). The official "point of departure" is always the "particular circumstances of China," though "beneficial experiences" of foreign courts and judicial management can be borrowed. In a high-level conference about the ongoing judicial reform, the president of the SPC expressly turned down the possibility of pursuing the type of judicial independence in the Western model of separation of powers, and reinstated the need for the party leadership and the "party control of [judicial] cadres."

The party can interfere with a judicial decision in several ways. First and most obvious, the president and vice presidents of any court are usually party members subject to party discipline. Since the president is held responsible for the whole court, the party can achieve effective control over the court through the presidential responsibility system. Further, it is still common for the party secretary of the Political and Legal Committee, often the same person as the chief of the Public Security Bureau, to discipline the court president with the party principles. Finally, the party is in fact responsible for initiating and pushing forward all major political and legal reform activities. The most recent amendment on "rule of law," for example, was first raised as a proposal in the CCP Charter during the 15th Party Congress before it was copied verbatim to the Constitution. Nor could the judicial reform be launched without approval of the major party leaders. Thus, both the mobility and the inertia of the Chinese judicial system depend crucially on the party. This brings into serious question the possibility of establishing a true independent judiciary in which individual judges are held ultimately responsible not to the political will, but to the law. After all, the administrative leadership and the trial committees are still an integral part of the court structure through which the party can step in and supervise judicial judgments whenever the cases are deemed "important," "complicated," or "difficult."

This chapter does not systematically analyze the rational incentives that set the Chinese judicial reform in motion; it might be legitimate to assume that good will for social justice is still present among the Chinese legal community and some political power holders. Since judicial reform was initiated by the party itself, however, it is inherently limited by the party's own imperatives. The goal of judicial reform is ostensibly to make the judiciary independent so that it can decide cases fairly and efficiently. Yet as soon as a judicial judgment touches a nerve of the party, political power is likely to contest the efficacy of the judicial judgment. Throughout Chinese history, the winner in this contention, when it arises, is always the political power. Thus it is perhaps impractical to expect that the current judicial reform, ambitious as it is, will make the Chinese judiciary truly independent by Western standards. Even if the ongoing judicial reform is otherwise successful, it will still be limited by the ultimate political bottom line: a party that is essentially above the law.

Is Judicial Reform Likely to Succeed in China?

This chapter has sought to answer the above question by analyzing the current political, legal, and social conditions. As I have shown, the prospect is a mixed one and changes with the fluctuating political climate in China. While Jiang Zemin, when he was the general secretary of the CCP, did promise on one occasion a degree of judicial autonomy, the phrase was quickly qualified to exclude the possibility of confusion with the Western notion of the separation of powers. Indeed, the Outline itself warns against any "deviation" from the party leadership. The recent public campaign against the Falun Gong sect further raises doubts about the credibility of the party's avowed effort at creating a government under rule of law rather than rule of man.

On the other hand, especially after its accession to the World Trade Organization, China is unmistakably merging with the rest of the world, and so must its legal system in general and its judicial system in particular. Only an independent and competent judiciary is capable of sustaining the long-term social and economic progress, which ultimately provides political legitimacy to the current government. The future of China in the new millennium critically hinges on the fate of judicial reform: while its success might prove to be the first step toward the end of the one-party dictatorship and the beginning of a relatively free, self-governed, and prosperous society, its failure may well portend the overall degradation of the Chinese living environment by jeopardizing the key elements necessary for carrying out a successful social reform—among others, basic order and stability, the control of official corruption, continuing economic growth, and technological innovation. It remains to be seen whether judicial reform in China can successfully resolve the contradictions between political imperatives and socioeconomic needs.

The bulk of this chapter was written at the time when the first five-year judicial reform was about to end. Now two years have elapsed, and the ruling party has changed leaders. The plan for the second reform has finally been unveiled. The delay itself reveals the delicacy and difficulties inherent in judicial reform taking place in the political context of a one-party monopoly. Just like its predecessor, the second plan contains hardly anything new except for procedural reform of death sentences. To be sure, there will be new progress, which will bring forth new hope for a better judicial system. But it is bound to remain within the orbit carved out by the ruling party, whose interests will prevent any reform from touching the untouchable. So the nature of politics ultimately defines the limits of judicial reform, which sets the limits for rule of law in China. In this sense, while democracy is conditioned upon and in some cases preceded by the establishment of rule of law, it may well be that rule of law also depends on democracy for healthy development. At least the experience of Chinese judicial reform seems to affirm the conventional wisdom that the fruits of law rarely grow out of despotic soil.

9

State Power and Unbalanced Legal Development in China

Yongshun Cai and Songcai Yang

Political and socioeconomic changes in China have assigned an unprecedented role to law, and rule of law is believed to be crucial to regime transition in China. That is why Pan Wei sees rule of law as one of the most important components of future regime building in China. Randall Peerenboom has much disagreement with Pan, but he also believes in the importance of rule of law to China and thinks that China should focus on creating the institutions and establishing a legal system that at a minimum meets the standards of a thin rule of law. There has not been a commonly accepted definition of rule of law, but "[v]irtually all definitions of rule of law agree on the importance of law's function to set limits to the exercise of private and state power."[1] Hence, a precondition for rule of law is to restrain state actors. Peerenboom also points to a series of daunting challenges in achieving a thin rule of law in China. This chapter aims to demonstrate some of those challenges by examining the problems encountered by legal professionals (i.e., lawyers) in China. It shows that for rule of law or its development to be possible in China, not only government agencies but also legal departments have to be restrained.

An emerging market economy, together with social and political changes, has expanded the role of lawyers in China. This is reflected in an increase in the number of law firms and lawyers. From 1989 to 2000, the number of law firms increased from 3,653 to 9,541, and the number of lawyers rose from 43,530 to 117,260.[2] The economic status of lawyers has also increased significantly. Successful lawyers belong to the high-income group in society and are among those who receive special attention from tax collection organizations in an effort to prevent income tax evasion. In Beijing in 2000, for example, according to a survey of about 200 law firms, over 90 percent of lawyers had an annual income of over 100,000 yuan, whereas the average salary of employees in the municipality was only 16,350 yuan.[3] In Guangzhou in 2001, among the ten people who paid the highest amount of personal income tax, two were lawyers.[4]

The economic success of some lawyers, however, does not imply that legal professionalism in China has achieved a high degree of maturity. The legal community still faces a number of problems that affect its level of development in China. First, many lawyers are inadequately trained and incompetent. Although the average education level of lawyers in China is higher than that of judges,[5] professional training is still inadequate. It is estimated that in the early 2000s, over 48 percent of lawyers had a primary college education (*dazhuan,* or an education between senior high school and college), while only about 40 percent had received a college education or higher.[6]

Second, the environment in which lawyers operate is still replete with social and political constraints. Chinese citizens have traditionally relied more on informal mediation than on the courts for dispute resolution, which has limited the role of lawyers.[7] In addition, lawyers have not had a good reputation.[8] This, to some extent, remains true in today's China because of the ethical problems among Chinese lawyers. Some lawyers have engaged in inappropriate or unlawful activities such as bribing judges, prosecutors, and arbitrators, whereas others have been blamed for overcharging clients, unruly conduct, and disrupting order in court.[9] Perhaps a more important constraint that lawyers face is in their relationship to the state. The legal system in China is still seen as an instrument of the party-state for maintaining social and political order. To this end, legal institutions remain in the "cage" of the party-state. For the same reason, lawyers' practices also have to be accepted by the party-state, which implies limited autonomy of lawyers when defending litigants against state actors.

While the many problems that plague professionalism among Chinese lawyers are not new, this chapter aims to address how these problems have shaped legal practice in China. How does lawyers' lack of autonomy affect their incentive to represent clients and thereby influence litigant interests? Lawyers are supposed to provide legal services to those who need legal advice. When clients have difficulty securing qualified lawyers to represent them, the credibility or the authority of the legal system is in question. Based on a survey of about 280 lawyers in Changsha, capital city of Hunan Province, and on secondary sources, this chapter explores the implications of state power for legal system progress in China.[10] It examines how the power of state agencies, together with economic calculations, has shaped lawyers' selective legal representation. As administrative litigation and criminal cases involve government or legal organs and possibly greater risks, lawyers are reluctant to accept such cases. In contrast, as cases concerning economic affairs often bring more financial benefit and involve less risk, lawyers are more inclined to represent parties in these cases. As a result, there is an under-representation of litigants involved in criminal and administrative cases. Lawyers' selective involvement may undermine the people's confidence in legal institutions, leading to an unbalanced development of the legal system in China. Therefore, China still has a long way to go to achieve rule of law.

Selection of Lawsuits by Chinese Lawyers

In China during the reform period, an increasing number of social and economic disputes have been resolved through legal channels. From 1990 to 2000, the number of cases accepted by the courts increased from 2,916,774 to 5,356,294—an increase of 83.6 percent.[11] But this increase does not directly reflect the participation of law-

Table 9.1

Types of Lawsuits Lawyers Are Most Reluctant to Take On (N = 268)

Category	Number of lawyers	Frequency (%)
Administrative litigation	183	68.3
Criminal lawsuits	51	19.0
Administrative and criminal litigation	6	2.2
Civil lawsuits	17	6.3
Economic lawsuits	5	1.9
Other	6	2.3
Total	268	100

Source: Authors' survey, Changsha, Hunan Province, 2002.

yers in litigation. Lawyers have been found to be more willing to represent litigants in cases of an economic or civil nature, rather than administrative or criminal cases. Our survey in Changsha points to this pattern. Of the 268 lawyers who were asked what types of cases they were most reluctant to take on, about 68 percent reported administrative litigation cases, and another 19 percent reported criminal cases (see Table 9.1). In contrast, less than 2 percent were most reluctant to represent parties involved in economic cases.

Indeed, a severe problem in China is that defendants involved in criminal and administrative litigation are underrepresented. It is estimated that in such cases, only 30 percent of them have defense lawyers.[12] In 2000, for example, the number of lawyers in Beijing was 5,495. The total number of criminal cases they took on was 4,300, which accounted for 10 percent of their cases. The annual average number of criminal cases taken on by each lawyer decreased from 2.64 in the previous years to 0.78 in 2000, although the number of criminal cases judged by the courts had increased. This implies that a significant number of criminal defendants did not have legal representation. "Impartial and fair trials require representation by someone who knows the law and is independent of the judges deciding the cases and the political authorities who made the laws."[13] The lack of such people undermines the credibility of legal institutions. Officials of the Ministry of Justice admit that this tendency is not conducive to the development of the legal system in China.

Why are lawyers reluctant to take on criminal or administrative litigation cases? We argue that the type of lawsuits taken on is largely determined by two factors. The first is the degree to which the government or its agencies or legal organs are involved in a case. When a case involves such organs, it often means that lawyers will face state power. Administrative litigations are directed at the government or its organs, whereas criminal cases involve the public security bureau that is responsible for the investigation, as well as the procuracy, which serves as the public prosecutor. The involvement of state organs not only implies risks but also reduces the likelihood of a success. The second factor pertains to economic benefits. State regulation of legal fees has shaped lawyers' incentives for taking on lawsuits. Lawyers often receive much more in fees for their services in economic lawsuits, as these fees are often based on the value of property involved in the lawsuit. In addition, such cases often involve business firms, which, compared to individuals, are better able to afford the legal fees. In contrast, the benefits received in administrative and criminal cases tend to be meager because they often (but not always) do not involve a large amount of property. In addition, economic disputes are often between individuals or firms (or other social organizations) rather than between individuals (or other social organizations) and state organs. Hence the incentive structure, which is embedded in the political structure, and economic benefits fuel lawyers' preference for lawsuits pertaining to economic disputes.

Economic Rationale and Lawsuit Selection

As noted above, successful lawyers in China have joined the high-income sector of society. A closer look at those who earned the highest incomes discloses that wealth distribution among lawyers is closely tied to the types of lawsuits they take on. For example, in 2001, the total business income of law firms in Shanghai was over 1.21 billion yuan. The income of 121 firms (with a business income of over 3 million yuan each) accounted for 70 percent of the total business income, although their lawyers constituted only 35 percent of the lawyers in the city. Those that obtained the highest income were predominantly those that represented parties involved in banking, securities, foreign trade, real estate, and other economic lawsuits.[14]

Our survey of the lawyers in Changsha also points to the pattern by which lawyers who take on economic cases are more likely to draw a higher income. Of the seven lawyers whose annual income was over 200,000 yuan, six reported that they focused on economic cases, whereas the remaining one accepted both economic and civil cases (see Table 9.2). In the group with the second-highest income, most take on economic cases. Table 9.2 illustrates the trend that as income level increases, the percentage of lawyers who focus on economic cases also increases, whereas it is the converse for lawyers who focus on criminal cases. Another finding is that only one out of the 275 lawyers reported that he focused on administrative litigation, and this person belonged to the lowest-income group.

Lawyers' willingness to take on economic disputes is partly due to the way in which legal fees are regulated. In 1990, the Ministry of Justice, the Ministry of Finance, and the National Price Bureau issued a directive regulating the fees charged for legal representation (see Table 9.3). These regulations have disparate implications for economic cases versus other types of cases. The regulated legal fees for taking on criminal cases are more or less fixed, whereas it is less so for economic disputes. For example, lawyers would be able to receive up to 150 yuan for their services in a criminal case. In economic cases, however, they could charge up to 3 percent of the value of the property involved in the case. This implies that lawyers who take on cases involving a large amount of property would be able to receive more payment regardless of the amount of work they have to do.

Table 9.2

Distribution of Lawyers' Income in Changsha (N = 275)

Income range	Number of lawyers	Type of cases preferred (%)						
		Criminal	Civil	Criminal and economic	Economic	Civil and economic	Administrative	No priority
Over 200,001	7	0	0	0	85.7	14.3	0	0
100,001–200,000	15	6.7	26.6	0	46.7	13.3	0	6.7
50,001–100,000	47	8.5	34.0	2.1	29.8	12.8	0	12.8
30,001–50,000	56	10.7	33.9	1.8	33.9	8.9	0	10.7
10,001–30,000	99	12.1	36.4	3	30.3	8.1	0	10.1
Less than 10,000	51	9.8	50.9	0	21.6	5.9	1.9	9.8
Total	275	29	100	5	87	25	1	28

Source: Authors' survey, Changsha, Hunan Province, 2002.

Table 9.3

Legal Fees Charged by Lawyers by Category of Lawsuit

Category of cases	Charges (yuan)
1. Consultancy	
a. Not involving property	1–5
b. Involving commercial property	10–30
2. Criminal cases	
a. First-instance trial	30–150
b. Second-instance trial only	30–150
c. Both first- and second-instance trials	30–50
3. Civil cases	
a. Not involving property	70–150
b. Involving property	100–200 + 0.5%–3% of amount of properties*
4. Economic disputes	0.5%–3%*
5. Administrative cases	
a. Public security cases	30–60
b. Patent cases	50–400
c. Labor disputes	30–50

Source: Bureau of Justice of Hunan Province, *Hunan lushi guanli shouce* (Handbook for the management of lawyers in Hunan province), 1999, pp. 81–83.

*The percentage is determined by the category to which the amount of property belongs.

The regulated fees of 1990 are too meager today and are largely ignored. A normal practice is for the fees to be determined through negotiations between lawyers and clients. As one lawyer reports, "The regulated legal fees (1990) are too meager. A divorce case is worth only 50 to 100 yuan, and no lawyer is willing to take it on. . . . The fees charged for a criminal case now are between 1,000 yuan and 2,000 yuan and can be between 5,000 yuan to 10,000 yuan for those clients with a higher income. Legal fees for a straightforward civil lawsuit are between 500 and 1,000 yuan."[15] As the negotiated price may be deemed too high by clients ex post, it is not rare that some refuse to pay the charges after the case is closed regardless of the outcome.[16] Some lawyers reported that about 30 percent of their fees could not be collected.

In this circumstance, some local governments have implemented new regulations for legal fees. As Table 9.4 suggests, the regulations vary from place to place, largely depending on the level of economic development. Yet, as in the directive issued by the three national organs in 1990, the fees regulated for economic disputes are largely determined by the value of property involved. Hence, lawyers receive higher payments for taking on such cases. This regulation has led to complaints from some lawyers: "Now fees are not charged based on the amount of work done and the degree of difficulty of the work. Instead, it depends on the value of property involved. This is unreasonable."[17] Government efforts have also failed to satisfy citizens, as they find that lawyers' fees are intolerably high.[18]

Table 9.4

Legal Fees Charged by Lawyers in Selected Places (in yuan)

	Shanghai[1]	Shenzhen	Shandong	Ningxia
Criminal cases				
a. Investigation period	2,000	2,000–10,000	300–1,000	500–2,000
b. Prosecution period	4,000	2,500–12,000	500–3,000	1,000–3,000
c. First-instance trial	8,000	3,000–15,000	1,000–6,000	1,500–5,000
Civil cases				
a. Not involving property	5,000	2,000–5,000	500–5,000	500–5,000
b. 100,000–1,000,000	1.5%	8%–2.5%[2]	3%–2%[2]	4%–3%[2]
c. one million and above	1%–0.75%	—	1%	3%–1%[2]
Administrative litigation[3]				
Not involving property	5,000	1,500–15,000	500–3,000	500–3,000

Source: Zhang Jingyuan, "Lushi shoufei: Kunhuo yu xuanze" (Lawyers' charges: Puzzles and solutions), *Banyuetan* (Biweekly forum), no. 5 (2002): pp. 18–22.
Notes:
1. The maximum fees a lawyer can charge.
2. The percentage depends on the range of the values of the property.
3. The criteria for such cases are the same as those for civil cases.

Given the economic incentive, lawyers "are most willing to take on civil and economic cases, especially those that involve a large amount of property."[19] Some of our interviewees reported how they had amassed wealth by taking on economic lawsuits. A lawyer admitted that the payment he received from a single economic lawsuit "alleviated his situation of poverty" overnight. After he obtained his license, he had been focusing on criminal cases. Although the amount of work in such cases was by no means light, the returns were meager. His income per year was about 20,000 to 30,000 yuan. His financial situation changed when he took on an economic case. The case he accepted involved a dispute between a state bank and a firm that failed to repay the bank 3 million yuan in loans. The lawyer in question acted as legal counsel to the bank, which promised that his law firm would receive 15 percent of the 3 million yuan if he could help secure payment of the loans. As the evidence pointing to the firm's failure to service the loans was beyond dispute, the lawyer did not have difficulty winning the case. The issue lay with the execution of the court ruling, as the firm tried to hide its assets.[20] Given the fact that the lawyer in question had been a police officer previously, he knew how to locate the firm's assets. In the end, the firm had to service its loans. As agreed, the lawyer received 250,000 yuan of the 450,000 yuan, with the rest being paid to his law firm. It is not rare that law firms and lawyers make what in China is nothing less than a small fortune by taking on economic lawsuits.

Law firms and lawyers are also more willing to focus on economic disputes because of the economic pressure arising from the reform. Lawyers are now no longer the "state's legal workers" but "society's legal workers." In 1999, the State Council issued a directive requiring the separation of law firms from public agencies. The directive regulated that law firms should completely separate from government organs or other public agencies before October 31, 2000, and those firms that failed to meet the deadline would have their business licenses revoked. The mode of ownership after the separation was either a partnership or a cooperative. With this reform measure, previous state law firms are now required to be financially independent, and lawyers acknowledged the pressure of survival. For example, by the early 2000s, 449 of 462 law firms (or 97 percent) in Beijing had adopted the system of partnership. Given the costs of operating the firms, it is natural for lawyers to take on cases that are more lucrative.[21]

Yet, the tendency to focus on economic cases might be curbed in that competition among lawyers would inevitably compel some to take on less profitable cases, like administrative litigation or criminal cases. This, however, is only part of the story, as there are other factors that affect the choice of lawsuits. China remains an authoritarian regime and state power is strong, so lawyers face uncertainties when taking on administrative litigation or criminal cases. The lawyers surveyed reported that, other things being equal, they were more likely to win economic disputes rather than administrative litigation or criminal cases. Among the 276 lawyers surveyed, over 32 percent reported that their odds of winning a case were not affected by the type of cases they took on. But it was also found that about 30 percent reported a higher likelihood of winning if they took on economic lawsuits as opposed to criminal cases (7.2 percent) or administrative litigation (1.1 percent). This implies that economic calculations may not be the only reason for reluctance to take on administrative litigation or criminal cases. Factors such as potential risks in administrative litigation and criminal cases are also significant in shaping lawyers' choice of lawsuits.

State Power and Lawyers: Administrative Litigation

With the dismantling of the collective farming system and the weakening of the work-unit system, direct interactions and conflicts between the state and citizens are more frequent than before. Since early 1990, the National People's Congress has enacted a number of laws, including the Administrative Litigation Law, the PRC Compensation Law, and the Administrative Review Law, to institutionalize state–society interactions. Chinese citizens have also used laws to protect their interests. The Administrative Litigation Law is an example. From 1990 to 2000, the number of administrative litigations increased from 13,006 to 85,760, and the total number of administrative litigation cases during the ten-year period was over 586,000.[22]

Yet there is still a significant gap between the making of a law and its implementation.[23] Thus far, the most important mode of settlement of these cases has been the withdrawal of lawsuits. In each year between 1995 and 1999, about 45 to 53 percent of administrative litigation cases were withdrawn.[24] The power of state agencies and the resulting pressure on litigants is an important reason for the withdrawal of lawsuits against these agencies.[25] Although some citizens who withdraw their lawsuits may have their claims partly attended to, violators of the law are seldom punished. "Some government officials do not take administrative litigations seriously. They either threaten the people or refuse to appear in court. Some of them even issue administrative orders to the court as leaders. Because of such pressure, some courts do not dare to accept certain cases or often rule with biased judgments, blatantly ignoring the law."[26] In Wuhan, for example, in the ten years from 1990 to 2000, the number of administrative litigations initiated totaled 4,250. About 67 percent (or 2,868) were withdrawn for various reasons. In all these cases, administrative leaders never appeared in court.[27] Lack of confidence in the system has led to the number of administrative litigations being rather limited in terms of its proportion to the total number of cases judged by the courts. Since the Administrative Litigation Law was enacted in 1990, the total number of administrative litigations stands at less than 2 percent of the total number of lawsuits.[28]

While it is common for citizens to be lacking in the willingness (*bu yuan*), the courage (*bu gan*), or knowledge (*bu hui*) to sue state agencies, such constraints have also led to lawyers' reluctance to take on administrative litigation cases. For one, lawyers feel that it is difficult to win such cases. According to our survey, only one out of the 275 lawyers surveyed reported that he was most likely to win in administrative litigations. Another factor is that lawyers may be seen as challenging state agencies when representing clients whose interests are encroached on by these agencies. The following section presents a case in detail to show the surprising degree to which a local government may abuse its power to punish lawyers, and the defenseless situation of individuals when they face state authority.

The Case of Zhang's Imprisonment

This case concerns a lawyer, Zhang Jun, in Xiyang county of Shanxi Province.[29] In 1989, a township government wanted to take a piece of land away from a village. The peasants resisted strongly because the land belonged to their village. The township government then launched a lawsuit against the village and won the case in the county court. Viewing the court ruling as being biased, the villagers approached Zhang, a lawyer and also the director of the Political and Legal Office of the Political Consultative Conference in Shanxi Province, a position of considerable social status. Despite Zhang's defense, the villagers lost the appeal as well. Given the peasants' refusal to surrender their land, the local government resorted to forceful execution in 1990. In March, the head of the intermediate court of Jinzhong District (to which Xiyang county belongs) led over 200 people from the legal departments of the county and township to the village for the execution. A number of villagers resisted, but they were beaten and arrested. Many more had to flee to the mountains. The county government not only searched and arrested protesters, but also set the police on those who lodged appeals in Taiyuan (the capital city of the province) and Beijing. The village head was caught when he lodged an appeal in the capital city. After his release, he continued to make appeals and, eventually, died on his way to higher-level authorities.

The leaders of the county and the district governments did not stop there. They believed that the villagers dared to resist because they were instigated by Zhang, and they publicly claimed that Zhang would be punished. In June 1990, Zhang was arrested in his office by police officers from Xiyang county. The next year, he was tried in the county court and was accused of accepting bribes from peasants, cheating, and instigating peasants to resist a court ruling. The court and the procuracy obtained the "evidence" by coercing a few villagers into making false accusations. When the trial was in session, over 1,500 people went to the county court to attend the hearing, but they were not allowed to enter the courtroom. The next day, when the court adjourned, Zhang's two lawyers were surrounded by scores of police officers. The head of the court asked the lawyers to withdraw their defense, but they refused. Unexpectedly, the head knelt down before them, begging them to relent. Angry policemen then started to beat the lawyers, who quickly fled to the bus station and left.

Despite Zhang's defense of himself, he was sentenced to fifteen years in prison. He then lodged an appeal to the intermediate court but lost the case again. After Zhang was jailed, the county court and the district court turned to his wife, who was also a lawyer and had helped Zhang in the case. The courts wanted to put her behind bars as they were worried that she would lodge appeals to higher-level authorities. In December 1991, the county court sentenced her to three years in prison on the charge that she was involved in accepting bribes, which was a false charge. When her sentence ended, the district court demanded that she should not lodge appeals for Zhang after her release, with the threat of a longer sentence. Zhang's wife agreed and was released.

Due to a serious illness, Zhang was allowed to return to his home under supervision in 1994. By that time, both Zhang and his wife had been dismissed by their employers. From then on, they began the long process of appeal; Zhang lodged 647 appeals in all.[30] They appealed to the provincial Party committee, the provincial people's congress, the provincial government, the provincial political consultative conference, the provincial court, and other organs. They also went to Beijing to appeal.

During the twelve years of appeals, this couple received the support of many people, but this story merely indicates the power of a county government over the power of the people. Peasants from the village that Zhang defended made appeals for him every year. They made a rule that nobody could become the village head if Zhang's innocence was not restored. The lawyers' association of Shanxi Province repeatedly reported the case to the Ministry of Justice, the Party committee, the government, and the people's congress of Shanxi Province. When the case was publicized, it shocked many lawyers in China. Lawyers from a number of provinces organized a meeting to discuss the case. About forty lawyers from different parts of China made appeals to the National People's Congress, the China People's Political Consultative Conference, the Central Political and Legal Commission, the Supreme Court, the Supreme Procuracy, the Ministry of Justice, the National Association of Lawyers, as well as the media.

Over the years, about 4,000 people appealed on Zhang's behalf, and the provincial Party secretary also urged a resolution of his case on a few occasions. Due to these efforts, the provincial high court finally decided to conduct a retrial and sent its people to Xiyang county in 1997 to investigate. When the high court encountered difficulties, it became hesitant in proceeding with the case. It was not until 2001 that the court passed the verdict that Zhang's crime of accepting bribes and cheating was unfounded. But the crime of inciting villagers to resist a court ruling remained. Zhang was sentenced to three years in prison for this crime. The reason why Zhang could not be judged "not guilty" was a political one. A former head of the provincial court admitted that the case was discussed among leaders of the court and the provincial political-legal committee. A leader of the provincial political-legal committee said that Zhang could not be claimed innocent, as that would affect the stability of Xiyang county. Thus, the leader of the provincial court told the collegiate panel to make the judgment based on the provincial leader's instructions. When the panel concluded that Zhang was innocent, a court leader demanded the minutes of the meeting be burned.

It is difficult to ascertain the number of similar cases in China, but cases of this nature indicate how laws may be abused. They also show the malleability of legal institutions in China and the tragic impact on the fate of some individuals. Such cases not only determine citizens' reluctance to sue law-violating state agencies but also undermine lawyers' willingness to represent clients. As one lawyer admitted in an interview, "To be frank, I have never taken on an administrative litigation. The chance of success is slim. Even if you win the case, the judgment may not be executed. In addition to the meager legal fees, lawyers are also unwilling to offend government agencies." While it may be true that lawyers everywhere are reluctant to challenge state power, Chinese lawyers face especially great risks in doing so.

Legal Departments and Lawyers: Criminal Cases

Lawyers also face state power when representing clients in criminal cases because they have to deal with the public security department and the procuracy, which investigate and prosecute criminal cases. Although legal organizations, such as the court and the procuracy, are weak versus the Party and the government, they possess unparalleled power when compared to individual citizens, including lawyers. The relationship between legal organs and lawyers in the settlement of criminal cases in China has been described as such: "The public security bureau cooks the food [*zhu fan*, or collecting evidence], the procuracy sends the food [*song fan*, or transferring the case to the court for public prosecution], the court eats the food [*chi fan*, or making the judgment], and the lawyers beg for food [*tao fan*]."[31] The relationships among the legal organs that administer the criminal process have two important implications. First, the cooperation of legal organs in criminal cases is a normal practice, and it is all the more so when the cases have been brought up for some political motive of a government organ.[32] Second, the position of the lawyers is weak because of the difficulties and risks involved in representing litigants in such cases.

The first problem faced by lawyers in taking up criminal cases is evidence collection, including difficulties in interviewing suspects, accessing files on the suspect, and carrying out investigations.[33] The Criminal Procedure Law and the Lawyers' Law

Table 9.5

Sources of Risks in Criminal Cases as Reported by Lawyers (N = 276)

Category	Number of lawyers	Frequency (%)
Legal organ	181	65.6
Litigant	31	11.2
Legal organ and litigant	13	4.7
Other	27	9.8
No risk	24	8.7
Total	276	100

Source: Authors' survey, Changsha, Hunan Province, 2002.

regulate that the lawyer has the right to meet with suspects. A directive by the central legal organs also states that "in criminal cases that do not involve national security, lawyers are entitled to speak with suspects without the approval of legal organs during the investigation period." But in practice, "when lawyers want to meet with suspects of cases that do not involve national security, they almost always need that approval. . . . Thus far, this problem has existed in almost all localities, including Beijing, in the country. It is common that lawyers are prevented from speaking with suspects."[34] Some frustrated lawyers have sued the legal organs for denying them the right to meet with suspects.

A more serious problem is the risk involved. Legal organs represent the state in criminal cases and may view legal defense as an obstacle to the outcome desired by legal departments or government officials. Some people in legal departments complain: "You lawyers only acknowledge the problems of the public security department, the procuracy, and court. Why can't you cooperate with legal departments?" Some leaders have even said that they do not believe that lawyers, unlike government officials or legal agents, have never violated laws. They have also threatened to take severe action if any illegal activities are ever uncovered.[35] What makes these threats credible is the power of legal and government agencies. This has also been reflected in our survey. Among the 275 lawyers, almost 66 percent reported that legal organs posed the most risks in taking on criminal cases, whereas only 8.7 percent reported that there was no such risk (see Table 9.5). A similar survey of 130 lawyers in Beijing showed that 62.4 percent reported that the greatest obstacles encountered in their practices stemmed from the legal departments, whereas 17.3 percent reported that state agencies posed the greatest difficulties.[36]

The risk posed by legal organs, especially the procuracy, is due to the regulations that grant more power to the procuracy while limiting the autonomy of lawyers. Article 306 of the revised Criminal Law promulgated in 1997 provides that the counsel or legal representative will be punished if he or she destroys or fabricates evidence, helps the litigant destroy or fabricate evidence, or threatens or induces the witness to change his or her testimony. The penalty for violation of Article 306 can be a prison sentence of three to seven years. While this law grants much power to legal departments, it does not regulate the reverse situation in which lawyers' rights are encroached upon. This is an important loophole that has been frequently exploited by the procuracy.[37]

A lawyer can be arrested under the charge of coaching the defendant to give false evidence if the defendant changes his or her statement after meeting with the lawyer. But as the public security department may extort a confession through torture, it is common for the accused to withdraw the false confession when he or she has an opportunity to do so. The lawyer can also be arrested when there are disparities between the evidence collected by the lawyer and the legal departments, because he or she would be suspected of coercing or inducing the witness into changing his or her testimony or providing false testimony.[38] In 1995, the Association of Chinese Lawyers received less than twenty appeals from its members for protection of their rights. After the Criminal Law was enacted in 1997, the number of appeals reached seventy every year. About 80 percent of these appeals pertained to accusations of "fabricating evidence" or "obstruction of evidence collection."[39] In recent years, at least ten lawyers have been arrested each year for defending criminal suspects. By the early 2000s, at least 150 lawyers had been arrested on the charge of falsifying testimony, although most of them were later proven innocent.[40]

In one example in Xinjiang Autonomous Region, a female lawyer was first detained by the procuracy and then arrested by the public security bureau in 2001 on the charge of "obstruction of evidence collection." She was sentenced to three years in prison, because the statements she had taken from the three witnesses differed from what the procuracy had obtained. There was in fact a good reason for the disparity. In order to obtain the type of evidence it needed, the procuracy required the three witnesses to surrender evidence to its anti-corruption bureau, which is well-known for its power in disciplining public agents. The predicament of the female lawyer in question also made other lawyers realize that it was necessary to have at least one other lawyer present when taking statements, or that it was better not to take on criminal cases in the first place.[41]

In other instances, lawyers were punished simply because they offended public prosecutors by refusing to give in to their unreasonable demands. In a high-profile case, a lawyer in Henan Province was released from prison and pronounced "not guilty" after being detained for four years. This lawyer, Li, was arrested when defending a corrupt cadre. Li was hired by the defendant's wife and had received payment for his work. When the head of the anti-corruption bureau of the procuracy met Li at the end of 1998, for an unknown reason, he asked Li to return the money to the defendant's wife. Li said that it was not against the law for a lawyer to receive payment for his or her services. The head said: "I know it is not against the law, but I can talk with the court to put you in prison." He beat Li and then asked the public security bureau to place Li in a detention house. Three days later, the procuracy issued an approval for Li's arrest with the charge of "helping to fabricate evidence."

During his detention, Li was tortured by the police. In his appeals, he stated: "A few policemen undressed me and forced me to run in the snow . . . they physically and verbally abused me . . . they handcuffed me and used me as a punching bag. When I fell, they pulled me up and hit me again. . . ." The police also interrogated him continuously without allowing him to sleep. Li's lawyer was only allowed to meet with him seven months later. Li was arrested in 1998 and pronounced "not guilty" and released in 2001, because the charges were unfounded. During the trial, as the legal departments lacked evidence, Li was first arrested under the charge of "exacting bribes." The charges were then changed to "cheating," "perjury," and "tax evasion." Indeed, Li's imprisonment was largely based on the two pivotal but flawed testimonies of the local public security bureau. In one testimony, the date was found to have been altered. In the other, the signature was dated 1998, but the paper had only been manufactured in 1999. Had it not been for the many efforts of the media, some delegates to the National People's Congress, and well-known scholars, it is highly uncertain if Li would have been judged "not guilty" and released.[42]

Another factor that undermines lawyers' willingness to take on criminal cases is intervention from higher-level authorities. This hinders a lawyer's work for two reasons: First, lawyers may unwittingly offend public prosecutors or government officials when taking on such cases. For example, a lawyer successfully defended a suspect in a criminal litigation. Yet some government officials were annoyed as they believed that the lawyer's success had made them "lose face." Consequently, the procuracy detained the lawyer for thirteen months under the charge of embezzlement. The truth behind this charge was that the law firm that the lawyer worked for had bought a cellular phone which the latter had borrowed.[43] Second, as some lawsuits are settled based on the will of leaders rather than on the facts, lawyers' defense is of limited use. As legal workers' practice is "not only based on the law but also based on the instructions of the Party committee,"[44] it is not surprising that lawyers are told, "the leaders have decided on the outcome of the case; how dare you defend the suspect?"[45] This is especially true in politically motivated cases where legal organs are supposed to cooperate to solve the case so as not to damage the image of the government.[46] Legal defense may thus be regarded as undesirable or unnecessary. In 1998, for example, the police of Shanxi Province solved a case in which pseudo-alcohol poisoned 140 people, with 32 of them dying and one losing his eyesight. This tragedy attracted much attention from the media and citizens alike. President Jiang Zemin made three phone calls inquiring about the case. As both the citizens and the local government were angry with the nine suspects, no local lawyer dared to accept the case. In the end, a lawyer from Beijing, who was also a vice chairman of the Association of Chinese Lawyers, defended the suspects. When the trial began, this lawyer was not allowed to speak. He then decided to leave the court to protest but was stopped by the court police.[47] Similarly, one lawyer gives his reasons for not taking up criminal cases:

> Due to the political considerations of those in power, intervention is common. From the very beginning, the judgment is based on the decision of leaders. When a lawyer gets involved in a case, he or she may find many questions and have some good cases to make. He or she may conduct investigations to collect evidence and make thorough preparations for the trial. But such efforts are often a waste because the outcome has already been decided ex ante. This is very frustrating.[48]

Moreover, in criminal cases, public prosecutors and lawyers often do not enjoy the same status in court. For example, the court often limits the time a lawyer can use to make his case, or interrupts him when he speaks. In the Xinjiang case mentioned earlier, the defendant's lawyer needed the approval of the court to speak, but the prosecutors could speak whenever they wanted.[49] In other cases, the judge has even ordered the lawyer to leave the court, not because the latter violated court rules but because his or her defense was seen to be offensive to the judge. In Fujian Province in 2001, a lawyer was ordered to leave the court when he asked why the daughter of the defendant who was in the visitors' seat was handcuffed. In Shanghai in 2001, a judge ordered a lawyer to leave escorted by the police after the lawyer asked the court to verify the defendant's confession that was provided by the prosecutor.[50]

Due to the factors discussed above, Chinese lawyers have good reason for not accepting criminal cases. One lawyer reported: "I have been a lawyer for four years. On the day I obtained my license, I told myself not to take on criminal cases."[51] A deputy minister of the Ministry of Justice admitted: "Due to the risks, some lawyers lack the courage to engage the court and lose their willingness to take on criminal cases. Some of them have even changed their jobs." He also stated the negative impact of state power on lawyers' choice of lawsuits:

> Lawyers' rights are frequently violated, which has resulted in a severe negative impact on their practice. . . . Due to the increased risks, lawyers' incentive and confidence are undermined . . . their involvement in criminal cases has not increased for years. The number of criminal lawsuits with legal representation is much lower than the total number of cases reviewed by the courts. . . . Such events have also undermined people's trust in lawyers and damaged their reputation. The responsibility of lawyers is to protect the legal rights of litigants, ensure the rightful implementation of the law, and promote justice. If lawyers cannot even protect their own rights, how can they defend the rights of others?[52]

As a result, when lawyers do take on criminal cases, they are cautious and tactful. As a lawyer reported:

> The reason that I have not been placed in a detention house thus far is that I learned a piece of advice in a class held by the Ministry of Justice in 1998. The teacher told us to never obtain a separate testimony from the witness. If it is inevitable, I would ask him or her to take the stand in court. For eight years, I have strictly adhered to this rule. Therefore, even when I have won over 10 criminal lawsuits, the legal departments cannot throw me in prison. But I have also taken precautionary measures by tailoring my work notes so that they can only be understood by me.[53]

Other lawyers have reported that at times when they interview detained suspects in criminal cases, they leave the phone numbers of their friends working in high-level legal departments or governments with their family members, in case they are detained or arrested. Others have reported that they hope to become delegates to the People's Congress. This reason is simple: if they become delegates, the legal department cannot detain or arrest them at will, because the arrest of such delegates requires the approval of the standing committee of the People's Congress.

Conclusion

This chapter explores some of the challenges faced by China in its "long march toward rule of law" by examining the interaction between state agencies and lawyers.[54]

Economic development and social changes in China have increasingly made legal institution building and the rule of law a necessity. As Lubman writes: "If China is to cope with the many problems that are by-products of economic reform, including a decline in social order, spreading corruption and a general crisis of values, it will need strong legal institutions and a legal culture that promotes the rule of law."[55] The Chinese government has realized the importance of a credible and viable legal system and has made efforts to promote the rule of law. The problem, however, is not only whether a law is enacted or not but also whether the law can be rigorously enforced. A fundamental problem with the legal system is the lack of effective constraints on the power of state agencies.[56]

This study shows that the power of state agencies, including government and legal organs, has affected the development of the legal system by influencing legal representation in China. A profound implication of the persistence of the great authority of these agencies is the unbalanced development of legal practice in China. Chinese lawyers are selective in taking on lawsuits and base their choices on cost–benefit calculations. They are more willing to take on cases pertaining to economic and civil affairs, as opposed to administrative litigation and criminal cases. In addition to the fact that lawyers benefit more financially by taking on economic or civil cases, the risks involved in administrative litigation or criminal cases serve as another deterrent. Administrative litigation often involve government agencies, so lawyers who defend their clients against state agencies may offend officials and risk punishment. Similarly, in criminal cases, the procuracy that acts as the public prosecutor has enormous power over lawyers. An institutionalized foundation for its power is the provision of the Criminal Law that governs misconduct of lawyers. While it is legitimate to regulate lawyers' conduct, the problem is that lawyers' rights are not adequately protected and the law has been abused by legal organizations.[57]

As lawyers are supposed to serve the interests of citizens, their reluctance to represent citizens in court will undoubtedly undermine the people's confidence in the legal system. As the more competent lawyers prefer to take on economic and civil lawsuits, those litigants involved in administrative litigation and criminal cases are often not well represented. Selective legal representation on the part of lawyers in China suggests that the legal community is deeply embedded in the political structure. To some extent, the situation of Chinese lawyers today reflects the continuation of the social, historical, and political factors that have shaped the legal profession ever since its emergence. Hence, the development of legal professionalism is more possible with legal, socioeconomic, and political changes that foster an environment in which lawyers have more autonomy, but are qualified and disciplined. Therefore, achieving an even thin rule of law in China remains challenging.

10

Law and Labor in Post-Mao China

Yunqiu Zhang

Pan Wei's proposal for building the rule of law in China shows an acute understanding of some fundamental problems with the current Chinese legal system and offers corresponding remedies for them. Should it be successfully implemented, China would be reasonably ranked as a country with rule of law. In Pan's proposal, nonelected technocratic elites—"neutral civil servants," "autonomous" judges, "independent" anticorruption agents, and "independent" auditors—would be central players in the rule of law structure. What is conspicuously absent is public participation—the participation of ordinary citizens.

In my opinion, any meaningful rule of law must directly engage ordinary citizens. Undoubtedly, as Pan suggests, a major function of rule of law is to regulate the state and particularly to discipline government officials and restrict their arbitrary acts. On the other hand, however, rule of law should also be directly concerned with society. Specifically, it should function to regulate social relations, especially to mediate conflicts or disputes among different social (or interest) groups, and above all to empower the underprivileged (e.g., workers) to protect themselves against encroachment by the privileged (e.g., employers). Since ordinary citizens are in a disadvantageous and vulnerable position vis-à-vis social elites, they particularly need law as a weapon for self-protection and they have the potential capacity to use the law. Therefore, the rule of law should be designed and built in such a way that it would meet the increasing needs of ordinary citizens and could be conveniently used by them for self-protection.

This chapter will address the necessity and possibility of involving ordinary citizens in building the rule of law by examining the interactions between law and a specific social group—workers.

With the deepening of the market-oriented economic reform in post-Mao China, the labor relationship has been becoming strained and labor disputes have been increasing. Given that most labor disputes are caused by employers' violations of workers' interests, workers are increasingly facing the challenge of finding effective means to defend their own interests. Recent scholarly studies have indicated that workers often responded to violations of their interests with street protests (demonstrations).[1] Numerous labor protests did indeed occur, especially in the late 1980s and the 1990s. However, protests were far from the principal strategy for workers to redress their grievances. As Blecher aptly argues, workers' protests remained "spasmodic, spontaneous and uncoordinated." The explanation Blecher offers for this lack of "coordinated challenge" on the part of workers is that "workers have become subject to hegemony of the market and of the state—workers have come to accept the core values of the market and of the state as legitimate." Blecher's assessment is objective and insightful—it acknowledges that workers and the state share some common values and concerns, and that the two sides are not necessarily mutually hostile or confrontational.[2]

The following pages will attempt to tackle the issue—why workers did not adopt street protests as a major strategy in defending their interests, or why there was a lack of radical or coordinated challenge from workers—from a different perspective, namely, the perspective of labor laws. This approach is based on the assumption that labor laws, which have proliferated in the reform years as a result of vigorous state legislative efforts, have provided workers with a new channel to settle their disputes with management and to express their concerns and to protect their interests, as well as the assumption that this legal channel—state-sanctioned or -supported—is less risky than protests (which are not endorsed by the state and could likely incur state reprisals) and therefore is preferable for most workers and could serve as an alternative to protests. To test this assumption, the following questions will be examined: What are the major labor legislation efforts made by the state? How did this labor legislation affect workers? Did labor legislation serve to restrain or enhance workers' capability to confront management? Were workers willing and able to seek legal action when getting involved in labor disputes? What were the challenges workers faced in taking legal action?

Primarily based on the author's field studies in Qingdao,[3] especially interviews with workers and investigation of some labor lawsuits, this chapter argues that labor legislation had a positive effect on workers—providing them with a useful weapon for self-protection; workers gradually developed an awareness of the rule of law and the willingness to use legal means in handling their disputes with management and, in so doing, they often succeeded. On the other hand, however, the legal weapon proved too heavy for ordinary workers to wield—they had to face enormous and often insurmountable barriers in lodging and winning lawsuits.

Labor Legislation

Labor legislation in post-Mao China started in the early 1980s and gained momentum in the 1990s. During the two decades, various kinds of labor laws (or regulations) were enacted and put into effect by both the central and local authorities. These labor laws addressed all major aspects of the labor relationship. While aimed at protecting the "lawful" interests of both labor and capital, they put overwhelming emphasis on labor's rights and interests. Take the *Regulations on Labor Management in Foreign-related Enterprises in Qingdao* (1993) as an example. This document consists of eleven chapters: (1) general provisions; (2) recruitment of workers; (3) labor contracts; (4) wages; (5) work hours and vacation; (6) social insurance and benefits; (7) labor training; (8) labor safety and sanitation; (9) labor disputes; (10) labor supervision; (11) legal responsibilities; and (12) additional notes. They can be divided into three groups in terms of their points of emphasis. Group one includes chapters 1 and 12, which outline the goals and principles of the regulation as well as the scope of its application. Group two includes chapters 2, 3, 9, and 10, which are neutral and constrain both labor and capital. Chapters 3 and 9 seem particularly important for the purpose of this study. The former stipulates that employers and workers must sign labor contracts on the principles of "voluntarism and equality and of negotiation and mutual agreement" (*ziyuan pingdeng, xieshang yizhi*); it also sets conditions for suspension of labor contracts. Chapter 9 is about channels or procedures for settling labor disputes: through enterprise-based mediation committees, or district- or city-level arbitration committees, or the court of law. Group three, including chapters 4, 5, 6, 7, 8, and 11, is the main body of the regulation, almost exclusively dealing with employers' obligations and workers' interests and rights. Chapter 4 provides for standards of wages: average wages should be 120 percent as much as those in the state enterprises of the same industry; minimum wages should not be lower than those in state enterprises; wage rates should be raised every year in proportion to growth in production; payment of wages should not be defaulted on. Chapter 5 stipulates that daily and weekly work hours should not exceed eight and forty-eight respectively; extra work hours should not exceed two hours daily, six hours weekly, and 120 hours annually; pay for working extra hours and holidays should be 50 percent and 100 percent higher than normal wages respectively; breaks (45 minutes during an eight-hour work day) and nursing time for women workers (twice daily, 30 minutes each time) should be allowed. Chapter 6 requires enterprises to pay a certain portion of fees for workers' pensions, unemployment insurance, and medical care as well as housing subsidies. According to chapter 7, employers should provide workers with vocational and technical training. Chapter 8 obliges management to take efficient measures to improve working conditions and strengthen labor protection and guarantee labor safety. Chapter 11 outlines legal penalties (mainly fines) that would be imposed on employers should they fail to fulfill their obligations.[4]

The most comprehensive national-level labor legislation is the Labor Law. In addition to all the main points covered in other labor legislation, the Labor Law contains new provisions, particularly concerning women's interests. Chapter 7, "Special Protection for Female and Non-Adult (between 16 and 18 years old) Employees," stipulates that female employees who are menstruating not be asked to work high above the ground, in low temperatures, in cold water, or to do jobs of high labor intensity (above grade three); female workers who are seven months' pregnant not be asked to work overtime and night shifts, and their maternity leave not be less than ninety days.[5] Within a year or so after the passing of the Labor Law, a set of more specific national-level labor regulations were promulgated as its supplements.[6] These labor laws were characterized by overwhelming and almost one-sided emphasis on workers' rights and interests and employers' obligations. The rationale for this legislative orientation was that labor was too weak and vulnerable vis-à-vis capital and hence needed more concern. Doubtless, these labor laws provided workers with a potentially powerful weapon in their struggle against encroachment by capital.

To ensure that the labor laws would function to benefit workers rather than remain dead letters, the Chinese regime and especially trade unions at different levels adopted a variety of measures such as promoting legal education and founding legal assistance centers. Legal education was intended to popularize labor laws among workers and to awaken workers to their "lawful rights and interests" (*hefa quanyi*), thereby enabling them to use the "legal weapon" for self-protection. In the city of Qingdao, for example, city- and district-level trade unions frequently organized study sessions on labor laws among workers. Between November 14, 2001, and February 20, 2002, the All-China Federation of Trade Unions launched a nationwide campaign—The Trade Union Law Knowledge Contest (*Gonghuifa zhishi jingsai*)—to propagandize the revised Trade Union Law. The contest questions, concerning all major issues on the rights of trade unions and workers, were published in major newspapers such as *Renmin Ribao, Gongren Ribao,* and *Fazhi Ribao.* Local unions and workers responded to this campaign enthusiastically. In Quanzhou of Fujian Province, 30,000 workers participated in the contest; in Nanning, trade unions, to prepare workers for the contest, distributed labor legislation materials and set up billboards with labor legislation information in public parks and streets; unions in Guizhou organized a preliminary labor law knowledge contest involving 120,000 workers. These activities helped to increase workers' awareness that there existed various labor laws and that they could use these laws to defend their own interests.[7]

As a further step to make labor legislation function for the benefit of workers, union organizations, backed by local governments, began in the mid-1990s to set up workers' legal assistance centers or agencies at different levels (city, district or county, and street) with the responsibility of providing legal services to workers.[8] The logic behind this effort was that many workers themselves, restrained by a shortage of resources at their disposal (especially money, time, and legal experience), were unable to fight legal battles against their powerful employers and therefore needed legal assistance from outside; such legal assistance, it was thought, would be conducive to the quick settlement of labor disputes and thus help maintain social stability.[9] By April 1996, most provincial and city-level trade unions had their own legal work departments (*falu gongzuo bu*) and legal service agencies (*falu fuwu jigou*). In that year, the All-China Federation of Trade Unions initiated a three-year program aimed at training 1,120 new union-affiliated lawyers, 6,000 labor arbitrators, and 300,000 labor law supervisors.[10]

The legal assistance agencies were staffed with professional legal personnel and financed primarily by government funds and donations from nongovernmental organizations and businesses. To address the shortage of full-time legal workers affiliated with the legal assistance agencies, local authorities called on "societal forces" (*shehui liliang*), especially independent law offices, to offer their help. In Guangzhou, law offices were required to provide voluntary assistance to the city's legal assistance centers and their records of working with these centers were linked to the annual review and renewal of their lawyers' licenses. Meanwhile, law students were mobilized to work as volunteers for the legal assistance centers. Services that were provided to workers by these legal assistance centers included offering consultation on labor issues, preparing complaints, filing lawsuits, and appearing in court on workers' behalf. Legal fees were charged at discounted rates for workers with union membership, and free legal service was granted to "particularly poor workers." During the five years from 1995 to 1999, Qingdao's legal assistance centers at the city and district levels provided 85,000 workers with free legal services—legal consultation, representing workers in 200 arbitration cases and lawsuits, writing 150 complaints.[11] In the city of Beipiao (in Liaoning Province), the Municipal General Trade Union's legal service department issued legal assistance cards to 10,000 staff and workers (union members) by 2001. The cards stated that workers would receive free consultation at the city's legal service agencies, including law offices, and that their lawsuits could be represented by the General Trade Union's legal assistance department.[12] To make legal services more readily accessible to workers, city or district-level unions in some localities also encouraged enterprise-level unions to set up and maintain their own legal assistance agencies. In Ningdu county of Jiangxi Province, for example, unions in twenty-one private enterprises hired lawyers as of December 11, 2001. These lawyers provided the following year-round services to workers: offering lectures on labor laws; reviewing labor contracts on workers' behalf; protecting workers' welfare (pensions, medical care, and social insurance); representing workers in mediation and lawsuits.[13]

Partly due to the legal education campaign and help from the legal assistance centers or agencies, workers increasingly became aware of their legitimate interests and rights and were ready to use the legal weapon in solving disputes with their employers. In so doing, they won most legal cases.

Labor Litigation

In the post-Mao era (the 1980s and the 1990s), the settlement of labor disputes in China involved the use of three mechanisms or institutions: mediation, arbitration, and two-level trial (*liang shen zhi*) by the (People's) Court of Law. Mediation occurred at the grassroots or enterprise level and was handled by the mediation committee composed of representatives of management, workers, and the trade union in the enterprise. Mediation was not a legal procedure, nor was it a required step in the process of settling a labor dispute. The decision reached by the mediation committee was not legally binding. If either of the two disputing parties deemed the mediation committee's decision unacceptable, they could apply for arbitration. They also could choose to bypass mediation from the outset and resort directly to arbitration.[14]

Arbitration was conducted at the city or district level by the arbitration committee, whose members included representatives from management, the trade union, and the government's labor agency (or department). The committee employed legal professionals and labor issue experts as full-time or part-time arbitrators and had the power to authorize them to form an arbitration court to settle a specific labor dispute case. The formation of the arbitration court was based on the principle of "one court for one case"; an arbitration court is formed for a certain case and is dismissed with the settlement of that case. Arbitration was a legal procedure indispensable for settling a labor dispute and could not be bypassed. The decision made by the arbitration court was legally binding on both parties involved in the labor dispute and could be executed compulsorily by the Court of Law. If either of the two parties disagreed with the arbitration committee's decision, it could present the case to the Court of Law.

Trial by the Court of Law was the final step in the process of settling a labor dispute. There was no specialized labor court in China. Labor dispute lawsuits were handled by the civil court. They were first tried by the lower-level (county or district) court. If the plaintiff or defendant felt dissatisfied with the lower-level court's verdict, he or she could chose to appeal to a higher-level (municipal) court, whose decision was final and had to be executed.[15]

Of the three institutions (mediation, arbitration, court trial), mediation was most critical in the settling of labor disputes. It appealed to all parties concerned (workers, management, and the government), primarily because of its low financial and social costs. The services rendered by the mediation committee were free and readily accessible to both workers and management; and settlement of labor disputes through mediation would not necessarily lead to deterioration of the labor–capital relationship, since mediation, primarily based on persuasion and negotiation or dialogue, did not always involve the kind of confrontation or animosity characterized with harsh mutual blaming or charges. By contrast, services provided by the arbitration committee and the Court of Law entailed the payment of service fees from workers and/or employers, and these fees had the effect of deterring the two parties concerned, especially individual workers, from actively pursuing a lawsuit. In addition, due to the influence of Chinese cultural tradition, which discredits litigation as disruptive of social harmony, many workers have tended to regard resorting to litigation as a disgraceful act to be avoided. To some workers, launching a legal battle against their employers, even if they won, might not result in improvement of their conditions, but it would instead bring about new problems for them, particularly reprisals from their employers, unless they chose to quit their jobs at the end of the litigation. As far as the government was concerned, litigation also was less desirable, since it cost state resources and functioned to embitter the labor–capital relationship and was therefore potentially conducive to social instability. This concern explains why the Chinese regime persistently gave the first priority to mediation as a means of settling labor disputes.[16]

Although mediation remained the primary channel for labor dispute settlement, arbitration increasingly became an important alternative to it in the latter half of the 1990s, as demonstrated by the dramatic increase in both the number of labor disputes handled by the arbitration committee and the number of workers involved (see Table 10.1). Behind these numbers lay the growing interest of workers in litigation and their willingness to exploit it. In a state-run enterprise in Qingdao, about half of the workers surveyed acknowledged that they had consulted with others on labor laws. Seventy percent of them promised that they would "go to the court" if their "legiti-

Table 10.1

Labor Disputes Accepted by Arbitration Committees

	1993	1994	1995	1996	1998
Number of cases	12,358	19,098	33,030	48,121	93,645
Number of workers involved	—	77,794	122,512	—	358,531

Sources: Zhongguo laodong tongji nianjian (Chinese labor yearbook) 1995, p. 491, 1996, p. 423, and 1999, p. 507; *1997 Zhongguo zhigong zhuangkuang diaocha* (Survey of the status of Chinese staff and workers in 1997), p. 111.

mate rights and interests were violated," and 60 percent vowed that even if a lawsuit lasted for several years, they would "continue the litigation until justice was won." Some employers and managers in the city of Qingdao confided that "nowadays" workers were so keenly aware of and fond of talking about their "lawful rights and interests," and so inclined to "seek litigation," that they needed to be dealt with carefully.[17] Such "litigiousness" of workers was further borne out by the testimonies of some workers who had involved themselves in labor lawsuits. One worker (in a private company), who had been dismissed by management a month before the expiration of his labor contract on grounds that there was not enough work, argued:

> One month's wages may make no big difference for my family's livelihood. But I felt I simply could not remain passive with regards to the injustice done to me by the cruel employer. What I wanted was justice. I sincerely believed that I was innocent and would win the lawsuit—that is why I directly applied for arbitration without going through mediation.

Another worker (in a private enterprise) whose wages were cut by management as a penalty for her refusal to do more overtime work, made a complaint first with the city's arbitration committee and then, dissatisfied with the decision of the committee, presented her case to the district court. Three months elapsed before the case was settled in her favor. She told this author emotionally:

> I already had been on overtime too much and felt exhausted. I needed rest and to spend more time with my family. Some employers really think that they are masters and can do anything to us workers. As an individual, I am indeed powerless; but there is law, which can help me. I was determined to seek a redress [*tao ge shuofa*] for the unfair treatment I suffered. So I lodged the lawsuit. Although in doing so I and my family encountered lots of difficulties, I am happy that I eventually won the case.

In another case, three workers were dismissed by the new management when their (state-owned) company was merged into another one. Having failed to persuade the management to withdraw its decision, they lodged a complaint with the city's arbitration committee and the committee ruled that the new company should resume the employment of these workers. Disagreeing with this decision, the management filed a complaint with the district-level court and won. In turn, the three workers appealed to the city-level court, only to find their appeal rejected. Frustrated, but not intending to give up, they vowed to appeal to the upper-level (provincial) court. One worker said:

> We are determined to defend our legitimate right to work and will continue to appeal to the higher authorities to redress our grievances. No matter what troubles are ahead, to seek justice, we will fight to the end even at the cost of our entire family fortune.

These workers indeed seemed "litigious"—they were ready to take advantage of the legal system to redress their grievances, or in their own words, "to seek a redress," and in so doing they proved persistent. "Seek a redress" (*tao ge shuofa*) became a catchphrase among many workers in the 1990s,[18] which demonstrated workers' growing awareness of the usefulness of litigation as a weapon for safeguarding their interests and their confidence in the prospect of the rule of law. In this regard, workers' level of literacy could make a difference. According to a survey by the ACFTU (All-China Federation of Trade Unions), employees with higher levels of education (college or university) were more prone to seek litigation than those with lower levels of education (elementary, middle school, and high school).[19] With technical or managerial expertise and skills that enabled them to find new employment, they needed not worry too much about potentially unfavorable repercussions that a lawsuit might bring about, particularly potential retaliation from employers. In most cases, however, workers preferred to settle their disputes with employers by mild or less confrontational means such as private talks or negotiations with management, mediation by a third party, petitioning of trade unions (especially at the city level) or government agencies; only when these means failed or when they felt deeply insulted by the employers' overbearing and callous attitudes toward their requests did they resort to litigation. Furthermore, in pursuing litigation, most workers simply attempted to seek fair redress of their verifiable grievances or to protect their "lawful interests and rights" rather than use exaggerated or alleged grievances as an excuse to extract excessive benefits from employers. Workers' "litigiousness" did not necessarily have to do with the nature or culture of the laboring class. Instead, it essentially resulted from the adverse circumstances under which they lived and worked. In other words, workers were driven to be litigious by the forces hostile to them and beyond their control.

In pursuit of litigation, notably arbitration (the main form of litigation), workers followed different paths and adopted a variety of strategies. Some, mostly those with good educations, chose to work on their own instead of seeking assistance from legal experts or lawyers. They took the initiative in filing complaints, prepared necessary documents themselves, and paid legal fees out of their own pockets. These workers were relatively well acquainted with labor legislation and confident about the prospects of their legal action. One worker in this category, who won a legal case entirely through his own efforts, explained why he had preferred to go it alone:

> In my case, it is crystal clear that my employer bluntly violated my lawful interests; from the very beginning, I knew that I had a strong case against him and that he would be doomed to lose if I sued him. Then why should I bother to hire or consult with any legal experts? It would be a waste of time and money![20]

Other workers, especially those who were in poor financial straits or less educated, tended to launch their legal crusades with the encouragement or help from legal assistance agencies. A worker in this category, who won a case in arbitration, confided:

> Initially I was reluctant to confront my boss [laoban] in the arbitration court, since I felt that I could not afford the arbitration fees and that as an ordinary individual worker I was powerless vis-à-vis the boss. On the other hand, however, I was unwilling to swallow the grievances. So with the suggestion of a friend of mine, I gathered courage and went to the legal assistance center, asking for help. A legal expert in the center reviewed my case and came to the conclusion that my boss was in the wrong and that given my family's economic situation, I was eligible for free legal assistance. So the center prepared and filed a complaint with the arbitration committee on my behalf. The center almost did everything for me.

To ensure the success of their legal battles, some workers were ready to explore and mobilize other resources such as mass media, local authorities, and personal connections. For example, they could release their stories—"grievances" or "injustices"—to journalists, who would in turn investigate the cases, particularly by visiting the employers concerned. This would likely bring pressure to bear upon these employers. Worried about the potential damage to their reputations that publicizing of the lawsuits might bring about, they might choose to seek a quick end to the disputes by taking a conciliatory tone (or making concessions to workers). Although the media are largely under the regime's control, reports about labor disputes and lawsuits did frequently appear in newspapers, local and national.[21] When cases were made public, especially if their settlement met with difficulties and lingered too long, they could easily attract intervention by local authorities. The latter, deeply concerned about social stability, were likely to urge legal institutions (the court and the arbitration committee, some of whose members concurrently worked with local government departments) to expedite settlement of labor disputes in favor of workers. These cases could also attract the attention of local, especially city-level (general), trade unions, which openly and unequivocally identified themselves as workers' organizations or representatives, and would come to offer their assistance to workers, providing free legal counsel and helping find legal experts or lawyers as their legal representatives. Sometimes, workers actively and directly appealed to local officials and unions for help with their legal battles. This strategy of publicizing a legal case and appealing to local leaders often worked in China, a country still without a sound or full-fledged modern legal system.[22]

The overwhelming majority of labor lawsuits were initiated by workers, with only a small portion by employers. Lawsuits initiated by workers accounted for 90.5 percent and 90.6 percent of the total lawsuits in 1993 and 1998 respectively.[23] Among the labor-initiated cases, most were concerned with workers' economic benefits—

wages (remuneration), work hours, labor contracts, labor welfare (labor insurance, pensions, and medical insurance), and labor protection. The root causes of these lawsuits were overt or covert violations of workers' interests by employers—being in arrears in wage payments, arbitrarily deducting wages, extending work hours without appropriate overtime pay, changing or terminating labor contracts without advance notice, failing to pay labor insurance or pensions, or refusing to cover medical costs related to on-the-job accidents.

Above all, arrears in wage payments seem most irritating to workers. Some surveys revealed that 76 or 90 percent of labor disputes were brought about by employers' default in paying their workers.[24] As far as capital-initiated lawsuits were concerned, most of them were related to workers' failure to honor labor contracts, for example, they left to work for new employers before the expiration of their labor contracts and without their employers' consent, which often caused interruptions of production. Some of these workers had received extensive and full-time technical or managerial training, even abroad, with the sponsorship of their employers, and their sudden departure did inflict economic losses on the enterprises.

What worried the employers most was that accompanying the departure of these employees, their "business secrets" would likely be disclosed to their competitors (other businesspeople). Under such circumstances, the employers concerned tended to use all means, including litigation, to recover their losses—demanding compensation from the workers and their new employers.[25] Employers could be rather persistent with the pursuit of litigation in defense of their interests. It often occurred that employers, after losing cases in arbitration, appealed first to the lower-level (district) court and then, if they lost again, to the higher-level (city-level) court. Sometimes they persisted in lawsuits even though knowing well that they, obviously in the wrong, would have no chance of winning the cases in the courtroom. Why were employers still willing to engage continuously in the legal battle (e.g., moving from arbitration to court trials) if there was no hope for victory? As a matter of fact, these employers were not sincerely seeking justice but rather playing a game or tactic, one of "wearing down or exhausting the workers." They believed that, as employers, they possessed more resources (notably money and time), and therefore could afford a protracted legal battle; by stark contrast, individual workers were in a disadvantageous situation and unable to sustain for long the time-consuming and costly lawsuits; thus if lawsuits dragged, workers would likely feel exhausted and choose to seek accommodation with employers or simply drop the cases. In reality, however, this tactic did not work in most cases, mainly because it was counterweighed by persistence on the part of workers.[26]

Litigation functioned well in settling most labor disputes and especially in protecting labor's interests and rights. The vast majority of cases that were filed received serious treatment and successful settlement either by the arbitration committee or the Court of Law. For example, 94 percent of all cases *accepted* by the arbitration committee in 1995 were *arbitrated* (settled) in the same year, and 98.5 percent were settled in the year of 1998 (see Table 10.2) Generally, labor dispute cases were handled fairly and in accordance with the law. When being interviewed by this author, the workers

Table 10.2

Cases of Labor Disputes Settled by Arbitration Committees

			Results of settlements		
Year	Accepted	Settled	Lawsuits won for employees	Lawsuits won for factories or companies	Lawsuits partly won by both parties
1995	33,030	31,415 (94%)	16,272 (51%)	6,189 (19.7%)	8,954 (28.5%)
1998	93,649	92,288 (98.5%)	48,650 (52.7%)	11,937 (13%)	27,365 (29.6%)

Sources: Zhongguo laodong tongji nianjian (Chinese labor yearbook) 1995, p. 491, 1996, p. 423, and 1999, p. 507; *1997 Zhongguo zhigong zhuangkuang diaocha* (Survey of the status of Chinese staff and workers in 1997), p. 111.

who had become involved in litigation and won their cases all acknowledged that they were treated fairly (by the arbitrators and judges) and were satisfied with the results of arbitration and court trials, although they also complained about the various difficulties they had encountered in the process of litigation. Some of them expressed their confidence in the legal system and litigation, vowing that they would not hesitate to take legal action in the future if they felt their interests were encroached upon again by management.

Litigation seems an effective weapon for workers to use in safeguarding their legitimate interests, as testified by the fact that workers won most labor dispute lawsuits. For instance, in 1995 workers won 51 percent of the total cases in arbitration compared to only 20 percent won by employers (the rest were won partly by both parties), and in 1998 the cases won by workers accounted for 52.7 percent, while those won by employers only constituted 13 percent (Table 10.2). According to other estimates, workers were winners of 60, 70, or even 93 percent of the lawsuits.[27] Workers would have had more chance of winning if they had not missed the so-called prescription (time limit—*shixian*). The Labor Law of the PRC stipulates that if workers or management intend to file a complaint with the arbitration committee, they must do so within sixty days of the date on which the labor dispute occurred. But many workers were unaware of this rule. Some of them brought their cases to the arbitration committee long after the time limit (or prescription) had passed and had to face rejection. Sometimes workers lost lawsuits because of failing to provide or keep relevant proof such as letters or notices from their employers, dismissals (or layoffs), reductions of wages, and the like.

Problems

As demonstrated in the previous pages, legal legislation generally functioned to the benefit of workers, serving as a useful weapon in defending their lawful rights and interests, and many workers indeed became increasingly willing to use this weapon. However, this legal weapon proved too heavy for workers to wield. In order to fight a successful legal battle with their employers, workers had to encounter and overcome various barriers.

First and foremost, workers were restrained financially and sometimes could not afford litigation fees. In Guangzhou, for example, payment of between 400 and 500 yuan was a precondition for applying for arbitration, and average lawyer fees for one case amounted to about 1,000 yuan, which was beyond many workers' financial capability. Although workers could apply for help from legal assistance centers, they had to meet certain criteria in order to be eligible for the assistance. In Guangzhou, before July 29, 2002, it was stipulated that only workers from families with a 380 yuan (or below) per capita income were eligible for legal assistance. Since July 29, 2002, the amount has been increased to 500 yuan or below, covering 20 percent of the population of the city.[28] Eligibility did not necessarily guarantee availability of legal assistance, since many legal assistance centers, underfunded, were plagued with a chronic shortage of money and personnel. This financial restraint deterred some workers from entering lawsuits.

Another obstacle workers often met in lodging lawsuits had to do with collecting and presenting evidence. Chinese civil law stipulates that whoever lodges the complaint is obliged to provide evidence (*shui zhuzhang, shui juzheng*). This principle applies to labor lawsuits.[29] Workers would have the obligation to provide relevant evidence if they wished to sue their employers. In practice, however, it was difficult and sometimes impossible for workers to collect evidence, primarily because of the employers' refusal to cooperate. To make things worse, some employers tried to hide, destroy, or even forge evidence. Fellow workers generally shied away from being witnesses, fearing potential reprisals from employers. Without sufficient and valid evidence, workers would have no hope of winning their cases although they may have suffered genuine injustices.[30]

Furthermore, workers sometimes found themselves in the dilemma of winning lawsuits without getting the benefits they had fought for. A court decision might be in the worker's favor, but its enforcement could be problematic. Specifically, it could be compromised or blocked by employers who were reluctant to honor the court decision. In one case, for example, the employer ignored the court verdict that he reemploy the worker he dismissed. Only under the court's repeated pressure did the employer call back the worker, but he neither assigned the worker a job nor paid him. For this, the employer incurred further intervention from the court and was penalized. Embarrassed and irritated, the employer vented his spite on the worker—chronically finding fault with him, and eventually forcing him to quit. Indeed, retaliation was a major concern for workers when they decided to enter a lawsuit against their employers, who could easily find an excuse to punish those "litigious" workers by laying them off, lowering their wages, and giving them less desirable job assignments.

The employers' reluctance or even refusal to carry out court orders for workers can be partly explained by their concern for "saving face"—protecting the dignity of their authority. To the employer, following a court order and reversing a decision of his own would well mean losing face—undermining his credibility and authority. In other cases, employers failed to redress injustices as the court ruled because of their inability to do so (especially when economic compensation and payment of defaulted wages were involved)—their businesses were unprofitable and even on the edge of bankruptcy. Under such circumstances, further judicial intervention would be to little avail. Generally, the court was loath to push an enterprise (especially if it was state-run) to bankruptcy by compulsory execution of its orders, for that would lead to the unemployment of more workers, which in turn had the potential of causing social instability. In this sense, even the court itself was constrained by the general economic and social conditions of the country.

Some difficulties that bothered workers in pursuing litigation were caused by the loopholes in the Labor Law itself. The Labor Law served as the basis of arbitration and court trials in labor dispute cases. Yet it was far from adequate: it only set forth general principles without giving consideration to specific circumstances, and it was not revised periodically to cover new problems that arose in the accelerated economic reforms. For example, in Henan Province an enterprise was sold by the township government, which caused the suspension of payment of pensions to the retirees. The latter collectively applied for arbitration and requested that the payment of their pensions be resumed. But the (county) arbitration committee refused to handle this case on the grounds that it resulted from a government act and hence was beyond the purview of labor dispute arbitration. The arbitration committee apparently denied that this was a labor dispute case, simply because it involved the government.[31] Certainly the committee could find an excuse for its decision in the Labor Law, which defined a labor dispute as one between labor and the management instead of one between labor and government. Thus, the inadequacy of the Labor Law meant genuine inconvenience for workers.

In addition, workers' use of the legal weapon was sometimes impeded by the shortage of qualified arbitration personnel, judges, and labor lawyers. Some members of the arbitration committee, without receiving systematic legal or judicial training, were not sufficiently acquainted with labor laws and regulations. Others lacked a "consciousness of the rule of law" and succumbed to influence or pressure from the government, especially when handling lawsuits involving state-run enterprises—this suggests that judicial independence was still an ideal to be realized in China. Besides, labor lawsuits kept increasing rapidly while there was no corresponding growth in the number of arbitration committee members, which could not but lead to a delay of labor lawsuit settlements and compromise the quality of an arbitration (especially when sufficient evidence could not be gathered due to the shortage of arbitration personnel). As far as lawyers were concerned, their number was too small compared to the number of workers—for example, as of April 1996, there were only 90,000 lawyers nationwide, while workers numbered 200 million. Some lawyers were unwilling to accept labor dispute cases, since legal service fees for this type of case were not only relatively low but also not guaranteed, given the clients' (mostly workers) generally poor economic conditions. By contrast, they were more interested in cases related to disputes over real estate, securities, finance, and intellectual property, which would bring them high profits. Besides, some lawyers were unfamiliar with labor legislation, partly due to the fact that most labor-related laws were promulgated only recently (since the mid-1990s).

Toward the Rule of Law in the Area of Labor

The previous discussion has suggested that in the post-Mao era, especially in the 1990s, labor laws (and regulations) proliferated owing to the unprecedented and vigorous legislative efforts by the regime, and litigation became an increasingly important channel for resolution of labor disputes. The labor laws, with their emphasis on labor's rights and interests, were exploited by workers as a weapon for self-protection. Partly due to the legal education campaigns, more and more workers became acquainted with labor laws and interested in using legal channels to settle disputes with their employers, as demonstrated by the fact that over 90 percent of labor lawsuits were initiated by workers. The legal weapon proved to be useful to workers, considering that they won the majority of labor lawsuits. Obviously, in the area of labor, China was already on the track toward building a modern legal system and the rule of law.

The use of legal channels to settle labor disputes marked a major departure from the practice of the Mao era. During that period, administrative or political means rather than legal means played the dominant role in the handling of labor issues. Party or state policies and officials' instructions were above the laws and used in labor management.[32] State bureaucrats exercised their power in settling labor disputes. Accordingly, labor legislation and the building of relevant legal institutions were neglected, especially after the completion of socialist transformation in the mid-1950s. They became simply nonexistent during the chaotic years of the Cultural Revolution (1966–1976). Under such circumstances, the working people, generally lacking a sense of the rule of law, could hardly come up with the idea of using litigation to redress their grievances. When involved in any labor disputes, their only option was to passively wait for official intervention. This lack of the rule of law was fundamentally shaped by the then prevailing command economic system, under which the state monopolized all major economic powers, not only owning but also directly managing all industrial and commercial enterprises, and deciding on such labor-related matters as employment, wages, vacations, and working conditions. Such overall economic control enabled the state to use administrative means in settling labor disputes. In addition, the labor relationship under the command economic system was essentially a relationship between workers and the state, and generally remained simple and stable. Intensive labor disputes hardly existed, since sources of labor disputes were few and limited, which was in turn largely due to the unified labor allocation and fixed wage systems and relatively safe working environment, as well as the regime's firm ideological control. Almost absent were the kind of serious violations of workers' interests (e.g., arbitrary deduction of wages, random extension of work hours, and dismissals). These socioeconomic conditions tended to render almost irrelevant labor legislation and the building of rule of law in the labor area.

Administrative intervention as a means for settling labor disputes gradually became obsolete in the post-Mao years, with the deepening of market-oriented economic reforms and the changing of labor relations. During the reforms, the state gradually relinquished its direct control over enterprises. Formerly state-owned enterprises increasingly became independent economic entities, operating according to the basic market principle of demand and supply. Private businesses, both Chinese and foreign, multiplied and flourished. In this new economic environment, labor relations underwent fundamental changes. No longer dominated by state power, there developed capitalist-style relations between labor and capital; no longer simple and stable, these relations became diverse, antagonistic, and unstable. Labor disputes kept arising and often erupted into strikes and stoppages. Acutely concerned with economic development and social order, the state was anxious to stabilize the ever-deteriorating labor relations. On the other hand, it became aware that the traditional way of handling the labor relationship—direct government intervention—was no longer workable (because of the diminution of state power over enterprises) and that new mechanisms needed to be found. The principal new mechanism that the state found was labor legislation. From the state's perspective, labor laws could be used to define more authoritatively the rights and obligations of labor and capital in market economic conditions and serve as an effective yardstick for the settlement of labor disputes; using the legal means to manage labor relations was consistent with international conventions and hence would be acceptable to both workers and employers, and especially to foreign investors. The state's efforts at labor legislation were thus necessitated by, or a response to, the dramatic changes in labor relations brought about by the market-oriented economic reforms. They implied that the state was no longer omnipresent and omnipotent, and had to succumb to market forces just as workers did.

Labor legislation was not an isolated legislative phenomenon. Instead, it was paralleled by legislation in other areas—civil, criminal, administrative, and the like. As a matter of fact, it was part of the Chinese regime's long-term and overall strategy of building the rule of law, which in turn constituted the core of political reform. From Deng Xiaoping to Jiang Zemin, Chinese leaders have been committed to implementing this strategy. As a result of the regime's persistent efforts, about 329 national-level laws (and regulations) and 6,200 local-level laws were passed between 1979 and 2000.[33] No longer simply a rubber stamp, the People's Congress—the legislative body—at different levels was strengthened and gained substantial power. Various new legal institutions such as law offices (private and foreign-operated) and legal assistance centers were set up. Legal education, a major means for the socialization of law, was promoted to train legal personnel and to enhance the public's legal consciousness. Particularly important was the change in the regime's perception of the nature of law. The regime tended to abandon its instrumentalist view of law, which regarded law simply as an instrument for the suppression of one class by another and especially for state control or domination of society in the name of proletarian dictatorship.[34] Meanwhile, the regime gradually came to embrace the principle of "all are equal before the law" and to see law as the embodiment of the will of the whole society, as a major channel to resolve conflicts and regulate social order, and as a weapon individuals could use to protect their legitimate rights and interests from encroachment by all forces, including state bureaucrats. Should law still be identified as a kind of means, it was to serve not only the interests of the state but also those of the general public. Such a perception of law became popular among more and more Chinese citizens, who were ready to use the law when the need arose. This popular legal awakening led to the steady increase in the number of civil lawsuits, a large proportion of which were related to compensation for property damage. Doubtless, in the post-Mao era, the rule of law has emerged and gained prominence in all areas, including that of labor, and the Chinese have proved receptive to modern ideas about the rule of law just as they did to ideas about the market economy.

It must be emphasized that the rule of law in the area of labor (as well as in other areas) in post-Mao China is still in its nascent stage. As outlined in the third section of this chapter, numerous problems exist in the current labor legal system, especially in the enforcement of labor laws and court verdicts. Overcoming these problems will take a long time, which in turn means that building a full-fledged modern legal system or law-ruled society will be a long and tortuous process in the Chinese context.

11

The Internet and Emerging Civil Society in China

Guobin Yang

The debate on the rule of law and democracy sparked by Pan Wei's essay assumes that neither rule of law nor democracy exists in China at the dawn of the twenty-first century. The Chinese government may have been building a legal system for decades, yet this system lacks transparency, accountability, and due process. It is not surprising, therefore, that Chinese citizens are increasingly resorting to contentious means in their struggles for a more just society. The Internet answers an immediate social need. It provides a new medium for citizens to speak up, link up, and act up against power, corruption, and social injustice. In this way, the Internet has influenced the development of civil society and given expression to grassroots impulses for political reform. No analysis of political change in contemporary China can afford to ignore these social forces. The goal of this chapter is to provide an empirical assessment of how the use of the Internet has influenced civil society development and thereby contributed, in explicit and implicit ways, to popular struggles for a more just society.

The Internet has been used in three key areas of Chinese civil society, namely, the public sphere, social organizations, and popular protest. With respect to China's public sphere, the Internet has fostered public debate and problem articulation and demonstrated the potential to play a supervisory role in Chinese politics. It enables citizens to speak up. In the realm of associational life, the Internet has facilitated the activities of existing organizations while creating a new associational form, the cyber-organization. It helps citizens to link up. Finally, the Internet has introduced new forms and dynamics into popular protest. It provides a space for citizens to act up.

Before I go on, a few caveats are in order. The first caveat is that the Internet is a contested area. Like other technologies, it is a double-edged weapon and can be used differently by different social actors. A study of the social impact of the Internet does not draw a linear causal arrow from the Internet to civil society. Rather, it shows how agents in civil society use the Internet and, in the process, strengthen civil society. It requires an understanding of the social activities online.

Second, because the Internet can be used for different purposes, one field of struggle is about who decides what technical functions it may have and how to obtain those functions.[1] These struggles shape the future of the technology, making it more or less open to democratic practices. In appearance, ordinary Internet users are not directly involved in these struggles, yet how they use the Internet, what functions they favor, and what meanings they attach to the Internet may bear on these struggles in important ways. The original designers of the Internet did not design it for democratic purposes. Had the Internet not been used for such purposes by millions of users, it would not have shown such potential in the first place. This suggests that even an understanding of the technical struggles surrounding the Internet depends on an empirical analysis of the actual activities online.

Third, it is imperative to study the Internet in proper historical and political contexts. The same technology has different social implications under different historical and social conditions. Thus, for example, the Internet may be important to social actors with no access to mass media and less so to those who control mass media. In assessing the social impact of the Internet in China, therefore, it is essential to take a historical and sociological perspective, that is, to show the specific ways in which the Internet is used under specific conditions. To set the social and historical context for the discussion, let us start with a review of the recent developments and current conditions of civil society in China.

Civil Society in China: Recent Developments and Challenges

The concept of civil society has four basic elements: (1) autonomous individuals and (2) civic associations in relation to the state,[2] (3) engaged in more or less organized activities in a (4) public sphere "outside the immediate control of the state but not entirely contained within the private sphere of the family."[3] The four elements are interrelated. Individual and organizational autonomy are the basic conditions of the public sphere; social organizations function to protect or extend the interests of individual citizens, often in the form of organized protest or social movements; the public sphere functions with "a critical public willing and able to hold government accountable for its actions."[4] A vigorous civil society is often taken to be foundational to democratic politics.

Studies of civil society in reform-era China have revealed three major areas of change that point to an emerging civil society:

- Existing forms of social organization have undergone change, new associational forms have appeared, and social organizations in general have proliferated.[5]
- Both social organizations and individual citizens enjoy more autonomy from state power than in the pre-reform decades, with some notable new developments since the 1990s.[6]
- With the changing functions of the media and the increase in spaces for public discussion, a nascent form of public sphere has emerged.[7]

Despite these achievements, Chinese civil society faces major challenges. First, as a civil society institution, the public sphere remains incipient and weak. Articulation of social issues and sharing of information are limited by the lack of institution-alized means of communication and public forums. Second, despite the proliferation of social organizations, these are mostly organizations of what B. Michael Frolic refers to as a state-led civil society. They lack sufficient autonomy from the state to function as a routinized social base against state power on behalf of citizens. Gordon White, Jude Howell, and Shang Xiaoyuan point to a new type of organization that they refer to as "interstitial or unrecognized."[8] While these appear to have more independence from the state, for the very reason that they are unrecognized, they lack the necessary political legitimacy to function effectively. Finally, organized protest in contemporary China is under strict state control, which means that routinized social movement organizations that systematically fight social injustices and politi-cal power still do not have a legitimate existence. Large-scale social movements have erupted in the past two decades in China. Yet, because of state repression and organizational weakness, these movements cannot develop long-term political goals and strategies. How might these challenges be met? Far from claiming that new information technologies are the solution, this chapter will show where the Internet has made notable differences.

Studying the Internet in China

Studies of the Internet in China have focused on the physical network and mecha-nisms of state control. Those that broach the topic of the social and political implica-tions do so with a cautious tone.[9] There are, however, a few notable exceptions. For example, Geoffrey Taubman argues that the sway of the party-state over the ide-ational and organizational character of China's domestic affairs will be diminished as a result of the Internet.[10] Eric Harwit and Duncan Clark, while focusing on political control, draw attention to the potential for independent group formation in light of the new technological tools. They conclude by noting the ambivalence of content control in China: "As for content, in the short run, political controls will remain schizophrenic as the value of an open network conflicts with conservative political philosophies and as the nature of the Internet's audience makes it an unlikely tool for precipitating socially disruptive forces."[11] This conclusion is highly instructive. While emphasiz-ing state control, it acknowledges its limits. This conclusion sounds a call for more systematic empirical research on the actual uses of the Internet in China.

While recognizing the role of the Chinese state in shaping Internet use in China, I concentrate on the social uses of the Internet. Such a view is consistent with an influ-ential bottom-up approach to the study of contemporary Chinese society and politics. This bottom-up approach recognizes that the Chinese state is not an omnipotent en-tity, but has numerous permeable holes, not the least of which is the lack of interest or sincerity at the local level in implementing central policies.[12] This view is confirmed for the Internet by a June 2001 report on Chinaonline.com, which has this to say on Internet control in China: "Internet regulations come from Beijing, but each province has a significant amount of control, and authorities in each city also have some local autonomy. Consequently, in different places, there is great variation in policy, regulations, service and price."[13]

My analysis is based on survey data and in-depth case studies collected through participant observation and immersion in China's emerging Internet culture from February 2000 to July 2001. This methodology may be described as "virtual ethnography."[14] It includes extensive participation in online activities and interactions with fellow users in cyberspace, as well as regular monitoring and recording of Internet content. What actually happens in Chinese cyberspace cannot be fully grasped except through such virtual ethnography.

Internet Control and Counter-Control

Since October 1997, CNNIC (China Internet Network Information Center) has conducted two surveys on Internet development each year. The surveys consistently show that the profile of a typical Chinese Internet user is a relatively young person (between twenty and thirty-five years old) with some college education.[15] This profile sets limits to any attempt to overgeneralize the social impact of the Internet in China, but it is an encouraging profile, because the relatively young age of China's Internet users implies a stronger likelihood that the impact of the Internet will keep growing.

The Internet offers a variety of applications. In China, as elsewhere, e-mail and search engines are favorites. A notable phenomenon in China is the popularity of chatrooms, newsgroups, and bulletin boards. Table 11.1 shows the most desired information by China's Internet users according to the five CNNIC survey reports published from June 1999 to December 2002. Table 11.2 shows the most frequently used network services for the same period.

As the tables show, China's Internet users crave information. News is clearly the most desired information, but technological and educational information is also widely sought. As indicated by the relatively high percentages of respondents choosing e-mail, chatrooms, newsgroups, and bulletin boards as the most frequently used network services, China's users rely heavily on the Internet for personal expression and interpersonal communication. This point should be kept in mind when discussing the impact of the Internet on Chinese civil society.

The development of the Internet has posed a dilemma for the Chinese government. While supporting the growth of this new economy, the government has attempted to exert control over Internet content. Since 1996, more than a dozen regulations concerning Internet uses and services have been promulgated by various government agencies. For example, the "Computer Information Network and the Internet Security, Protection and Management Regulations," consisting of five chapters and twenty-five articles, was promulgated by the Ministry of Public Security on December 30, 1997, and outlined the duties and responsibilities of China's Internet service providers. Regulations specifically targeting bulletin boards were announced in November 2000, stipulating that users are responsible for the information they release, that they cannot release information harmful to national interests, and that bulletin board services should follow a licensing

Table 11.1

Most Desired Information Among China's Internet Users,
June 1999–December 2002 (multiple options, in percentages)

Type of information	June 1999	Dec. 1999	June 2000	Dec. 2000	June 2001	Dec. 2001	June 2002	Dec. 2002
News	84	65.5	82.0	84.38	63.5	74.0	75.8	78.0
Computer software and hardware	68	51.7	59.1	58	44.2	55.6	60.3	53.4
Entertainment	47	38.8	50.9	52.66	44.1	46.5	41.3	44.6
Electronic books	52	38.0	46.0	45.99	32.8	37.4	35.6	3.6
Science and education	41	31.4	N/A	35.77	31.4	31.8	28.8	30.1
Job hunting	19	19.3	26.1	29.12	19.8	22.2	19.0	22.1
Financial information	26	21.2	31.1	22.88	19	16.4	11.8	11.0
Travel	14	12.0	19.3	12.55	12.5	11.4	7.3	7.6
Medical information	10	9.4	14.5	11.78	7.6	7.7	4.9	4.9
Dating	9	8.2	12.1	9.3	4.7	4.5	2.8	2.9

Source: CNNIC survey reports: July 1999, January 2000, July 2000, January 2001, July 2001, January 2002, July 2002, January 2003.

procedure. In 2003, the State Broadcasting, Film, and Television Administration issued regulations for the control of content dissemination. Also in 2003, the Ministry of Culture tightened the registration and management of Internet bars.[16] Besides these regulations, Chinese government agencies intervene directly in Internet use, for example, by exercising sophisticated filtering of Internet traffic.[17]

The growing control of the Internet undoubtedly dampens Internet use in one way or another. But as Jayanthi Iyengar puts it insightfully, "There are two digital Chinas—the much publicized one of political repression and blocking 'forbidden' content—but that one is dwarfed by the booming digital China of shopping, trading, chatting and playing games. And that's where the boom is."[18] Indeed, there is a palpable irony here. While Internet control has visibly increased, Internet activism has persisted. Among the countries with the largest numbers of Internet users, China is unique in its combination of high levels of Internet control and Internet activism. Frequent efforts at control are accompanied as frequently by outbursts of cyber protests. Since the popularization of the Internet in China in 1998, not a year has passed without some influential cases of Internet activism. Scholars have yet to account for this paradoxical situation. Such an account has to begin with empirical studies of how Chinese citizens use the Internet.

In reality, actual practices among users and dotcom companies vary in ways that often go beyond the parameters of state regulations. The management of bulletin

Table 11.2

**Most Frequently Used Network Services Among China's Internet Users,
June 1999–December 2002** (multiple options, in percentages)

Network service	June 1999	Dec. 1999	June 2000	Dec. 2000	June 2001	Dec. 2001	June 2002	Dec. 2002
Email	90.9	71.7	87.7	87.65	74.9	92.2	92.9	92.6
Search engine	65.5	50.4	55.9	66.76	51.3	62.7	63.8	68.3
Software upload or download	59.6	44.2	50.7	50.56	43.9	55.3	51.0	45.3
Information inquiry	54.8	39.3	49.3	44.65	39.5	46.7	40.3	42.2
Chat online	29.2	25.5	38.8	37.53	21.9	22.0	45.5	45.4
Games and entertainment	15.8	13.6	17.7	18.94	15.8	17.1	18.6	18.1
Newsgroups	21.4	17.0	25.4	19.33	10.7	13.4	20.4	21.3
Bulletin board systems	28.0	16.3	21.2	16.72	9.0	9.8	18.9	8.9
Free personal homepage	21.6	13.5	19.7	15.58	8.4	11.8	8.6	6.8
Online shopping	3.2	7.8	14.1	12.54	8.0	7.8	10.3	1.5

Source: CNNIC survey reports: July 1999, January 2000, July 2000, January 2001, July 2001, January 2002, July 2002, January 2003.

boards, for example, varies in the degree of control and censorship. Bulletin Board Systems (BBS) managers monitor and censor posts, but they also have an interest in keeping their forums up and running, and running with good traffic. For their part, users have various ways of contesting censorship and evading filtering. For example, in May 2000, in the online protest surrounding the murder of a Beijing University student, users of the popular bulletin board "Strengthening the Nation Forum" (*Qiangguo luntan*) found that posts containing the characters for "Beida" (Beijing University) would be blocked. They beat the filters by inserting punctuation or other symbols between the two Chinese characters for "Beida," posting messages with phrases like "Bei.Da," and "Bei2Da." This suggests that while Chinese state agencies attempt to keep Internet activities under control, users have counter-control strategies. The various uses of the Internet to be discussed below take place under these conditions of control and counter-control.

The Internet and the Public Sphere

As formulated by Habermas, the concept of the public sphere has the following elements: (1) publics composed of autonomous individuals that engage in rational debate; (2) spaces where publics may freely assemble for such debate; and (3) media of communication, such as newspapers and books.[19] Habermas is often criticized for his idealized conception of the public sphere, since in reality, power and inequality often creep in. This chapter emphasizes the public sphere as open spaces for communication. These may be spaces for public debate and problem articulation, or they may simply fulfill a social function by providing spaces for social interaction. The development of the Internet in China has given rise to online communication spaces, including chatrooms, listservs, newsgroups, electronic magazines, and bulletin boards. These spaces are fulfilling important functions in China's nascent public sphere.

In the broadest sense, China's online spaces are not restricted to Web sites supported by computer servers physically located in China, nor are they restricted to Chinese-language sites. Some popular news sites about China, such as *China News Digest* (cnd.org), have English-language services. This chapter focuses on Chinese-language Web sites and network services. As long as access from within China is available, the actual server locations are not important.[20]

It is hard to estimate how many Chinese-language online spaces exist, not the least because new ones keep appearing while old ones may disappear. A rough estimate of the active bulletin boards would put the number in the thousands. Many Chinese universities have BBSs,[21] as do commercial portal sites. For example, as of April 11, 2001, chinaren.com maintained 33 BBS forums, sina.com had 96, and netease.com had more than 600. Several Web sites maintain rankings of Chinese-language forums worldwide. As of April 11, 2001, creaders.net had a list of 244 popular BBS forums; geocities.com had 103, while cwrank.com listed 30 "most popular" Chinese-language forums. Topforum.com not only has a ranking of 60 Chinese-language forums, but also maintains a daily collection of about 300 frequently read posts. As of June 18, 2001, the posts were selected from among 1,007 forums.

Online "publics" have proliferated along with online forums. Online publics form around forums of different thematic categories, such as leisure and entertainment, romance, sports, science and technology, education, economy, art and literature, politics, news, and others. They may reside inside or outside of China, but are more or less interconnected. The Internet facilitates such connection—messages in one forum are often cross-posted in another—so that issues brought up in one forum may be rapidly broadcast to others. With the existence of numerous online forums and publics, a wide range of issues is brought into the forums and to public attention. Take the popular "Strengthening the Nation Forum" (*Qiangguo luntan*, hereinafter QGLT), for example.[22] On December 20, 2000, topics brought up included relations with Japan, implications of Bush's presidency for China, amendments to China's marriage law, the passage of a homosexual marriage law in the Netherlands, corruption of Chinese government officials, the hardships of laid-off workers, end-of-year analysis of China's stock market, debate about the rule of law and rule of man, complaints about growing tuition fees in China's higher education institutions, and the history of China's Cultural Revolution.

Not all issues stimulate discussion equally, and discussions may be as short as several threads or as long as several dozen. Despite censorship, the discussions in QGLT are more wide-ranging and elaborate than in conventional media or many other bulletin boards.[23] In June 2001, I studied four popular Chinese-language news and politics bulletin boards. Two of them, QGLT and Beida Online (www.beida-online.com/list.php3?board=Beida_Forum), are based in China; the other two are run by Muzi.com (http://lundian.com/forum/normal/chinese/10001.html) and Creaders.com (www.creaders.org/cgi-bin/mainpage.cgi) respectively, both based in North America. I found that QGLT not only has the most posts (2,321 for June 11 and 2,798 for June 12), but also the highest percentage of responses (60 percent for both June 11 and 12), indicating a high level of discussion in the forum.[24] One good example of such a discussion concerns the functions of this and other bulletin boards in Chinese politics. Many argue that it should be used to promote democratic governance, as a place "for hearing people's voices and providing input for government decision-making" (Beidou,[25] February 24, 2000). Others emphasize democratic participation: "The forum should become a people's democratic square" (New Leftist, January 6, 2000). A persistent demand is that the space be used to promote democratic politics in China (Xingfu, November 9, 1999). The debate also targets undemocratic practices in the forum. A user named Haohao rejected personal attacks:

> Some net friends [*wangyou*], for lack of a rational attitude to their own and other users' viewpoints, would become angry when they are stuck in their arguments. They cannot control their anger, thus resulting in personal attacks and slandering. These net friends have a superficial knowledge of the world. They thought they could shut others up with personal attacks. In fact, as soon as you launch a personal attack, you discredit both your own viewpoints and your character. (Haohao, February 1, 2000)

Another made the following suggestion:

> I think the key issue in the management of the forum is to establish a clear and precise set of rules. These rules should be publicized. Whether the rules are just or reasonable enough is not a big problem (after all, this is a forum of a party newspaper—it cannot be free from its own biases). The important thing is to follow rules. Then net friends will not have so many complaints. (New Great Wall, October 28, 1999)

This debate about democratic and undemocratic practices in online discussions is not an isolated example. Similar discussions are common in other forums, indicating a high degree of engagement with public issues among China's netizens. In the middle of these online discussions, a new type of political action, critical public debate, entered contemporary Chinese life. In his study of political participation in Beijing, Tianjian Shi enumerates twenty-eight political acts used by citizens in Beijing to articulate interests. With the exception of big-character posters, none of these involves public debate. Most acts, such as "complaints through labor unions" or "complaints through the bureaucratic hierarchy," involve the airing of personal grievances without the possibility of opening up these grievances for public discussion.[26] Only in extraordinary times such as the student movement of 1989 did public debate occur. The Internet provides alternative spaces for public debate.

China's online spaces also help to articulate social problems. Habermas underscores the "problem articulation" function of the public sphere, noting that "the communication structures of the public sphere are linked with the private life spheres in a way that gives the civil-social periphery, in contrast to the political center, the advantage of greater sensitivity in detecting and identifying new problem situations."[27] Tianjian Shi's study discusses the political acts Beijing citizens may use to articulate their interests. The above-mentioned examples of "complaints through labor unions" and "complaints through the bureaucratic hierarchy" are such acts. Regardless of how effective these complaints are, it is clear that these channels can only reach a limited audience. Some complaints may reflect problems of general concern, yet there are no institutionalized channels for bringing personal problems to public attention. Personal problems articulated on the Internet, if of sufficient social importance, can attract more attention. One example is the online diary of Lu Youqing. Lu suffered from cancer. In the summer of 2000, when his doctor told him he had only about three months left to live, he decided to record his feelings and experiences in diary form and publish the diary on the Internet. Lu's online diary quickly attracted a large online readership and aroused heated debate among readers on the meaning of life and death in the contemporary world. As Duncan Hewitt reports from Shanghai, "Mr. Lu's very human and often philosophical account of dying fits in with a growing strand of confessional literature in China—which has challenged traditional taboos and the belief that personal matters should remain private."[28]

Finally, China's online spaces have played a supervisory role in government affairs and public life. The importance of this supervisory role is in direct proportion to the nebulous nature of the decision-making process in China. The Internet has helped to expose a number of cases concerning serious bureaucratic problems. It was through the Internet, for example, that a November 1999 report spread on how mismanagement of over 200 blood donation facilities in Henan Province may have spread HIV to large numbers of people in the province during the early 1990s.[29] Another case concerns a fatal disaster in a tin mine in Nandan, Guangxi. The accident occurred on July 17, 2001, and killed eighty-one miners. After the accident happened, the local government and mine authorities covered it up for about half a month. Amid murderous threats from local mine authorities, a few journalists from the *People's Daily* managed to get the story out onto the Internet, leading to a full investigation of the disaster and the conviction of local government officials and mine owners involved in the cover-up scheme.[30]

The arguments just outlined are supported by recent survey data produced by social scientists in China. A survey of the Internet in five Chinese cities shows that China's non-Internet users rely heavily on TV and newspapers for information, while for communication and personal expression, they do not have effective channels. In contrast, for Internet users, although TV and newspapers are still important sources of information, the Internet clearly plays a prominent role. With regard to communication, Internet users enjoy an overwhelming advantage over non-users. Thus, as media for expressing personal views, 14.2 percent of non-users selected TV, 21.9

Table 11.3

Which Medium Can Better Meet Which of Your Following Needs?
(N of internet Users =1,045)

	TV	News-papers	Maga-zines	Internet	Books	Radio	None of the above
Learning about current affairs in China and overseas	86.5	69.5	21.1	61.9	15.0	23.4	1.1
Acquiring information for personal life (e.g., shopping, travel information)	56.6	52.6	32.7	58.9	14.5	11.7	3.6
Acquiring educational information	28.6	35.8	21.1	56.1	61.2	7.9	3.1
Entertainment or personal hobbies (e.g., games, music)	59.1	23.0	26.3	67.7	20.8	19.6	4.3
Expressing personal views and opinions or publishing writings	10.0	22.7	14.6	62.8	8.5	4.0	17.0
Exchanging views or information with others	8.8	9.4	6.8	73.4	4.6	4.0	15.5
Participating in social activities	19.8	16.8	8.2	44.5	5.2	7.1	34.6
Promoting personal emotions (e.g., making friends or maintaining relationships with friends and colleagues)	9.5	6.4	6.0	63.6	6.1	4.8	27.0

Source: Guo Liang and Bu Wei, "Report on the Conditions of the Internet in Five Cities in China in Year 2000 Conducted by the Center for Social Development of the Chinese Academy of Social Sciences," 2001. www.chinace.org/ce/itre/. Accessed June 18, 2001.

percent selected newspapers, and 10.9 percent selected magazines. Added together, the proportion for non-Internet users relying on these three dominant conventional media for expressing views is 46 percent, while 62.8 percent of Internet users chose the Internet as a medium for expressing views. The same pattern holds when it comes to exchanging views with others. Of non-users, 13.9 percent selected TV as a medium for exchanging views with others, 14.2 percent selected newspapers, and 6.8 percent selected magazines. These numbers are insignificant compared with the 73.4 percent of Internet users who find the Internet to be a medium for exchanging views with others.[31] Table 11.3 summarizes the percentage of Internet users relying on different media for purposes of information or communication. Table 11.4 shows the

Table 11.4

Which Medium Can Better Meet Which of Your Following Needs?
(N of non-internet users =1,086)

	TV	News-papers	Maga-zines	Internet	Books	Radio	None of the above
Learning about current affairs in China and overseas	91.6	71.2	19.4	11.1	12.8	31.4	1.0
Acquiring information for personal life (e.g., shopping, travel information)	63.7	60.7	25.6	10.4	12.8	19.2	5.8
Acquiring educational information	43.0	44.0	20.1	12.0	48.7	12.9	6.5
Entertainment or personal hobbies (e.g., games, music)	65.2	26.5	18.6	14.7	14.3	24.0	13.6
Expressing personal views and opinions or publishing writings	14.2	21.9	10.9	14.4	6.2	4.9	50.2
Exchanging views or information with others	13.9	14.2	6.8	19.3	4.2	4.9	53.4
Participating in social activities	19.4	16.6	5.4	12.3	2.8	8.1	55.7
Promoting personal emotions (e.g., making friends or maintaining relationships with friends and colleagues)	14.7	10.0	5.3	17.3	5.6	4.4	58.6

Source: Guo Liang and Bu Wei, "Report on the Conditions of the Internet in Five Cities in China in Year 2000 Conducted by the Center for Social Development of the Chinese Academy of Social Sciences," 2001. www.chinace.org/ce/itre/. Accessed June 18, 2001.

percentage of non-Internet users relying on different media for purposes of information or communication.

It is important to note that discourse in Chinese-language online spaces is not always civil, as befitting the ideals of a *civil* society. The debate on democratic and undemocratic practices on QGLT attests to the existence of undemocratic practices. These undemocratic practices should sound a cautionary note to observers, but do not invalidate my argument about the role of the Internet in civil society activities. In fact, they probably reflect a greater degree of openness on the Internet. After all, one key difference between China's online spaces and its offline public sphere is the greater diversity of the online spaces. As in other areas of social life, diversity entails differences, including differences that may appear offensive.

The Internet and Civic Associations

Volunteer organizations are important components of civil society. Although social organizations have proliferated in China, they are mostly corporatist in nature and lack sufficient political autonomy. The impact of the Internet should be considered against this background.

Impact on Existing Organizations

The Internet reduces the barriers of geographical and social locations to voluntary associational life. People in different physical locations can now more easily find or join organizations. Existing organizations use the Internet for publicity, recruitment, fund-raising, and public education. Of particular interest is the growing number of environmental NGOs, many of which maintain active Web sites. A review of the Web sites of several environmental NGOs reveals some common characteristics in their uses of the Internet.[32] First, they carry information about their organizations, including mission statements, membership information, events, and activities. Second, they publish information about the environment and feature environmental problems in China. Third, they maintain links to other Web sites related to environmental protection, including Web sites of China's governmental environment protection agencies and international environmental organizations. Some Web sites have discussion forums; others maintain archives of government regulations on environmental issues. While serving to propagate knowledge about the environment, they also function as information centers for volunteers willing to commit time and effort to their causes. In several cases, such as Green-Web and Greener Beijing, the Internet is clearly indispensable to their existence. With a membership of more than 1,000, Greener Beijing boasts of being "the first and the most active Internet-based environmental NGO in China."[33]

The Emergence of Cyber-Organizations

Cyber-organizations are voluntary organizations that "exist only or primarily on the Internet and maintain relatively fewer . . . offline resources."[34] Elsewhere, I have referred to these organizations as web-based. They are digital formations.[35] They may be more or less organized, with the less organized ones resembling what Howard Rheingold calls virtual communities.[36] They usually form in chatrooms, BBS forums, newsgroups, and listservs.

There are numerous such cyber-organizations and virtual communities in China. One active virtual community has formed around a BBS forum called "China Educated Youth Forum" (*Huaxia zhiqing luntan*, or HXZQ).[37] The forum was set up in

June 1998 by two individuals interested in the historical experience of China's educated youth generation. By May 2000, it had attracted a daily average of 700 hits and ranked fifteenth in the list of top-ranking Chinese-language bulletin boards maintained by geocities.com. In July 2000, through online discussions, the core members of the forum established the "China Educated Youth Internet Studio" (*Huaxia zhiqing gongzuoshi*), a collective management entity, to plan, develop, and fund the operations of its BBS forum and associated Web sites. The studio sets for itself two missions: to build a virtual home for friendship, education, entertainment, and mutual help, and a "Virtual Educated Youth Museum" for publishing and archiving documents about the "Up to the Mountains and Down to the Countryside" (*shangshan xiaxiang*) movement. While it has attracted some younger visitors, the forum is mainly a gathering place for a group of individuals of the "educated youth" generation.

This virtual community does not operate online only. Social ties forged in the forum have extended into offline life. I have been a regular visitor to the forum since February 2000 and have read many stories about real-life visits among community members. At least two members residing in Southern California have visited their online friends in Guangzhou and Shanghai. One person in Beijing toured Guangzhou to see Guangzhou-based members. Another living in Wuhan visited Beijing-based members on a business trip. Furthermore, this community has a complex and transnational online network. HXZQ started with a bulletin board. It then added a chatroom, two more bulletin boards, and a well-designed, content-rich homepage. The homepage contains historical photos and music, archives on historical documents about the "Up to the Mountains and Down to the Countryside" movement and retrospective stories and current debates about the historical experience of the generation, links to personal homepages owned by community members, and, as of October 7, 2001, an address book of 212 former educated youth. Of these 212 core members of the community, 97 listed their current country of residence. Nineteen of these 97 are in the United States, 3 in Canada, 3 in Japan, 2 in Australia, 1 in New Zealand, 1 in Germany, 1 in Hong Kong, and the rest in mainland China. Thus, HXZQ serves as a virtual nexus of a network of former educated youth in and outside of China.

An example of a cyber-organization is the environmental group Greener Beijing Institute. This group started as a Web site in November 1998. In its first few years of existence, the Web site won prizes in national Web design competitions and was widely publicized in newspapers and TV news programs. Its "Environmental Forum" became a popular online bulletin board with thousands of registered users. Members of Greener Beijing engage in three kinds of activities to promote a green culture—operating a Web site; conducting environmental protection projects; and organizing volunteer environmental awareness activities. While Greener Beijing conducts some on-the-ground work, its central activity is maintaining the Web site and fostering online discussions. Its BBS forums spurred "offline" environmental activism. For example, in 1999 one of the early online discussions on the recycling of used batteries inspired students at the Number One Middle School of Xiamen City (Fujian Province) to organize a successful community battery recycling program. Another impressive online project of Greener Beijing was the launching of a "Save the Ti-betan Antelope Web Site Union" in January 2000, which drew national attention to this endangered species. With the launching of the Web site union, Greener Beijing and environmentalists from twenty-seven universities jointly organized environmental exhibit tours on many university campuses.

Cyber-organizations may be subject to the typical constraints of Internet control. Compared with offline organizations, however, they have more elbow room. Their virtual existence gives them some degree of freedom such as transregional mobilization and transmembership recruitment. Such virtual existence undoubtedly has its weaknesses. Social ties built this way are relatively weak. Besides virtual membership and a Web presence, cyber-organizations rarely have the necessary organizational resources to provide for more permanent operations. Yet in China's political environment, the rise of such organizations contributes to the growth of civil society and thus constitutes an important new dimension of civil society development.

The Internet and New Dynamics of Popular Protest

The use of the Internet to organize offline protests became widely known recently in the anti-Japanese demonstrations in April 2005. In fact, such Internet-organized protests had happened before in China, as they happen frequently in other parts of the world. Not only is the Internet used to organize offline protests, protests happen daily in cyberspace as well. In China, where organized protests are strictly sanctioned, the possibility of using the Internet for protests has important implications for the dynamics and forms of popular contention. Yet little is known of exactly how the Internet is used for protests. How does protest diffuse? How are people mobilized? What are some of the new dynamics and forms of contention? A unique case study allows us to provide some preliminary answers to these important questions.

The case concerns the protest activities surrounding the rape and murder of Qiu Qingfeng in late May 2000.[38] Qiu was a student in Beijing University. She was found raped and murdered on May 20, 2000, having been attacked on her way back to the university's rural Changping campus. Upon learning of the murder, university authorities decided to hold back the news. The case happened at a sensitive time—about two weeks before the eleventh anniversary of the suppression of the 1989 student movement. Students at Beijing University had been among the most active in that movement. Clearly, university authorities attempted to cover up the case in order to forestall any unexpected turn of events around the anniversary date. News of the murder first broke on Beijing University's "Triangle" (*Sanjiaodi*)[39] online bulletin board at 11:19 P.M. on May 22. The posts quickly triggered a wave of protest in BBS forums across China. Beginning on May 23, there was a dramatic increase in the number of visits to the Triangle forum. The total number of hits in this forum was 408 for May 21 and 689 for May 22. It jumped to 11,863 on May 23. The number reached a record high of 12,073 on May 24 and tapered off after that, though still maintaining a level much higher than that prior to the protest.

While the number of visits to the Triangle forum increased dramatically, so did the number of posts. The Triangle forum was set up on December 25, 1999. From then until May 22, 2000, only 303 posts appeared. Beginning on May 23, this number increased sharply. Altogether 423 messages were posted on May 23 alone. This number peaked to 1,842 on May 24. Between May 23 and 26, a total of 3,692 messages were posted, all related to the murder.

News about the murder case shot through the country on the Internet. One of the first two messages that appeared on the Triangle forum was cross-posted to the "Perspectives on Current Affairs" forum of Shantou University at 8:44 A.M., May 23, to the "News" forum of Xi'an Jiaotong University at 9:29 A.M., to the "Current Affairs and News" forum of Netease.com at 3:46 P.M., and to the "Focus" forum of Sohu.com at 10:19 P.M. No posts about the murder appeared on "Strengthening the Nation Forum" on May 23, but fifty-six did on May 24.

The patterns of diffusion of protest highlight two key features about online protest: speed and openness. In a matter of hours after the first message about the murder case was posted on Beijing University's Triangle forum, the news had spread across China's numerous bulletin boards. This would be unimaginable without the Internet, because the conventional media remained reticent on the matter. During the period of online protest discussed here, major national and regional newspapers such as *People's Daily, Guangming Daily, Legal News Daily, Beijing Daily,* and *Beijing Youth Daily* made no mention of the murder case. *Legal News Daily* usually carries some news about crimes, but it did not report this case. It was the Internet that gave Chinese citizens an opportunity to make their voices heard.

Also interesting are the connections between online protests and campus protest activities. Such connections were manifest in the mutual influences between protests on online forums and campus demonstrations and sit-ins. In the protest period, the Internet was used to discuss and formulate goals and demands and organize campus demonstrations. One post demanded the resignation of university administrators in charge (FINA, May 23, 2000, "Triangle"). Another suggested that university authorities should compensate the victim's parents, improve security conditions on and around the campus, and show more respect and care for students (Anew, May 26, 2000, Netease.com). A widely circulated third post announced a planned demonstration march from neighboring Qinghua University to Beijing University.[40] Another important connection between online and offline protest was the almost instantaneous online broadcast of campus events. This broadcast kept interested users in other parts of the country informed of campus activities. Thus, one post reports:

At 8:00, I checked out things online in the library. I thought people probably had already left [for the gathering]. I packed up my books and went in search of the crowd. In the small plaza in front of the big hall, quite a lot of people had gathered. White candle lights swayed and flickered. Students sat silently together in circles, in groups of 7 or 8 or several dozen. On the stairs near the Triangle area, a huge heart-shaped pattern was laid with flickering candles, with little white-paper flowers in the middle of the heart. I saw the following netfriends: Caishen, Hubing, Xsy, Littlefisher kansg, Lhx, Cc, Bigfatcat, Tiank. (Young, May 23, 2000, 21:08, "Triangle")

The Internet was not only used for protest, but itself became an object of struggle. This has to do with the specific conditions under which the Internet is used in China. China's netizens tend to perceive the Internet as a space for exercising their right of free speech, while the government tries to keep control. Where these interests conflict, protest may arise from among the users. Thus, despite its relative openness, the Internet is not a perfectly free space. In May 2000, China's Internet users were aware of possible social control efforts on the part of the authorities and consciously and sometimes tactically contested control. For example, in anticipation of possible control action by the university administration, posts appeared on Beijing University's BBS forums that asserted the constitutional right of free speech and warned the authorities against containing protest by shutting down the BBS. Knowing that explicitly hostile language could backfire, some users warned that the protest should proceed in a forceful but rational manner. Below is one example:

> Please make good use of the BBS. At present, the BBS management has made positive responses to our sentiments. In case the management comes under pressure [from the authorities], please show your understanding. (FINA, May 23, 2000, "Triangle")

Thus, while protest developed on the BBS forums, its meanings expanded among discussions and debates. Although the protest was still about the murder case, it quickly became a struggle for freedom of speech on the Internet. As the following post shows, Internet users were excited about the possibilities of freedom of speech opened up by the new technology:

> On the 22nd, the news began to circulate on the BBSs of Beijing University and Qinghua University. Out of indignation at the university leadership's response, the students in these two universities, with the online support of students from other universities, decided to hold memorial services for their schoolmate. This was in order to break through the deliberate control of information and suppression of memorial activities by the authorities. The information circulated on the Internet indicates that similar cases have happened in other universities, but have almost all been covered up. It may be believed that if it had not been for the Internet, and if it had not been because of the students' indignation, this case would also have been covered up. ("Triangle Forum," May 27, 2000, cross-posted on Netease.com on May 29, 2000)

As an important component of civil society, popular protest is a powerful means of resisting political power and protecting citizen rights. Until recently, the major protest events in the PRC, from the Red Guard Movement to the student demonstrations of 1989, all happened because of some kind of state initiation. This was due to a peculiar state–society relationship in China, a relationship characterized by the state's penetration of civil society and by its dependence on political campaigns and mass mobilizations to deal with social, political, and economic problems. Historically, this relationship turned the state into the unwitting initiator of popular protest. As Zhou puts it, "Participating in state-initiated political campaigns provides an opportunity for individuals and groups to pursue their own agendas and exploit new opportunities. State-initiated political campaigns provide opportunities for unorganized groups and individuals to act together."[41] The rise of online protest indicates the changing dynamics of popular protest as well as a change in the state–society relationship. The Internet facilitates the key conditions for the emergence of popular protest. It helps to disseminate information, formulate goals and strategies, identify opponents, and organize protest events. All of this happens speedily, at low costs, and without incurring the kinds of risks facing street demonstrators. Online protest has brought new elements into the art of protest.

Explaining the Impact of the Internet on Chinese Civil Society: Conditions and Obstacles

The technological development of the Internet in China as elsewhere depends on government policy and economic incentives. Just as the Internet was initially developed as a government-sponsored military project in the United States, so too its introduction into China was guided directly through government action. In both the United States and China, market incentives brought the Internet within the reach of the general public, who then began to use it in ways not necessarily in the interest of political elites. It is fair to say that state and economy directly shaped the rise of the Internet in China.

For the Internet to exert influence on civil society, however, political power and market forces are insufficient conditions. People attach meanings to technology and these meanings shape how they use it. At the same time, the particular meanings they attach to particular technology depend on a host of other factors. My discussions suggest that China's users value the Internet as a means of communication and expression; yet without an understanding of the history of political communication in China, the cultural meaning of the Internet cannot be fully grasped. In this regard, suffice it to mention that political communication and dissent depended mainly on the risky business of putting up big-character wall posters.[42]

If state power and market forces have given birth to the Internet as a new sphere of social and political life, will the same forces take away this life? This is a key question for future research. Observers are wary of this possibility but remain hopeful that this is not a preordained struggle. To understand the future struggle over the Internet in China, it is necessary to understand the pressing obstacles. These obstacles are of two kinds, internal and external. By internal obstacles, I refer to those elements that hinder democratic participation in online communication. Participants on online forums want their voices to be heard, but there are "bullies" who attempt to deprive fellow participants of their voice, for example by making them feel that they are inadequate discussants. Similarly, to carry on a meaningful discussion, participants should be able to articulate ideas, take positions, and inquire into interlocutors' positions. It takes time and practice to gain these skills. A final internal obstacle is stylistic and rhetorical indecency: online discourse can be very uncivil. These internal obstacles are not insurmountable. As long as participants are prepared to engage in online discussions, it is likely that a culture or environment will evolve in the form of a community ethos to regulate conversations within reasonable bounds.

External obstacles are economic and political in nature. Politically, given that state elites are wary of the politically corrosive effects of civil society and of the Internet's role in it, they are likely to step up control. The economic obstacle has two sides to it. On the one hand, China has not developed to a point where the Internet may be popularized nationally. The digital gap is deep. With continuous economic development, we can expect the Internet-using population to grow steadily, a hopeful sign that this aspect of the economic obstacle will lessen and not worsen. On the other hand, with further economic development, the trend toward commercialization of the Internet may become stronger. Commercialization represents a different kind of barrier to civil society development. As often happens in the conventional media, commercialization of the Internet could squeeze out the political action that now takes place there. In view of these two daunting obstacles, it is hard to foretell to what extent the Internet will continue to strengthen Chinese civil society. This will depend on how the economic and political obstacles are reduced. At the same time, the possibility of the Internet's continual influence on Chinese civil society cannot be foretold either. How the political and economic obstacles are reduced depends on whether and how China's Internet users will continue to use the Internet for such civil society activities as public debate, organization, and protest. At this moment, there are no signs that they will abandon the Internet.

Conclusion

Evidence presented in this chapter shows that the Internet has opened up new possibilities of meeting the challenges of civil society in reform-era China. It has contributed to public participation in information exchange and debate; it facilitates the articulation of social problems and the exposure of social injustices. Civic associations have developed an online presence while new, Internet-based organizational forms have appeared. Finally, because of the Internet, new forms and dynamics of protest have emerged.

Public debate, voluntary organizing, and protest that take place on the Internet in China are linked with the global community, including the Chinese diaspora around the world. Despite government efforts to block selected sites, Internet users in China can access Web sites overseas, or "link up" (*chuanlian*)—a term of heavy political import—with overseas individuals and groups for information exchange, solidarity building, or protest. The virtual community of the "China Educated Youth Forum," for example, clearly crosses national boundaries. The porous and networked nature of the Internet thus ties Chinese civil society to the global community, and vice versa.[43] Their interpenetration is a source of energy for China's incipient civil society. Such interpenetration enhances information flows critical to civil society activities.

By using the Internet to speak up, link up, and act up, Chinese citizens participate in Chinese politics uninvited. Their multifarious online activities express their political aspirations. As the empirical evidence in this chapter shows, these are not neces-sarily lofty aspirations involving grand political designs. They are people's mundane struggles for basic citizenship rights—the right to voice their opinions on govern-ment policies, to be informed of issues that affect their lives, to freely organize them-selves and defend their interests, and to publicly challenge various kinds of authorities and social injustices. Whichever type of political institution can best guarantee these basic rights—democracy, the rule of law, or both—should be on the priority list for political reform.

12

The Internet and Single-Party Rule in China

Tamara Renee Shie

Pan Wei's argument that there exists another alternative between Western-style democracy and Chinese-style communism, a government characterized by rule of law without democracy, appears to be one logical direction in which an information technology–driven Chinese government could proceed. Elements of how the Internet and information technology (IT) can help bring about this change are evident in the patterns of growth, usage, and successful regulation of the Internet in China. One does not have to agree with Pan's depiction of Western democracy or of Chinese social equity to acknowledge the potential truth to his argument that Chinese governance might develop according to a different paradigm than that of the West. He argues persuasively that Chinese historical, cultural, and political traditions are unlike those in the West and thereby shape Chinese views of political principles differently. Chinese political traditions, which lend themselves to a rule of law government, rested on political equality exemplified by the nondiscriminatory civil service exams, a fair amount of economic liberation in a largely classless agricultural society, and a government that ruled by means of persuasion and morality. The Internet has the potential to support a return to such traditions that have been obscured in modern Chinese history. Internet use has already forced the governing CCP to admit mistakes and be more forthcoming with information. It is revolutionizing a public system of checks and balances not unlike a Social Consultation Committee on a national scale whereby officials may gauge and even concede to public opinion on a variety of issues voiced via the Internet. Economically, rapid Chinese development has been introducing a social cleavage most obvious between the eastern and western provinces. Business, educational, and cultural opportunities are concentrated along the eastern seaboard. However, the Internet could counteract that trend by providing such opportunities online, as well as even market access, to Chinese regardless of location. Finally, social persuasion and pressure are at the very heart of Internet control in China. The government has found its greatest success in managing usage through self-censorship. The Internet might also be used as a powerful tool to sway public opinion on anything from commercialism to advancing nationalistic agendas. Many CCP statements regarding the need for Internet regulation appeal to concerns over morality. Pan Wei's system of governance characterized by rule of law without democracy sheds some light on the role the Internet may play in such a political transformation.

Nevertheless, Pan Wei does not leave the reader without questions. If indeed China is a country without a strong experience of large sociopolitical groups (nor, as Pan implies, a desire to create them) and the rule of law is not about regulating those who are ruled but about regulating the government, then this is where the Chinese system of Internet filtering and Pan's vision diverge. The Internet is not only being used to curb corruption and foster greater government transparency, but also to keep political dissidence in check. Although there has been a general loosening of controls over speech, press, assembly, and association, and the Internet has to an extent furthered those freedoms, it has at the same time allowed the Chinese government to limit such freedoms where they continue to threaten central party power.

This chapter will examine the Internet's potential capability to transform governance in China by exploring such questions as: Is the theory plausible that increased access to information vis-à-vis the Internet will lead to Chinese democratization? Or can the CCP successfully limit access to information online, while simultaneously utilizing the Internet's economic potential and maintaining political power? Could the Internet potentially bring about greater freedom without democracy? Does the Internet offer promise or peril for the Chinese Communist Party? The chapter first explores the hypotheses connecting the spread and use of information technology with democratic movements. This section is followed by a brief look at the extraordinary growth of the Internet in China and a systematic presentation of the various methods that the Chinese government has thus far employed to control the Internet. The next section observes how these measures have been successful in promoting the Chinese dual strategy of maintaining power and supporting economic development, and in some ways are even strengthening CCP authority. In conclusion, this chapter debunks the argument that the introduction of the Internet into countries under authoritarian rule, and in particular China, will inevitably lead to democratization. This conclusion does not, however, rule out some kind of political change.

Linking the Internet with Democracy

Mueller and Tan call the theory that greater levels of freedom of communication and information are inextricably linked to more democratic societies the *expectation of convergence:* according to this theory, as countries like China modernize and reform, their political and economic institutions naturally converge toward Western-style democracy.[1] This theory of democratic convergence coupled with the construct of *technological determinism*—"the belief that new technologies have an intrinsic, autonomous power to shape and transform society"[2]—forms the determinedly optimistic view that modernization inevitably involves embracing the "information age" and all the subsequent freer flow of information included, and thereby democracy. The advent of the Internet has only intensified such beliefs and the predictions that such democratic revolutions have begun, are in the process, or are only around the corner across the globe.

This theorized link between the Internet and democracy became solidified in the late 1980s and early 1990s as many communist and authoritarian regimes fell concurrently with the development and proliferation of information technology. Kedzie called this phenomenon the "Coincident Revolutions."[3] The concept of the "Dictator's Dilemma,"[4] a chief premise of these revolutions, suggests that the struggle between an autocratic ruling party and information technology is a zero-sum game. A totalitarian government must choose either between retaining power or obtaining economic growth through the adoption of information technology; the two are mutually exclusive and cannot be simultaneously achieved. Such a theory attributes certain positive qualities to information technology like "good," "liberating," or "democratic." In the waning years of the Cold War, Western, particularly American, politicians wholeheartedly embraced this principle. Acknowledging such convictions, in 1985, then U.S. secretary of state George Shultz wrote:

> The free flow of information is inherently compatible with our political system and values. The communist states, in contrast, fear this information revolution perhaps even more than they fear Western military strength. . . . Totalitarian societies face a dilemma: either they try to stifle these [information and communication] technologies and thereby fall further behind in the new industrial revolution, or else they permit these technologies and see their totalitarian control inevitably eroded. In fact, they do not have a choice, because they will never be able entirely to block the tide of technological advance.[5]

Again in 1991, after the fall of the Soviet Union and the end of the Cold War, U.S. secretary of state James A. Baker made this pronouncement: "No nation has yet discovered a way to import the world's goods and services while stopping foreign ideas at the border. It is in our interest that the next generation in China be engaged by the Information Age. . . . For this we determine the U.S. feels that the Internet and information technology is a way in which democratic ideas will flourish and assist in managing the change that will come some day."[6]

The Internet was all but officially proclaimed a "technology of freedom."[7] Kedzie's innovative 1997 RAND study analyzed the correlation between the penetration of information technology, or "interconnectivity," and the democracy ratings of 144 countries. Using multiple regression analyses, he concluded that "in all cases, the results show electronic network interconnectivity to be a substantial and statistically significant predictor of democracy."[8] Yet at the same time he concedes that a strong correlation does not conclusively determine causality, and that many other factors besides information technology may be at work in countries transforming from authoritarian regimes to democracies. There are also a significant number of other factors to be considered in qualifying Kedzie's results (to be discussed in the conclusion of this chapter). However, this has not drowned out the ardent voices of technological libertarians, and China is their greatest test. Even faced with less than conclusive evidence of the Internet's liberalizing influence, many politicians and pundits continue to determinedly laud the Internet's eventual triumph over autocracy.[9] Media and opinion pieces often present a distorted, schizophrenic view of China's ground realities—on the one hand lambasting the growing control over the Internet while on the other hand purporting an increase in online freedom or waxing nostalgic for a time when such freedom theoretically existed.[10] Although there have been a growing number of critical voices, academic scholars are no less convinced. In his provocatively entitled book *The Coming Collapse of China,* Gordon C. Chang declares that although "the regime may patrol cyberspace, it cannot help but be changed in the process." He argues that the Communist Party is unprepared for the force of the Internet.[11] David Gompert, former director of the National Defense Research Institute at the RAND Corporation, asserts that information technology has great potential to bring about democracy in China. He writes, "the information revolution both liberates and requires liberation," and that in China, "its growing investment in and reliance on information technology will intensify pressures for further economic and political liberalization."[12] And yet the Chinese leadership feels it can follow the path of a market economy with Chinese characteristics, and that the Internet can be used to improve both economic growth as well as Party control.

The Internet in China

Since China was first connected to the World Wide Web in 1993, the Internet has grown by leaps and bounds. From very modest beginnings of approximately 2,000 Internet users in 1993, the number surged to approximately 94 million users by the start of 2005.[13] China now has the world's second largest number of citizens online after the United States' 201 million. Although this number as yet still represents only 7 percent of China's total population of over 1.3 billion, the country continues to have extraordinary growth potential. The figures for January 2005 represent a more than fourfold increase over the 22.5 million users in 2000. Various predictions place the number of "netizens" in China to be between 120 million and 134 million by the end of 2005, representing a 28 percent increase over 2004.[14] China represents the fastest growing IT and telecommunications markets in the world. In 2002 the number of personal computers in use in China was 36 million, third in the world after the United States with 190 million and Japan with 49 million. With the sales of personal computers in China doubling every twenty-eight months, China will rapidly close the gap with the United States. The People's Republic of China (PRC) is currently the world's second largest personal computer market. Not only is the sale of personal computers widening the reach of the Internet, so too is the expanding subscription to telecommunication services. By the end of 2001, China had surpassed the United States to have the largest number of mobile phone subscribers in the world. By November 2004 there were 329 million mobile users and the number was expected to surpass 400 million in 2005.[15] With land-fixed line phone subscribers at 313 million, the total number of Chinese phone subscribers reached more than 640 million. As more households purchase personal computers, mobile phones, and telephone subscriptions, the Chinese Internet population can be expected to rise exponentially. Information technology promises to attract much needed foreign investment and technology.

Contrary to the assumptions of foreign pundits who argue that the Internet spells an inevitable end to China's one-party rule, the CCP has embraced information technology, making it a cornerstone of its modernization plans by means of "driving industrialization with informatization." During an April 2005 visit to Bangalore, India, Chinese premier Wen Jiabao declared the coming of the IT Asia Century through the combined efforts of China and India. Beijing has launched a number of initiatives to connect the entire country to the Internet as rapidly as possible. One of these initiatives is a three-pronged approach to bring all government ministries, Chinese businesses, and finally every Chinese citizen online.

The Chinese government declared 1999 as Government Online Year. On June 22, 1999, the Government Online Project was launched—a concerted effort by the Chinese government to have all government offices online and accessible to the public. In April 2004 there was a total of 11,764 governmental Web sites.[16] While many Web sites only offer limited information, they do offer citizens the potential ability to access government information previously unavailable. Not only do Web sites increase the transparency of government agencies, they also improve many public services that formerly would have been very time-consuming or nearly impossible for many citizens to access. For example, the Ministry of Education has opened online schools. Web sites for such agencies as the People's Bank of China, the Customs Administration, the State Administration of Industry and Commerce, the State Tourism Bureau, the Ministry of Labor and Social Security, the Ministry of Health, and the State Administration of Taxation allow Chinese to do their banking online, book hotels, apply for import and export quotas, search for employment, find answers to health questions, and complete tax or customs forms. It is expected that all of the PRC's central authorities, provinces, municipalities, autonomous regions, and embassies in foreign countries will be connected to the Internet and offer Web sites by 2010. By August 2004, 90 percent of China's 336 largest cities had launched Web sites.[17] However e-governance is still in its early stages. In the most recent China Internet Network Information Center (CNNIC) statistical report on Internet development in China, 36.2 percent of respondents answered that although they had heard of it, they did not understand the meaning of the term "e-governance." Eleven percent answered they had never heard the term. While 7.5 percent of respondents indicated they often sought information online from e-goverment sources, 9.8 percent signaled they were still dissatisfied with information provided on e-government sites. Yet this is an increase over the 2002 statistics in which only 2.5 percent retrieved information from government Web sites and 1.4 percent utilized online government services.[18] The Chinese government remains aggressively committed to improving e-governance, and plans to introduce additional online services, such as online voting.

Anticipating China's entry into the WTO, Beijing realized that Chinese businesses, only a small percentage of which had Web sites, were at a disadvantage from overseas competition. A Business Online Facilitation Association was founded in early January of 2000 in order to facilitate and promote use of computers and the Internet in business, in addition to pooling and sharing the knowledge of those businesses already online. Following the establishment of this association, it was announced that the year 2000 would be "Business Online Year." On July 7, 2000, the State Economic and Trade Commission, the Ministry of Information Industry (MII), China Telecom Group, and the Economic Information Center of the State Economic and Trade Commission jointly established the Business Online Project with the aim of rapidly linking 1 million small, 10,000 medium, and 100 large enterprises to the Internet.[19] With the demand for e-commerce on the rise, there are increased incentives for Chinese businesses to provide web access to their products.

Finally, it is the 1.3 billion Chinese that the CCP hopes to win over to the Internet. The China Family Online project began in May 2000 with the introduction of the Web site Sinohome.com. In order to introduce families to the Internet and the China Family Online Web site, a CD-ROM guided new users through the start-up process and even offered three free hours of connection time. The MII, the All-China Women's Federation, the Central Committee of the Communist Youth League, the Ministry of Science and Technology, and the Ministry of Culture together formally initiated the "Project of Family Internet Access" on December 20, 2001. In 2002 the central government also began the National Information-Sharing Network, intended to link libraries, museums, art galleries, and research institutes across the country.[20] Part of the purpose of the Network, to be completed in 2005, is to increase the ability of those in China's poorer western provinces to access information. As more telephone lines and newer vehicles for delivery of the Internet become available, information sharing will expand its reach throughout China.

Methods of Internet Control

Claims of the transformative power of the Internet rest on the argument that authoritarian governments will find it increasingly difficult to control the flow of information as greater numbers of their citizens go online. Although the Internet developed relatively regulation-free and bottom-up in Western democracies, Beijing is attempting to control the Internet much in the same way it has controlled other information media, with top-down approaches. Due to the open two-way communication nature of the Internet, the Chinese government has had to implement more creative measures in its attempts to assert its authority over the expansion and use of the Internet. What they have designed is a sophisticated system of control utilizing multiple methods that target both Internet content and access at various levels. Some methods the CCP has implemented to do this are: organizing the infrastructure controlling the Internet, introducing rules and regulations regarding the Internet, controlling Internet Service Providers (ISPs) and Internet Content Providers (ICPs), flooding the Internet with approved sites, blocking or censoring Internet content, regulating public Internet outlets, and encouraging self-censorship.

Organizing the Infrastructure and Controlling the Internet

In China the Internet is state-owned and -operated. When the Internet first took off, there were few rules and regulations or a clear authority governing its control. As

Beijing realized its potential and the number of users grew, the CCP leadership quickly acknowledged that it would need to rein it in. In 1995, the development of the Internet was placed under the control of four government agencies—the Ministry of Posts and Telecommunications (MPT), the Ministry of Electronics Industry (MEI), the Chinese Academy of Sciences (CAS), and the State Education Commission (SEC). Later in 1998, the MPT and MEI were merged to create the Ministry of Information Industry (MII), which now holds the major responsibility for regulating the growth of IT in the PRC and reports to the Party Central Committee. The organ of the State Council involved with the Internet is the Leading Group for Information (LGI), which drafts the regulations and standards pertaining to the operation of the Internet, sets fees and services, and monitors the performance of Internet networks. Other state agencies are also involved in the administration of the Internet. The MII is primarily involved with controlling the physical networks, such as the ISPs, but the State Administration of Radio, Film, and Television, the State Council and Information Office, and the Ministry of Public Security share regulation of Internet content.[21] In addition, a commercial service, China Internet Corporation (CIC), owned and operated by Xinhua News Agency, was established, giving the Propaganda Department a semi-monopoly over Internet news distribution. The CNNIC "manages Internet addresses, domain names and network resource directories and provides related information services."[22] It was founded on January 3, 1997, and is administratively operated by the Computers Network Information Center of the CAS, but also reports to the MII.

China's Internet networks are divided into two types: interconnecting and access networks. There are currently seven such interconnecting or backbone (*fulian*) networks granted licenses in China, which connect China with the international global network. They are the China Network (ChinaNet), China 169 (which includes the China Network Communication [CNCNET]), China Scientific Net (CSTNET), China Unicom Public Computer Interconnection Network (UNINET), China Education and Scientific Research Net (CERNET), China Mobile Network (CMNET), and the China International Electronic Transaction Net (CIETNET). As of early 2005, two additional networks, the China Great Wall Net (CGWNET) and the China Satellite Net (CSNET), were under construction. This is up from the four original *fulian* networks available in 2000. These backbone networks are closely linked to government agencies: ChinaNet is operated by China Telecom; the Ministry of Education (formerly the State Education Commission) runs CERNET; the Chinese Academy of Science heads up CSTNET; UNINET is run by China Unicom, China's second largest telephone operator; the Ministry of Commerce is affiliated with CIETNET. The access networks work like ISPs in the West and do not have to be affiliated with the interconnecting networks. Although ISPs can be privately owned, they must operate through the *fulian* in order to be licensed and to connect with global cyberspace. ChinaNet is the largest and most extensive of the interconnecting networks; over two-thirds of China's net users subscribe through its ISP. This system effectively creates a large China-wide *intranet* with only a few controlled portals to the global World Wide Web. Xinhua's CIC works like an America Online service provider. Incoming and outgoing e-mail is connected to the world's Internet, but all other services are within China only.

Introducing Rules and Regulations Regarding the Internet

Premier Li Peng signed China's first Internet regulations, the "Provisional Directive on the Management of International Connections by Computer Information Networks in the PRC," into law on February 1, 1996. As the Internet has expanded in China, the government has passed a succession of regulations to oversee its implementation.[23] While many of these provisions contain regulations of content or access, such as pornography or information related to state security, which one would expect in any country, others explicitly exert state control over the Internet. Article 15 of the "Measures for the Administration of Internet Information Services" lists the content that is illegal on the Internet:

1. information that goes against the basic principles set in the Constitution;
2. information that endangers national security, divulges state secrets, subverts the government, or undermines national unification;
3. information that is detrimental to the honor and interests of the state;
4. information that instigates ethnic hatred or ethnic discrimination, or that undermines national unity;
5. information that undermines the state's policy for religions, or that preaches evil cults or feudalistic and superstitious beliefs;
6. information that disseminates rumors, disturbs social order, or undermines social stability;
7. information that disseminates pornography and other salacious materials; that promotes gambling, violence, homicide, and terror; or that instigates the commission of crimes;
8. information that insults or slanders other people, or that infringes upon other people's legitimate rights and interests; and
9. other information prohibited by the law or administrative regulations.

Regulations concerning the Internet have become more specific, although some sections remain ambiguous (such as what might constitute information that endangers national security or disturbs social order) and at the same time reflect greater security consciousness.[24] The regulations have progressively shifted more responsibility onto the providers of Internet services as well as Internet users—each and every web user, whether an individual, a service provider, or a sponsor of electronic bulletin boards or chat rooms, is held accountable for their actions online and for any content they access and send. Users can be punished for writing or distributing content that endangers "state secrecy" or security. In March of 2005 the MII announced that all China-based Web sites—commercial, governmental, personal, and even "blogs"[25]— must register with the ministry by June 30 or face closure. Notably, these regulations do not represent formal laws but rather serve as general guidelines for the use of the Internet. Nonetheless, while enforcement is frequently lax, the primary purpose of the regulations is to serve as a warning to Internet users and providers.

Controlling of Internet Service Providers (ISPs) and Internet Content Providers (ICPs)

In addition to requiring ISPs and ICPs to license and register with one of the *fulian,* the government places responsibility for any infractions of the regulations squarely at their doors. ISPs and ICPs must receive approval from the network providers for anything distributed on their sites, with the exception of information already openly distributed through other media. Any ISP or ICP that fails to report infractions on their Web sites is subject to severe penalties. This not only follows the premise of "those who go online will be held responsible," but also introduces "those who provide information online will be held responsible." The service and content providers that make up the "access networks" are required to obtain personal information on all subscribers (including account numbers, addresses or domain names of Web sites, and telephone numbers). The providers are obligated to pass on users' personal details to the CNNIC and to keep the above records for two months to hand over to state authorities upon request. In January 2002 and May 2003, respectively, the MII and the Ministry of Culture issued additional regulations requiring ISPs and ICPs to register themselves and users with national and local authorities. The 2002 regulations require ISPs working in "strategic and sensitive sectors" to install software that will archive all messages sent and received by users. If the ISP uncovers an illegal message, a copy is to be sent to the Ministry of Information Industry, the Ministry of Public Security, and the Bureau for the Protection of State Secrets.[26] The 2003 provisions require ICPs to register with their central or provincial office in addition to any other registrations under previous rules.[27]

Flooding the Net with Approved Sites

The CCP is moving to inundate the Internet with approved sites and content to keep netusers logging on but distracted from potentially subversive material. Initiatives like Governments and Enterprises Online are rapidly adding attractive sites to the Internet. Some of China's top Web sites are *Renmin Ribao,* Xinhua News Agency, China Radio International, *China Daily,* and the China Internet Network Information Center, all state-owned media outlets. Although Chinese government Web sites (with the domain gov.cn) make up only 1.5 percent of total Web sites, many government-related Web sites do not have .gov designations (for example, the *People's Daily,* Xinhua News Agency, the Chinese Academy of Sciences, the Communist Youth League of China). Many of these Party-controlled organizations are opening clever, glossy Web sites with help from foreign firms. By January 2005 there were an estimated 668,900 Chinese Web sites. This is a dramatic increase over the 27,289 Web sites recorded in CNNIC's

July 2000 survey report. With 1.3 billion citizens in the PRC alone, Chinese has the potential to become the most commonly used language on the web. According to September 2004 figures maintained by Internet marketing consultancy Global Reach, Chinese is the second most common language used online, representing 13.7 percent of the world's total online population. As more Chinese language Web sites are introduced in cyberspace, more users are logging on and turning to domestic sites.[28]

Blocking or Censoring of Internet Content

Early in the Chinese Internet revolution, Party officials had hoped to establish a China-only intranet, essentially closing China off from access to the global Internet. The project was called the Golden Bridge Project, or the China World Web (CWW). The project began in 1993 by setting up Internet protocol connections between government ministries and state-owned enterprises, and in October 1996 services were first offered to the public.[29] Unfortunately for the CCP, demand for Internet access, particularly for economic growth, rapidly outstripped the project's creation. The idea of a complete intranet was abandoned. The government, however, has found some success in limiting access to the global web through various methods, such as channeling users through the state-owned networks or rapidly introducing domestic sites. Additionally, the CCP has instituted measures to block sensitive sites and censor online information.

Despite the emphasis on the potential openness of the World Wide Web, the Chinese government has built what has become known as "The Great Firewall of China" with the help of foreign companies. A quarter of the vendors at the Security China 2000 trade show, many of them foreign firms, were marketing products aimed at enhancing China's "Golden Shield." Cisco Systems, a U.S. company known for building corporate firewalls to block viruses and hackers, was hired by the Chinese government to build a firewall on a national scale.[30] Cisco designed a router device, integrator, and firewall box specifically tailored to the PRC's telecommunications system. Routers can be used to intercept information and also to conduct keyword searches. The firewall can block forbidden, politically sensitive Web sites by recognizing the unique addresses encoded for each Web site. Nortel Networks, a Canadian firm, is also involved in assisting China to censor its web users. The company developed a "Personal Internet" strategy that allows the network to identify subscribers when they log on, match their names with their IP addresses, and be aware of trends in content accessed over time.[31] Some sensitive Web sites that have been periodically blocked in China include those of CNN, the BBC, the *New York Times,* and the *Washington Post,*[32] as well as sites for the Falun Gong or known Chinese dissident groups. In early September 2002, several foreign search engines, most notably Google and AltaVista, were blocked for several days without explanation. More recently the Chinese government has adopted a less overt strategy to filter Internet traffic. Previously, blocking was mostly in the form of prevention of access to certain sites; now those sites can be accessed, but keyword searches on "sensitive issues" generally do not result in hits.

Regulating Public Internet Outlets

The Chinese central government is also putting more pressure on owners of Internet cafes, or Internet bars, to police themselves. A 1999 circular issued by the Ministry of Public Security, the MII, the Ministry of Culture, and the State Administration of Industry and Commerce makes it compulsory for Internet cafes to register names and addresses of users, number of terminals, employee information, and agency agreements with local telecommunications officials. In addition, after obtaining licenses from local commercial administration departments, owners of Internet cafes must register with local public security bureaus before opening for business. While enforcement of these rules is irregular, the penalties for breaking the laws when there is a crackdown can be severe. Sweeps and closures occur on a fairly regular basis. Unlicensed Internet cafes are regularly closed, while licensed cafes have been ordered to install monitoring software and equipment.[33]

Encouraging Self-Censorship

Perhaps the greatest tool the CCP has employed to manage online usage is applying pressure on users to self-police. Before going online, Internet users have to sign an Internet Access Responsibility Agreement in which they pledge not to engage in activities online that would threaten state security or undermine public safety. Those found guilty of breaking the laws pertaining to Web use could suffer severe penalties. In January 1999, Lin Hai became the first Chinese to be tried and sentenced for Internet misuse.[34] He was sentenced to two years in jail and lost his political rights for one year. Activist Wu Yilong was given an eleven-year prison sentence for distributing articles on the China Democracy Party via the Internet.[35] In a June 2004 report, Reporters Without Borders, an international NGO for press freedom, cited China as the "world's biggest prison for cyber-dissidents."[36]

For users unwilling to censor themselves, there are the "Big Mamas," Web site employees who lead groups of volunteers who scan the Internet for any sensitive material and delete it. Provinces and cities across China are also hiring their own Internet police.[37] In April 2005 the Suqian city government formed an "Internet Commentator Team" to sway public opinion in Internet chat rooms. In addition to individual self-censorship practices, businesses are jumping on the bandwagon. Since 2002 hundreds of Chinese Internet businesses have been pressured to sign the Internet Society of China's "Public Pledge of Self-Regulation and Professional Ethics for China's Internet Industry" to practice self-discipline and follow the cardinal principles of "patriotism, observance of the law, fairness, and trustworthiness" in the Internet industry.[38] Even foreign Internet companies are ready to concede to Beijing's requests to get a foot in the door of China's burgeoning market. In 2002, the American Internet search engine company Yahoo! signed the pledge. Google and Microsoft have also agreed to censor news on their Chinese web portals.[39]

Measures of Success

Not only has the Chinese government successfully employed multiple methods of Internet control, but it has also managed to reap major political and economic benefits from its expansion. The Internet may actually be increasing CCP government efficiency in a number of ways. Initiatives like the Government Online or Enterprises Online projects are reducing bureaucracy and improving transparency. In a country as large as China, Beijing has often had difficulty keeping in contact with and exerting influence over far-off provinces. The Web provides an opportunity for greater communication and cooperation between provincial and municipal governments and the central government. By the same token, more government and enterprise information is available to the Chinese public. Some ministries have established anti-corruption bulletin boards, and a few officials have made their e-mail addresses public in order to receive comments or questions from constituents. In December 2003, China's foreign minister took part in the country's first online chat session with a senior government official.[40]

While the medium fosters a modicum of open access for the user, at the same time Internet chat rooms, bulletin boards, and the occasional message monitoring allow the government to gauge political opinion. A two-year study funded by the Markle Foundation and carried out by the Chinese Academy of Social Sciences found that a majority of respondents (between 60 and 80 percent), both users and nonusers, agreed that the Internet would provide more opportunities for people to express their political views, to criticize government policies, to increase their political knowledge, and to help government officials to understand the political views of common people. The survey also found that a majority of users trusted the content they found online and believed some control of the Internet was necessary. Increased government accountability is another potential by-product of the information technology revolution. News stories on local disasters that are not published in national newspapers have sometimes found their way onto the Internet. These stories have sometimes forced the central government to become more forthright with information. Moreover, the net has provided a forum to foster nationalism and to monitor and track dissidents. Dissidents may use the World Wide Web to communicate with each other and to disseminate information, but the real question is whether greater freedom of information will lead more citizens to take the substantial risks involved in organized opposition to the government. A 2002 RAND study found that dissident use of the Internet was not enough to truly challenge the Chinese government and that, at least for the time being, Beijing's approaches to counter dissident use of the Internet have been successful.[41]

Continuing economic prosperity and the rising standard of living are also aiding the Party in improving its image. For many net users in the PRC, the Internet is primarily for e-mail, chatting, researching, and entertainment. The Internet also increasingly serves as an opportunity for the growing middle class to go shopping. China's e-commerce is on the rise. Banking on that growth, the U.S. online auction company eBay bought out EachNet, China's leading e-commerce site, in 2003. The appeal of using the Internet primarily for personal communication and leisure purposes, combined with its expanding commercialization, may eclipse any concerted efforts at online activism.[42]

Often, proponents of the Internet's freeing potential point out the increasing difficulty Beijing will have in controlling the online environment. Theoretically, because the government is unable to screen all messages, block all objectionable Web sites all the time, and arrest or imprison all persons who send, post, or read subversive content on the Web, the tide of democratic change cannot be stemmed. However, at times monitoring and posturing can be just as effective, or even more so, as absolute control. In the case of Singapore, Rodan points out that monitoring is a relatively easy and inconspicuous means to control the Internet, and "when extensive networks of political surveillance are already in place and a culture of fear about such practices exists, the impact of monitoring is likely to be strong."[43] Perception can be a very strong motivating factor. If one perceives the threat of being monitored, an environment of self-censorship is easily created. As one Singapore official declared, "Censorship can no longer be 100 percent effective, but even if it is only 20 percent effective, we should not stop censoring."[44] Singapore was in fact the first country in the world to adopt Internet censorship regulations in 1995. With one of the world's highest Internet connectivity rates, Singapore has successfully implemented a variety of regulations governing the Internet, from establishing the Internet as a medium subject to the same laws as traditional media, requiring all ICPs and ISPs to register with the government and block Web sites the government deems objectionable, to instituting serious fines and jail sentences for offenders, and restricting political content and activity online. Although Singapore's small size and political system notably facilitate its ability to contain the Internet, governments elsewhere have taken notice, in particular China.[45]

In contrast to the idea of greater freedom of communication, Internet censorship and regulation have been steadily increasing. Online surveillance is actually more prevalent than one might suppose, and with the rise of Internet use and e-commerce, and as a result of measures taken after the September 11 terrorist attacks on the United States, it is only increasing. Within Asia, recent scholarship has indicated that the links between democracy and the advancement of the Internet have been decidedly mixed and in general have not borne out the forecasts of technological libertarians. Across Asia and the world, in Vietnam, Iran, Cuba, Myanmar, Syria, Saudi Arabia, Zimbabwe, and Australia, governments have been moving to limit the reach of the Internet.[46] While Singapore may have provided Chinese leaders with a model for Internet control—another Confucian society with a high level of economic development and strict government control—China is now serving as an archetype for other authoritarian regimes. Governments around the world that desire to restrict online content and access are no doubt closely observing China's apparent success in "nailing" the Internet while reaping its benefits. For if a large country like China is able to accomplish this, then conceivably any country could.

Conclusion

Looking more closely at Kedzie's study of interconnectivity and democracy, several questions arise concerning its validity and applicability to the Chinese (and other) cases. First is that of the time factor. Kedzie published his study in 1997 using 1993 interconnectivity data. In 1993, the use of the Internet was far from widespread. It was not even introduced into China until 1993. Even by 1997, the first CNNIC survey reported only 620,000 Chinese Internet users. Second, the roles of geography, history, and culture are given a backseat to the interconnectivity variable. Although Kedzie acknowledges that the former Soviet Union, Estonia, Latvia, and Lithuania had greater levels of interconnectivity and democracy in part due to their proximity to Western Europe, there was less emphasis on their acceptance of such communication technologies as a result of those bonds. The Chinese for their part frequently argue that their unique history and culture set them apart. Third, the "counter examples," where ruling parties utilized new information and communication technologies to maintain authoritarianism, are too easily dismissed as examples only of technologies that fall within the comfort level of dictators. Fourth, Kedzie's analysis fails to account for examples in which countries with increased levels of Internet connectivity may have actually become less democratic (Venezuela, for example), where communication technology primarily and undemocratically benefits the elites,[47] or aids nonstate actors whose ambitions do not coincide with Western democratic ideals.[48] Fifth, despite the proclamation of "all cases" indicating a high correlation between interconnectivity and democracy, Kedzie identifies Singapore as a dominant outlier. He does not go so far as to say Singapore is an exception to the rule, but only that the data suggest a smaller, less optimistic correlation coefficient. Singapore's high level of interconnectivity per capita is downplayed for its small absolute statistics in relation to all the Western democracies. However, Singapore's status as an outlier and Kedzie's reasoning for its relative unimportance is significant because Singapore has served as a model to China in its Internet filtering, and in absolute terms China has more people online than any other country excepting the United States.

It is interesting that Pan Wei also uses Singapore as an example of a government already successfully implementing rule of law without democracy. Singapore's primary objective too was to attain "modernity, instead of democracy" and its economic development has been nothing short of extraordinary. The city-state enjoys one of the world's highest standards of living, a robust economy built with a highly technical workforce, advanced use of information technology, and fair levels of civic activism without political agitation. Kedzie labels Singapore a "partially free" country and says, "While not ideal from the western perspective [Singapore's level of democracy] would be a welcome improvement for a third of the countries and more than 40 percent of the world's population."[49] This begs the question of whether the West could also accept a "partially free" China?

Finally, Kedzie's study fails to account for the full impact of adaptation, in information technology, control strategies, and governance. For example, the definition of "interconnectivity," encompassing only e-mail traffic, resembles only a fraction of what the Internet offers today. Although Kedzie does address this issue, indicating that e-mail, more than any other online service, provides the hypothesized democratic criteria—"multi-directional discourse across borders in a timely and inexpensive manner, unbounded by geographic and institutional constraints"—the proliferation of other Internet-based communication media such as Web sites, chatrooms, and blogging are not addressed. Even though one might expect greater means of interconnectivity to increase tendencies toward democracy, *unbounded institutional constraints* is hardly an accurate description of the regulation environment surrounding the Internet today, even in the West. One might envision that over time the Internet, too, could fall within the authoritarian's comfort level. Additionally, the portrayal of the Internet as an instrument of autonomy assumes that citizens will choose to exercise that autonomy. A combination of social engineering, censorship, and political apathy can reduce incentives to use the Internet for activism.

Imagine instead that the Internet *has* already taken hold in China. The rapid spread of telecommunications and information technology belie the impression of a China still waiting to enter the Information Age. China's leaders are far from shirking the introduction of the Internet, and are instead embracing it and succeeding. Rather than viewing the Internet as an inevitable threat to Communist Party rule, CCP leaders appear to view the Internet as a "powerful weapon" that can be harnessed to the CCP's plans for China's modernization. The premise of the "Dictator's Dilemma" has not been borne out. The belief that the Internet will somehow help bring "freedom" to China is fundamentally misguided. The Internet will not bring democracy to China by itself because it is neither inherently revolutionary nor liberating; the Internet is a function of those who use it, whether governments, activists, gamers, shoppers, or terrorists. Beijing has thus far proven adept at expanding both information technology and economic growth while instituting various regulations of the Internet.

This is not to say that the Internet is not changing China, just that the transformation is not nearly as extensive nor does it yet resemble what Western democracy proponents might hope for. Fundamentally, we must ask ourselves what is meant by the terms *freedom* and *democracy*. Are these not terms characterized by greater economic prosperity, educational opportunities, access to information, freedom of expression, governmental transparency and efficiency, opportunity for citizens to make their political views known to officials, and ability for officials to survey public opinion? If so, then the Internet is playing a key role in China's political transformation. To what end, we do not yet know. Pan Wei's case for a rule of law government without a liberal, politically plural democracy in China outlines a potential model for this transformation. Definitively, it is too early to know the impact of the Internet on political transformation and single-party rule in China's future. Connectivity rates, although growing, cover less than 10 percent of the population. However, for the time being and probably for some time to come, the Internet may be more of an asset than a liability for Chinese single-party rule.

13

Toward a Rule of Law Regime

Political Reform Under China's Fourth Generation of Leadership

Suisheng Zhao

Although scholars have continued to debate the feasibility of Pan Wei's consultative rule of law regime, political reform in post-Mao China has moved steadily toward governing the country by law (*yifa zhiguo*) or governing the government according to law (*yifa zhizheng*). This trend can be observed in the following three important aspects of political reform after the transition of the CCP leadership from the third generation led by Jiang Zemin to the fourth generation under Hu Jintao:[1] institutionalization of the leadership system with an emphasis on the normative rules and procedures; the effort to make government more accountable to an increasingly plural society; and the improvement of citizens' constitutional rights. These aspects of political reform reveal what the rule of law regime is.

Institutionalization of the Leadership System

Institutionalization of China's leadership system, one of the most important aspects of political reform, is also an effort to build a rule of law regime as it emphasizes the normative rules and procedures in the decision-making process. It started in the 1980s when Deng Xiaoping realized that "the lack of effective institutions and checks on arbitrary authority had helped bring about disasters in the Mao years."[2] Significant reform measures have included regular Party and state body meetings according to constitutional schedules; constitutionally mandated two-term limits for the premier and president; a retirement age for all Party and government posts; and a personnel policy emphasizing youth and education.

One of the most important consequences of institutionalization is the enhancement of formal institutional authority and a decline in the informal personal authority of top leaders. By definition, personal authority revolves around individual personage and derives from the charismatic nature of strong leaders, which supersedes impersonal organization in eliciting the personal loyalty of followers. In contrast, institutional authority derives from and is constrained by impersonal organizational rules. In an ideal type, such authority rests not on individual charisma but on a leader's formal position in an institutional setting. Insofar as a leader can issue commands under institutional authority, it is the function of the office he or she holds rather than of any personal quality.

For many years in PRC history, personal authority was more important than institutional authority in top-level politics. This was particularly true during the 1980s when retired senior leaders possessed great personal prestige and influence over newly promoted and younger top office-holders.[3] Although Deng gave up most of his formal titles voluntarily at the peak of his power, with the exception of chairman of the Central Military Commission (CMC) that he retained for two more years after stepping down from the Politburo Standing Committee in 1987, he still exercised ultimate authority due to his personal stature, connections, and breadth of experience. He cashiered two of his chosen successors (Hu Yaobang and Zhao Ziyang), organized the crackdown on student demonstrators in Tiananmen Square in 1989, and regularly intervened in policy matters until he became incapacitated in the mid-1990s. Deng's ultimate authority was reflected crucially in the secret resolution of the 13th Party Congress in 1987 to refer all important matters to him for final decision, as was revealed later. As a result, Deng ruled China even when his only formal position was honorary chairman of the Chinese Bridge Players' Society.

Institutional authority has advanced to take a more important position than personal authority since the demise of the senior revolutionary veterans in the 1990s, which completed a transition of Chinese leadership from the revolutionary to the postrevolutionary generations. The rise of the third generation of leadership under Jiang began the transition. The rise of the Hu leadership has completed it. This is the first generation of leadership in the PRC without significant personal memory of the revolution years or any wartime military experience. As a result, since Deng's death in 1997, there have not been any retired senior leaders who ever practiced footloose informal power as Deng did. As noticed by Dittmer, "After retirements, Yang Shangkun, Yang Baibing, Wan Li, Qiao Shi, Liu Huaqing, and Zhang Zhen seem to have vanished into political oblivion without a trace."[4] Even though Jiang Zemin sought to follow the lead of Deng since his stepping down from the Party boss position at the 16th Party Congress, he was not able to exercise the level of informal authority that Deng was able to wield because Jiang did not have the kind of prestige and stature that Deng had. Jiang's authority depended at first upon the approbation of the elders and, later, on his institutional positions. That is why Jiang tried to retain the CMC chairmanship and keep his name and photograph appearing ahead of Hu Jintao's in the official media for quite a while after the 16th Party Congress, while Deng could afford to have his name and photographs appear behind those of Zhao Ziyang after the 13th Party Congress in 1987. In fact, there was a surprisingly strong anti-Jiang sentiment among the Party elites after Jiang decided to keep his CMC post at the 16th Party Congress. It was reported that in a rare move, a group of influential Communist Party elders wrote to the Communist Party Central Committee in June 2003 urging Jiang to give up his chairmanship of the CMC by the end of the year. The elders said Jiang's departure would "speed up rejuvenation in the leadership" and that it "would have beneficial effects on the smooth running of the party and state affairs."[5] With the advance of institutionalization, Jiang's ability to wield power via personal influence dramatically declined.

After taking office, Hu Jintao has moved further in the direction of institutionalization of the leadership system and, in particular, has emphasized the importance of preserving the normative rules and procedures of collective leadership in decision-making processes. At the highly publicized first Politburo meeting after the 16th Party Congress, Hu emphasized the rule of law and the Constitution. Since then, the Politburo and its standing committee meetings have been routinely publicized in the official media. In addition to regular Politburo meetings, Hu started a system of collective study sessions to help his colleagues make decisions based on more educated information. At the State Council's first executive meeting presided over by Premier Wen Jiabao on March 19, 2003, two days after his assuming the position, a set of working codes for the cabinet were worked out that emphasized administration by law and enhancing supervision in government work. Wen called for the new administration to strive to make breakthroughs in three aspects: First, important decisions should be made collectively on the basis of thorough investigations, feasibility studies, and soliciting opinions from all walks of life. Second, in making decisions concerning the nation's economic and social development, cross-departmental and cross-subject hearings should be conducted and the government should make better use of experts and research institutes. Third, an accountability system should be put in place. Those who violate the decision-making procedures and cause major losses should be held directly responsible for their mistakes.[6]

In a move to institutionalize a decision-making system in the State Council, Wen stopped making decisions at premier work meetings (*zongli bangong huiyi*), which did not have any legal status but were held regularly by his predecessors. Instead, he has made decisions at the State Council executive meetings (*guowuyuan changwu huiyi*) and State Council plenary meetings (*guowuyuan quanti huiyi*), which were regulated by the Constitution and State Council Organic Law. Wen's predecessors Li Peng and Zhu Rongji relied heavily upon the premier work meetings to make State Council decisions. It was reported that within the five-year tenures of both premiers, each held about 150 such meetings. Both Li and Zhu liked the premier work meeting because it was called upon by the premier, its participants were at the discretion of the premier, and it gave the premier a lot of discretionary power in the decision-making process. In contrast, both the State Council executive meeting and its plenary meeting are clearly stipulated by the Constitution and law. The participants of executive meetings must include the premier, vice premiers, state councilors, and State Council secretaries general. They should be convened at least once a month. The participants at plenary meetings are all members of the State Council. They should be held every two months or once a quarter. It was reported that 37 executive meetings were held between March 19, 2003 and January 29, 2004, about 3–4 meetings each month. One Chinese scholar indicated that the new practice "reflects the institutionalization of the State Council decision-making system, [and] avoids the rule of man in the decision-making process. This is a major method toward ruling the country according to the Constitution and laws." It quoted another Chinese scholar that the reform was "a step toward legalization, institutionalization, and regularization in the operation of the State Council."[7]

Another significant move toward institutionalization of leadership politics is the decision in July 2003 to abolish the annual series of informal central work conferences at the summer resort of Beidaihe. The informal central work conference started in Mao's years and was held in various locations. Many major policy decisions were made at these conferences, although their existence and jurisdiction were never stipulated in the CCP or PRC constitutions. The central work conference survived the post-Mao transition as "it served as a forum for consensus building in which important members of the political elites make bargains with each other. . . . Since most members of the top elite are now aged and cannot move around easily, the location of the meetings has basically been fixed at Beidaihe, a coastal summer resort about three hundred miles from Beijing."[8] Major policy and personnel decisions were made at the month-long Beidaihe conferences. Vacationing and participating in these informal meetings, retired elders exercised undue influence. The decision to abolish the Beidaihe informal conferences and to rely upon formal meetings of the Politburo and its Standing Committee is certainly a major advance toward institutionalization of decision making at the top. As a Hong Kong reporter indicates, the cancellation of the Beidaihe conferences is "a new effort to regularize [government] procedures and institutions" and "testimony to Hu's determination to curtail rule of personality and to run the party and country according to law and institutions."[9]

Under these circumstances, it is not surprising to read such a bold statement as the following by an official in the Research Office of the Central Party School: "A modern society demands a modern government whose administration should be kept open, honest, transparent and efficient." To build a modern government, he suggests, "State laws and regulations of governments at all levels should not be changed frequently willy-nilly."[10] Continuing institutionalization of the leadership system in this direction is certainly an important development for building a rule of law regime. The top CCP leaders will tend to have less and less personal authority as the institutionalization of leadership politics continues. In this case, in the years to come, Hu Jintao, no matter how capable he is, will have less personal authority than Jiang and, as a result, is less likely to become a strongman after his retirement than Deng or even Jiang. The lack of a strongman in the leadership should at least make members of the CCP leadership more willing to follow normative rules and procedures in decision making. This formal structure of collective leadership would in turn further strengthen the process of institutionalization of the decision-making system.

Cadre Accountability

Another aspect of political reform is to make the government officials/cadres more responsive to societal demands and more accountable for their bad performance in response to the legitimacy crisis that the CCP suffered after the inception of market-oriented economic reform and opening up to the outside world. In Mao's years, the government authority of the communist state was enforced by official ideology and party discipline. State authority began to erode when economic reform led to the decline of official ideology as a guide to correct political action, lax party discipline, and the paralysis of party organizations in grassroots levels. As a result, the state's control has become more formalistic and less substantive, while the people's response to state authority has become increasingly cynical, with general acceptance on the surface, but subtle and sometimes blatant noncompliance on many issues in reality. The state has gone through the motions of governing without checking too carefully on how thoroughly its orders are carried out, as long as no systematic opposition is organized. To an extent, the role of the communist state has reverted to that of traditional government by feigned compliance and the highly ritualized Confucian state, particularly at the grassroots levels.

This system worked well in imperial China because traditional Chinese social order was relatively simple and could be held together by the bonding spirit of Confucianism. However, it has become more and more difficult for the Communist leadership to receive compliance without normal inputs from the society, as "China's economy and society have become more complex and ever great[er] functional specialization and social differentiation have created an ever richer diversity of interests."[11] To make the situation worse, the devastating rise of rampant corruption has severely damaged party legitimacy. As a result of the rapid emergence of the market economy and of the absence of checks over the government officials, the politically connected have reaped a vastly disproportionate share of the benefits from China's economic boom. Corruption and abuse of power have become widespread throughout China, breeding resentment and anger among Chinese people who do not have institutional means of voicing or redressing their grievances and defending themselves against predation.

In response, Deng's political reform in the 1980s began to imply that the responsibility of the state was to expand socialist democracy rather than exercise dictatorship, although it never defined democracy in Western terms. Carrying out political reform to accommodate a more pluralist society, as Minxin Pei indicated, the party has developed a strategy of opening up peripheral parts of the political system while allowing no challenge to its power.[12] Opportunity for voluntary participation in politics has been increased at both the grassroots and national levels, as indicated in Chapter 2 of this book.

Since Hu Jintao came to power, the effort to rebuild regime legitimacy has continued. In particular, the new leadership has tried to promote a new image of *qinmin* ("be nice to the people") government by working closely with the masses, especially the disadvantaged. On March 18, 2003, the day after assuming the presidency, vowing before the TV cameras, Hu proposed what has been known as "three new people's principles" (*xin sanmin zhuyi*): to use power for the people (*quan weimin shuoyong*), to link sentiments to the people (*qing weimin shuoji*), and to pursue the interest of the people (*li weimin shuomo*). On the same day, Wen Jiabao, the new premier, quoted a poem as his motto: "In life or death, act for the country's benefit."[13] These efforts have been known as the "Hu-Wen New Deal" (*Hu-Wen xinzheng*) since then.

One of the institutional innovations of the "Hu-Wen New Deal" has been the set-up of a cadre accountability/responsibility system (*ganbu wenze zhi*) according to which, if any official is found unable to prevent mishaps ranging from epidemics to labor unrest, they will face tough penalties or dismissal. This system was triggered primarily by the SARS (severe acute respiratory syndrome) crisis in 2003. After a whistleblower exposed lies about the outbreak, Chinese people began demanding basic rights to information and the World Health Organization and the foreign media clamored for accountability. In the hospitals, the virus crept into the ranks of the Communist Party. Unlike in the past, the drama was chronicled in real time on the Internet. Realizing the danger that SARS could pose to the country and the state, Hu made an unusual move at an unscheduled Politburo meeting on April 17 in acknowledging that the government had lied about the disease. To show his commitment to all-out war against an epidemic sweeping the country and the capital, three days later, he fired Beijing's mayor and the country's health minister for covering up the actual number of SARS patients. Prime Minister Wen Jiabao, in a show of remorse and regret, apologized for mistakes while attending a regional SARS Summit in Bangkok in late April. A *People's Daily* commentary later admitted that "The spread of SARS has something to do with the initial belated reporting of the true situation and the negligence and dereliction of duty on the part of some government officials. The belated, incomplete reporting resulted in the government's failure to fully carry out its duties in the initial, but crucial period of the SARS outbreak." This commentary continued, "Modern forms of government are characterized by transparency and openness. The Chinese Government has not, in the past, been accustomed to public disclosure of its activities."[14]

Partially in response to the media exposure and domestic as well as international pressure with regard to the initial cover-up of the epidemic, the new Chinese leadership worked hard to build an image as the champion of ordinary Chinese people by calling for government officials to be more professional and accountable. As one Western scholar observed, "The SARS crisis—and the Chinese government's deceitful early response to it—has underlined the urgent need for systemic political reform."[15] In response, the Hu-Wen administration made efforts to find new ways of communicating with the Chinese people and made a change in style of governance toward a more transparent and rule-binding administration. After admitting to the cover-up of the severity of SARS in Beijing, the central leadership insisted that the media must honor the people's *zhiqing quan* ("right to know"), and ministries, provinces, and cities must establish a news dissemination system to boost government transparency. A cadre responsibility system was set up whereby leading officials were required to show greater accountability and to report truthfully on the epidemic situation. As a result, it was reported that the behavior of China's usually docile media had changed.

Television stations are carrying an unprecedented number of news conferences and interviews live. Newspapers are reporting news as it breaks, not days or weeks afterward. Reporters are asking sharp questions, and publications are printing their findings, whether about SARS patients escaping from hospital or SARS-related violence erupting in the provinces.[16]

One Chinese journalist reported that "Nearly 1,000 government officials, including former Minister of Health Zhang Wenkang, were sacked or otherwise penalized in 2003 for either concealing lax efforts to prevent the SARS outbreaks or even concealing the epidemic."[17] Since then, major accidents and environmental disasters such as mine explosions have been routinely exposed in the media and responsible officials have been routinely removed or even punished.

Although it is hard to say how much such changes show an acceptance of liberal democratic principles or entail complete opening of the political system, the Hu-Wen administration has certainly been under pressure to reform the system to reflect the tumultuous pace of transformation in China, from technology that often outpaces efforts to control information, to globalization and foreign influences that vie with Communist Party doctrine. As a Western reporter pointed out, "In a way, the SARS epidemic helped crystallize some political reforms and the rule of law in China; the Communist Party appears to have opened up to public scrutiny and accountability . . . as politics stabilize and people's power and prerogatives emerge."[18]

To express the government's responsiveness to the voice of disadvantaged people and regions, the new leadership has made some fine adjustments in policy emphasis to balance out reform in the nation's economic and social landscape and identified some new fronts in the country's continuing reform drive, so that the rapid progress made to date in some sectors of the economy and society is matched in others. After taking over the helm of party leadership, Hu made his first trips to Xibaipo in Hubei Province, a CCP revolutionary shrine, and Inner Mongolia, a relatively poor and inland region. His message was not primarily to distinguish himself from Jiang with different sources of legitimacy and social-economic agenda. Rather, it was to strike a balance between the priority of economic efficiency and the importance of narrowing disparities in society, and between the continuity of opening up along the coast and the development of the remote rural areas. As one observer indicated, "Hu Jintao's recent engagement in favor of China's disadvantaged should not be seen as a sign of his opposition to Jiang Zemin's statist visions. Jiang's statist vision is about political stability. Hu Jintao reflects the concerns of the Chinese power elite about social stability. The two are not opposites but complementary."[19]

These changes and adjustments have made the Hu-Wen administration more responsive to popular demands than its predecessors, but it is far from building institutions and systems of governance that would guarantee effective supervision of the rulers. Although the cadre accountability system is designed to make cadres more responsive to societal demands, the way it has worked is actually to make the cadres responsive only to their hierarchical superiors. This is not what is perceived as accountability in a genuine sense of democracy.

From this perspective, it is a reform toward the rule of law rather than democratization. As a matter of fact, the Hu-Wen administration, like its predecessors, has not hesitated to put a damper on the changes that threaten the CCP's monopoly of power. This explains why, while the party asked the media to report any breaking news in a "timely, objective way" during the SARS epidemic, the authorities at the same time set clear limits. Immediately after the government's calls for a more open approach to combating the disease, propaganda officials upbraided the editor-in-chief of the popular tabloid *Beijing Star Daily*. His offense was using an overly large front-page headline to announce the firing of the health minister and Beijing's mayor for mishandling the epidemic, in contrast with the *People's Daily*, which ran a brief item below the front-page fold. Other casualties include two local newspapers that belong to the *Nanfang Daily* Group, based in Guangzhou. The group's *Southern Weekend*, a high-brow, nationally circulated weekly whose investigative reports frequently riled senior officials, went through its second top-level personnel changes in three years. This time a provincial propaganda official, Zhang Dongming, was named editor of the paper and deputy editor of the parent company to ensure that party policies are followed. A sister paper, *21st Century World Herald*, was temporarily closed for running several controversial articles on Chinese politics.[20]

Constitutional Reform

Market-oriented economic reform has required the CCP to build a legal framework that can post clear rules of transaction, check the arbitrariness of state power, protect property rights, and instill business confidence in the Chinese market. Thus, building a legal system, or *fazhi,* a Chinese word which means both "rule of law" and "rule by law," has become one of the most important aspects of political reform. Reformist leaders have worked hard to pass laws and promote the supremacy of the Constitution in maintaining an authoritarian stability.

The progress in legal reform has been very impressive in recent years. As Peerenboom indicated Chapter 3 of this book, "Even in the eyes of the harshest critics, China's legal system has come a long way in just over twenty years. Two decades of reform have produced remarkable changes in institutions, laws, and practices." In particular, constitutional reform has become a hotly debated issue in China's political reform agendas.

The Constitution is supposed to define the composition and power of political structures of the regime and regulate the relations of the various institutions to one another and to the citizens. However, for many years in PRC history, the Constitution has borne little relation to the actual government of China. Constitutional documents and traditions in liberal democracies take the general form of a contract or an agreement between the ruled and the rulers, and "limitations on the rulers are exacted by the ruled in exchange for allowing the rulers to preserve some elements of their right to govern and for preserving the stability of the governing system itself."[21] The Constitution in the PRC, however, has largely been a declaration of general political aims used to legitimize the CCP's power, and has therefore become an extension of party rule. The status of the Constitution is ambiguous. It has not functioned as a set of fixed principles against which specific laws and practices are measured and over-turned if found to be at odds. Although all Chinese constitutions have included the standard statement of freedoms and rights, these freedoms and rights are limited by the degree to which people's exercise of them is considered acceptable by the party. If one's actions are stamped anti-party, the wrath of the people's dictatorship could legally be executed toward the citizen. Therefore, the Chinese Constitution has been seen as "an element in a broader structure of the political constitution" by some West-ern scholars.[22]

The PRC has been governed by four constitutions. Four amendments have been made to the current Constitution. The making and amending of the Constitution have provided not only an indication of the constitutional reform, but also "a good barom-eter for China's political, economic and social changes."[23] Each constitution has not only come with a new power structure of the state but also "contained a clear indica-tion of the policy direction the current leadership at that time intended to take."[24] While the first constitution in 1954 detailed the state structure of the new People's Republic, its normal function became obsolete when the Cultural Revolution resulted in the disruption of the established institutional arrangement and produced new struc-tures and processes that had little, if any, constitutional validity. The second constitu-tion, known as "the Cultural Revolution Constitution" (*wenge xianfa*), was written in 1975. After the inception of economic reform, the third constitution, known as the "Four Modernizations Constitution" (*sige xiandaihua xianfa*), was adopted in 1978, marking the initial attempts to restore the pre–Cultural Revolution political system and reorient party policy toward economic development. The formal structures gov-erning the Chinese political system barely gained legitimacy with the 1978 Constitu-tion, when the fourth constitution, known as the "Reform and Opening-up Constitution" (*gaige kaifang xianfa*), was passed in 1982.

To reflect the new policy direction of post-Mao reforms, many changes were made in the 1982 Constitution. Among them are the following three important ones. First, it downgraded the importance of class struggle in Chinese society. The definition used in the 1975 and 1978 constitutions of China as "a socialist state of the dictatorship of the proletariat" was replaced by "a socialist state under the people's democratic dictator-ship," a concept similar to the 1954 definition of China as a "people's democratic state." Second, in an effort to establish a rule of law regime, the 1982 Constitution stipulated that "no organization or individual is privileged to be beyond the Constitu-tion or law." It made an attempt to free the state from the grip of the party although, in practice, the state's freedom for political maneuver is still circumscribed and limited. Unlike the constitutions of 1975 and 1978, reference to the party as the "core of lead-ership" was dropped, as was the claim that it is the citizens' duty to support the party. Mention of party control now only appeared in the preamble, where its leading role was acknowledged in the four basic principles. The third major change is the emphasis on the equality of all citizens before the law, a restoration of the 1954 stipulation to this effect. Notably, the renewed emphasis on citizens' rights and duties and on the need to treat people in accordance with known rules and regulations is reinforced by the fact that the chapter on Fundamental Rights and Duties of Citizens is now placed second in the Constitution, whereas in all previous Constitutions it stood third, after the chapter on the state structure. Interestingly, the 1982 Constitution did drop two citizens' rights from the 1978 Constitution, namely, the freedom of the "Four Bigs" (the right to speak loudly, air views fully, hold great debates, and write big-character posters), which was considered too closely associated with the style of expression during the Cultural Revolution, and the freedom to strike, the deletion of which was largely influenced by events in Poland with the rise of Solidarity at the time.

Functioning to regularize the framework for political life in China, the 1982 Constitution was amended four times—in 1988, 1993, 1999, and 2004—in response to the policy adjustments at the 13th, 14th, 15th, and 16th Party Congresses. The fact that it was amended, rather than replaced by new constitutions, suggests an important development in Chinese politics and a consensus among China's leaders on the fundamental goal of economic modernization. It was reported that after the 13th Party Congress in 1987, when the Chinese leaders discussed the first amendment to the Constitution, they laid down two principles. First, the reform should abide by the law while the law should serve the reform. Second, amendment of the Constitution is confined to articles that would hinder the reform if they were not changed; articles would remain as they are where the amendment is less significant, and some problems would be solved through interpretation of the Constitution. "By doing so, the Constitution can maintain its stability and so can the country."[25]

Indeed, largely reflecting already existing and approved economic and political practices, these amendments provided ideological justification of the party's economic reform policies and helped the reformist leaders "to create a more predictable system based on a clearer separation of roles and functions and a system of clearly defined rules and regulations applicable to everyone."[26] They moved China toward international norms on legal issues. Among the most important items in the amendments, the 1988 amendment introduced provisions on private economy while the 1993 one replaced the concept of "socialist market economy" with the concept of "planned economy on the basis of socialist public ownership." In the 1999 amendment, the role of the private sector was elevated from being "a complement to the socialist public economy" to "an important component of the socialist market economy." The phrase "counter-revolutionary activities" was changed to "crime jeopardizing state security." Significantly, "the constitutional amendments explicitly avow, for the first time in the constitutional history of the People's Republic, to 'govern the state according to law' (yifa zhiguo) and 'establish the socialist state of rule of law.'"[27]

Among the 2004 amendments, the most politically motivated change is the incorporation of the concept of the "Three Represents" into the preamble of the Constitution, a reflection of Jiang Zemin's desire to enshrine his political legacy. The Three Represents are Jiang's modification of Marxist theory and require the Communist Party represent the interests of all the people, including business owners, rather than just the working class. The Three Represents came across to most Westerners as communist gobbledygook, just as the concept of the "socialist market economy" once seemed a laughable oxymoron. But both terms provided indications of the way in which the Chinese economic and political systems would evolve. The essence of the Three Represents is that the CCP "should represent the elite rather than the masses and it should bind the country together rather than dividing it through struggle and class dictatorship."[28] It aims to transform the CCP from a revolutionary party to a conservative ruling party that is more inclusive and relevant to economic modernization objectives.

The second notable revision is that the "Citizens' legal private property is not to be violated . . . the state protects citizens' private property rights and inheritance rights according to law." This change puts private assets of Chinese citizens on an equal footing with public property, both of which are "not to be violated." The word "private" has long been the center of attention and the focus of much debate among Chinese officials, scholars, and the public over its place. For many years after the founding of the PRC, the word "private" and such terms as private interests, private property, and private concerns were targets of attack. Post-Mao reform has loosened the strict social and economic controls exercised by the state and produced a new private sector. However, for a rather long period they could only be called *minying* (citizen-operated) enterprises, not private enterprises. Obviously, the practice of encouraging the private sector of the economy, but avoiding reference to its existence in the Constitution, cannot sit well with the rising private sector. Many private entrepreneurs have been afraid that their assets would be subject to state takeover without a legal guarantee in the Constitution. It was reported that before the third constitutional amendment in 1999, many legal scholars had appealed to add an article on the inviolability of private property, but the proposal was abandoned due to strong opposition within the party.[29] Since then, it has become a key demand of China's newly emerged entrepreneurs. Such an amendment would certainly encourage more private investment and initiative, which the party needs to raise the living standards of the Chinese people and to remain in power.

The private property amendment to the Constitution is significant not only for the protection of private entrepreneurs but also for the protection of the private assets of ordinary Chinese. According to a Xinhua news report, China's private assets surpassed 11 trillion yuan (US$1.33 trillion) by the end of 2002, exceeding state assets by about 1 trillion yuan (US$121 billion). Most of these private assets are owned by ordinary citizens who need more protection in the Constitution because their right to hold their own assets is more likely to be infringed upon by the state and the rich. One most discussed infringement on private property rights in recent years is the forcible relocation of urban and rural residents during real estate development projects or the construction of economic projects. Millions of urban and rural residents have been forced to leave their homes with inadequate compensation. To address this problem, the proposed constitutional amendment adds "the State should give compensation" to the original stipulation that "the State has the right to expropriate urban and rural land," although "exactly what kind of compensation should be given is not stated in the amendment because during the constitutional revision process there was conflicting debate over this issue."[30]

The third important constitutional revision is that "the State respects and protects human rights." This amendment is obviously a response to Western criticism of China's human rights record. Although it is ambiguous and makes no mention of political freedom, this amendment, together with the private property protection and the stipulation that the "State should give compensation," are major steps forward in defining "limitations on those who rule at the highest level in a nation-state, a primary goal of all modern national constitutions whatever form they may take."[31] The Constitution not only bestows legitimate authority on the CCP leadership but can also be used by citizens to limit the behavior of the state. In a commentary on the constitutional amendments, one scholar indicated, "For a government that not too long ago persecuted private property owners and denounced 'human rights' as an alien western concept, these are monumental improvements."[32]

While the top-down approach toward constitutional reform has set limitations to the scope of the amendments, Liu Xiaobo, a Chinese political dissident known for his role in the 1989 Tiananmen pro-democracy demonstrations, acknowledges that "a constitution for the party authority [*dangquan xianfa*] has been transformed into a constitution to limit the party authority [*xianquan xianfa*]." Evidence of the transformation, according to Liu, is that the emphasis of legal education has shifted from educating citizens to obey the law to educating officials to follow the law. Reading the Chinese official statement and the proposal for the fourth constitutional amendment, he finds at least four aspects of positive change. One is the official acknowledgement that the most fundamental function of the Constitution is to protect citizens' rights while regulating state authority. The second is the confirmation of popular sovereignty in the Constitution, namely, the state deriving its authority from the consent of its citizens. The third is the positive response of the CCP to the constitutional principle of division of power and checks and balances. And the fourth is Hu Jintao's "new three people's principles," which reflect his constitutional consciousness of the principles of protection of citizens' rights and limitation of the state authority. Liu believes that the most important driving force for these changes is pressure from society, especially the rights-protection (civil rights) movement (*weiquan yundong*) that has developed in recent years.[33]

Indeed, protection of constitutional rights has become a hot topic in China's media, as ordinary Chinese have developed an understanding of the legal rights they are supposed to enjoy and try to make them real. This development has produced rights consciousness and activism, including a series of protests against the government infringement on citizens' rights. Among the major incidents, the debate over excessive police powers raged after a young man named Sun Zhigang was beaten to death in police custody, leading to a decision to revoke the detention and repatriation regulation giving police extensive powers to detain and repatriate people found without urban residency permits in cities in June 2003. The regulation, which was passed in

1982 and covered the provision of shelter for vagrants and beggars in urban areas and their repatriation, was widely criticized by human rights activists for violating its original purpose of providing assistance to the homeless. The decision came after the death of twenty-seven-year-old Sun Zhigang on March 20 while in custody. Sun was a university graduate from Wuhan and was detained by police in Guangzhou after he failed to produce his temporary residence permits. He was sent to a detention center and died three days later. Sun's tragic death caused a public uproar after its exposure by the media. Three young legal scholars made a petition to the National People's Congress and challenged the legality of Detention and Repatriation. This petition was followed by a national outcry over the unexplained beating death of Sun. In response, Guangzhou courts sentenced a detention center nurse and one of her patients to death, and sixteen others were given prison sentences for Sun's death.[34] The old Detention and Repatriation system was replaced with a comprehensive relief program. Although these actions were to help the Hu leadership establish an image as "cadres of the masses,"[35] they are a positive response to the demands for protecting individuals' constitutional rights. According to one reporter, "Sun's tragic death merits special attention because going by past standards, similar instances of abuse of power by the police were considered so routine his maltreatment would not even make it into the local press. . . . At least on the surface, these developments testify to President Hu Jintao's commitment to rule by law."[36]

Since then, Chinese media have carried many stories of citizens' actions to protect their constitutional rights with positive results. The official Xinhua News Agency reported on China's first discrimination case when two Henan residents filed a lawsuit against the Shenzhen Public Security Bureau in Guangdong Province on April 15, 2005, as they were offended by police posters displayed in public areas suggesting that Henan migrants were involved in crime. These two Henan residents said that the police action violated the Chinese Constitution's principle of equity and infringed on the rights of Henan people, damaged their reputation and caused them mental distress. They asked the police to apologize for their action in the national media. It was reported that Shenzhen police apologized to the two residents and other Henan people in a local newspaper, in which Liu Kuanzhi, director of the police substation, was quoted as saying: "The banner targeting Henan-native gangs has hurt people from Henan Province and we sincerely apologize to them." According to the report, local police went door-to-door in the district involved, where many people from Henan live, to apologize. All the posters were removed.[37]

Other than the cases of the struggle to defend individuals' constitutional rights, in a few places, when independent candidates tried to run for election to local people's congresses that have usually been reserved for the party nominees, the authorities allowed them to run and even take office. An entrepreneur in Hubei, arrested on trumped-up charges, was released after public opinion rallied behind him. In particular, a small but growing band of Chinese who were forcibly relocated by local authorities without adequate compensation protested with temerity to demand that the government respect private property rights. The government has given ground modestly over forced evictions in order to assuage public anger. In late 2003, central and local authorities began to clamp down on the "savage" methods used by some companies to force residents out of their homes. Then the central government issued a policy document in January 2004 calling for fairer and more transparent procedures to set the level of compensation, in light of the fourth constitutional amendment, which required the state to protect private property and human rights. One Western reporter suggested that "recent cases have shown that it is possible for public opinion to force China's Communist Party to cede greater civil rights. . . . Eventually Beijing may find that accepting an independent judiciary and wider participation in government is the only way to resolve conflicts that threaten to upset social stability."[38]

It is worth noting that all these stories had been openly reported and hotly discussed in Chinese media. Beijing's popular magazine *Xinwen Zhoukan* (News Week) titled its special 2003 year-end issue "2003: New Civil Rights Actions." A commentator from the magazine wove together many of these stories and saw "an unusual linkage among these seemingly random incidents." The commentator believed that "along with new civil rights actions, the call for maintaining the supremacy of the constitutional system has forcefully arisen above the water."[39] The rise of constitutional rights consciousness has brought about many new concepts among Chinese people. Guangzhou's bimonthly magazine *Nanfeng Chuang* (South Wind Window) listed ten "concepts of the year" in 2003. Most of them are closely linked with constitutional consciousness, such as *yimin weiban* (people are the original source of political authority), *yixian zhiguo* (to rule the country according to constitution), *zhiqing quan* (the right to information), *zunzhong minyi* (respect the people's will), and *lianjia zhengfu* (low-cost government).[40]

The popularization of these new concepts came together with a rising tide of open debate on constitutional reform by Chinese intellectuals. While the official proposal for the fourth constitutional amendment was discussed behind closed doors before it was made public, many intellectuals demanded the amendment be openly debated and responsive to public concerns. *Fenghuang Zhoukan* (Phoenix Weekly) published a group of cover-page stories about the intellectual debate in July 2003. One story featured a legal scholar, Cao Siyuan, who was known for writing on, appearing for, and organizing conferences about constitutional reform. Although Cao was detained after the 1989 Tiananmen massacre and expelled from the party, he has managed to run a nongovernmental research consulting firm in Beijing. It was to the surprise of many observers that Cao successfully organized a conference on constitutional reform in the city of Qingdao on June 19–20, 2003. At the conference, forty-one Chinese legal scholars and a few former government officials, including Jiang Ping, former president of the Chinese University of Politics and Law, and Zhu Houze, former director of the CCP Central Propaganda Department, presented papers and engaged in dialogues on constitutional reform. Some of the proposed reforms overlapped with those in the official proposal, such as the guarantee of private property rights. Some others, however, went beyond the official bounds, such as the constitutional right of citizens to choose their leaders and even some steps toward a multiparty political system. At the conference, Cao and some others lambasted Jiang's efforts to enshrine the Three Represents into the Constitution on the grounds that the Constitution should be free from all ideology. Cao presented a radical proposal of ten specific areas of constitutional amendment, including the principle of supremacy of citizens' rights, separation of powers, constitutional review by a Constitutional Commission, judiciary independence, and direct elections of leaders. He was even able to collect signatures on the Internet to support his constitutional amendment proposal.[41]

The development of legal reform has certainly resulted in significant liberalization and other positive changes in China's political life. However, these changes obviously fall far short of establishing a liberal democracy. For example, although the decision to abolish the Detention and Repatriation regulation represents progress toward the rule of law, it is more a way to pacify the public outcry over unchecked police power. In fact, while the positive response is a welcome sign, the process by which the decision was reached lacked transparency and involved little participation by the public or public debate of the substantive issues. Reporters were barred from the court during the trial of the Sun case. The decision to abolish the regulation was made by the State Council three days after the three young legal scholars submitted a petition to the NPC for a constitutional review. If this petition had been formally accepted by the NPC and processed according to procedure, that would have been big progress in rule of law. Instead, the state adopted the administrative measure to quell public anger. This is exactly the opposite of rule of law, and at most rule by law. China still has a long way to go to build a liberal democracy.

The Rule of Law Regime and Proceduralism

Political reform comprises a thin end of the wedge in the rigid authoritarian system, and the new generation of leaders has tried to establish an image of a new stripe—less hide-bound, more open-minded, and more rule-abiding. However, these advances have been very modest, and it is not entirely clear if Pan Wei's consultative rule of law regime would lead to a genuine system of rule of law. Paradoxically, one of the main purposes of the reform has been to head off threats that might eventually increase pressures for democratization. It is interesting to read an article in a June 2003 issue of the official *Outlook Weekly* by Sun Zaifu, a member of the party's central disciplinary commission. While openly urging the party to pursue democratic reform and embrace market forces, Sun made it clear that the notion of democracy put forward by the Chinese leaders was highly circumscribed. "We must not blindly follow the West," he stated, saying China was not ready for popular elections. "While casting one's ballot to elect officials was a constitutional right, democracy in action meant cadres having the interests of the broad masses in mind when they made decisions and implemented policies."[42]

Bruce Gilley has characterized the recent development of institutionalization and the rule of law regime in China as "proceduralism" that has resulted in an "end of politics" and a form of "crypto-politics." According to him, "Proceduralism is an attempt to deal with decisions through processes that are blind to outcomes. It is a key to the notion of 'technocracy'—officialdom guided by markets and scientific expertise." He suggests that the doctrine of proceduralism has come with "a trend in China's politics that has been growing since the mid-1990s: the repression of political debate among the party and state elite." The Constitution is seen as "the pediment of the procedural temple," and, "Constitutionalism, as envisaged by Mr. Hu and others, is a way to establish a reign of quiescence over those who would contest party and state decisions. It is a constitutionalism stripped of the political life that makes constitutions powerful symbols of deliberative agreements in other countries."[43]

While Gilley may be too negative toward the rule of law regime, he made a useful distinction between institutionalizing open political competition and "proceduralism." It is particularly interesting to see the doctrine of proceduralism in the context of a grand policy consensus built by Deng and advanced by Jiang and Hu over the primacy of concentrating on economic modernization and political stability in order to maintain the CCP one-party rule. It has been a long-held party belief during the reform years that keeping economic growth moving and prosperity on the rise is crucial to the party's progress and efforts to maintain one-party rule over an increasingly savvy society. Its legitimacy can be maintained without abolishing the one-party rule, as long as the Communist Party's rule can be improved to deliver economic growth.

The doctrines of proceduralism and economic primacy have so far stood the state as well as the reformist leaders in good stead, as the party's legitimacy in China has become increasingly tied to its ability to maintain a rule of law regime, raise incomes, and deliver year after year strong GDP growth. In this case, "When the party considers itself under assault, no law, treaty or right contains its fury. Despite nominal guarantees of freedom of association in China's Constitution, the police treat religious and labor groups that operate without official approval as seditious."[44] As one Western reporter indicated, while praising the fact that "China has edged toward more pluralism and openness in recent years, the authorities still punish those who dare to undermine the Communist government's power, for instance by organizing a political party or a workers' protest."[45]

The real test of political reform, therefore, is whether the party and state are willing to accept constitutional curbs on their ultimate power by, among other things, an independent constitutional review process, expansion of direct local elections, dilution of party control of the judiciary, and, in practice, permitting people to exercise such rights as freedom of assembly. It is hard to expect the Hu leadership to make such a breakthrough as the new leadership wants to do better than its predecessors and improve the system that they oversee—not bring it down. It has worked to govern an increasingly complex polity rather than to strike out in a new political direction. Quoting a Western scholar, one Western reporter wrote, "We see nothing in Hu's history to suggest he is any different from good members of the Communist Party, and none of them really believes in democracy."[46] In addition, most members of the current leadership were technically trained as professional technocrats. The most important feature of the technocrats is that they are ideologically agnostic and have nothing, or very little, to do with any ideology, communism and liberalism alike. The current leaders have "experienced ideological disillusionment twice. The first time was with Marx's communism and Mao's socialism. The second time was with economist Adam Smith's 'invisible hand.' . . . As a result, new leaders are more interested in discussing issues than defending 'isms.'"[47] They are believers in Deng's "cat theory" and tend to be very pragmatic. Lucian Pye's description of the operational characteristics of the Jiang leadership could be readily applied to the Hu leadership as well. That is, these pragmatic leaders "want governing to be a normal, routine matter, nothing dramatic or extreme. They want government to be just the practice of management, not of politics, for that would involve contending over values. In contrast to the constant drama and excitement over new departures that characterized the Mao and Deng eras, public affairs under Jiang have become a prosaic, almost colorless activity."[48] This is a typical picture of political life under the rule of law regime.

14

Reflections on the "Consultative Rule of Law Regime"

A Response to My Critics

Pan Wei

I

My earlier chapter in this book, which explains why China has so far not embraced electoral democracy, was initially drafted on the eve of Hong Kong's return in 1997. Like most authors revisiting their old works, I find in it many places for regret. However, witnessing what has happened in China in the past decade, my confidence in the six-pillar "consultative rule of law regime" has been growing. Instead of revising what I wrote before, I would rather begin by saying what I intend to do with that earlier chapter.

1. Bring back old knowledge on the pattern of sociopolitical change: A particular regime is rooted in a particular *social structure* and a particular *value system;* and both are rooted in a particular *division of labor,* as well as a particular *mode of production.* This pattern guides my explanation.

2. Demonstrate, according to the above pattern, the unique social origins that shaped the Chinese traditional polity.

• Compared to the European societies that were marked by highly differentiated and somewhat fixed hierarchies, the Chinese traditional society was an essentially undifferentiated one, based on free, equal, and self-sufficient farm families. Independent family farms in China effectively barred primogeniture, hence, "No rich family could be sustained for more than three generations" *(fu bu guo sandai).* In such a "society" of tens of millions of equal, free, independent, and self-sufficient farm families, kinship was vital, but keeping lineage ties was already difficult, and organizing sociopolitical groups would mean very high "transaction costs," easily suffering internal betrayal and external "divide-and-rule."

• Out of such difficulty of social organization, the Chinese people developed little consciousness of social class or interest group. They instead believed *junzi bu dang* ("decent people do not form or join parties"), and felt little need for protecting/promoting their own interests by forming a group/party to get hold of a part of government power. There was among the Chinese a lack of a power-politics mentality or of a consciousness of a "society," so to speak. The Chinese people expected a government that could be neutral and just, serving the welfare of "all the people"; a massive bottom-up rebellion would otherwise be justified.

• The above social structure and value system led to a regime dominated by the emperor-led civil service. This unique traditional polity consisted of three parts: first, an official ideology of Confucianism, which believed that the government, no matter how it comes to power, exists only for the purpose of the welfare of all the people (i.e., *minben zhuyi*), or it is destined to be overthrown; second, a government of meritocracy in which officials are selected through levels of open civil service exams and promoted through performance evaluations (in reality, patron–client ties played a key role); and third, a dominant governing policy of a Taoist nature, namely, small government with very limited functions. This regime had been very stable before modern times. The threat to the traditional Chinese government, not the polity though, had come from only two factors: first, the degradation of successors to the throne, which led to the deterioration of the civil service; second, the invasion by nomadic tribes from the north. When those two factors were combined, it was time for the alternation of dynasties.

3. Explain the rise of the Chinese Communist Party as the instrument for China's "modernization." The traditional polity of two thousand years would have lasted even longer without China's encounter with the "nation-state"—an innovation of social organization in Europe. Unlike modern revolutions in European societies, the Chinese revolution of the twentieth century was not for equality, liberty, or elections based on social classes and/or interest groups; it was for mobilizing scattered, equal, free, selfish, and self-sufficient farm families to resist foreign imperialist powers and build a "nation-state" out of merely a category of civilization. Modernization or "nation-building" in China can be defined as three sequential tasks:

• mechanical solidarity of political integration;
• organic solidarity of economic interdependence among citizens;
• a stable political system/regime credible to the general public.

China felt the need for this modernization due to its encounter with "modern nations," which was a materially and psychologically painful experience. Psychologically, the constant defeats by the imperialist powers destroyed Chinese self-confidence. Materially, China lost to Russia a territory of 3 million square kilometers, half of which was equivalent to the territorial combination of Britain, France, Germany, and Poland, and the other half of which was lost to the Soviet-manipulated independence of the People's Republic of Mongolia. The last war reparations that China was forced to pay to the imperialist powers occurred in 1900, after the "Boxer's Movement." The amount was 450 million taels of silver, namely, each Chinese, man and woman, old and young, should pay a tael (roughly an oz.t.). According to the then official U.S. dollar/silver tael exchange rate in the reparations treaty, 450 million taels of silver was equivalent to the price of over 46.4 times the Alaska purchase. The money was paid off in 1940, and, with 4 percent interest, the total amount paid was nearly 1 billion taels of silver. Chinese have a notorious habit of spitting in public. Those 20,000 foreign soldiers who were pieced together from eight countries to invade China would have been drowned by spittle if the 450 million Chinese farmers had been able to organize themselves to spit at them instead of each paying one tael of silver. Not long before, in 1895, China had just paid 200 million taels of silver for the Japanese invasion, an equivalent to the price of over twenty Alaskas. And those were just the last two war reparations in a series. Until the mid-1940s, Japan still occupied half of the Chinese territory. Therefore, mobilizing and organizing the selfish and independent farmers for collective self-defense and for other tasks of building a strong, modern nation became China's top social demand, which overwhelmed the tiny number of elites indulged in importing Western liberalism. Undoubtedly, the Leninist Party was then the most efficacious instrument for mobilizing and organizing Chinese farmers. Before that, China had tried to learn from the Japanese constitutional monarchy, the European parliamentary systems, as well as the German system under Hitler's Nazis. All had failed except the Communist way, which was a modified Soviet model. Every one of us has seen the Communist Party's achievement in nation-building after 1949, and the miracles have extended to today.

4. Explain the historical linkage between the Chinese traditional polity and the Communist regime. The Party-state obviously differs from the traditional polity:

- Being a highly disciplined organization for mobilization, the Party turns all the officials into "cadres," namely, politicians instead of civil servants.
- The Party controls all the government and semi-government organs which are much more extensive and visible than the traditional government.
- Highly committed to modernization, the Party-state abandons the traditional Taoist policy of governance and is infatuated with the effectiveness of intervention into socioeconomic life.

Despite those differences, the Party-state's linkage to the traditional polity is also obvious and obviously strong, reflecting the fact that China is still an undifferentiated society of high social mobility with a weak mentality of power politics:

- The Party is like a collective emperor, above the law.
- Like the traditional government, and different from the parties in parliamentary systems, the Communist Party has no particular social base; it is presumably an elitist Party neutrally representing the interests of modernization of "all the people."
- Like the traditional ideology, the official ideology is still *minben zhuyi*, expressed in the slogan "Government is to serve the people." While people are still not used to being economically and politically divided, meritocracy continues to be the dominant principle for selecting and promoting government officials, though often mixed with patron–client ties.

5. Explain the current demand for political reforms. The new market system, particularly the success of it, provides rich opportunities for rampant corruption. This leads to a radical deterioration of the Party, as well as that of the quality of government. The Chinese regime would enjoy fairly high credibility if it could bring corruption under control. We all agree that the corruption problem comes from the concentration of power in the hands of the Party, and all levels of Party officials tend to abuse their power. Yet there are radical disagreements as to how to end the Party's monopoly of power in order to curb corruption. Those disagreements can be summarized as follows.

- The further development of the market mechanism per se would naturally curb corruption, because it means constant reduction of the government role. Few people now believe this, because it does not endure the test of history anywhere.
- Electoral democracy, or to be precise, popular elections of top-level officials, could curb corruption. I proposed in my chapter an "iron triangle" among politicians, electorates, and money suppliers, arguing that there is a built-in mechanism of corruption in the electoral game of relative majority. That is to say, elections do not curb corruption; they increase corruption by creating another major source of it.
- Rule of law could curb corruption. By "rule of law," I mean three things: first, the principle of the supremacy of the Constitution based on "Basic Law" (or natural law) and modern liberties; second, judicial independence and the neutrality of the civil service to ensure the implementation of the above principle; and third, the implementation of meritocracy in selecting and evaluating the judiciary and civil service, so as to ensure judicial independence and impartial law enforcement.

According to the image of Hong Kong's polity, I proposed a six-pillar "consultative rule of law regime." The pillars are:

- a neutral civil service;
- an independent judiciary;
- an independent anti-corruption agency;
- an independent auditing agency;
- extensive consultative institutions based on levels of the People's Congress;
- the principle of four liberties to be observed by all five institutions, namely, the freedoms of speech, press, association, and assembly.

That six-pillar "consultative rule of law regime" is about the government, which is separated from the Party. When I am asked about the role of the Communist Party, the image of Singapore's People's Action Party comes to mind. An elitist party that produces neutral politicians derives itself from the tradition of Confucianism.

It is often kindly suggested that I read Max Weber, learn about Taiwan's "successful" democracy, and know that Hong Kong and Singapore are really just two cities instead of large countries. Scholars from the West are familiar with the power competition among parliamentary parties that represent class/group interests, and often consider this the only and universally fair way to govern. I suggest that it could be worth a little leisure time to look at another type of regime, which is dominated by the civil service, and is different from Max Weber's market-rationality-based modern bureaucracy. In the Chinese traditional regime, politicians emerged from the ladder of civil service, not political agitations in TV shows. The social base for those political leaders is not the market mechanism, but an undifferentiated society and a popularly and deeply embedded belief in meritocracy instead of group competition for government power. That kind of regime, existing in the largest country of the world, survived social changes of more than two thousand years. And the Chinese Communist regime today clearly bears its genes. So understood, the civil-service-dominated polity in Hong Kong and Singapore is not an accident at all, but the offspring of a long-sustaining social structure and culture in the largest nation of the world. The major difference among them is that Hong Kong and Singapore imported British legalism, and China imported Soviet communism. And in China's soil it is easier to turn communism into legalism than into democracy. Moreover, what failed the Soviet Union and Taiwan occurred right before our eyes.

II

Some scholars suggest that my chapter should omit the part on China's social history and focus on polity options. Yet a polity does not come from nowhere; it is not just the options or "strategies" of a few politicians. I wrote about China's social history for an understanding of the social origins of a polity. A nation could certainly import a political system, or have one imposed upon it, but few such nations have worked up to expectations. In a foreign soil, one might plant dragon seeds but harvest only fleas.

Some outsiders export a political system for entertainment—to satisfy their own "belief" or their sense of the superiority of their own political civilization. Some others do so for nefarious purposes. For the targeted country, however, a political system heavily affects its people's lives; it had better fit into their own social structure and cultural-historical roots, or they will simply suffer, miserably. For the people in China, a change of political system is suggested not for entertainment or for some alien beliefs; it is for very practical purposes—curbing corruption in particular. That seems very "superficially" instrumental. Yes, the Chinese have been secularized for more than two thousand years.

I have been wondering why the entire West has become indulged in spreading free elections. I understand that elections have worked well and will continue to work well in certain social structures of stable cleavages and cultures with a strong mentality of power politics. That has clearly endured the test of history. Yet, why the eagerness to vehemently spread it to all corners of the world, even with wars of mass destruction and the destruction of a nation?

I thought that it was all about "democracy." Yet I later found that any workable definition of democracy would be called "too simplistic." Ousting tyrants, majority principle, political participation, liberty and equality, law and order, economic prosperity, international peace, and so on—everything good is included in the contemporary concept of "democracy." Confucius had no problem with the broadly defined God, and I love the "broadly defined democracy" like anyone else does.

My challenge goes only to the myth of free elections—a "narrow" or "parochial" or "simplistic" definition of democracy. The arrogant attempt to export "electoral democracy" has led to some significant "conflict of civilizations." Like Christianity, it is supposedly a method of polity good for all nations, and superior to all other methods. To all the perceived "authoritarian" regimes, "free elections" is a fixed prescription from the West. If it does not work, the patients are blamed instead of the prescription.

So it is argued that China will eventually need to become an electoral democracy after the installation of rule of law, or even that there cannot be rule of law without first installing electoral democracy. What about China's achievements without free elections? Of course, there are no achievements, and even if there were, they would be the starting point for a deadly disaster. What about the existing disasters with the installation of free elections? They are, of course, either the necessary cost of the perpetual good, or the elections are not free enough. Free elections has become the biggest religion in the post–Cold War world. To support the "consultative rule of law," I must therefore demystify the mechanism of free elections.

It is true that "one man, one vote" helped abolish feudalism in Europe. China, however, never had that kind of feudalism, and few Chinese people identified themselves with groups, so that it was not necessary to grab a part of the government power to protect and promote their "group" or "class" interests. This case can be "theoretically" explained as follows.

1. Free elections do not foster "political equality." While the majority principle destroyed the legal hierarchy in European feudal society, it did not create "political equality." The majority procedure creates a new form of political inequality between electorates and politicians, between votes for losers and votes for winners, and absolute inequality between the absolute minority and majority. In fact, equality is not the natural feature of politics. By definition, all kinds of "-cracy," or "government," suggest an elitist minority leading the majority, which is essentially based on the monopoly of the means of violence. According to Rousseau, and I agree with him, there has never been a true democracy—government by the people—and there never will, for it is against the natural order. After all, elections, like examinations and evaluations, are to choose a few elites capable of leadership. Realistic political equality for the people has only one form: equality before the law.

2. Free elections do not give individuals "free" choice, but involve the politics of group leaders. In a national election today, the political influence of an individual vote is close to zero, and a ballot of real free choice would basically be a wasted vote, for the most likely free choice might be a vote for the voter himself or one of his relatives or close friends. Instead of representing the power of the people, a very tiny number of politicians capable of gathering the votes and finally winning the election are true power holders. Even politicians' TV image designers are perhaps much more

powerful than electorates because they "gather" votes. Moreover, the game rule for most elections stipulates the choice of one out of two candidates, and yet they are said to have provided the people with "free" choices to represent "people's power." It is a pure lie to claim that the people have freely "picked" their leader. The leaders have themselves elected with the help of the rules of the game.

3. Free elections do not create accountability to the people of the absolute minority and, most often, not even to the people of the absolute majority. Logically, the majority principle does not protect or promote the interests of the minority; the principle of equality before the law does. What about the accountability to the majority? If a society were divided into two groups, 50 percent plus one vote would make the absolute majority. With three groups, 33.3 percent plus one vote would make the majority, and with four groups, 25 percent plus one vote. We could continue this counting with five, six, seven groups. Is there a society that is only divided into two social groups? The result is that the so-called "majority" in free elections would always mean a relative majority and an absolute minority. That is to say, with free elections, we do not really even get the government's accountability to a real majority. That problem is "solved" with the "game rule" that people have to choose one between the two, which is ridiculously called "accountability" to the people's demands. In short, the majority principle creates accountability to the strongest groups in the society, not the largest number of people. Without rule of law, free elections end up with "The strong do what they want, and the weak suffer what they have to," namely, a pure game of power politics.

4. Free elections are not the only method of periodically replacing leaders. It is often said that free elections for leaders' alternation is not the best, but there is no better alternative. I know that "no better" means exactly "the best." A periodic opportunity to change the leader with the relative majority's support has lots of benefits in a certain time and certain social context, but may produce more costs than benefits in some other social context and time. A periodic opportunity to change leaders is not the key; the key is whether there are other valid ways to do so. Carefully look around the world or just at China; we could count more than one hundred ways to periodically replace leaders, and a system of relative majority support is only one of them. Falling into a "belief," one tends to compare only advantages of the principle of the relative majority with the disadvantages of the other methods, such as age limits, meritocracy through ladders of examination, and constant evaluations.

5. Free elections do not promote basic rights of liberty. The majority principle does not include the idea of liberty, and it has nothing to do with protecting the basic rights of an absolute minority. Elected lawmakers, given the way in which they gain power, cannot be impartial, and they are much less impartial than a professional civil service. Although modern democracy has incorporated the notions of liberty, these notions are logically and historically irrelevant to free elections. The invention of the notions of liberty or basic human rights dates long before the installation of free elections, and they are now accepted by most peoples in their modern constitutions. Yet liberty in constitutions is easy, as in India and the Philippines; liberty in practice depends on the rule of law, an independent judiciary, and effective law enforcement.

6. Free elections can oust dictators, but they also create dictators. There is no clear boundary between an elected leader and a dictator. The boundary can only be set by the mechanism by which the elected leaders are placed under the law. So the U.S. president-elect has to "swear in" in front of the nonelected chief justice of the Supreme Court, pledging loyalty to a constitution written more than two hundred years ago. Free elections without rule of law lead to either tyranny or disorder.

7. Free elections do not promote social solidarity. Social cleavages worsened by free elections could be quickly mended if the people strongly identify with the principle of power politics. While there is certainly an evangelical attempt to "enlighten" the peoples who do not take the majority principle for granted, we need to remember that the numbers game has nothing to do with justice and science. We are far from certain that the numbers game is even fair play. Therefore, in certain countries of different cultural traditions, open and periodic competition for government power could become periodic social disintegration into political agitation, promoting a politics of hatred.

III

Democracy and *authoritarian regime* have become the two most useless concepts in the academic research of our time. The former wildly includes even the occupation of Iraq and the Iraqis' obedience in the face of the American soldiers' gunpoint; the latter summarizes the Chinese governments from the first emperor of over two thousand years ago to today's Communist regime. The former includes too many varieties of a contradictory nature, and the latter describes no variation across the "nondemocratic" world from ancient history to the present. These two concepts are now easy labels used by ignorant politicians and lazy scholars. They have become favorites in Hollywood action movies. That is the reason that I turn to the more concrete term *free election.*

The aim of my previous chapter is more about explaining China's failure in building a parliamentary electoral system than proposing a new regime. Nevertheless, having closely studied the results of rural grassroots elections and witnessed the electoral experiences in Taiwan, I have strongly felt the danger of building an electoral system before installing rule of law. Ever since Hong Kong's return, I have written extensively on this issue in Chinese, and have taught thousands of students at Peking University. The idea has gained its own life now, becoming a visible competitor to the election-centered yardstick in measuring China's progress.

I consider the rule of law regime not a blueprint for the future government, but a direction for political reforms. And it is an issue-driven and problem-solving process, not about values. Its major task is to curb corruption. That sounds very instrumental, and I intend precisely to find a problem-solving instrument. Nevertheless, I have spelled out my differences with a major value in the West, namely, the majority principle, rooted in the mentality of power politics. I argue that these differences are derived from the different social structures and cultures. Tolerance of differences, I believe, should be the core spirit of liberalism.

Notes

Notes to Chapter 1

1. Jiang Zemin, "Report to the 15th Party Congress" (section six), September 12, 1997.

2. Alexis de Tocqueville, *Democracy in America,* trans. George Lawrence, ed. J.P. Mayer, p. xiii (Garden City, NY: Doubleday, 1969).

3. Ibid., p. 12.

4. Talcott Parsons, *Societies: Evolutionary and Comparative Perspectives* (Englewood Cliffs, NJ: Prentice Hall, 1966).

5. For a fairly complete discussion on the idea of "democratic peace," see Bruce Russett, *Grasping the Democratic Peace: Principles for a Post-War World* (Princeton, NJ: Princeton University Press, 1993), chapter 7; and Russett, "Can a Democratic Peace Be Built?" *International Interactions* 18, 3 (Spring 1993): 277–282.

6. Robert A. Dahl, *On Democracy* (New Haven: Yale University Press, 1998), Part II, III. Dahl makes it clear that those are conditions for "ideal" democracy. His "actual democracy" is even more confusing: (1) elected officials; (2) free, fair, and frequent elections; (3) freedom of expression; (4) access to alternative sources of information; (5) associational autonomy; (6) inclusive citizenship. Having read this, do we have any need to discuss such important differences as "liberal" democracy and "nonliberal" democracy, say, the Philippines and Germany?

7. Thomas Hobbes, *Leviathan* (1651), chapter 17 (Orchard Park, NY: Broadview ed., 2005).

8. Robert Dahl, *Polyarchy: Participation and Opposition* (New Haven: Yale University Press, 1971).

9. Dahl, *On Democracy,* chapter 5.

10. Thucydides, *The Peloponnesian War,* Crawley translation, revised by T.E. Wick (New York: Modern Library, 1982), Book V, 89, p. 351.

11. Joseph A. Schumpeter, *Capitalism, Socialism and Democracy,* 3rd ed. (New York: Harper & Brothers, 1950), chapter 22.

12. The most famous discussion on this is still in the works of Marcus Tullius Cicero (106–43 B.C.E.). Cicero, *Oratio pro Cluentio,* 53; and his *De Legibus* (On law), vol. 3, chapters 7–18.

13. John Locke wrote, "Where there is no law there is no freedom." "Where law ends, tyranny begins." *Two Treatises of Government* (New Haven: Yale University Press, 2003), chapter VI, 57, XVIII. Sartori has a very clear discussion on the relationship between law and liberty. See his quotations from Cicero, Locke, Paine, and Rousseau. Giovanni Sartori, *The Theory of Democracy Revisited* (New York: Chatham House, 1987), chapter 11 (Liberty and Law), pp. 298–336.

14. Gabriel A. Almond and Sidney Verba, *The Civic Culture* (Thousand Oaks, CA: Sage Publications, 1989), chapter 13.

15. Singapore officials claim that before building an autonomous ICAC, the Hong Kong government sent officials to train to Singapore's CPIB.

16. Weber's typology of authority clearly indicates the idea of traditional-legal dichotomy. The "legal-rational" authority is considered modern, with charismatic authority as an in-between transitional type. Similar ideas had already been discussed before Weber, such as in the works of Tonnies and Durkheim. Ever since Parsons, nearly all the later "modernization" theorists in the United States centered their discussion on the emergence of legalism in one way or another. See Max Weber, *The Theory of Social and Economic Organization,* trans. A.M. Henderson and Talcott Parsons (New York: Free Press, 1964), Part I, chapter 3; Ferdinand Tonnies, *Community and Society,* trans. C.P. Loomis (New York: Harper & Row, 1963), vol. I; Emile Durkheim, *The Division of Labor in Society,* trans. George Simpson (New York: Free Press, 1964), vol. I; Parsons, *Societies, Evolutionary and Comparative Perspectives.*

17. *Beijing Wanbao* (Beijing evening news), June 29, 2001, p. 3.

18. Economic freedom refers to a free flow of the three basic economic elements—land (where the production materials come from), labor, and money. For example, "liberalism" in international economic relations advocates the free flow of goods and money, but does not support the free flow of labor across national boundaries; that is not only incomplete liberalism but unequal "liberalism" to the less-developed countries.

19. Confucius, "Weizheng Pian" (Chapter on governance) in *Lun Yu* (Comments from Confucius), in *Sishu Wujing* (Four books and five classics) (Chengdu: Bashu Shushe, 1996), p. 91.

20. For an early study on this, see Hsiao-Tung Fei, *China's Gentry* (Chicago: University of Chicago Press, 1953), and a more recent work by Vivienne Shue, *The Reach of the State: Sketches of the Chinese Body Politic* (Stanford: Stanford University Press, 1988).

21. See, for example, Larry Diamond, "Rethinking Civil Society: Toward Democratic Consolidation," *Journal of Democracy* 5, no. 3 (July 1996): Sheri Berman, "Civil Society and the Collapse of the Weimar Republic," *World Politics* (April 1997); Sidney Verba, Key Lehman Schlozman, and Henry E. Brady, "The Big Tilt: Participatory Inequality in America," *American Prospect,* no. 32 (May–June 1997); David Rieff, "The False Dawn of Civil Society," *The Nation,* February 22, 1999; and Thomas Carothers, "Think Again: Civil Society," *Foreign Policy* (Winter 1999–2000).

22. All Hong Kong government sections have their own consultation committees, the number of which was close to 500 in 1996 before the handover, with a total of nearly 6,000 members. They were developed as a symbol of the colony's "shared rule" with the local people. Relevant data can be found in the *Hong Kong Yearbook* of various years.

23. Deng Xiaoping, "Speech on 3 June 1988," in *Deng Xiaoping Wenxuan* (Selected works of Deng Xiaoping) (Beijing: Renmin chubanshe, 1993), vol. 3, p. 267. A government television program even aired the video recording of Deng saying this. See Zhongyang wenxian yanjiushi (Central Documents Research Office), *Deng Xiaoping,* transcript of the 12-episode documentary TV series (Beijing: Zhongyang wenxian chubanshe, 1997), pp. 249–250.

Notes to Chapter 2

1. Samuel P. Huntington, *Third Wave: Democratization in the Late Twentieth Century* (Norman, OK: University of Oklahoma Press, 1993).

2. Daniel V. Dowd, Allen Carlson, and Mingming Shen, "The Prospects for Democratization in China: Evidence from the 1995 Beijing Area Study," in *China and Democracy,* ed. Suisheng Zhao, pp. 189–206 (New York: Routledge, 2000).

3. Che-po Chen, "The Political Pragmatism of Chinese University Students at the Dawn of the Twenty-first Century," in *China and Democracy,* ed. Suisheng Zhao, pp. 207–232 (New York: Routledge, 2000).

4. Suisheng Zhao, "A Tragedy of History: The Chinese Search for Democracy in the Twentieth Century," *Journal of Contemporary China,* no. 3 (1993): 18–37.

5. Jie Chen, "The Impact of Reform on the Party and Ideology in China," *Journal of Contemporary China,* no. 9 (Summer 1995): 22–34.

6. Deng Xiaoping, "Dang he Guojia Lingdao Zhidu de Gaige" (The reform of the party and state leadership system), in *Deng Xiaoping Wenxuan* (Selected works of Deng Xiaoping) (Beijing: Renmin chubanshe, 1983), pp. 280–302.

7. Ren Zhongyi, "Zaitan Jianchi Sixiang Jiben Yuanze" (Upholding the four cardinal principles reconsidered), *Nanfang Zhoumo* (Southern weekend), May 5, 2000, p. 4.

8. Richard Madsen, *China's Catholics: Tragedy and Hope in an Emerging Civil Society* (Berkeley: University of California Press, 1998), pp. 3, 8.

9. Sylvia Chan, "Research Notes on Villagers' Committee Election: Chinese-Style Democracy," *Journal of Contemporary China* 7, no. 19 (1998): 510.

10. Rong Hu, "Economic Development and the Implementation of Village Elections in Rural China," *Journal of Contemporary China* 14, no. 44 (August 2005): 427.

11. Chan, "Research Notes on Villagers' Committee Election: Chinese-Style Democracy," p. 520.

12. Guo Zenglin with Thomas P. Bernstein, "The Impact of Elections on the Village Structure of Power: The Relations Between the Village Committees and the Party Branches," *Journal of Contemporary China* 13, no. 39 (2004): 275.

13. Paul Grove, "Reforming Chinese Politics," *Asiaweek,* September 5, 1997, www.asiaweek.com/asiaweek/97/0905/feat.html.

14. Tianjian Shi, "Economic Development and Village Elections in Rural China," *Journal of Contemporary China* 8, no. 22 (November 1999): 440.

15. Guy Hermet, Richard Rose, and Alain Rouquie, eds., *Elections Without Choice* (London: Macmillan, 1978).

16. Julie Chao, "Chinese Congresses Refuse to Follow All Party Dictates," *Washington Times,* March 9, 2001.

17. Murray Scot Tanner, *The Politics of Lawmaking in Post-Mao China: Institutions, Processes and Democratic Prospects* (Oxford, UK: Clarendon Press, 1999). Kevin J. O'Brien, *Reform Without Liberalization: China's National People's Congress and the Politics of Institutional Change* (New York: Cambridge University Press, 1990).

18. Stanley B. Lubman, *Bird in a Cage: Legal Reform in China after Mao* (Stanford, CA: Stanford University Press, 2000), p. 174.

19. Xia Ming, "China's National People's Congress: Institutional Transformation in the Process of Regime Transition (1978–98)," in *Parliaments in Asia,* ed. Philip Norton and Nizam Ahmed, p. 119 (London: Frank Cass, 1999).

20. Chao, "Chinese Congresses Refuse to Follow All Party Dictates."

21. For a detailed study of political reform and the resulting dual structure of leadership, see Suisheng Zhao, "Political Reform and Changing One-Party Rule in Deng's China," *Problems of Post-Communism* 44, no. 5 (September/October 1997): 12–21.

22. This article was first printed by *Zhongguo Qingnian Bao* (China youth daily) as an internal circular in September 1991. It was leaked overseas and published in the December 1992 issue of *Zhongguo Zhichun* (China spring) in New York City.

23. Guo Daohui, "Quanwei, quanli haishi quanli, dui dang yu renda guanxi de falu sikao" (The authority, the power, or the right, thoughts on the legal principles of the relationship of the party and the NPC), *Faxue Yanjiu* (Legal studies), March 1994.

24. Elisabeth Rosenthal, "China's Communists Try to Decide What They Stand For," *New York Times,* May 1, 2002, p. A3.

25. Bao Tong, "Three Represents: Marking the End of an Era," *Asian Wall Street Journal,* August 27, 2002. Available at http://online.wsj.com/public/resources/documents/a-baotong20020827.html.

26. Willy Wo-lap Lam, "Appealing to Modern Comrades," *South China Morning Post,* November 1, 2000 (online version).

27. Ibid.

28. Andrew Scobell, "After Deng, What: Reconsidering the Prospects of a Democratic Transition in China," *Problems of Post-Communism* 44, no. 5 (September/October 1997): 24.

29. Fred Hiatt, "For China, the Most Difficult Reforms Lie Ahead," *Los Angeles Times,* April 1, 2001, p. B7.

30. Willy Wo-Lap Lam, "New Generation Pushes China Democracy," March 13, 2001. Available at www.cnn.com/2001/world/asiapct/east/03/china.ccp.willy/index.html.

Notes to Chapter 3

1. It is indeed consistent with a position I have advocated elsewhere. See "Ruling the Country in Accordance with Law: Reflections on the Rule and Role of Law in China," *Cultural Dynamics,* no. 11 (November 1999): 315–351; *China's Long March Toward Rule of Law* (Cambridge: Cambridge University Press, 2002).

2. See, generally, David Kairys, ed., *The Politics of Law* (New York: Basic Books, 3rd ed., 1998).

3. Gary S. Becker, "A Theory of Competition Among Pressure Groups for Political Influence," *Quarterly Journal of Economics,* no. 98 (August 1983): 371–400; Jonathan R. Macey, "Promoting Public-Regarding Legislation Through Statutory Interpretation: An Interest Group Model," *Columbia Law Review,* no. 86 (March 1986): 223–268.

4. For a detailed discussion of both progress toward rule of law and continuing obstacles, see Peerenboom, *China's Long March.*

5. Between 1996 and 2000, only 27 to 37 percent of Latin Americans expressed satisfaction with democracy. Support for democracy in 2002 was lower than in 1996 in all but four Latin American countries. According to the Latinobarometer, Latin Americans have lost confidence in democracy because of the lack of economic growth, the deterioration of public services, the rise of crime, and the persistence of widespread corruption. As a result, there is little trust in democratic institutions, including political parties (19 percent), parliaments (22 percent), and the judiciary (26 percent). Nevertheless, Latin Americans are reluctant to return to the recent past of authoritarian military regimes. In contrast, several authoritarian regimes in Asia have been successful in providing growth, improving public services, ensuring stability, and curtailing corruption. Thus, whereas Latin Americans see no alternative to democracy, many Asians see some form of soft authoritarianism or nonliberal democracy as viable options. See Comisión de Promoción del Perú (Commission for the Promotion of Peru), available at www.peru.info/peru.asp; Latinobarómetro: Opinion Publica Latino Americana (Latinobarometer: Public Opinion in Latin America), available at www.latinobarometro.org. See Juan Forero, "Latin America Is Growing Impatient with Democracy," *New York Times,* June 24, 2004. Available at www.nytimes.com/2004/06/24/international/americas/24PERU.html?ex=1089065297&ei=1&en=7f452d7bbb6ecb14. A United Nations report finds that 56 percent of Latin Americans said economic progress is more important than democracy. Massive discontent has led to the downfall of six elected leaders after violent unrest, growing support for neo-authoritarian leaders, and the granting of extrajudicial powers to effective leaders. There have even been calls in Peru for the return of Alberto Fujimori, who was run out of office on corruption charges.

6. Robert Pinkney, *Democracy in the Third World* (Boulder, CO: Lynne Rienner, 2003), p. 65.

7. Amartya Sen, "Freedoms and Needs," *The New Republic,* January 10 and 17, 1994, p. 34; see also Sen's *Poverty and Famine* (New York: Oxford University Press, 1981).

8. I discuss the obstacles and prospects for democracy at greater length in *China's Long March,* pp. 513–557.

9. See, for example, Yali Peng, "Democracy and Chinese Political Discourses," *Modern China* 24 (October 1998): 408–444; Minxin Pei, "Racing Against Time: Institutional Decay and Renewal in China," in *China Briefing,* ed. William A. Joseph, pp. 11–49 (Armonk, NY:

M.E. Sharpe, 1997). Pei cites polls showing that two-thirds of the people thought that the economic situation was improving while one-half thought their own living standards were improving, and that the majority of respondents (54 percent) placed a higher priority on economic development than democracy. Over two-thirds of those polled supported the government's policy of promoting economic growth and social stability, and 63 percent agreed that "it would be a disaster for China to experience a change [similar to] that in the former Soviet Union." Even 40 percent of non-CCP member respondents said they voluntarily supported the same political position as the CCP. Another study showed Chinese to be the least tolerant of diverse viewpoints among all of the countries surveyed. It also found little support for a free press and the publishing of alternative views. Andrew Nathan and Shi Tianjian, "Cultural Requisites for Democracy in China: Findings from a Survey," *Daedalus,* no. 122 (Spring 1993): 95–124.

10. Judith Shklar, "Political Theory and Rule of Law," in *Rule of Law: Ideal or Ideology,* ed. Allan C. Hutchinson and Patrick Monahan (Toronto: Carswell, 1987). For additional critiques of rule of law generally and from within China, see *China's Long March,* pp. 126–187. While I think many of the critiques are overstated, in some cases, as with Pan, rule of law is held out to be a miraculous cure to all that ails contemporary societies, which it clearly is not. For several criticisms about the inflated expectations of rule of law to promote and protect human rights, see Randall Peerenboom, "Human Rights and Rule of Law: What's the Relationship?" *Georgetown International Law Review* 36, no. 1 (2005).

11. See, for example, Robert Summers, "A Formal Theory of Rule of Law" *Ratio Juris,* no. 6 (1993): 127–142; cf. Joseph Raz, "Rule of Law and Its Virtue," in *The Authority of Law,* ed. Joseph Raz, pp. 210, 211 (New York: Oxford University Press, 1979).

12. For similar but not identical lists, see Lon Fuller, *The Morality of Law* (New Haven: Yale University Press, 1976); Geoffrey de Q. Walker, *Rule of Law* (Carlton, Victoria: Melbourne Press, 1988).

13. For a summary of the various debates surrounding "Asian Values," see Randall Peerenboom, "Beyond Universalism and Relativism: The Evolving Debates About 'Values in Asia,'" *Indiana International and Comparative Law Review,* no. 14 (2003): 1–85.

14. For an overview of competing thick conceptions of rule of law in Asia, see, generally, Randall Peerenboom, ed., *Asian Discourses of Rule of Law: Theories and Implementation of Rule of Law in Twelve Asian Countries, France and the U.S.* (New York and London: RoutledgeCurzon, 2004).

15. The general consensus is that the new law and development, much like the previous law and development of the 1960s and 1970s, has failed, with some notable exceptions, to produce functional legal systems that meet the requirements of a thin rule of law. Compared to most developing countries, China is a success story. China has made remarkable progress in a short time in improving the legal system, having essentially begun from scratch in 1978. As of 2002, China's legal system ranked in the 51st percentile on the World Bank's rule of law index, having risen from the 32nd percentile in 1996.

16. Harold Berman, *Law and Revolution* (Cambridge: Harvard University Press, 1983), p. 294.

17. Liu Junning, "Cong fazhiguo dao fazhi" (From Rechsstaat to rule of law), in *Zhengzhi Zhongguo* (Political China), ed. Dong Yuyu and Shi Binhai, p. 233 (Beijing: Jinri Zhongguo chubanshe, 1988).

18. Su Li, "Ershi shiji Zhongguo de xiandaihua he fazhi" (Twentieth-century China's modernization and rule of law), *Faxue Yanjiu,* no. 20 (1998): 9.

19. As the legal system is inevitably embedded within a broader social and political context, a thin rule of law will inevitably be embedded within some thick conception of rule of law. The existing thick framework is closest to the statist socialist ideal type I have sketched elsewhere. Pan Wei's consultative rule of law is more similar to the soft or neo-authoritarian ideal type. My own preferences would be for a version of the communitarian ideal type, though most likely with more liberal elements than is typically found in Asian variants of communitarianism.

For a discussion of the statist socialism, neo-authoritarian, communitarian, and liberal democratic ideal types, see Peerenboom, *China's Long March.*

20. See Randall Peerenboom, "Social Networks, Civil Society, Democracy and Rule of Law: A New Conceptual Framework," in *The Politics of Affective Relations: East Asia and Beyond,* ed. Hahm Chaihark and Daniel Bell, pp. 249–276 (Lanham, MD: Lexington Books, 2004).

21. "Zhongguo xingzheng fazhi fazhan jincheng diaocha baogao" (Survey report on the development and progress of China's administrative rule of law), 348, ed. Jiang Mingan, 1998 (hereinafter "Administrative Rule of Law").

22. Ibid., at 58.

23. Ibid., at 280. More generally, less than 0.4 percent of public security decisions were challenged in Anhui Province between 1994 and 1996. Ibid., at 438.

24. The economic success of the Asian Dragons is often attributed to their strong governments. Economic development and transition states require tough and timely decisions. Authoritarian governments are able to make these choices. For a contrary view, see José María Maravall, "The Myth of the Authoritarian Advantage," *Journal of Democracy,* no. 5 (1994): 17–31.

25. Peter Schuck, *Foundations of Administrative Law* (New York: Oxford University Press, 1994), p. 6. According to Schuck, "agencies' behavior is shaped far less by the episodic decisions of reviewing courts than by institutional politics and other nonlegal phenomena such as agency culture, market forces, and professional norms."

26. See Peerenboom, *China's Long March,* pp. 394–449.

27. See, for example, *Jiang Zemin's Congress Report,* FBIS, September 23, 1997, FBIS-CHI-97–266 (hereinafter "Jiang's Report") (the report was delivered at the 15th National Party Congress).

28. Richard Baum and Alexei Shevchenko, "The 'State of the State' in Post-Reform China," in *The Paradox of China's Post-Mao Reforms,* ed. Merle Goldman and Roderick MacFarquhar, pp. 333–360 (Cambridge: Harvard University Press, 1999).

29. Michael William Dowdle, "Of Parliaments, Pragmatism, and the Dynamics of Constitutional Development: The Curious Case of China," *New York University Journal of International Law & Politics,* no. 35 (2002): 1.

30. Sean Cooney, "A Community Changes: Taiwan's Council of Grand Justices and Liberal Democratic Reform," in *Law, Capitalism and Power in Asia,* ed. Kanisha Jayasuriya, p. 253 (London: Routledge, 1999); see also, Kun Yang, "Judicial Review and Social Change in the Korean Democratizing Process," *American Journal of Comparative Law,* no. 41 (1993), who notes a more aggressive role for Korean courts as reforms continued, pp. 1–8.

31. See David Bourchier, "Magic Memos, Collusion and Judges with Attitude," in *Law, Capitalism and Power in Asia,* ed. Jayasuriya, p. 233.

32. See Linda Chelan Li, "The 'Rule of Law' Policy in Guangdong: Continuity or Departure? Meaning, Significance and Processes," *China Quarterly,* no. 161 (March 2000): 199, 208–214.

33. Carol Jones, "Politics Postponed: Law as a Substitute for Politics in Hong Kong and China," in *Law, Capitalism and Power in Asia,* ed. Jayasuriya, p. 45.

34. Larry Diamond, "Is the Third Wave Over?" *Journal of Democracy,* no. 7 (July 1996): 20–37.

35. See Randall Peerenboom, "Rights, Interests and the Interests in Rights in China," *Stanford Journal of International Law,* no. 31 (1995): 359–386.

36. Kevin O'Brien and Lianjiang Li, "Selective Policy Implementation in Rural China," *Comparative Politics,* no. 31 (January 1999): 167–186.

37. The system would have to be structured so as not to provide incentives to local officials to minimize violations. For instance, officials would receive points for voluntarily addressing certain issues. In addition, outside monitors could be used for auditing purposes. If the moni-

tors discovered that local governments were covering up problems to avoid losing points, they would be penalized by a loss of several times the amount of points at stake.

Notes to Chapter 4

1. An Chen, "Rising Class Politics and Its Impact on China's Path to Democracy," *Democratization* 10, no. 2 (Summer 2003): 147. The Gini index "measures the extent to which the distribution of income . . . among individuals or households . . . deviates from a perfectly equal distribution." Zero represents perfect equality and 100 perfect inequality. World Bank, *World Development Report 2005* (New York: Oxford University Press, 2005), p. 250.

2. World Bank, *World Development Report 2005,* pp. 258–259.

3. Ibid., p. 258.

4. An Chen, "Rising Class Politics," p. 148.

5. Ibid., p. 145. If one takes account of surplus rural labor seeking jobs in the cities, An Chen reports that the overall unemployment rate may have been as high as 27.6 percent in 2000.

6. Nicholas R. Lardy, "Sources of Macroeconomic Instability in China," in *Is China Unstable?* ed. David Shambaugh, pp. 59, 57, 60, 61 (Armonk, NY: M.E. Sharpe, 2000).

7. Ibid., p. 58.

8. Morris Goldstein and Nicholas R. Lardy, "What Kind of Landing for the Chinese Economy?" Institute for International Economics, *Policy Briefs in International Economics,* no. PB04–7. Available at www.iie.com/publications/pb/pb04–7.pdf.

9. Martin King Whyte, "Chinese Social Trends: Stability or Chaos?" in *Is China Unstable?* ed. Shambaugh, p. 148. See also An Chen, "Rising Class Politics."

10. These trends and concepts are documented in Minxin Pei, *China's Trapped Transition: The Limits of Developmental Autocracy* (Cambridge, MA: Harvard University Press, 2006).

11. Merle Goldman, "The Potential for Instability Among Alienated Intellectuals and Students in Post-Mao China," in *Is China Unstable?* ed. Shambaugh, pp. 123–124.

12. On the advantages of gradual, liberalizing change in allowing for the emergence of a system of "mutual security" between competing political forces, see Robert A. Dahl, *Polyarchy: Participation and Opposition* (New Haven, CT: Yale University Press, 1971), pp. 33–41. Dahl concludes that a "disproportionately large number of the stable, high-consensus polyarchies seem to have come about by . . . peaceful evolution" (p. 41). This early finding bears some kinship with the subsequent enthusiasm of O'Donnell and Schmitter, among others, for a gradual, pacted transition. See Guillermo O'Donnell and Philippe Schmitter, *Transitions from Authoritarian Rule: Tentative Conclusions About Uncertain Democracies* (Baltimore, MD: Johns Hopkins University Press, 1986). Among the postcommunist states, Michael McFaul (among others) has emphasized the value of a revolutionary break with the past regimes. See McFaul, *Russia's Unfinished Revolution: Political Change from Gorbachev to Putin* (Ithaca, NY: Cornell University Press, 2001). However, gradual economic and political reform in Hungary did help to make for a relatively smooth and successful transition to democracy, and as the experience of many post-Soviet states shows, a sudden collapse of the old (Soviet) order did not in most cases bring about a thorough displacement of the old Soviet elite.

13. Singapore is rated as one of the least corrupt countries in the world, but it is also well below the median level for civil liberties (not to mention political freedom). For most of the past twenty years, Singapore has been rated a 5 on the Freedom House 7-point scale of civil liberties (with 1 being most free and 7 least free). This is the same rating it has on political rights. While Singapore exhibits efficiency and integrity in economic governance, and a rule of law that is autonomous and well respected in business and ordinary criminal affairs, Singapore is very far from allowing the freedoms of speech, press, assembly, and association that Pan Wei advocates (eventually) for China. In fact, in recent times, there have been only two

nondemocracies in the world with civil-liberties scores below the mid-point of 4 on the Freedom House scale: Tonga, and Antigua and Barbuda. Both of these are island states of around 100,000 people. Neither is even faintly imaginable as a model for China.

14. Andreas Schedler, Larry Diamond, and Marc F. Plattner, eds., *The Self-Restraining State: Power and Accountability in New Democracies* (Boulder, CO: Lynne Rienner, 1999).

15. Guillermo O'Donnell, "Horizontal Accountability in New Democracies," in *The Self-Restraining State,* ed. Schedler, Diamond, and Plattner, pp. 29–51.

16. Andreas Schedler, "Restraining the State: Conflicts and Agents of Accountability," in *The Self-Restraining State,* ed. Schedler, Diamond, and Plattner, pp. 333–350.

17. An Chen, "Rising Class Politics."

18. These trends and concepts are documented and developed in Pei, *China's Trapped Transition.*

19. Erik Eckholm, "China's Party Bosses Thwart Local Leaders," *New York Times,* April 25, 2002, p. A8.

20. Erik Eckholm, "China's Man to Watch Steps into the U.S. Spotlight," *New York Times,* April 27, 2002, p. A3.

21. The framework of three ideal types of political centers—uninhibited (as in Maoist times), inhibited, and subordinated (in essence, democratic)—were first developed by Thomas A. Metzger and further refined through discussions with Ramon H. Myers. Metzger introduced these concepts in his preface to *Two Societies in Opposition: The Republic of China and the People's Republic of China After Forty Years,* ed. Ramon H. Myers, p. xvii (Stanford, CA: Hoover Institution Press, 1991). For an application of these ideal types to the Taiwan experience, see Linda Chao and Ramon H. Myers, *The First Chinese Democracy: Political Life in the Republic of China on Taiwan* (Baltimore, MD: Johns Hopkins University Press, 1998), particularly pp. 7–9.

22. Robert A. Scalapino, "Will China Democratize? Current Trends and Future Prospects," *Journal of Democracy* 9, no. 1 (1998): 38–39.

23. Linda Chao and Ramon H. Myers, "How Elections Promoted Democracy in Taiwan Under Martial Law," in *Elections and Democracy in Greater China,* ed. Larry Diamond and Ramon H. Myers, pp. 23–45 (Oxford and New York: Oxford University Press, 2001). See also Chao and Myers, *The First Chinese Democracy.*

24. Richard Baum, "Democracy Deformed: Hong Kong's 1998 Legislative Elections—and Beyond," and Robert A. Pastor and Qinshan Tan, "The Meaning of China's Village Elections," in *Elections and Democracy in Greater China,* ed. Diamond and Myers, pp. 75–100 and 126–148.

25. Tianjian Shi, "Cultural Values and Democracy in the People's Republic of China," in *Elections and Democracy in Greater China,* ed. Diamond and Myers, pp. 176–195.

26. Lianjiang Li and Kevin J. O'Brien, "The Struggle over Village Elections," in *The Paradox of China's Post-Mao Reforms,* ed. Merle Goldman and Roderick MacFarquhar, pp. 137 and 140 (Cambridge, MA: Harvard University Press, 1999).

27. Ibid., pp. 140–142.

28. On the politics of this movement, see Chao and Myers, *The First Chinese Democracy,* and Yun-han Chu, *Crafting Democracy in Taiwan* (Taipei: Institute for National Policy Research, 1992).

29. Larry Diamond, "Anatomy of an Electoral Earthquake: How the KMT Lost and the DPP Won the 2000 Presidential Election," in *Taiwan's Presidential Politics: Democratization and Cross-Strait Relations in the Twenty-first Century,* ed. Muthiah Alagappa, pp. 48–87 (Armonk, NY: M.E. Sharpe, 2001).

30. See, for example, Samuel Huntington, *The Third Wave: Democratization in the Late Twentieth Century* (Norman: University of Oklahoma Press, 1991), p. 7; Philippe C. Schmitter and Terry Lynn Karl, "What Democracy Is . . . and Is Not," *Journal of Democracy,* no. 2 (Summer 1991): 75–88; and for recent empirical and conceptual reflections on this debate,

Larry Diamond, "Elections Without Democracy: Thinking About Hybrid Regimes," and Andreas Schedler, "Elections Without Democracy: The Menu of Manipulation," *Journal of Democracy,* no. 13 (April 2002): 21–35 and 36–50.

31. O'Donnell, "Horizontal Accountability in New Democracies."

Notes to Chapter 5

1. Bernard Silberman, "The Structure of Bureaucratic Rationality and Economic Development in Japan," in *The Japanese Civil Service and Economic Development,* ed. Hyun-ki Kim et al., pp. 135–173 (Oxford: Clarendon, 1995).

2. Analysts differ on how to categorize Singapore. Some label it authoritarian. Some semi-authoritarian. Some semi-democratic. Some a very, very flawed democracy, certainly more open than much of the U.S. South before the implementation of the 1965 voting rights act.

3. Cf. Edward Friedman and Bruce Gilley, eds., *Asia's Giants: Comparing China and India* (New York: Palgrave Macmillan, 2005).

4. Jeffrey Sachs, *The End of Poverty* (New York: Penguin, 2005), chapters 7 and 8.

5. Juan Linz and Alfred Stepan, *Problems of Democratic Transition and Consolidation* (Baltimore: Johns Hopkins University Press, 1996), pp. 139, 391.

6. Peter Perdue, *China Marches West* (Cambridge: Harvard University Press, 2005).

7. Lee Kuan Yew, "China Must Teach Youngsters Not to Let Its Might Threaten Neighbors," *The Star* (Malaysia), May 17, 2005.

8. Perdue, *China Marches West.*

9. Mussolini's fascists likewise dismissed so-called Anglo-Saxon democracy as irrelevant.

Notes to Chapter 6

This is a slightly shortened version of an article first published in the German journal *ASIEN,* no. 94 (January 2005): 7–24. The reprint was authorized by the German Association for Asian Studies.

1. Catherine Jones Finer, ed., *Social Policy Reform in China: Views from Home and Abroad* (Aldershot: Ashgate, 2003); Zhang Junhua, "The Construction of a Social Security System in the PRC—A Critical Account" (in German), *China aktuell* 32, no. 7 (July 2003): 866–975 (part I); 32, no. 8: 986–997 (part II); Zhu Yukun, "Recent Developments in China's Social Security Reforms," *International Social Security Review* (Oxford) 55, no. 2 (2002): 39–54; Sarah Cook, *After the Iron Rice Bowl: Extending the Safety Net in China* (Brighton: Institute of Development Studies, 2000).

2. For a general account of the situation of urban migrant workers, see Dorothy Solinger, *Contesting Citizenship in Urban China: Peasant Migrants, the State, and the Logic of the Market* (Berkeley: University of California Press, 1999).

3. See Thomas P. Bernstein and Lü Xiaobo, "Taxation Without Representation: Peasants, the Central and the Local States in Reform China," *China Quarterly,* no. 143 (2000): 742–763.

4. Hsiao Pen, "Separating the Party from the Government," in *Decision Making in Deng's China,* ed. Carol Lee Hamrin and Suisheng Zhao, pp. 153–168 (Armonk, NY: M.E. Sharpe, 1995); see also former CP General Secretary Zhao Ziyang's report, "Striving Along the Road of Socialism with Chinese Characteristics," delivered at the 13th Party Congress in October 1987 and reprinted in *A Selection of Important Documents Since the CCP's 13th National Congress* (Beijing: Renmin chubanshe, 1991), pp. 4–61.

5. Li Lianjiang, "The Two-Ballot System in Shanxi Province: Subjecting Village Party Secretaries to a Popular Vote," *China Journal,* no. 42 (July 1999): 103–118; for a more comprehensive account and critical assessment of recent institutional innovations to establish more intra-Party democracy, see Gang Lin, "Leadership Transition, Intra-Party Democracy, and Institution Building in China," *Asian Survey* 44, no. 2 (March–April 2004): 255–275.

6. The establishment of a socialist rule of law system was written into the state constitution in early 1999. For critical accounts of the Communist leadership's efforts to create a "socialist rule of law system," see *Understanding China's Legal System: Essays in Honor of Jerome A. Cohen,* ed. C. Stephen Hsu (New York: New York University Press, 2003); Randall Peerenboom, *China's Long March Toward Rule of Law* (New York: Cambridge University Press, 2002); Pitman B. Potter, *The Chinese Legal System: Globalization and Local Legal Culture* (London: Routledge, 2002); Eduard B. Vermeer, *China's Legal Reforms and Their Political Limits* (Richmond: Curzon, 2002); Guo Sujian, "Post-Mao China: The Rule of Law?" *Issues & Studies* 35, no. 6 (November/December 1999): 80–118.

7. These divergent viewpoints have been nicely juxtaposed in a recent edition of the *Journal of Democracy* on "China's Changing of the Guard," 14, no. 1 (January 2003): 5–81, containing contributions by Andrew J. Nathan, Bruce Gilley, Bruce J. Dickson, Wang Shaoguang, Yang Dali, Chen An, Xiao Gongqin, He Qinglian, and a concluding article by Pei Minxin.

8. See for example, Frederick C. Teiwes, "The Problematic Quest for Stability: Reflections on Succession, Institutionalization, Governability, and Legitimacy in Post-Deng China," in *China Under Jiang Zemin,* ed. Tien Hung-mao and Chu Yun-han, pp. 71–95 (London: Lynne Rienner, 2000); Richard Baum and Alexei Shevchenko, "The State of the 'State,'" in *The Paradox of China's Post-Mao Reforms,* ed. Merle Goldman and Roderick MacFarquhar, pp. 333–360 (Cambridge: Harvard University Press, 1999); Jean-Pierre Cabestan, "The 10th National People's Congress and After: Moving Towards a New Authoritarianism, Both Elitist and Consultative?" *China Perspectives,* no. 47 (May–June 2003): 4–20.

9. Andrew J. Nathan, "Authoritarian Resilience," *Journal of Democracy* 14, no. 1 (January 2003): 6–17; Yang Dali, "State Capacity on the Rebound," *Journal of Democracy* 14, no. 1 (January 2003): 43–50; Xiao Gongqin, "The Rise of Technocrats," *Journal of Democracy* 14, no. 1 (January 2003): 60–65.

10. Bruce Gilley, "The Limits of Authoritarian Resilience," *Journal of Democracy* 14, no. 1 (January 2003): 18–26; Bruce J. Dickson, "Threats to Party Supremacy," *Journal of Democracy* 14, no. 1 (January 2003): 27–35; Wang Shaoguang, "The Problem of State Weakness," *Journal of Democracy* 14, no. 1 (January 2003): 36–42; He Qinglian, "A Volcanic Stability," *Journal of Democracy* 14, no. 1 (January 2003): 66–72. Bruce Gilley has been even more outspoken in another recent contribution, in which he suggests a diminution of formal and informal contestation and the rise of "cryptopolitics" in China's political system; see "The 'End of Politics' in Beijing," *China Journal,* no. 51 (January 2004): 115–135.

11. For more comprehensive accounts of recent intellectual discourse on democracy and political reform in post-Tiananmen China, see Merle Goldman, "Politically Engaged Intellectuals in the Deng-Jiang Era: A Changing Relationship with the Party State," *China Quarterly,* no. 145 (March 1996): 35–52; Thomas Heberer and Nora Sausmikat, "Political Discourses, Intellectuals and Political Change: Discourse Change in Post-1998 China and Its Implications" (in German), *ASIEN,* no. 82 (January 2002): 35–60; Ding Yijiang, "The Conceptual Evolution of Democracy in Intellectual Circles: Rethinking of State and Society," in *China and Democracy: The Prospect for a Democratic China,* ed. Suisheng Zhao, pp. 111–140 (New York and London: Routledge, 2000); for a thought-provoking critique of contemporary Chinese intellectuals' depoliticization only covered by their flawed conceptualization of "enlightenment" and modernity, see Ben Xu, "Postmodern-Postcolonial Criticism and Pro-Democracy Enlightenment," *Modern China* 27, no. 1 (January 2001): 117–147.

12. The objective of "building a socialist democracy with Chinese characteristics" was written into the 1982 state constitution. For an account of the Chinese discourse on the concept of "socialist democracy," linking it to the system of people's congresses (as done most often), see Du Lun, *Perfection of "Socialist Democracy with Chinese Characteristics"* (in German), Project Discussion Paper No. 8/2001, Institute of East Asian Studies, University of Duisburg-Essen.

13. Victor N. Shaw, "Mainland China's Political Development: Is the CCP's Version of

Democracy Relevant?" *Issues & Studies* 32, no. 7 (July 1996): 59–82 (at 79–81). Most visibly, the reform agenda resulted in a dual structure of Party leadership materializing in the post-1989 era: the Communist Party relinquished its role as a mobilizing force in economic and social institutions at the local level and restricted its power to retaining ultimate control over all government bodies. See Suisheng Zhao-, "Political Reform and Changing One-Party Rule in Deng's China," *Problems of Communism* 44, no. 5 (September/October 1997): 12–21.

14. See, "Political Liberalization Without Democratization," chapter 2 of this volume, p. 41.

15. Pan Wei, "Toward a Consultative Rule of Law Regime in China," *Journal of Contemporary China* 12, no. 34 (2003): 3–43. I will mainly refer to this article for making my argument more comprehensible to those who do not read Chinese. For Pan Wei's Chinese articles on the topic, see "Fazhi yu weilai Zhongguo zhengti" (Rule by/of law and the future of China's political system)," in *Zhanlue yu guanli* (Stategy and management), no. 5 (1999): 30–36; "Minzhu yu zhengzhi: xiangfu er xiangcheng" (Democracy and politics: Complementing each other), in *Zhanlue yu guanli,* no. 2 (2001): 116–120. The Chinese version of the English article quoted here has recently been republished as the first chapter of an essay collection carrying the same title: *Fazhi yu "minzhu mixin"* (Rule by/of law and the "democracy superstition") (Hong Kong: Hong Kong Press for Social Sciences, Ltd., 2003). Pan Wei maintains a website containing a complete collection of his articles, both published and unpublished, which can be accessed via www.sis.pku.edu.cn/panwei/.

16. As a matter of fact, Pan Wei is highly critical of present-day Communist rule, even if he rejects the Western concept of liberal democracy for China. He demands a thorough rejuvenation of the Party and the institutionalization of a free press and independent consultative bodies to keep the Party in check. Consequently, he is as much criticized by Western and Chinese liberals as by many Party officials, who are highly suspicious of any external control over the CCP.

17. For such a critique see Edward Friedman, "A Comparative Politics of Democratization in China," *Journal of Contemporary China* 12, no. 34 (2003): 103–123.

18. The consultation function of the people's congresses makes sure that the regime becomes "accountable to various social demands," though it would not "surrender to those demands."

19. According to the "Three Represents" officially announced by Jiang Zemin on July 1, 2001 (and written into the Party Charter during the 16th National Party Congress in late 2002), the Communist Party represents the development of the advanced productive forces, China's advanced culture, and the fundamental interests of the overwhelming majority of the people.

20. Randall Peerenboom, "A Government of Laws: Democracy, Rule of Law, and Administrative Law Reform in the PRC," *Journal of Contemporary China* 12, no. 34 (2003): 45–67 (at 51).

21. As Peerenboom has noted, "even assuming Pan's five-pronged reform agenda is implemented, by itself it will not be sufficient. A wide range of other administrative and legal reforms are required, and legal reforms must be complemented by changes in the political, social and economic realms." See Peerenboom, "A Government of Laws," p. 58.

22. Guo, "Post-Mao China: The Rule of Law?" p. 116.

23. Peerenboom, "A Government of Laws," p. 61.

24. As a matter of fact, Kevin O'Brien and Li Lianjiang's notion of "rightful resistance" observed in the Chinese countryside does capture well the rise of a rights awareness among peasants, who seem to be more and more inclined to pursue their interests by means of collective action. See Kevin O'Brien, "Rightful Resistance," *World Politics* 49, no. 1 (1996): 31–55; Li Lianjiang, "Elections and Popular Resistance in Rural China," *China Information* 15, no. 2 (2001): 19.

Notes to Chapter 7

1. Randall Peerenboom, *China's Long March Toward Rule of Law* (New York: Cambridge University Press, 2002), p. 41.

2. Joseph Raz, *The Authority of Law: Essays on Law and Morality* (Oxford: Clarendon Press, 1979), p. 212.

3. Harold J. Berman, *Law and Revolution: The Formation of the Western Legal Tradition* (Cambridge: Harvard University Press, 1983), p. 9.

4. Harold J. Berman, *Law and Revolution II: The Impact of the Protestant Reformations on the Western Legal Tradition* (Cambridge: Belknap Press of Harvard University Press, 2003), p. 5.

5. Berman, *Law and Revolution,* pp. 532, 537.

6. Ralph V. Turner, *Magna Carta Through the Ages* (New York: Longman, 2003).

7. Berman, *Law and Revolution II,* pp. 248–255.

8. Xia Yong, *Fazhi yuanlu: Tongfan yu xifang* (Origins of the rule of law: East and west) (Beijing: Chinese Social Sciences Press, 2004), p. 74. Xia Yong is the director of the Institute of Law, Chinese Academy of Social Sciences.

9. Jacques Gernet, *A History of Chinese Civilization* (New York: Cambridge University Press, 1996), p. 80.

10. Wang Yu-chuan, "An Outline of the Central Government of the Former Han Dynasty," in *Studies in Governmental Institutions in Chinese History,* ed. John L. Bishop, p. 138 (Cambridge: Harvard University Press, 1968).

11. H. Lyman Miller, "The Late Imperial Chinese State," in *The Modern Chinese State,* ed. David Shambaugh (New York: Cambridge University Press, 2000).

12. Gernet, *A History of Chinese Civilization,* p. 116.

13. Charles O. Hucker, "Governmental Organization of the Ming Dynasty," in *Studies in Governmental Institutions in Chinese History,* ed. John L. Bishop, p. 66 (Cambridge: Harvard University Press, 1968).

14. For a classic study on the career advancement of the Chinese gentry class, see Ping-ti Ho, *The Ladder of Success in Imperial China: Aspects of Social Mobility, 1368–1911* (New York: Columbia University Press, 1962).

15. Peerenboom, *China's Long March,* pp. 28, 32, 33.

16. Suzanne Ogden, *Inklings of Democracy in China* (Cambridge: Harvard University Press, 2002), p. 51.

17. Yang Hefu, *Zhongguo gudai falü sixiang lun ji* (Essays on ancient Chinese legal philosophies) (Beijing: Chinese University of Politics and Law Press, 2003), p. 84.

18. See Xia Yong, *Fazhi yuanlu,* p. 78.

19. See Yang Hefu, *Zhongguo gudai falü sixiang lun ji,* pp. 198–207.

20. Brian Downing, *The Military Revolution and Political Change: Origins of Democracy and Autocracy in Early Modern Europe* (Princeton: Princeton University Press, 1992), p. 19.

21. Henry Spruyt, *The Sovereign State and Its Competitors* (Princeton: Princeton University Press, 1994), pp. 52–53.

22. S.E. Finer, *The History of Government* (New York: Oxford University Press, 1997), pp. 890, 894, 895.

23. Downing, *The Military Revolution and Political Change,* p. 22.

24. Samuel P. Huntington, "The West Unique, Not Universal," *Foreign Affairs* 75, no. 6 (1996): 32.

25. Joseph Strayer, *Feudalism* (New York: Van Hostrand Reinhold, 1965), p. 13.

26. Finer, *The History of Government,* pp. 867–868.

27. Downing, *The Military Revolution and Political Change,* p. 21.

28. Ibid., p. 31.

29. Berman, *Law and Revolution,* p. 533.

30. Finer, *The History of Government,* p. 873.

31. Berman, *Law and Revolution,* p. 12.

32. Finer, *The History of Government,* pp. 862, 863, 888.

33. John Locke, *Two Treatises of Government,* ed. Peter Laslett (Cambridge: Cambridge University Press, 1964), Second Treatise, p. 326.

34. The above discussion draws from Finer, *The History of Government,* pp. 877, 911, 1279–1280, 1332–1335.

35. Thomas Eartman, *Birth of the Leviathan: Building States and Regimes in Medieval and Early Modern Europe* (New York: Cambridge University Press, 1997), pp. 167–169.

36. Finer, *The History of Government,* p. 905.

37. Eartman, *Birth of the Leviathan,* p. 168.

38. Finer, *The History of Government,* p. 1274.

39. Eartman, *Birth of the Leviathan,* pp. 168, 177.

40. Finer, *The History of Government,* pp. 1335, 1343.

41. Ibid., pp. 1298–1303.

42. For more details, see Pan Wei, "Fazhi yu Zhongguo de weilai zhengti" (The rule of law and China's future political system), *Zhanlue yu guanli* (Strategy and management), no. 5 (1999).

43. Randall Peerenboom, "Varieties of Rule of Law: An Introduction and Provisional Conclusion," in *Asian Discourse of Rule of Law,* ed. Randall Peerenboom, p. 40 (London and New York: Routledge, 2004).

44. Niall Ferguson, *Empire: The Rise and Demise of the British World Order and Lessons for Global Power* (New York: Basic Books, 2003).

45. Alfred Stepan and Cindy Skach, "Constitutional Frameworks and Democratic Consolidation: Parliamentarism Versus Presidentialism," *World Politics* 46, no. 1 (October 1993).

46. Lam Peng Er, "Singapore: Rich State, Illiberal Regime," in *Driven by Growth: Political Change in the Asia-Pacific Region,* ed. James W. Morley (Armonk, NY: M.E. Sharpe, 1999).

47. Fareed Zakaria, "The Rise of Illiberal Democracy," *Foreign Affairs* 76, no. 6 (November/December 1997): 26.

Notes to Chapter 8

1. Cai Dingjian, *History and Evolution: The Historical Course of the Construction of the Legal System of New China (Lishi yu biange: Xinzhongguo fazhi jianshe de licheng)* (Beijing: China University of Politics and Law Press, 1999), pp. 179–197.

2. For a review of the contribution of the nongovernment sectors (the NGOs) to the Chinese rule of law, see C. David Lee, "Legal Reform in China: A Role for Nongovernmental Organizations," *Yale Journal of International Law,* no. 25 (2000): 363.

3. For the achievements and limitations of Chinese legal reform, of which judicial reform is a part, see Stanley Lubman, *Bird in a Cage: Legal Reform in China After Mao* (Stanford: Stanford University Press, 1999); Pitman Potter, ed., *Domestic Law Reforms in Post-Mao China* (Armonk, NY: M.E. Sharpe, 1994); Randall Peerenboom, "Globalization, Path Dependency and the Limits of Law: Administrative Law Reform and Rule of Law in the People's Republic of China," *Berkeley Journal of International Law,* no. 19 (2001): 161.

4. Gong Depei, "The Phenomenon of Judicial Partiality Must be Eliminated" (Yao dujue sifa bugong de xianxiang), *People's Court Daily (Renmin fayuan bao),* April 28, 2000.

5. *Xinhua Daily,* October 25, 1999, p. B1.

6. Article 126 of the Constitution provides that the Chinese courts have "the judicial power according to the provisions of law, and are not to be interfered with by administrative agencies, social organizations, individuals." Article 8 of the Judges Law goes even further: a Chinese judge is entitled to "(1) the power and working conditions for carrying out the judge's professional responsibility; (2) trial of cases according to law, free from the interference of administrative agencies, social organizations and individual persons; (3) freedom from dismissal, demotion, retirement or penalties without the cause and procedure determined by law." For the distinction between the Chinese understanding of judicial indepen-

dence embodied in the court as a collective entity and Western independence of individual judges, see Andrew Nathan, *China's Transition* (New York: Columbia University Press, 1997), p. 239.

7. As Mencius puts it famously: "Virtue alone is insufficient for ruling; mere laws cannot carry themselves into practice." *Mencius,* 4A: 1, Benjamin I. Schwartz, trans., *The World of Thought in Ancient China* (Cambridge, MA: Harvard University Press, 1985), pp. 322–323. For the revitalization of the notion of *renzhi* ("rule of man," which I think is a serious misnomer for the meaning it is supposed to convey) among Chinese legal scholars, see Su Li, "Taking Rule of Man Seriously" (Renzhen duidai renzhi), *Journal of the East China Institute of Law and Politics* (*Huadong zhengfa xueyuan xuebao*), no. 1 (1998): 8–13.

8. *Zhongyang Zhengfu guanyu Jiaqiang Renmin Sifa Gongzuo de Zhishi* (Directive of the central government on strengthening legal work of the people), November 3, 1950.

9. He Rikai, "Judicial Reform: From Power to Authority" (Sifa gaige: Cong quanli zouxiang quanwei), *Law Science* (*Falü kexue*), no. 4 (1999): 30–38.

10. Tie Li and Lu Jingbi, "A Defective Judicial Reform: A Study of Important Events in the Legal Community Since the Establishment of the State" (Yichang you quexian de sifa gaige: Jianguo yilai faxuejie zhongda shijian de yanjiu), *Jurisprudence* (*Faxue*), no. 6 (1998): 2–5.

11. Even back in 1991, there were 138,000 persons above the rank of assistant trial member (*zhushenyuan*), with only 47,000 lawyers. In 1997, the number of lawyers in China increased to 100,000, but the number of judges above the assistant rank increased to 247,000 due to the local expansion of capacity (*zengbian*). See Wang Chengguang, "Judicial Efficiency and the Reform of the Internal Operating System of the Courts" (Ban'an xiaolü yu fayuan neibu yunxing tizhi de gaige), *Jurisprudence* (*Faxue*), no. 10 (1998): 46–51.

12. Ma Junju and Nie Dezong, "The Existing Problems in Our Current Judicial System and the Strategies for Improvement" (Dangqian woguo sifa zhidu cunzai de wenti yu gaijin duice), *Review of Legal Studies* (*Faxue pinglun*), no. 6 (1998): 25–30.

13. Cai Dingjian, "Preliminary Comments on the Reform of the Court System" (Fayuan zhidu gaige chuyi), *Strategy and Management* (*Zhanlüe yu guanli*), no. 1 (1999): 97–102.

14. See Wang Yinghui, "Governing the State According to Law and the Judicial Reform" (Yifa zhiguo yu sifa gaige), *Studies on Law and Commerce* (*Fashang yanjiu*), no. 2 (1999): 47–50.

15. See He Weifang, "The Road Toward Judicial Reform" (Sifa gaige zhi lu) (Part II), *Beijing University Law Information* (*Beida falü xinxi*) 4, no. 3 (2000). Part of the reason is that the judgments of the Chinese courts lack a clear place in the hierarchy of law. Formally speaking, China, in imitating the continental legal style, does not recognize court decisions as part of the "law."

16. See He Weifang, "The Road Toward Judicial Reform" (Sifa gaige zhi lu) (Part II), *Beijing University Law Information* (*Beida falü xinxi*) 4, no. 3 (2000).

17. Hao Tiechuan, "On Governing the State According to Law in the Transitional Period of Chinese Society" (Lun Zhongguo shehui zhuanxing shiqi de yifa zhiguo), *Chinese Jurisprudence* (*Zhongguo faxue*), no. 2 (2000): 7.

18. Pi Chunxie and Deng Dandan, "Study on the Chinese Judicial Reform (II): The Dilemma of Administrative Litigation and Thoughts on Its Reform," *The Jurist* (*Faxuejia*), no. 2 (1998): 97–99.

19. Wu Xiaodong, "Three Problems That the Reform of the Trial Operating System Needs to Resolve" (Shenpan yunxing jizhi xu gaige de san wenti), *People's Court Daily,* June 2, 2000.

20. Liu Han and Zhang Gengda, "Four Problems for the Reform of the Judicial Panel System" (Heyiting zhidu gaige si ti), *People's Court Daily,* May 5, 2000.

21. See "Vindicating Judicial Fairness by Rigid Institutions," *Xinhua Daily,* July 27, 2000, p. A2.

22. Tan Shigui, "A Study of Chinese Judicial Reform" (Woguo sifa gaige yanjiu), *Modern Jurisprudence* (*Xiandai faxue*), no. 5 (1998): 67.

23. "Xiao Yang Requires That over Half of the Basic-level Courts Must Implement the Trial Leader and Single Judge Selection System This Year" (Xiao yang yaoqiu jinnian guoban jiceng fayuan shixing shenpanzhang duren shenpanyuan xuanren zhi), *Legal Daily*, June 24, 2000.

24. For supporting arguments made by the former president of the SPC, see Zheng Tianxiang, *On Governing the State According to Law* (*Lun yifa zhiguo*) (Beijing: People's Court Press, 1999).

25. Wan Exiang, "Deepening Judicial Reform, Guaranteeing Judicial Fairness," *Law Review* (*Falü pinglun*) 17, no. 3 (1999): 1–2.

26. Zhang Cuiling, "The Wave of Judicial Reform" (Sifa gaige langcao), *Beijing Youth News*, November 28, 2000.

27. For judicial opposition to this option, see Ma Junju and Nie Dezong, "The Existing Problems in Our Current Judicial System and the Strategies for Improvement," p. 24.

28. Han Yuanheng, "Report on the Reform of the People's Courts in Botou City" (Botoushi renmin fayuan gaige jishi), *People's Court Daily*, May 8, 2000.

29. Chen Ruihua, "The Road Toward Judicial Reform" (Sifa gaige zhi lu) (Part I), *Beijing University Law Information* (*Beida falü xinxi*) 4, no. 2 (2000).

30. For objections from a Chinese judge, see You Zhenhui, "On the Internal Competition for the Posts Within the Courts" (Fayuan neibu jingzheng shanggang bian). Available at www.china-judge.com/fnsx/fnsx950.htm.

Notes to Chapter 9

1. John Reitz, "Constitutionalism and the Role of Rule of Law: Theoretical Perspectives," in *Democratic Theory and Post-Communist Change*, ed. Robert D. Grey, p. 112 (Englewood Cliffs, NJ: Prentice Hall, 1997).

2. See *China Law Yearbook 1990*, p. 1009; *China Law Yearbook 2001*, p. 903.

3. *Jiangnan shibao* (Jiangnan times), May 8, 2002; *Chinese Statistical Yearbook 2001*, p. 135.

4. *Xinxi shibao* (Information times), July 7, 2002.

5. By the early 2000s, the number of judges had reached 240,000. Many of them had no formal training in law. Among the heads and deputy heads of the courts in the country, only about 19 percent had a college education. Among the judges, only 15.4 percent of them had a college education, often not in law. Liu Jinhuai and Guo Chunyu, "Jiceng fayuan zouxiang gaige xuqu" (Local courts start reform), *Liaowang* (Perspective), no. 29 (2000): 28–29.

6. Liu Guiming, "Zhongguo lushi mianlin shida nanti" (Chinese lawyers face ten problems), *Fazhi yu jingji* (Law and economy), no. 3 (2002): 4–9.

7. Philip C.C. Huang, *Civil Justice in China: Representation and Practice in the Qing* (Stanford: Stanford University Press, 1996); T'ung-Tsu Ch'u, *Local Government in China Under the Ch'ing* (Cambridge: Harvard University Press, 1962).

8. Alison W. Conner, "Lawyers and the Legal Profession during the Republican Period," in *Civil Law in Qing and Republican China*, ed. Kathryn Bernhardt and Philip C.C. Huang, pp. 210–248 (Stanford: Stanford University Press, 1994).

9. Wang Guangxin and Liu Shanshu, "Faguan yanzhong de lushi" (Lawyers in the eyes of judges), *Zhongguo lushi* (Chinese lawyer), no. 8 (1998): 16–17.

10. This survey was carried out in Changsha of Hunan Province between February and March of 2002. At the time we conducted the survey, Changsha had about 97 law firms, and our survey covered all the law firms, but the number of valid answers varies across questions. We chose Changsha as the site of the survey for two reasons. First, as the capital city of Hunan Province, the level of economic development in Changsha is neither very advanced nor backward. It can thus be representative of less developed but not undeveloped areas. Second, we had access to interviewees there.

11. *China Law Yearbook 1991,* p. 933; *China Law Yearbook 2001,* p. 1256.

12. Wang Chao, "Xingshi lushi zeren huomian: toushi yu qianzhan" (The immunity of criminal responsibilities of lawyers in criminal cases: An analysis and predictions), *Lushi yu fazhi* (Lawyer and law), no. 5 (2002): 4–6.

13. Randall Peerenboom, *China's Long March Toward Rule of Law* (New York: Cambridge University Press, 2002), p. 8.

14. *Laodongbao* (Labor news), May 20, 2002.

15. Wang Chenguang and Gao Qicai, "Lushi zhiye de xianzhuang diaocha" (An investigation of the current situation of lawyers), *Zhongguo lushi* (Chinese lawyer), no. 12 (2000): 5–13.

16. Zhang Jingyuan, "Lushi shoufei: Kunhuo yu xuanze (Legal fees: Problems and solutions), *Banyuetan* (Biweekly forum), no. 5 (2002): 18–22.

17. Wang and Gao, "Lushi zhiye de xianzhuang diaocha."

18. Zhang, "Lushi shoufei: Kunhuo yu xuanze."

19. Wang and Gao, "Lushi zhiye de xianzhuang diaocha."

20. For a discussion of the execution of court judgments, see Donald Clarke, "The Execution of Civil Judgments in China," *China Quarterly,* no. 141 (1995): 65–81.

21. *Beijing qingnian bao* (Beijing youth), March 18, 2002.

22. *Fazhi ribao* (Legal daily), September 27, 2000.

23. Minxin Pei, "Citizens vs. Mandarins: Administrative Litigation in China," *China Quarterly,* no. 152 (1997): 832–862.

24. See *China Law Yearbook,* various years.

25. Jiang Wujun, "Wunai de chesu" (No choice but to withdraw the case), *Lushi yu fazhi* (Lawyers and law), no. 5 (1998): 24–25.

26. Li Zhonghe, "Xingzheng susong renzhong daoyuan" (Administrative litigations: A long way to go), *Fazhi ribao* (Legal news daily), October 10, 2000.

27. See the Web site of NetEase, www1.163.com/news/item/0,1567,70579,00.html.

28. See *China Law Yearbook,* various years.

29. Zhang Xiaolei, "Gongzheng: lu manman qi xiuyuan xi" (Obtaining justice: a long way to go), *Gongan yuekan* (Public security monthly), no. 6 (2002): 4–8; and no. 7 (2002): 4–9.

30. Most such appeals were not legal appeals lodged with upper-level courts; instead they were lodged with Party and government agencies.

31. *Zhongguo qingnian bao* (Chinese youth), November 28, 2001.

32. See Murray Scot Tanner, "State Coercion and the Balance of Awe: The 1983–1986 'Stern Blows' Anti-Crime Campaign," *China Journal,* no. 44 (2000): 93–128.

33. Li Pingzhang, "Lushi diaocha quzheng de kunhuo" (The problems with lawyers' investigation and evidence collection), *Zhongguo lushi* (Chinese lawyer), no. 8 (1998): 21–22.

34. Tian Wenchang and Zhou Jihan, "Xingshi susong: Lushi weini er kunhuo" (Criminal litigations puzzle lawyers), *Zhongguo lushi* (Chinese lawyer), no. 11 (2000): 39–42.

35. Jiang Fei, "Lushi xingbian de kunhuo" (The puzzles in lawyers' defense in criminal cases), *Zhongguo qingnian bao* (Chinese youth), July 3, 2002.

36. Zhang Kangan, "Beijng lushijie zhuangkuang diaocha baogao" (A report on the situation of lawyers in Beijing), *Zhongguo lushi* (Chinese lawyer), no. 8 (1998): 14–15.

37. Wang, "Xingshi lushi zeren huomian: toushi yu qianzhan."

38. Wang Xinhuai, "Lushi diaocha quzheng heshi buzainan?" (When will evidence collection by the lawyer not be difficult?), *Fazhi yu xinwen* (Law and news), no. 3 (2002): 8–12.

39. Wang, "Xingshi lushi zeren huomian: toushi yu qianzhan."

40. Zhong Fawang, "Lushi bei zuchu fading de sikao" (Some thinking on lawyers' being ordered to leave the court), *Lushi yu fazhi* (Lawyers and law), no. 5 (2002): 32–35.

41. Xin Lu, "Guanzhu Xinjiang shouli fanghai zuozheng'an" (Paying attention to the first case of preventing bearing witness in Xinjiang), *Lushi yu fazhi* (Lawyer and law), no. 3 (2002): 26–29.

42. Dong Fumin, "Diyuzhimen zouchu de wuzui lushi" (An innocent lawyer who came out of the inferno), *Lushi yu fazhi* (Lawyer and law), no. 3 (2001): 2–6; Liu Da, "Zhongyuan dalushi Li Kuisheng chen yuan zhaoxue" (Li's imposed charges were removed), *Fayuan* (Legal realm), no. 2 (2001): 8–11.

43. Jiang, "Lushi xingbian de kunhuo."

44. Zhang Tiefeng, "Wo lan de ban xing'an" (I am tired of taking criminal cases), *Zhongguo lushi* (Chinese lawyer), no. 11 (2000): 48–49.

45. Jiang, "Lushi xingbian de kunhuo."

46. In other cases where such political influence is not as strong, there may be conflicting views between legal organs and other public agencies. See Anthony Dicks, "Compartmentalized Law and Judicial Restraint: An Inductive View of Some Jurisdictional Barriers to Reform," *China Quarterly*, no. 141 (1995): 82–109.

47. Li Gongyin, "Weizhengzui ling lushi wang xingquebu" (The crime of perjury makes lawyers unwilling to take criminal cases), *Beijing qingnian bao* (Beijing youth), March 26, 2002.

48. Zhang, "Wo lan de ban xing'an."

49. Xin, "Guanzhu Xinjiang shouli fanghai zuozheng'an."

50. Zhong, "Lushi bei zuchu fading de sikao."

51. Jiang, "Lushi xingbian de kunhuo."

52. "Xia daliqi zhuahao lushi weiquan gongzuo" (Making more efforts to promote the work of protecting lawyers' rights), *Zhongguo lushi* (Chinese lawyer), no. 7 (2000): 23–25.

53. Jiang, "Lushi xingbian de kunhuo."

54. Peerenboom, *China's Long March Toward Rule of Law*.

55. Stanley Lubman, "Introduction: The Future of Chinese Law," *China Quarterly*, no. 141 (1995): 1–21.

56. Stanley Lubman, *Bird in a Cage* (Stanford, CA: Stanford University Press, 1999).

57. For this reason, a lawyer in Shaanxi Province who was elected a delegate to the National People's Congress, together with other delegates, proposed to revoke Article 306 of the Criminal Law. News reported in *Zhongguo lushi* (Chinese lawyer), no. 5 (2000): 6.

Notes to Chapter 10

1. Yongchun Cai, "The Resistance of Chinese Laid-off Workers in the Reform Period," *China Quarterly*, no. 170 (June 2002): 327–344; William Hurst and Kevin J. O'Brien, "China's Contentious Pensioners," *China Quarterly*, no. 170 (June 2002): 345–360; Feng Chen, "Subsistence Crises, Managerial Corruption and Labor Protests in China," *China Journal*, no. 44 (July 2000): 41–63.

2. Marc J. Blecher, "Hegemony and Workers' Politics in China," *China Quarterly*, no. 170 (June 2002): 283–303. For similar views about state–labor relations, see Yunqiu Zhang, "An Intermediary: The Chinese Perception of Trade Unions Since the 1970s," *Journal of Contemporary China* 6, no. 14 (Spring 1997): 139–152; and Zhang, "From State Corporatism to Social Representation: Local Trade Unions in China in the Reform Years," in *Civil Society in China*, ed. T. Brook and B. Frolic, pp. 124–148 (Armonk, NY: M.E. Sharpe, 1997).

3. Located in Shandong peninsula, the Qingdao region covers an area of 10,654 square km and is administratively composed of the (provincial-level) city of Qingdao and its five satellite

272 NOTES TO CHAPTER 10

(county-level) cities. Under the jurisdiction of these cities' authorities are large rural areas including small towns and numerous villages. The political and economic center of this region is the city of Qingdao, one of the original fourteen coastal open cities designated by the central government in 1984. Primarily due to its advantageous location, the Qingdao region has been a favorite destination for foreign investments in the post-Mao years. Since the early 1990s, I have been monitoring the socioeconomic developments of this region, especially the situation of labor relations. In 2001, I spent two months in Qingdao, doing my field studies on labor issues. With cooperation from some of my friends, I did surveys in three state-owned enterprises and interviewed two trade union cadres and twenty-five individual workers, twelve of whom came from state-owned enterprises, eight from foreign-invested ones, the rest from Chinese-owned township and private enterprises. Some of these workers were my former neighbors and their acquaintances and friends. The interviews took the form of casual conversation—the interviewees were not aware that I was doing research on labor issues.

4. *Zhonghua renmin gongheguo difangxing fagui huibian* (Compilation of local laws and regulations of the PRC) (1992–1994) (Beijing: Zhongguo falu chubanshe, 1995), pp. 1162–1167; 1118–1122.

5. "Zhonghua renmin gongheguo laodong fa" (The labor law of the PRC), in *Laodong fa quanshu* (A complete book of labor legislation) (Beijing: Yuhang chubanshe, 1994), pp. 3–9.

6. They include Regulations on Minimum Wages, Regulations on Employees' Work Hours, the Labor Contracts Law, the Social Insurance Law, the Unemployment Insurance Law, the Safe Production Law, Regulations on Employees' Injuries During Work in Enterprises, and Regulations on Labor Supervision, in *Zhongguo laodong tongji nianjian* (Chinese labor yearbook) (1995–96), p. 155.

7. *Gongren ribao* (Workers' daily), November 14, 15, 2001; December 13, 25, 2001.

8. Beside union-sponsored legal agencies, there was another type of legal assistance agency, which was set up or sponsored by the judiciary institutions at different levels.

9. Guan Huai, "Lun dui woguo zhigong de falu yuanzhu" (On legal assistance to workers in our country), *Faxue zazhi* (Law science magazine), no. 5 (2000): 5–7.

10. Quanguo zonggonghui zhengci yanjiushi (All-China Federation of Trade Unions Policy Research Office), ed., *1997 Zhongguo zhigong zhuangkuang diaocha* (Survey of the status of Chinese staff and workers in 1997) (Beijing: Xiyuan chubanshe, 1999), p. 238. Hereafter cited as *ZZZD*.

11. Interviews in Qingdao, July 2001.

12. *Gongren ribao,* March 22, 2002.

13. *Gongren ribao,* December 11, 2001.

14. "Zhonghua renmin gongheguo laodong fa" (The labor law of the PRC), in *Laodong fa quanshu*; "Zhonghua renmin gongheguo qiye laodong zhengyi chuli tiaoli" (Regulations on handling labor disputes in enterprises within the PRC), in *Zhonghua renmin gongheguo falu quanshu* (A complete book of statutes of the PRC) (Changchun: Jilin renmin chubanshe, 1993), pp. 690–693.

15. Deng Baohua, ed., *Laogong shensheng de weishi—laodong fa* (The guard of the sacredness of labor—The labor law) (Shanghai: Shanghai renmin chubanshe, 1997), p. 322.

16. Zhu Jiazhen, "Jianshao mangmu xing, zongqiang zijue xing, nuli kaituo laodong zhengyi chuli gongzuo de xin jumian" (Refrain from blind action, enhance awareness, and strive to open up a new phase for the work of labor dispute settlement), *Zhongguo laodong tongji nianjian* (Chinese labor yearbook), 1995–96, pp. 113–118.

17. The testimonies below are based on interviews in Qingdao in 2001.

18. This catchphrase originally came from the movie *Qiuju da guansi* (Qiuju enters a lawsuit), which depicts how Qiuju, a rural woman in the post-Mao era, persistent and determined, overcomes various obstacles in filing and eventually winning a lawsuit against the village leader who had done some physical harm to her husband. Qiuju's reason for pursuing the lawsuit was, in her own words, *"tao ge shuo fa,"* which has since become so popular among the

Chinese, especially among those who have suffered injustices, that they use this catchphrase when seeking to redress their grievances.

19. Over 11 percent of workers with university degrees used litigation to solve their latest labor disputes in 1997, compared to 5.22 percent of those with high school education and 1.29 percent of those who were illiterate. See *ZZZD*, p. 1522.

20. Interviews in Qingdao in 2001.

21. *Gongren ribao,* for example, carried numerous reports on legal cases concerning labor disputes. Almost without exception, these reports were in favor of workers, exposing employers' "unreasonable" treatment of workers, and difficulties that workers encountered in the legal process, and requested fair settlement of the legal cases.

22. Interviews in Qingdao in 2001.

23. *Zhongguo laodong tongji nianjian,* 1994, pp. 90–91; 1999, p. 509.

24. *Gongren ribao,* October 24, 2000; January 15, 2001.

25. Zhang Buhong and Zhang Luhao, eds., *Laodong fa xin leixing anli jingxi* (Analyses of new types of labor lawsuit cases) (Beijing: Renmin fayuan chubanshe, 1997).

26. Below is based on interviews in Qingdao in 2001.

27. *Gongren ribao,* April 11, 1996, October 23, 2002, and October 23, 2000.

28. *Jinyang Network,* July 30, 2002.

29. Deng Baohua, ed., *Laogong shensheng de weishi—laodong fa,* p. 343.

30. *Gongren ribao,* November 17, 2000. This problem was partly mitigated by a new regulation issued by the Supreme People's Court of the PRC obliging employers to present evidence in lawsuits arising from disputes over dismissal of workers, termination of labor contracts, reduction of remuneration, and calculation of workers' years on the job, even if it was the workers who initiated the lawsuits. See the Supreme People's Court of the PRC, "Guanyu shenli laodong zhengyi anjian shiying falu ruogan wenti de jieshi" (Interpretations of various issues on applied laws regarding trials of labor dispute cases), *Gongren ribao,* May 17, 2001.

31. Jin Bei and Peng Changxiang, "Rang laodongzhe zhangwo falu wuqi" (Let the workers take the legal weapon), *Gongren ribao,* May 28, 2001.

32. Cai Dingjian and Liu Dan, "Cong zhengce shehui dao fazhi shehui" (From a policy-dominated society to a law-ruled society), in *Zhongguo fazhi zhilu* (The road to the rule of law in China), ed. Huang Zhiying, pp. 83–93 (Beijing: Beijing University Press, 2000).

33. Lu Desheng and Ji Rongrong, "Ershi nian lai fazhi jincheng de huigu yu qianzhan" (Review and prospect of the process of the building of rule of law in the past twenty years), in *Zhongguo fazhi zhilu,* ed. Huang Zhiying, pp. 37–57.

34. This argument, which stresses the transitional nature of Chinese legal ideas, differs from two other major views about the Chinese perception of law. Edward J. Epstein holds that in the post-Mao era Chinese leaders still took "an instrumentalist approach to law" and law played an "instrumentalist role" in Chinese society. See his "Law and Legitimation in Post-Mao China," in *Domestic Law Reforms in Post-Mao China,* ed. Pitman B. Potter, pp. 19–55 (Armonk, NY: M.E. Sharpe, 1999.

Notes to Chapter 11

1. This is a key thesis in Lawrence Lessig's influential work, *Code and Other Laws of Cyberspace* (New York: Basic Books, 1999).

2. Adam Seligman emphasizes the idea of the autonomous individual as the basis of civil society. See *The Idea of Civil Society* (New York: Free Press, 1992), p. 179. Yet as Thomas Gold points out, the relationship between civil society and the state is fluid and dynamic, and thus autonomy is not an absolute. See Thomas Gold, "Bases for Civil Society in Reform China," in *Reconstructing Twentieth-Century China: State Control, Civil Society, and National Identity,* ed. Kjeld Erik Brodsgaard and David Strand, p. 164 (Oxford: Clarendon Press, 1998).

3. Craig Calhoun, *Neither Gods nor Emperors* (Berkeley: University of California Press, 1994), p. 190.

4. David Strand, "Civil Society and Public Sphere in Modern Chinese History," in *Chinese Democracy and the Crisis of 1989,* ed. Roger V. des Forges, Luo Ning and Wu Yen-bo, p. 54 (Albany: State University of New York Press, 1993).

5. See Deborah S. Davis, Richard Kraus, Barry Naughton, and Elizabeth Perry, eds., *Urban Spaces in Contemporary China* (Washington, DC and New York: Woodrow Wilson Center Press and Cambridge University Press, 1995); and Timothy Brook and B. Michael Frolic, eds., *Civil Society in China* (Armonk, NY: M.E. Sharpe, 1997).

6. Wang Shaoguang, "The Politics of Private Time: Changing Leisure Patterns in Urban China," in *Urban Spaces in Contemporary China,* ed. Davis et al., pp. 149–172; Michel Bonnin and Yves Chevrier, "The Intellectual and the State: Social Dynamics of Intellectual Autonomy During the Post-Mao Era," in *The Individual and the State in China,* ed. Brian Hook, pp. 149–174 (Oxford: Clarendon Press, 1996); and Ruth Hayhoe and Ningsha Zhong, "University Autonomy and Civil Society," in *Civil Society in China,* ed. Brook and Frolic, pp. 99–121. On new developments since the 1990s, see Benjamin L. Read, "Democratizing the Neighbourhood? New Private Housing and Home-Owner Self-Organization in Urban China," *China Journal,* no. 49 (January 2003): 31–59; Jude Howell, "New Directions in Civil Society: Organizing Around Marginalized Interests," in *Governance in China,* ed. Jude Howell, pp. 143–171 (Lanham: Rowman & Littlefield, 2004); Zhang Xin and Richard Baum, "Civil Society and the Anatomy of a Rural NGO," *China Journal,* no. 52 (2004): 97–112; and Yang Guobin, "Environmental NGOs and Institutional Dynamics in China," *China Quarterly,* no. 181 (Spring 2005): 46–66.

7. Craig Calhoun, "Tiananmen, Television and the Public Sphere: Internationalization of Culture and the Beijing Spring of 1989," *Public Culture* 2, no. 1 (1989): 54–71; Dai Jinhua, "Rewriting Chinese Women: Gender Production and Cultural Space in the Eighties and Nineties," in *Spaces of Their Own: Women's Public Sphere in Transnational China,* ed. Mayfair Yang, pp. 191–206 (Minneapolis: University of Minnesota Press, 1999). Also see Philip Huang, "'Public Sphere'/'Civil Society' in China: Paradigmatic Issues in Chinese Studies, III," *Modern China* 19, 2 (1993): 216–240; and Frederic Wakeman, "The Civil Society and Public Sphere Debate: Western Reflections on Chinese Political Culture," *Modern China* 19, no. 2 (1993): 108–137.

8. Gordon White, Jude Howell, and Shang Xiaoyuan, *In Search of Civil Society* (Oxford: Clarendon, 1996), p. 106.

9. Jack Linchuan Qiu, "Virtual Censorship in China: Keeping the Gate Between the Cyberspaces," *International Journal of Communications Law and Policy* 4 (1999/2000): 1–25; Kathleen Hartford, "Cyberspace with Chinese Characteristics," *Current History* (September 2000): 255–262; Nina Hachigian, "China's Cyber-Strategy," *Foreign Affairs* (March/April 2001).

10. Geoffrey Taubman, "A Not-So World Wide Web: The Internet, China, and the Challenges to Nondemocratic Rule," *Political Communication,* no. 15 (1998): 255–272.

11. Eric Harwit and Duncan Clark, "Shaping the Internet in China: Evolution of Political Control over Network Infrastructure and Content," *Asian Survey* 41, no. 3 (2001): 408.

12. See Lynn White III, *Unstately Power* (Armonk, NY: M.E. Sharpe, 1998); Kate Xiao Zhou, *How Farmers Changed China* (Boulder, CO: Westview, 1996); Xueguang Zhou, "Unorganized Interests and Collective Action in Communist China," *American Sociological Review* 58, no. 1 (1993): 54–73.

13. See www.chinaonline.com/issues/Internet_policy/newsarchive/secure/2001/June/C01060150.asp.

14. Christine Hine, *Virtual Ethnography* (London: Sage, 2000).

15. The gender gap among users has been narrowing over the years, from about 7 percent female and 93 percent male in June 1998 to 40 percent female and 60 percent male in December 2001.

16. For a complete list of Internet regulations in China, see CNNIC's official Web site, www.cnnic.net.cn.

17. OpenNet Initiative, "Internet Filtering in China in 2004–2005: A Country Study," April 14, 2005. Available at www.opennetinitiative.net/studies/china/ONI_China_Country_Study.pdf. Accessed May 24, 2005.

18. Jayanthi Iyengar, "Digital China Is Booming," *Asia Times Online,* February 17, 2004. www.atimes.com.

19. Jurgen Habermas, *The Structural Transformation of the Public Sphere* (Cambridge, MA: MIT Press, 1989).

20. According to a 2001 survey, 76.2 percent of the Web sites used by Internet users in China are Chinese-language Web sites based in China, 14.61 percent are Chinese-language sites based outside of China, while 9.19 percent are foreign-language Web sites.

21. BBSs enjoy great popularity in Taiwan. Yet because there is little evidence that users in mainland China access them, I have not included them in my discussion.

22. Affiliated with the online edition of *People's Daily,* QGLT was originally launched for public protest against the NATO bombing of the Chinese embassy in Belgrade. Apparently because of its official affiliation, QGLT has a more strictly enforced censorship system than other BBS forums in China. Contents are filtered while hosts maintain synchronous monitoring of posts. Discussion topics are supposed to be related to the strengthening of the Chinese nation. But this may be defined so broadly that basically any serious discussion about any issue can be considered to fall under the themes of the forum. In reality, the posts that tend to be deleted are those that have explicit anti-government messages. According to a news report of the *People's Daily* (May 17, 2000), QGLT had nearly 30,000 registered user names by early May 2000, with about 100,000 daily hits. From May 9, 1999, to September 4, 2000, it had a total of 1,258,720 posts, a daily average of 2,600 (www.geocities.com/Paris/Lights/4323/top20.html). As of mid-July 2001, QGLT still maintained a daily average of about 1,500 posts.

23. Another empirical study of the same forum confirms this point. See Chin-fu Hung, "Public Discourse and 'Virtual' Political Participation in the PRC: The Impact of the Internet," *Issues and Studies,* no. 39 (December 2003): 1–38.

24. Creaders has 177 posts on June 11 and 443 on June 12; Muzi has 57 posts on June 11 and 47 on June 12; Beida has 82 posts on June 11 and 132 on June 12.

25. "Beidou" is the user name, followed by the date the message was posted. I will use the same citation format throughout this chapter. All posts were originally in Chinese. They are cited here in English translations of my own rendering.

26. Wenfang Tang and William Parish devote substantial space to a discussion of political participation and interest articulation. While they found "incipient changes" in new, individualistic modes of political participation, their analysis makes no mention of how private interests may be channeled into public debate, indicating the lack of such channels in China's public life. See Wenfang Tang and William Parish, *Chinese Urban Life Under Reform* (Cambridge: Cambridge University Press, 2000).

27. Jurgen Habermas, *Between Facts and Norms* (Cambridge, MA: MIT Press, 1996), p. 381.

28. Duncan Hewitt, "Online Diary of Dying Man," http://news.bbc.co.uk/hi/english/world/asia-pacific/newsid_1039000/1039309.stm. Accessed October 11, 2001. I thank Sun-Ki Chai for bringing the story to my attention.

29. Report of the U.S. Embassy in Beijing, "Kids, Cadres and 'Cultists' All Love It: Growing Influence of the Internet in China." Accessed May 10, 2001, from www.usembassy-china.org .cn/english/sandt/index.html.

30. Zheng Shengfeng, "Nandan kuangnan de chenggong jielu liugei renmen de qishi" (Lessons from the successful exposure of the mine disaster in Nandan), *Xinwen zhanxian* (News frontier), no. 9 (2003).

31. Guo Liang and Bu Wei, "Report on the Conditions of the Internet in Five Cities in China

in Year 2000 Conducted by the Social Development Research Center of the Chinese Academy of Social Sciences." The primary investigators of this project were partners of the UCLA Internet Project (www.ccp.ucla.edu/pages/Partners.asp). The research design was modeled on the UCLA project. The report contains a detailed discussion of methodological issues. See www.chinace .org/ce/itre/. Accessed June 18, 2001.

32. Guobin Yang,"Weaving a Green Web: The Internet and Environmental Activism in China," *China Environment Series,* no. 6 (2003): 89–92.

33. Accessed October 7, 2001. Greener Beijing has since changed its name to Greener Beijing Institute.

34. Lori A. Brainard and Patricia D. Siplon, "Toward Nonprofit Organization Reform in the Voluntary Spirit: Lessons from the Internet," *Nonprofit and Voluntary Sector Quarterly* 33, no. 3 (September 2004): 443.

35. Robert Latham and Saskia Sassen, eds., *Digital Formations: IT and New Architectures in the Global Realm* (Princeton: Princeton University Press, 2005).

36. Rheingold defines virtual communities as "social aggregations that emerge from the net when enough people carry on those public discussions long enough, with sufficient human feeling, to form webs of personal relationships in cyberspace." See Howard Rheingold, *The Virtual Community: Homesteading on the Electronic Frontier* (Reading, MA: Addison-Wesley, 1993), p. 5.

37. The Web site for the bulletin board has migrated several times. A long-time serving board was at www.zqsc.org/huaxia/wwwboard/index.html. It was later replaced by http://bj.netsh .com/bbs/80472/. Its current main Web site, www.hxzq.net, was registered in July 2001.

38. The following analysis is based on data I collected from six Chinese BBS forums. They represent three main types of BBSs in China—university-based, commercial, and official. Three are university BBSs (Beijing University, Shantou University, and Xi'an Jiaotong University). The "Strengthening the Nation Forum," affiliated with the *People's Daily,* has an official status. The other two are run by popular commercial portal sites (Sohu.com and Netease.com). From May 23 to June 4, 2000, I followed the discussions closely, spending an average of six hours daily to read the posts and download information.

39. The news forum of Beijing University's BBS is called "Triangle" (*Sanjiaodi*). It is named after the famous Triangle area on campus, the unofficial center for information, public gatherings, and protests at Beijing University.

40. The message announced that demonstrators would meet in front of the auditorium at Qinghua University at 20:30 and then march from there to Beijing University's centennial hall. The message was posted by users in the following order: cind, May 23, 2000, 02:29, Qinghua University BBS; Rocktor, May 23, 2000, 08:40 Qinghua University BBS; onlooker, May 23, 2000, 08:55, Triangle.

41. Xueguang Zhou, "Unorganized Interests and Collective Action in Communist China," *American Sociological Review* 58, no. 1 (1993): 61.

42. For a historical survey of the use of wall posters in Chinese politics, see Hua Sheng, "Perspective on Free Speech in China: Big Character Posters in China, a Historical Survey," *Journal of Asian Law* 4, no. 2 (1990): 234–256.

43. A prominent case in this respect is the use of the Internet by Falun Gong practitioners in and outside of China. See Nan Lin, *Social Capital: A Theory of Social Structure and Action* (Cambridge: Cambridge University Press, 2001).

Notes to Chapter 12

This chapter reflects the author's opinion and not necessarily that of the National Defense University, the U.S. Department of Defense, or the U.S. Government.

1. Milton Mueller and Zixiang Tan, *China in the Information Age: Telecommunications and the Dilemma of Reform* (Westport, CT: Praeger, 1997), p. 7.

2. Henry Jenkins and David Thorbun, eds., *Democracy and New Media* (Cambridge: MIT Press, 2003), p. 5.

3. Christopher R. Kedzie, *Communication and Democracy: Coincident Revolutions and the Emergent Dictator's Dilemma* (Santa Monica, CA: RAND, 1997). Available at www.rand.org/publications/RGSD/RGSD127.

4. The term was first coined by Dr. Lawrence Press in 1996 (see http://som.csudh.edu/cis/lpress/devnat/nations/cuba/asce.htm) in regards to Cuba and telecommunications, and further developed by Christopher Kedzie. The concept has existed longer.

5. George P. Shultz, "Shaping American Foreign Policy: New Realities and New Ways of Thinking," *Foreign Affairs* 63, no. 4 (Spring 1985): 716.

6. James A. Baker, "America in Asia: Emerging Architecture for a Pacific Community," *Foreign Affairs* 70, 5 (Winter 1991/1992): 16–17.

7. From Ithiel de Sola Pool's seminal work on communication technology, *Technologies of Freedom* (Cambridge, MA: Belknap Press, 1983).

8. Kedzie, *Communication and Democracy,* p. 38.

9. See Geoff Long, "Why the Internet Still Matters for Asia's Democracy," in *Asian Cyberactivism: Freedom of Expression and Media Censorship,* ed. Steven Gan, James Gomez, and Uwe Johannen, pp. 68–95 (Bangkok: Frederic Naumann Foundation, 2004); Peng Hwa Ang, "Why the Internet Will Make Asia Freer," *Harvard Asia Quarterly* 5, no. 3 (2001): 48–50; Babak Rahimi, "Cyberdissent: The Internet in Revolutionary Iran," *Middle East Review of International Affairs* 7, no. 3 (2003): 101–115; Peter Ferdinand, ed., *The Internet, Democracy and Democratization* (London: Frank Cass, 2000).

10. For example, a newspaper piece on the unveiling of strict penalties for online distributors of pornography, which included a discussion of the narrowing of censorship in China and across Asia, began with "As the Internet sweeps across Asia, it is bringing with it a strong challenge to the region's authoritarian governments: a freer exchange of information and ideas." Kathleen McLaughlin, "Internet Prods Asia to Open Up," *Christian Science Monitor* (September 9, 2004), at www.csmonitor.com/2004/0909/p06s01-woap.html. An op-ed piece published by a conservative Washington, DC think tank on China's big-brotherish Internet restrictions began, "The Internet once promised to be a conduit for uncensored information from beyond China's border, and for a brief, shining instant in modern Chinese history, it was a potential catalyst for political and human rights reform in China." John J. Tkacik, "China's Orwellian Internet," *The Backgrounder* (October 8, 2004), at www.heritage.org/Research/AsiaandthePacific/bg1806.cfm.

11. Gordon C. Chang, "Future @china.communism: Is the Communist Party Ready for the Internet," *The Coming Collapse of China* (New York: Random House, 2001), pp. 90, 93.

12. David C. Gompert, "Right Makes Might: Freedom and Power in the Information Age," (May 1998), available at www.rand.org/publications/MR/MR1016/MR1016.chap3.pdf, pp. 47, 49.

13. China Internet Network Information Center (CNNIC), *15th Statistical Survey Report on the Internet Development in China.* Available at www.cnnic.net.cn/download/2005/2005012701.pdf, p. 5.

14. "China Expects 120 Million Netizens by the End of 2005," ChinaDaily.com (January 3, 2005), at www.chinadaily.com.cn/english/doc/2005–03/01/content_420724.htm.

15. "Mobile Phone Short Messages Register Record High," China Internet Network Information Center (November 23, 2004), at www.china.org.cn/english/Life/115729.htm.

16. "Nation to Quicken E-government Drive," China Internet Network Information Center (April 5, 2004), at www.china.org.cn/english/government/92143.htm.

17. "Make E-Governance Effective Public Service," China Internet Network Information Center (August 10, 2004), at www.china.org.cn/english/China/103546.htm.

18. Randy Kluver and Jack Linchuan Qiu, "China, the Internet and Democracy," in *Rhetoric and Reality: The Internet Challenge for Democracy in Asia,* ed. Indrajit Banerjee (Singapore: Eastern Universities Press, 2003), p. 41.

19. Jinhong Tang, "Recent Internet Developments in the People's Republic of China: An Overview," *Online Information Review* 24, no. 4 (2000): 316–321 (available on ABI/INFORM Global).

20. Xinhua News Agency, "Information Network Planned to Link Nation" (April 24, 2002), at www.china.org.cn.

21. Kathleen Hartford, "Cyberspace with Chinese Characteristics," *Current History* 99, 638 (September 2000): 255–262.

22. Article 6 of the March 6, 1998, "Implementation Measures Relating to the Temporary Provisions for the Management of Computer Information Networks in the People's Republic of China that Take Part in International Information Systems."

23. Some are: the "PRC Measures on the Regulation of Public Computer Networks and the Internet" on April 9, 1996; the "Regulations on the Security and Management of Computer Information Networks and the Internet" on December 11, 1997; the "Implementation Measures Relating to the Temporary Provisions for the Management of Computer Networks in the PRC that Take Part in International Internet Systems" on March 6, 1998; the "Provisions on Secrecy Management of Computer Information Systems on the Internet" on January 1, 2000; the "Measures for the Administration of Internet Information Services" on September 20, 2000; the "Circular on Tightening the Internet Culture Market" pertaining to the standardization of public Internet providers such as Internet cafes on May 16, 2002; and the "Interim Provisions on the Administration of Internet Culture" on May 10, 2003. Rules regarding business operations on the Internet as well as rules specific to the Shanghai and Beijing municipalities were also passed in 2000. See "The Battle for Cyberspace," in *The China Reader: The Reform Era,* ed. Orville Schell and David Shambaugh, pp. 256–259 (New York: Vintage Books, 1999); Robert Perrins, *China Facts and Figures Annual and Handbook, 1999,* (Gulf Breeze, FL: Academic International, 1999), pp. 340–344; *2000,* pp. 282–284; *2001,* pp. 317–320, available at www.opennetinitiative.net/studies/china/ONI_China_ Country_Study.pdf, pp. 8–19.

24. Not only have the rules become more specific but their focus has also narrowed, from national rules to rules pertaining to certain municipalities and businesses. In addition, the issuing agency has become increasingly security-oriented. The Ministry of Post and Telecommunications issued the regulations of April 9, 1996. The regulations of December 11, 1997 were circulated by the Ministry of Public Security, and the Bureau for the Protection of State Secrets put out the regulations of January 1, 2000. The Ministry of Information Industry has introduced many of the regulations since 2002.

25. "Blog," short for Web log, is a frequently updated online journal that reflects the personal thoughts and opinions of the author, or blogger, on a wide variety of issues from personal goals to current events.

26. "Beijing in Hard Drive to Patrol Net Users," *South China Morning Post,* January 18, 2002, and "China Sets New Net Rules," *South China Morning Post,* January 21, 2002. Although these articles were available during initial research in 2003 and 2004, in 2005 neither article appears in the *South China Morning Post* archives.

27. OpenNet Initiative, *Internet Filtering in China 2004–2005: A Country Study,* p. 15.

28. A survey of Internet use in China found that despite the greater number of sites offered overseas and in foreign languages, Chinese Internet users spend nearly 80 percent of their time accessing mainland China Web sites. Guo Liang, *Surveying Internet Usage and Impact in Twelve Chinese Cities* (October 2003), at www.markle.org/downloadable_assets/chinainternet_usage.pdf, p. 38.

29. Zixiang Tan, William Forster, and Seymour Goodman, "China's State-Coordinated Internet Infrastructure," *Association for Computing Machinery Communications of the ACM* 42, no. 6 (June 1999): 44–52.

30. Ethan Gutmann, "Who Lost China's Internet?" *Weekly Standard* 7, no. 23 (February 2002): 24–29. OpenNet Initiative, *Internet Filtering in China 2004–2005: A Country Study,* pp. 6–8.

31. Jack Aubry, "How Nortel Helps China Quash Dissent: Rights Group Report Says Technology Used for Surveillance, Infiltration," *Ottawa Citizen,* October 18, 2001.

32. For a list of some sites which were periodically blocked in 2002, see http://cyber.law.harvard.edu/filtering/China/China-highlights.html. The *New York Times* was removed from the blocked list in August of 2001 after a personal appeal by the paper's top editors to Jiang Zemin; see Steve Friess, "China Re-Blocks New Sites," *Wired News* (September 26, 2001), at www.wired.com/news/politics/0,1283,47121,00.html.

33. For news articles related to closures, see "China Cracks Down on Internet Cafes," *BBC News* (February 2, 2000), at http://news.bbc.co.uk/hi/english/world/asia-pacific/newsid_628000/628432.stm; Hamish McDonald, "China Shut 8600 Internet Cafes in 3 Months," *The Age* (May 7, 2004), at http://theage.com.au/articles/2004/05/07/1083881475636.html; Lucy Sherriff, "China Shuts 1,600 Cybercafes," *Register* (November 1, 2004), at www.theregister.co.uk/2004/11/01/china_net_crackdown; "China Net Café Culture Crackdown," *BBC News* (February 14, 2005), at http://news.bbc.co.uk/2/hi/technology/4263525.stm. For articles related to the installation of monitoring equipment see "China Cracks Down on Cybercafes," *BBC News* (November 21, 2001), at http://news.bbc.co.uk/hi/english/world/asai-pacific/newsid_1668000/1668335.stm and "Shanghai Cameras Spy on Web Users," *BBC News* (April 22, 2004), at http://news.bbc.co.uk/2/hi/asia-pacific/3648813.stm.

34. Ronald J. Deibert, "Dark Guests and Great Firewalls: The Internet and Chinese Security Policy," *Journal of Social Issues* 58, no. 1 (Spring 2002): 148.

35. Shanthi Kalathil, "The 'C' Word," *Dangerous Assignments* (Summer 2000), at www.ceip.org/files/Publications/cword.asp?p+5&from+pubdate.

36. Reporters Without Borders, "China" (June 22, 2004), at www.rsf.org/article.php3?id_article=10749&Valider=OK.

37. Reuters, "China Says Provinces Setting Up Internet Police" (August 6, 2000), at www.tibet.ca/wtarchive/2000/8/8_7.html.

38. Editorial, "China's Internet Industry Wants Self-Discipline," *People's Daily* (March 27, 2002), at http://englishpeopledaily.com.cn/200203/26/eng20020326–92885.shtml.

39. Will Knight, "Google Omits Controversial News Stories in China," *New Scientist* (September 21, 2004), at www.newscientist.com/article.ns?id=dn6426, and Associated Press, "Democracy a 'Bad Word': Microsoft Censors Blogs at its New Chinese Portal," *CNN.com* (June 14, 2005), at www.cnn.com/2005/TECH/internet/06/14/china.microsoft.ap.

40. Tom Zeller, "Beijing Loves the Web Until the Web Talks Back," *New York Times,* December 6, 2004, p. C15.

41. Michael Chase, *You've Got Dissent!* (Santa Monica, CA: Rand, 2002).

42. Jason P. Abbot, "Democracy@internet.asia? The Challenges to the Emancipatory Potential of the Net: Lessons from China and Malaysia," *Third World Quarterly* 22, no. 1 (February 2001): 110–111.

43. Garry Rodan, "The Internet and Political Control in Singapore," *Political Science Quarterly* 113, no. 1 (Spring 1998): 75.

44. Quoted in "Singapore to Censor Part of the Internet," *United Press International* (July 7, 1995), as cited in Rodan, "The Internet and Political Control in Singapore," p. 80.

45. Terence Lee, "Emulating Singapore: Towards a Model for Internet Regulation in Asia," in *Asian Cyberactivism: Freedom of Expression and Media Censorship,* ed. Gan, Gomez, and Johannen, pp. 162–196; and Melinda Liu, "The Confucian Solution: Singapore Shows China How to Have the Web and Control It, Too," *Newsweek,* April 2, 2001, p. 25.

46. John Neilson, "Australian Government Introduces Internet Censorship Laws," *World Socialist Web Site* (June 11, 1999), at www.wsws.org/articles/1999/jun1999/cens-j11.shtml; "Watch Out: Arabs and the Internet," *Economist,* July 10, 2004, p. 53; "Zimbabwe: Plan to Censor E-Mail," *New York Times,* June 2, 2004, p. A12; Maziar Bahari, "Closing the Cybergates; Iran Is Trying to Lure Internet Users to a Government Network with the Promise of Five Gigabytes of Storage," *Newsweek* (international edition), November 8, 2004, p. 57; Associated

Press, "Vietnam Adopts New Internet User Policies," May 13, 2004; "Middle East Politics: Arabs, Censorship and the Internet," *EIU ViewsWire* (July 12, 2004) (available on ProQuest); Shanthi Kalathi and Taylor C. Boas, *Open Networks, Closed Regimes* (Washington, DC: Carnegie Endowment for International Peace, 2003); and the Reporters Without Borders Web site at www.rsf.org.

47. Abbot, "Democracy@internet.asia?"; Binod C. Agrawal, "Communication Technology and Democracies of South Asia: The Danger of Curbing Freedom," in *Communication and Democracy,* ed. Slavko Splichal and Janet Wasko, pp. 221–232 (Norwood, NJ: Ablex Publishing, 1993); Vergel O. Santos, "The Internet and Philippine Democracy: A Frail Connection," in *Rhetoric and Reality,* ed. Banerjee, pp. 235–258; Men Kimseng, "Online Opposition: The Sam Rainsy Party Website in Cambodian Politics," in *Asian Cyberactivism,* ed. Gan, Gomez, and Johannen, pp. 592–621.

48. Zafarullah Khan, "Cyber Jihad: Fighting the Infidels from Pakistan," pp. 442–470 and Kasun Ubayasiri, "A Virtual Eelam: Democracy, Internet, and Sri Lanka's Tamil Struggle," in *Asian Cyberactivism,* ed. Gan, Gomez, and Johannen, pp. 474–512; Timothy L. Thomas, "Al Qaeda and the Internet: The Danger of 'Cyberplanning,'" *Parameters* (Spring 2003): 112–123, at http://carlisle-www.army.mil/usawc/Parameters/03spring/thomas.pdf.

49. Kedzie, *Communication and Democracy,* p. 69.

Notes to Chapter 13

1. According to China's official account, the PRC has been led by four generations of leaders, represented respectively by Mao Zedong, Deng Xiaoping, Jiang Zemin, and Hu Jintao. The current Hu Jintao leadership began to take over the helm at the 16th Party Congress in 2002. With the retirement of Jiang Zemin from the Central Military Commission in October 2004, the fourth generation of leaders has been in full charge.

2. Frederick C. Teiwes, "Normal Politics with Chinese Characteristics," *China Journal,* no. 45 (January 2001): 74.

3. Suisheng Zhao, "The Structure of Authority and Decision-making: A Theoretical Framework," in *Decision-making in Deng's China,* ed. Carol Lee Hamrin and Suisheng Zhao, pp. 236–237 (Armonk, NY: M.E. Sharpe, 1995).

4. Lowell Dittmer, "The Changing Shape of Elite Power Politics," *China Journal,* no. 45 (January 2001): 59.

5. Willy Wo-Lap Lam, "Jiang Urged to Give Up Forces Role," CNN.com, June 16, 2003.

6. Commentary, "New Leaders Spearhead New Ideas," at http://english.peopledaily.com.cn/200308/05/eng20030805_121723.

7. "Wen Jiabao quxiao zongli bangong huiyi ruhua gaoceng renzhi shecai" (Wen Jiabao abolishes the premier work meeting to weaken the rule of man at the top), Chinesenewsnet.com, February 10, 2004.

8. Suisheng Zhao, "The Feeble Political Capacity of a Strong One Party Regime: An Institutional Approach Toward the Formulation and Implementation of Economic Policy in Post-Mao China," *Issues & Studies* 26, no. 1 (January 1990): 76.

9. Willy Wo-lap Lam, "China: Breaking with the Past?" CNN.com, July 23, 2003.

10. Zhou Tianyong, "Build Up Credible Government," *China Daily,* November 21, 2002, p. 8.

11. Lucian W. Pye, "Jiang Zemin's Style of Rule: Go for Stability, Monopolize Power and Settle for Limited Effectiveness," *China Journal,* no. 45 (January 2001): 48.

12. Minxin Pei, "China's Ruling Party Cannot Have It All," *Financial Times,* January 13, 2004, p. 13.

13. Commentary, "Chinese New Leadership Wins Trust," *People's Daily Online English,* June 30, 2003.

14. Commentary, "SARS, a Valuable Lesson for Chinese Government to Learn," *People's Daily,* June 8, 2003.

15. Richard Baum, "Political Reform: Is China Ready to Listen to its People?" *South China Morning Post,* June 28, 2003.

16. John Pomfret, "Outbreak Gave China's Hu an Opening," *Washington Post,* May 13, 2003, p. A1.

17. Zhao Huanxin, "Tightened Reins Make Gov't Accountable," *China Daily,* March 14, 2004, p. 5.

18. Eric Teo Chu Cheow, "SARS and East Asia's Four Transformations," *PacNet,* no. 28, June 26, 2003, at www.csis.org/component/option,com_csis_pubs/task,view/id,428.

19. Michal Korzec, " Absorption of the Party by the State," *South China Morning Post,* January 29, 2003, p. 14.

20. Kathy Chen, "SARS Brings New Freedom to Rule-Bound China Media," *Wall Street Journal,* May 22, 2003.

21. Robert L. Maddex, *Constitutions of the World* (Washington, DC: Congressional Quarterly, 1995), p. x.

22. Flemming Christiansen and Shirin Rai, *Chinese Politics and Society: Introduction* (New York: Prentice Hall, 1996), p. 82.

23. Tony Saich, *Governance and Politics of China* (New York: Palgrave, 2001), p. 110.

24. Guo Shujian, *Post-Mao China: From Totalitarianism to Authoritarianism* (Westport, CT: Praeger, 2000), p. 102.

25. "People to Get More Rights," *Beijing Review,* January 15, 2004, p. 17.

26. Saich, *Governance and Politics of China,* p. 110.

27. Qianfan Zhang, "The People's Court in Transition: The Prospects of the Chinese Judicial Reform," *Journal of Contemporary China* 12, no. 34 (2003): 69–70.

28. William H. Overholt, "China's Party Congress: The New Vision," *South China Morning Post,* November 16, 2002.

29. Xinhua, "Constitution to Clarify Private Rights," January 5, 2004, at www.china.org.cn.

30. Ibid.

31. Maddex, *Constitutions of the World,* p. xiii.

32. Minxin Pei, "China's Ruling Party Cannot Have it All," *Financial Times,* January 13, 2004, p. 13.

33. Liu Xiaobo, "Zhonggong xianfa guan de chubu bianhua" (The preliminary changes in the CCP's constitutional outlook), Chinesenewsnet.com, January 14, 2004.

34. Daniel Kwan, "Powers of Police to Detain Migrants Will Be Scrapped," *South China Morning Post,* June 19, 2003.

35. Editorial, "The New Rules, Which Will Take Effect on August 1, Have Been Welcomed," *People's Daily Online English,* June 30, 2003.

36. Willy Wo-Lap Lam, "Is Hu Using Scandal to Embrace His Rivals?" CNN.com, June 10, 2003.

37. Xinhua, "Battle Against a Bad Name," at www.chinaview.cn 2005–05–26.

38. Hugo Restall, "China's Rising Rights Consciousness," *Dow Jones,* January 16, 2004.

39. Qiu Feng, "Xin minquan xingdong nian" (New civil rights action year), *Xinwen zhoukan* (News week), December 23, 2003, pp. 52–53.

40. *Nanfeng chuang* (South wind window), December 15, 2003, pp. 47–52.

41. Yong Zhi, Hufei, "Dalu minjian xiuxian bufa jijing" (Radical steps have been taken to revise constitution on the mainland), *Fenghuang zhoukan* (Phoenix weekly), July 2003, pp. 14–17.

42. Nailene Chou Wiest, "Top Cadre Urges Party to Pursue Democracy," *South China Morning Post,* August 6, 2003.

43. Bruce Gilley, "The End of Politics in Beijing," *Asian Wall Street Journal,* January 28, 2004.

44. Joseph Kahn, "Democratic Hopes Test China's Political Limits," *New York Times,* March 2, 2003.

45. Elisabeth Rosenthal, "Chinese Freer to Speak and Read, But Not Act," *New York Times,* February 12, 2003, p. A3.

46. Joe McDonald, "President Hu Jintao's Call for a More Democratic China," Associated Press, October 2, 2003.

47. Li Chen, "Mystery behind the Myths," *South China Morning Post,* June 11, 2001, at http://china.scmp.com/lifestyle/ZZZXXELDPNC/html.

48. Pye, "Jiang Zemin's Style of Rule: Go for Stability, Monopolize Power and Settle for Limited Effectiveness," p. 46.

About the Editor and Contributors

The Editor

Suisheng Zhao is professor and executive director of the Center for China–U.S. Cooperation at the Graduate School of International Studies, University of Denver. He is founder and editor of the *Journal of Contemporary China* and on the Board of Directors of the U.S. Committee of the Council for Security Cooperation in the Asia Pacific (USCSCAP). A 1999–2000 Campbell National Fellow at Hoover Institution of Stanford University, he was associate professor of Political Science/International Studies at Washington College in Maryland, associate professor of Government/East Asian Politics at Colby College in Maine, and visiting assistant professor in the Graduate School of International Relations and Pacific Studies, University of California–San Diego. He received a PhD in political science from the University of California–San Diego, an MA in sociology from the University of Missouri, and an MA in economics from Peking University. He is the author and editor of six books. His most recent books are *A Nation-State by Construction: Dynamics of Modern Chinese Nationalism* (2004), *Chinese Foreign Policy: Pragmatism and Strategic Behavior* (2003), *China and Democracy: Reconsidering the Prospects for a Democratic China* (2000), and *Across the Taiwan Strait: Mainland China, Taiwan, and the Crisis of 1995–96* (1999). His articles have appeared in *Washington Quarterly, Political Science Quarterly, China Quarterly, World Affairs, Asian Survey, Journal of Northeast Asian Studies, Asian Affairs, Journal of Democracy, Pacific Affairs, Communism and Post-Communism Studies, Problems of Post-Communism, Journal of East Asian Affairs, Issues and Studies, Journal of Contemporary China,* and elsewhere.

The Contributors

Yongshun Cai is assistant professor in the Division of Political Science at Hong Kong University of Science and Technology.

Larry Diamond is senior fellow at the Hoover Institution, co-editor of the *Journal of Democracy,* and co-director of the International Forum for Democratic Studies of the National Endowment for Democracy. He is currently co-editing a collaborative study on democratic consolidation in Taiwan.

Edward Friedman, a professor in the Department of Political Science at the University of Wisconsin, Madison, specializes in both Chinese politics and the challenges of democratization. Recent books include: *What If China Doesn't Democratize? Implications for War and Peace* (2000); and *National Identity and Democratic Prospects in Socialist China: The Politics of Democratization* (1995).

Pan Wei received his PhD from the University of California at Berkeley in 1996 and is currently associate professor of political science at the School of International Studies, Peking University. He conducts research in such areas as contemporary rural China, comparative political systems, and China's foreign relations.

Randall Peerenboom is professor of law at UCLA Law School. He often serves as an expert witness on PRC legal issues, and has been a consultant to the Ford Foundation and the Asian Development Bank on legal reforms and rule of law in China. He has written more than sixty articles and authored and edited several books on Chinese law and philosophy. Recent works include *China's Long March toward Rule of Law* (2002), and *Asian Discourses of Rule of Law: Theories and Implementation of Rule of Law in Twelve Asian Countries, France, and the U.S.* (editor, 2004).

Gunter Schubert is chair professor of Greater China Studies at the Institute of Chinese and Korean Studies, University of Tuebingen, Germany. His research fields are Chinese and Taiwanese politics, cross-strait relations, Chinese nationalism, comparative studies on democratization, and transition theory.

Tamara Renee Shie is research assistant for East Asia at the Institute for National Security Studies of the National Defense University in Washington, DC. From February to July 2004 she was a visiting fellow at the Pacific Forum CSIS in Honolulu, Hawaii. She holds an MA in International Policy Studies from the Monterey Institute of International Studies and an MA in Southeast Asian studies from the National University of Singapore. She has spent extensive time in East Asia, including China, South Korea, Japan, the Philippines, Indonesia, and Singapore. Her research interests cover a wide range of nontraditional security issues in East Asia such as maritime security, separatist conflicts, transnational crimes, and the complex nexus between national and human security objectives.

Guobin Yang is associate professor in the Department of Asian and Middle Eastern Cultures, Barnard College, Columbia University. He has published works on China's environmental NGOs, the Internet and Chinese civil society, the Red Guard movement, the 1989 Chinese student movement, and collective memories of the Cultural Revolution. His articles have appeared in *Asian Survey, China Quarterly, Modern China, Journal of Contemporary China, China Review, Sociological Forum, Sociological Quarterly, Theory and Society,* and *Media, Culture & Society.* In the 2003–2004 academic year, he was a fellow at the Woodrow Wilson International Center for Scholars in Washington, DC.

Songcai Yang is associate professor in the School of Law at Hunan University in China.

Baohui Zhang is associate professor of politics at Lingnan University in Hong Kong. He taught as associate professor of government at Daemen College in Buffalo, New York. With a PhD in government from the University of Texas in Austin in 1994, his research interests include democratization, Chinese politics, and U.S.–China relations.

Qianfan Zhang obtained his PhD in government from University of Texas at Austin in 1999. He then taught comparative public law at Nanjing University Law School, and is now teaching at Peking University. He is the associate director for the Constitutional and Administrative Law Center at Peking University and the vice president of the Chinese Constitutional Law Society. He has published several books and numerous articles on constitutional and administrative law, including *Market Economy and Its Legal Regulations* (1998), a two-volume treatise entitled *The Constitutional Systems in the West* (2nd ed., 2004/2005), *Introduction to the Study of Constitutional Law* (2004), and *Constitutionalism, Rule of Law, and Economic Development* (first author, 2004).

Yunqiu Zhang is assistant professor of East Asian studies at North Carolina A&T State University. His publications include articles on Chinese trade unions, labor relations, local state entrepreneurship, Daoism, and Chinese historiography.

Index